Art Causes School Evacuation

Wisconsin Bill Would Permit Blind to Hunt Deer

Squad Helps Dog Bite Victim

HOSPITAL SUED BY 7 FOOT DOCTORS

Unwanted Workers Get Shot at Jobs

TREES CAN BREAK WIND

Iowa Cemeteries Are Death Traps

POLICE DISCOVER CRACK IN AUSTRALIA

London Man Slain With Turnip

Queen Mary is Having Her Bottom Scraped

DEAD MAN GETS JOB BACK

Enraged Cow Injures Farmer with Ax

HIGH-SPEED TRAIN

Could Reach Valley in Five Years

Contemporary newspaper design

À VOIR

A FAIRE

Margie Gillis, la danse de la vie

THE TIMES

HONI·SOIT·QUI·MAL·Y·PENSE

DIEU·ET MON·DROIT

WORLD

LA PRENSA GRÁFICA

CULTURA

La nueva Biblioteca de Alejandría

La legendaria biblioteca resurgirá este día en la ciudad del mismo nombre, en el mismo lugar donde fue consumida por el fuego en el año 47 a.C. El edificio costó $220 millones.

AGENDA CULTURAL

Feria del Libro en Guadalajara

Arte salvadoreño en el corazón de Manhattan

La pintora Sonia Melara se ha afincado en Nueva York. "Es parte de mi desarrollo como artista", afirma. Ahora expone en la gran ciudad una colección que muestra el arte salvadoreño a través de una desgarradora visión del dolor y la figura humana.

Creación salvadoreña

Trayectoria artística

Comment & Analysis

'...eat music' Letters, page 17

The child support ...than a fiasco — it ...a national tragedy

...ell in a ...lbag

Andrew Roth

The new McCarthyites

Thatcher said: 'Lone parents, what are you going to do about them?'

...buoyant as he ...es 'new partner'

Balletrobics

Star athletes sweat by a former ballerina's stretching regimen, B3

...n-binding vote on marriage as Commons returns

BILL GETS EARLY TEST

Murder, politics collide in California

...hip of Indonesia has underpinned its foreign policy. Now it has a difficult path to tread

...ce Australia fair

The lucky country

Gazette

FINANCIAL POST

Canada finishes well ahead of U.S. as OECD tests teenage students

Rocky Mount...

Baghda...

81

NZZ am Sonntag

Kultur

Liebeskummer

Sie dürfen alles, schätzen grausame Phantasien und brauchen Gin Tonic gegen die Liebe: die Frauen der «Generation Ally».

Seite 83

Bücherliebe

Helen Hanff lebt in New York. Ihr Buchhändler in London. Sie schreibt Briefe, er schickt Pakete.

Seite 83

Eleganz

Der Dirigent Philippe Herreweghe feiert die Leichtigkeit von Bach und Brahms.

Seite 85

Freundschaft

Harald Szeemann zu Jean Tinguely, Marcel Duchamp und seiner Ausstellung im Tinguely-Museum Basel.

Seite 87

Einsicht

Kreativität lässt sich nicht herbeizaubern. Am Fernsehen schon gar nicht. «Hotel B.» wurde eingestellt.

Seite 93

Bester Film? Beste Regie? Robert Altman «Gosford Park» hat sieben Oscar-Nominationen (Fabrice Trombert/Retna)

Der Herr von Gosford Pa...

Robert Altman lässt Agatha Christie und Jean Renoir sich begegnen ... beste Darstellerriege bei Laune – und uns auch. *Von Martin Walder*

Mord – doppelt gemoppelt

Marcel Duchamp: Roue de Bicyclette (Pro Litteris/AKG)

DIE ZEIT

...ZEITUNG FÜR POLITIK · WIRTSCHAFT · WISSEN UND KULTUR

Erlaubt das Klonen

Unser Los ist Davos

Politik im Container

Ewige Vergangenheit

VALOR ECONÔMICO

Crise agravada na Argentina afeta o Brasil

...nton defends U.S. policy on Mid...

...cipants at ...n criticize ...e on Israel

AMERICA AND ISLAM IN A GLOBAL WORLD

THE WILLIAM J. CLINTON PRESIDENTIAL FOUNDATION

Contemporary newspaper design

Shaping the news in the digital age: typography & image on modern newsprint

Edited by John D. Berry
Foreword by Roger Black

MARK BATTY PUBLISHER

Library of Congress Cataloging-in-Publication Data
Contemporary newspaper design : shaping the news in the digital age : typography & image on modern newsprint / edited by John D. Berry. – 1st ed.
p. cm.
Includes bibliographical references and index.
ISBN 0-9724240-3-2 (alk. paper)
1. Newspaper layout and typography – Case studies. I. Berry, John D., 1950–

Z253.5.C64 2003
686.2'252 - dc22
2003024822

Printed and bound in Jordan

First Edition
10 9 8 7 6 5 4 3 2 1

ISBN: 0-9724240-3-2

Mark Batty Publisher LLC
6050 Boulevard East, Suite 2H
West New York, NJ 07093

www.markbattypublisher.com

Acknowledgments

Thanks to *Eye* magazine and Simon Esterson for permission to reprint his article “Kit of parts,” which was originally published in *Eye* no. 44 vol. 11, Summer 2002; to Jim Parkinson, for permission to reprint his “More than you ever wanted to know about nameplates,” which was originally published as a small booklet given out to attendees at one of the SND conferences; and to Matthew Carter and Font Bureau, who generously allowed us to use the typeface Miller for the text of this book.

CONTENTS

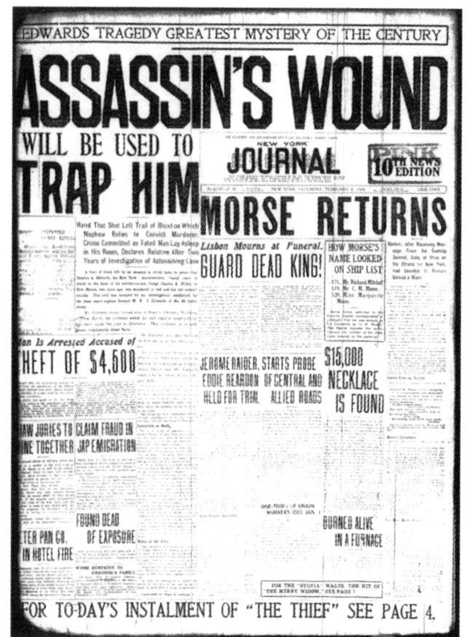

EDWARDS TRAGEDY GREATEST MYSTERY OF THE CENTURY

ASSASSIN'S WOUND

WILL BE USED TO

TRAP HIM

NEW YORK JOURNAL

10TH NEWS EDITION

MORSE RETURNS

Lisbon Mourns at Funeral.

GUARD DEAD KING!

HOW MORSE'S NAME LOOKED ON SHIP LIST

Man Is Arrested Accused of THEFT OF $4,500

JEROME RAIDER, STARTS PROBE OF CENTRAL AND ALLIED ROADS

EDDIE REARDON HELD FOR TRIAL

$15,000 NECKLACE IS FOUND

FOUND DEAD OF EXPOSURE

BURNED ALIVE IN A FURNACE

FOR TO-DAY'S INSTALMENT OF "THE THIEF" SEE PAGE 4.

Front pages from the *New York Journal* of Feb. 8, 1908 (above), and the *Rocky Mountain News* of July 11, 1904 (right).

VOL. XLV: NO. 193. DENVER, COLORADO, MONDAY, JULY 11, 1904.—10 PAGES.—PRICE 5 CENTS. ESTABLISHED 1859.

MOST NOTORIOUS BANDIT AND TRAIN ROBBER OF THE WORLD IS BURIED IN THE MOUNTAINS

CAPTAIN OF THE HOLE-IN-THE-WALL GANG LED RIO GRANDE RAILWAY HOLDUPS

Harvey Logan, Who Broke Jail in Tennessee, Killed Himself When Cornered by Posse in Colorado.

EAST ASKS FOR MORE

Indications That New Yorkers Will Insist on Hill's Choice of Man to Run Campaign.

THE OLD HOLE-IN-THE-WALL GANG OF OUTLAWS.

HARVEY LOGAN

THE DEAD BANDIT OF RIFLE, COLO.

SEVENTEEN SLAIN IN RAILWAY WRECK

NOT TOO COARSE FOR P. C. KNOX

TRAGIC CONFESSION BEFORE DEATH

DOMINATE PORT ARTHUR

Japanese Batteries Are Strongly Entrenched So as to Command All Parts of the Fortress.

MAY SEND FLEET TO FORCE SULTAN

WATCH THE 78,234 INCREASE

WILLIAM B. CHILDERS,

The News and The Times Want the Small Ads of the People. They Guarantee All Such the Greatest Circulation Ever Attained in the West

Foreword

Roger Black

Newspaper design is changing at a rate we haven't seen since the days of Hearst and Pulitzer. A hundred years ago, when dailies were the first line of news, there was an extraordinary explosion of graphic experiment. Spurred by the swirling technology of teletype, Linotype, stereotype – and photoengraving – newspapers were quickly finding new ways to grab attention. They were the first of the mass media. A convulsive series of graphic developments established the forms we still see today. Printed photographs, still wildly new things, began to appear on front pages. Vigorous typefaces, borrowed from advertising posters, vied with robust new text types to spell out lurid stories about shocking crimes and stupendous personalities. It was thrilling.

But as the proprietors became prosperous and powerful, the look of newspapers settled down. By 1920, the big-city dailies they owned had become enormously influential institutions, and they started taking themselves seriously. Pulitzer's *New York World* hired sleek intellectuals and polished critics. The wild-eyed reporters of the Teens, like H. L. Mencken, became columnists or moved to the new magazines. Innovation turned into formula; formula devolved into convention. While there were interesting waves of change in newspaper design in the 1950s, led by Edmund Arnold, and then again in the 1970s, led by a new association, the Society of Newspaper Design, newspapers did not fundamentally change. From the outside they looked much the same. They have become generic, and in a world of bright pixels not a little dull. Taken for granted. Scarcely read. Most readers don't even call their daily by name. They say, "Did you see it in the paper?"

Publishers and editors were fast to deny the threat of proliferating electronic media and steered complacently toward the cliff. First radio took away their ability to be the first bearer of news to their readers. Newsreels, then television stole their visual thunder. Now the Internet has usurped their role as the key conduit of correspondence, linking communities with threaded discussion groups, blogs...and classified ads.

For 30 years various pundits, starting with Marshall McLuhan, have blandly predicted the death of newspapers. Business experts have suggested they are going the way of the passenger railroads, and for the same reasons. But they survive. And, compared, say, to airlines and grocery stores they do a very profitable business. It is not unusual to hear of net profits of 30 percent. How can this be? The glossy predictability of TV may be a factor. The medium seldom lives up to its potential. The scripts are fatuous and repetitious. The reality programs are slow as all hell. And on the news side, hair-styled talking heads have replaced documentary journalism. TV is all sound these days, and no pictures.

One cause of the papers' continued existence is that, well, they continue to do a number of services better or at least more efficiently than anyone else. They attract readers with an offering of local news and sports not available elsewhere, combined with local retail ads. (And most publishers have found a way to combine their employment and other classified ads with a web site.)

But the chief reason this dodo is still alive is the inherent economy in the medium of writing and reading. A single writer (or a single photographer) can go out and cover a story, and then produce it in a way that it is interesting to an individual reader. It's the narrative, the storytelling that keeps newspapers going. A well-written piece of text, with a beginning, a middle and an end, can connect two people directly and efficiently, without the clanking production costs of television.

As editors and publishers are beginning to reinvent the medium, adding pieces of visual journalism, and shortening and intensifying the text, we are seeing a new wave of newspaper design, led by a very talented array of art directors and consultants. Lucie Lacava and Mario Garcia, Simon Esterson and Ally Palmer, are transforming newspapers with elegant, custom typefaces and a variety of presentation techniques. Retro styles mix with contemporary layouts in a way that underscores the diversity of the dailies' content. With more color, better printing and more sophisticated advertisements, newspapers have started to look really different for the first time in a century.

This book proves the point. John Berry, one of the best design writers and editors of the past decade, has assembled an energetic group of case studies of recent newspaper design projects. The span of this work is only a few years. If the editors can keep to the course and if designers can keep building the momentum, I'm ready to say they are going to save the whole industry. Newspapers may yet be around for a long time to come. ‹

Introduction

John D. Berry

Technology and economics propel a constant evolution in the design of daily newspapers

Newspaper design is something that most people take for granted. Readers don't even notice how their daily paper looks – until it changes; then they notice right away, and usually they complain. Newspaper readers are the most conservative audience on earth.

So a redesign will be undertaken only when there's something wrong with the previous design – or when some change makes it no longer appropriate. New management may want to establish its presence by stamping its own image on the paper; or a newspaper's circulation may be falling, so as part of an effort to reverse that trend, management decides to try changing the way the paper looks. In those rare instances where a brand-new paper springs into being, it's the design, just as much as the choice of stories and the editorial voice, that sets the tone.

When a new design is needed by a daily paper, it may be done by the paper's own staff, keeping all the work in-house; or it may be done by calling in outside designers, to give a fresh perspective. Quite often the process is some combination of the two. No matter how it's done, there has to be cooperation and coordination between the designers and the people who will implement their design – the editors and the production staff of the paper.

When a newspaper brings in outside design talent, it's usually a professional consultant who specializes in newspaper redesigns – someone who makes a practice of analyzing the paper's strengths and weaknesses, listening carefully and asking questions, defining what the paper's owners want to accomplish, and then creating not just a new design but the tools that the newspaper's staff will need in order to carry it out and maintain it in the long run.

The number of people who specialize in this field is small, and some of them have contributed to this book. They nearly all work collaboratively, with the local staffs and with each other; they have to, since every project is different and each one involves a different conjunction of people, place, and ideas.

A big influence on newspaper design, at least in North America, was the advent of *USA Today* in the early 1980s. Newspapers have traditionally been based in a particular city, however far their reach might extend; in some European countries, the major newspapers of the capital penetrate the entire country, making them in effect national newspapers. In the United States, which is large and sprawling, the closest thing to a national newspaper was *The New York Times*, which emanated not from the political capital but from the cultural capital. You could find *The New York Times* in most major cities, and its voice was lis-

NATIONAL POST, SATURDAY, JUNE 7, 2003

SASKATCHEWAN

Farmers say more cattle being slaughtered by feds

REGINA • Saskatchewan farmers say the Canadian Food Inspection Agency is ordering the slaughter of hundreds more cattle from herds that were never quarantined. Dr. Brian Evans of the agency said the animals being taken off the farms are those suspected either of having a genetic connection to the infected cow or having eaten the same feed.

'It undermines the credibilit

Quebec choice angers, shocks RCMP officials

RIFT

Continued from Page A1

Asked why, Mr. Lapointe replied: "Other articles [of the Criminal Code] are equally as appropriate. I cannot say which ones for the moment because the file is still being reviewed." Mr. Lapointe refused to elaborate, but said criminal charges will be laid in the near future.

The RCMP outlined other offences the two IRB judges were allegedly involved in, including obstruction of justice, fraud, forgery, conspiracy and possession of property obtained by crime. Those carry sentences of only two to 10 years in jail.

The Quebec Justice Department's decision has shocked and angered the RCMP, whose officials decided to try to force the Quebec prosecution service's hand and press for the more serious judicial bribery charges, government officials said.

The RCMP asked Daniel Bellmarre, an assistant deputy attor-

for 18 months, but was partially unsealed by Mr. Justice Colin McKinnon of the Ontario Superior Court following an application by the *National Post, The Montreal Gazette* and another media outlet.

Mr. Bourbonnais and Mr. Colavecchio have been suspended with pay from the IRB since the RCMP raided their Montreal government offices October, 2001.

The RCMP allegations about bribery and organized crime influencing federal immigration and refugee decisions yesterday reverberated in Parliament.

Inside and outside the Commons, the leaders of several opposition parties called for an immediate overhaul of how IRB judges are selected.

Critics of the appointment process for IRB judges have for years complained that both Liberal and Conservative governments have used the board as a patronage den to reward faithful party organizers and friends with high-paying jobs, yet the people

Detail from an interior news page of the *National Post* (above). Opposite: detail from the front page of *Cinco Días* (top; designers, Ally Palmer and Terry Watson), using Knockout and Capitolium for display and News Miller for text; detail from the Dutch newspaper *Trouw* (middle) using Gerard Unger's typeface Swift for text; and an example of the new agate type for financial listings in *The Wall Street Journal* (bottom).

tened to by everybody, even those who disdained it. The idea behind *USA Today*, however, was different: to be national not by weight and prestige but by universal coverage, without a focus on any one city or region, and to be distributed throughout the country.

USA Today made its position by aspiring to be national, rather than local to any one place, and by following through on its universal distribution. But it affected the look of other newspapers because of its design: colorful, visual, designed for the eye. *USA Today* was one of the first American newspapers to fully embrace the possibilities of color; it became famous for its "infographics," the charts and maps and visual aids that turned the words of the news into images that a reader could quickly grasp. A whole generation of newspapers struggled to either incorporate that style or respond to it.

But that was twenty years ago. The design of newspapers has absorbed that lesson and moved on; even *USA Today* has evolved. Full-color printing and sophisticated visual collage are common on the pages of most newspapers today; infographics are old hat (if still difficult to execute effectively). Look at the front pages, the interior pages, the supplements and sections, and you'll see a rich visual stew, a range of typography, photography, tables and charts, dramatic juxtaposition, "entry points" to the news, headlines and subheads and decks and pull-quotes – all serving up the news and its accompanying entertainment to the newspaper's regular readers every day.

It's interesting that some of the most dramatic new design has come in newspapers that began fresh with the intention of becoming national papers – *USA Today*, or more recently Conrad Black's *National Post* in Canada. It's not surprising, though: since they were start-ups, they had to establish their identity from the outset, and they used design to help do that. Both of those newspapers represent a fairly conservative political approach, but there's nothing unique to the right wing about good design: at the other end of the political spectrum, *The Guardian* in the UK and *Libération* in France both set standards for dramatic and careful presentation of the news.

Despite the importance of photography and various kinds of graphic images, the fundamental visual identity of a newspaper is set in its type. The text type is what we actually read, when we read a story; the display type is where we get the gist of what's there to peruse. The secret history of newspaper design – a history that's in plain sight, but that most readers know nothing about – is in its typography.

Newspaper typefaces have evolved as a special subset of type design for more than a century, from the "legibility faces" of the 1930s to the finely graded weights of a digital typeface like Poynter Oldstyle (designed to compensate for subtle variations of paper and printing, so that sections printed on different papers or presses will have the same visual texture when they're set side by side). Like every other kind of typography, newspaper type has been changed enormously by the changes in typesetting technology of the last twenty years: from hot-metal type to phototype to several distinct generations of digital type, and from Linotype machines to Atex systems to distributed networks of Macs or PCs running a page-layout program like QuarkXPress.

The fundamental building block of a newspaper page is awkward: a narrow column of text, usually justified. The lines are so short that it's hard to avoid ugly spaces within the lines, and sometimes misleading or nonsensical hyphenation. (We've all seen ridiculous examples of words broken badly between one line and the next, when an automated program decides where to put the hyphen, and no human eye has caught the absurdity in time.) Some newspaper designers get around this by setting the text with a ragged right-hand margin, rather than justified; but this creates a busier-looking page, and in compensation the overall layout has to be quieter and more strictly defined. As a rule, newspaper readers tend to resist ragged-right text, especially in the United States; when it comes to their daily paper, they resist anything they're not already used to. So the designers of typefaces for newspapers try to make faces that can fit a lot of letters on each line, without looking cramped, and that will look larger than they really are, while still appearing perfectly ordinary and unremarkable to the eye of the reader.

There are many more typefaces available today than ever before, and among those there are quite a lot of faces designed specifically for use in newspapers. The Poynter family of typefaces, designed by Font Bureau as a project of the Poynter Institute, offers complementary serif and sans serif typefaces that can be put to use by any number of newspapers in different ways. Matthew Carter's Miller (which is the face you're reading now) has been adopted by both newspapers and magazines around the world, sometimes in slightly customized forms. French designer Jean-François Porchez made his reputation by designing a completely new set of typefaces for *Le Monde*, the most prestigious newspaper in France, and has performed the same design feat for other newspapers around the country. Gerard Unger's type family Gulliver, which he designed as a solution to exactly the kind of problem mentioned in the last paragraph, has been put to use in such diverse ways that this one typeface has given entirely different personalities to different papers, depending on how it's used (see "Gulliver's travels" in this book), and several of his other typefaces are used in newspapers around Europe. Tobias Frere-Jones created HTF Retina as an "agate" face for the tiny financial listings of *The Wall Street Journal*, where appearance hardly matters but legibility is key. This list is far from comprehensive.

Special sections of newspapers have been with us for decades. In 1980, Anthony Smith pointed out in *Goodbye Gutenberg: The Newspaper Revolution of the 1980s* that newspapers were already responding to competition from television by specializing, and by publishing individual sections on different topics: sports, business, entertainment, real estate, science. Often these were once-a-week sections; the "Science Times" appears in *The New York Times* every Tuesday, for instance. In the late '70s, the big news (in the United States) was targeting by Zip codes, the postal codes that could subdivide a city or region more finely than any political or administrative subdivision. (Some other countries had even more finely divided postal codes, and the United States introduced a more localized nine-digit code a few years later. But the old five-digit coding by neighborhood or postal district was what made this kind of targeted marketing practical in the first place.) Newspapers could use this system to tailor local editions to individual parts of the region they served, taking ads and presenting extra material targeted to a specific audience.

Today, we take it for granted that newspapers will have separate sections for special subjects, and

HOY LUNES: EL NUEVO DIARIO, MÁS ATRACTIVO Y CON

Cinco Dí

Madrid Lunes 6 de octubre de 2003 www.cincodias.com Año XXV Nú

ENTREVISTA EXCLUSIVA CON EL VICEPRESIDENTE DEL GOBIERNO

Rodrigo Rato: "Esto disponible para Raj

BANCOS Y CAJAS: "Del regulador y del Gobierno todo el mundo se queja"

VIVIENDA: "Un

Trouw MENSEN

Laten zien wat de oorlog is

Hoe gaan we in de krant om met gruwelijke beelden? „Gaan we een bepaalde rand over dan willen de mensen niet meer kijken."

door Wilfried van der Bles

Oorlog: geschoten wordt er niet alleen door soldaten, 'geschoten' wordt er ook door fotografen. Een fractie daarvan komt in de kranten terecht. En dat pakt nogal divers uit. Op dezelfde dag, woensdag 2 april, dat *NRC Handelsblad* een dode baby liet zien, speen nog bijna in de mond, stond in *Trouw* en *de Volkskrant* de foto van een rouwende Irakees bij de kist van zijn moeder. Zij was bij dezelfde aanval van Amerikanen waarvan ook de baby het slachtoffer was, omgekomen.

NRC Handelsblad valt op met de keuze voor soms harde foto's, zoals van het vierjarig meisje dat aan haar oog gewond is geraakt. Met haar gruwelijk verwonde oog en bebloede hoofd staat ze groot op pagina drie. *De Volkskrant* en nog sterker *Trouw* lijken in hun fotoselectie terughoudender.

Het aardige is dat de drie kranten hetzelfde uitgangspunt hanteren: laten zien wat oorlog is. Jean Paul van der Wijk, chef van de fotoredactie van *NRC Handelsblad*: „Dat kun je niet doen zonder lijken te laten zien. Daar kunnen we niet omheen. Maar we kiezen echt niet per se voor de meest schokkende foto's. Beslissend is of de foto's het nieuws van de dag goed weergeven. Na de aanslag op de markt in Bagdad hadden we kunnen kiezen voor lijken met afgerukte ledematen. Dat hebben we bewust niet gedaan. Niet omdat we die foto's te schokkend vonden, maar omdat we een ander beeld beter vonden weergeven wat daar gebeurd is."

Volgens Van der Wijk valt het aantal lezersreacties op de foto's in zijn krant tot nu toe mee. Dat is dan opvallend. Wellicht kan de *NRC*-lezer meer hebben dan die van *de Volkskrant*. Fotoredacteur Gerrit-Jan van Ek en zijn collega's van *de Volkskrant* weten alles van wat foto's met lezers kunnen doen. De pontificale plaatsing op de voorpagina van de foto van de vermoorde Pim Fortuyn in mei vorig jaar leverde vele woedende telefoontjes op. Hetzelfde gold voor de reeks beelden van de executie van een Taliban-strijder in Afghanistan. Van Ek: „Dergelijke beelden roepen grote weerstanden op. De argumenten zijn steeds dezelfde, zoals: onze kinderen krijgen die krant ook onder ogen. Toch zie ik het als onze plicht hiermee door te gaan. De lezers moeten weten wat oorlog is. En tegen lezers die boos opbellen zeg ik: u moest eens weten wat er aan afschuwelijk materiaal niet door de selectie komt. Lezers denken altijd dat de fotoredactie uit is op de meest gruwelijke beelden. Maar dat is niet zo. Juist de wat minder afschuwelijke foto's hebben de grootste impact. Ga je een bepaalde rand over, dan willen de mensen niet meer kijken, vermoedelijk omdat ze in onze cultuur nauwelijks meer iets gewend zijn."

Wim Jansen, adjunct-hoofdredacteur van *Trouw* en dagelijks nauw betrokken bij de fotoselectie is het daarmee eens: „Je wilt als krant alle aspecten van de oorlog laten zien. De vraag is welke middelen je daarvoor inzet. Er is een breed scala van heel subtiele foto's tot buitengewoon wrede, rechttoe rechtaan foto's. Het is niet gezegd dat die laatste aan hun doel beantwoorden. Sterk confronterende beelden kunnen de aandacht ook afleiden van dat wat je wilt laten zien. Toon je afgerukte ledematen dan loop je de kans dat de lezers alleen nog maar staren naar een uitstekend stuk bot. Of ze willen de foto helemaal niet meer zien. Lijken in de krant zijn niet verboden, maar ze zijn al gauw te shockerend."

Met het tegendeel van de harde foto – het mooie plaatje – heeft Jansen trouwens even grote problemen. Het gaat er immers wel om iets van de rauwe werkelijkheid weer te geven. Van Ek van *de Volkskrant* vond vooral in het begin van de oorlog de esthetiek veel te overheersend in zijn krant: plaatjes van Amerikaanse macho-soldaten, vliegdekschepen en tanks, mooi met tegenlicht genomen. Maar veel anders werd er in het begin ook niet aangeleverd, volgens hem. „We kregen nauwelijks de kans een compleet beeld van de oorlog te geven. Natuurlijk waren er op dat moment ook minder beelden van slachtoffers dan nu. Maar toch hadden we het idee: we kijken niet goed. Die beelden zijn wel mooi, maar geven ook weinig informatie. Eind vorige week hebben we het roer omgegooid. Toen plaatsten we de foto van Iraakse lijken met op de achtergrond de doorzeefde bus."

Natuurlijk hebben de fotografen ter plaatse te maken met Amerikaanse censuur. Foto's van dode Amerikanen of Britten worden door de westerse persbureau's niet aangeleverd. Zelfcensuur doet vermoedelijk de rest, want de Amerikaanse media staan ook nog eens onder enorme druk van hun kijkers en lezers.

Per saldo resteert de vraag: is de werkelijkheid van de oorlog – gefilmd, beschreven of gefotografeerd – ooit weer te geven? Nee, natuurlijk. Wat *Trouw*-columnist Koen Koch vorige week over de live-verslaggeving op tv schreef, geldt ook voor de fotografie: „De doodsangst, de moordlust, de stank van de volgescheten broeken, de honger, de dorst, de intense vermoeidheid na dagen vechten, we kunnen het niet weten."

Wednesday, October 8, 2003

Capital Corp.: 2.07% 30 days; 2.07% two months; 2.10% three months; 2.10% four months; 2.10% five months; 2.11% six months.
Dealer Commercial Paper: High-grade unsecured notes sold through dealers by major corporations: 1.02% 30 days; 1.03% 60 days; 1.06% 90 days.
Certificates of Deposit: 1.06% one month; 1.10% three months; 1.11% six months.
Bankers Acceptances: 1.06% 30 days; 1.06% 60 days; 1.08% 90 days; 1.08% 120 days; 1.09% 150 days; 1.09% 180 days. Source: Prebon Yamane (USA) Inc.
Eurodollars: 1.08% - 1.06% one month; 1.09% - 1.06% two months; 1.10% - 1.08% three months; 1.11% - 1.09% four months; 1.11% - 1.09% five months; 1.16% - 1.13% six months. Source: Prebon Yamane (USA) Inc.
London Interbank Offered Rates (Libor): 1.1200% one month; 1.1500% three months; 1.1800% six months; 1.3400% one year. Effective rate for contracts entered into two days from date appearing at top of this column.
Euro Libor: 2.10413% one month; 2.13613% three months; 2.15206% six months; 2.25875% one year. Effective rate for contracts entered into two days from date appearing at top of this column.
Euro Interbank Offered Rates (Euribor): 2.103% one month; 2.134% three months; 2.149% six months; 2.246% one year. Source: Reuters.
Foreign Prime Rates: Canada 4.50%; European Central Bank 2.00%; Japan 1.375%; Switzerland 2.13%; Britain 3.50%.
Treasury Bills: Results of the Monday, October 6, 2003, auction of short-term U.S. government bills, sold at a

different editions for different markets. In Europe, it's not unusual for the same paper to have sections in different formats – such as the broadsheet *Guardian* with its tabloid cultural section, *G2*. Sunday and weekend editions may take a different form from the weekday edition, and in North America the Sunday magazine section is a common part of most metropolitan dailies.

The newspaper is no longer just one thing. Every paper is a congeries of information, thought, advertising, and entertainment, packed into a few pages of newsprint and sold at a ridiculously low price every day.

Newspapers get redesigned surprisingly often. *Le Monde* has gone through two redesigns in recent years (though conceivably they could be considered two phases of the same process); the staid *Wall Street Journal* and the *International Herald Tribune* both debuted new designs on the same day; the *San Francisco Examiner*, after being bought from the Hearst Corporation by the Fang family, went through several different designs before settling on one that reflected the paper's new role and identity. A glance at Jim Parkinson's article in this book will give some idea of how many newspapers have had their distinctive nameplates "restored" and "repaired" without the readers, in most cases, being any the wiser. A newspaper's design is its identity, and that identity is a valuable asset; that's why most redesigns are attempts to focus and sharpen the way the paper already looks, rather than to introduce something radically new. But the desire to keep changing things is constant, and both economic pressure and technological change are forces that overwhelm any newspaper that tries to stand still.

Despite the inherent conservatism of newspaper readers, and the way designers often have to slip their changes in so that nobody notices that anything is different (ideally, they just notice that somehow, inexplicably, the paper seems to be looking better), the design of daily newspapers over the last fifteen years has changed quite a bit.

Technology and economics have driven this change. Changing methods of composition and printing, changing competition (from television and now the Web), consolidation of ownership, and most importantly the advent of color, have shaped the newspaper we see and buy today. Even the staid *New York Times* features large, full-color photographs on its front page; and if its news pages have labored mightily to appear just the same as they always looked (even the recent advent of a new family of coordinated headline faces was simply meant to make the *Times* look more like itself), the paper's other sections have blossomed into quite dramatic visual entities – a process that has been seen at many other papers too.

There is more international influence on local papers, as more design trends jump from one country to another – partly because of the way the same consultants get hired to work on redesigns all over the world. (Also because so many papers these days are owned by a conglomerate based in another city or even another country.) National prejudices and preferences certainly do define how a country's newspapers will look, but often enough there's more variety of approach between different newspapers in the same city than there is between comparable papers in different countries.

In North America, the gradual switch in printing facilities to the 50-inch web press, which is narrower than the older presses, has led many broadsheet newspapers

Herald

THE WORLD'S DAILY NEWSPAPER PUBLISHED BY

Commodities: a bad-news 'buy' in rough times

MONEY REPORT | 13

Remembering the liber

2 Europes separated by one currency

Britain is expected to buy some time on joining the euro

By Alan Cowell

LONDON: When Britons finally decide whether or not to join the European single currency, they will ultimately be making a political choice about where they belong: in Europe or somewhere on its fringes.

On Monday, when the chancellor of the Exchequer, Gordon Brown, announces to Parliament whether Britain has met five tests he has devised to discover whether the country needs the euro, the political choice will be

Internet va-t-il démanteler l'éc

En passant en ligne, l'éducation devient la nouvelle frontière de la Netéconomie

EDUCATION.COM contre Education.fr: la bataille de la marchandisation de l'enseignement est ouverte. Selon deux des « six scénarios pour l'école de demain » que le Centre pour la recherche et l'innovation dans l'enseignement de l'OCDE a présentés en avril 2001 aux ministres de l'éducation des pays de l'organisation, le Réseau risque ni plus ni moins de précipiter « le démantèlement des systèmes scolaires ». Dans cette école des années 2015-2020, l'enseignement serait de plus en plus privatisé, et les établissements publics ne subsisteraient que « pour les exclus du numérique », courant le risque de se transformer en « dépotoirs ». Pour Jack Lang, ministre de l'éducation

pour moderniser notre système éducatif et pour faire entrer le multimédia et Internet à l'école ».

Si elles sont alarmistes, les prévisions de l'OCDE n'en révèlent pas moins plusieurs évolutions que suit l'éducation en passant en ligne, à commencer par une marchandisation accrue. Car même si les éditeurs scolaires n'ont pas attendu Internet pour faire leur beurre de l'éducation, l'e-learning se dessine comme le nouvel

Details of a front page from the *International Herald Tribune* (top) and of the front page of a special section from *Le Monde* (above). Opposite: detail of the front page of *The New York Times* on the first day using new headline typefaces (top), and an article from the same issue explaining the change (bottom).

to adapt themselves to a narrower page size – which in turn requires adjustments to the design.

Newspapers tend to come in one of two general formats: broadsheet or tabloid. While there is no precise definition of either term, the broadsheet format is bigger – the broad, long page, folded horizontally in the middle, that we think of first when we think "newspaper" – and the tabloid format is smaller in both dimensions, usually not folded except along the spine – in theory "half size." For a long time, tabloids have been thought of as rougher, cruder, more popular and vulgar than broadsheets; "the tabloids" is virtually a synonym for "the popular press," and often for the right-wing popular press (akin to the "shock jocks" of recent radio). The British tabloids are notorious for their gigantic, one-thought headlines, their "Page Three Girls," their xenophobia, and their obsession with football. American supermarket tabloids cater to simple tastes and credulous readers. A French tabloid's headline I once saw, displayed on a folding wooden sign-board, stole a march on the British tabs by declaring, "*Elizabeth n'est pas la vraie reine!*" ("Elizabeth is not the true queen!"). There have been attempts to snatch the tabloid format away from the simple-minded right wing – for example, an abortive attempt to start a left-wing popular tabloid in Britain in the 1970s – but the real change in the nature of the tabloid has been more recent and more pragmatic: it's simply an economical, practical format in which to publish a newspaper.

It used to be – and in North America it still is – that the real distinction between broadsheets and tabloids was class. You can see this in New York City, where so many people ride to their jobs on public transit of one kind or another. *The New York Times* is a broadsheet, ample enough to read in comfort on a commuter train coming in from the suburbs; the more working-class *New York Post* and *Daily News* are tabloids, easy to fold once vertically and hold in one hand while standing on a crowded subway train. There may be plenty of working-class riders on the commuter trains, and a surprising number of men and women in business suits ride the subway (including the current New York mayor, Michael Bloomberg), but the distinction is real – and the physical difference between the newspapers is practical.

But that smaller, narrower, more portable tabloid is gaining ground, especially in Europe. Perhaps it's the influence of alternative weekly papers, which have almost always chosen the tabloid format, but for whatever reason, tabloids seem to be defying expectations. As Simon Esterson points out in "Kit of parts," tabloid is the preferred format in Spain, and British newspapers as diverse as *The Guardian* and *The Times* have gone to tabloid for their "second" sections.

The newspaper of the future? Some pundits have predicted that it will be smaller, in tabloid format, with full use of color, and more closely focused on information and ideas – what makes a newspaper different from a Web site or the TV news. It's intriguing to try to guess what format might be favored if we really achieve "smart paper," a single sheet that can morph into any page you want; even if you don't hold the entire daily newspaper in your hand at one time, the same need for design and presentation of the news is present, although in a new form. And those who think carefully about the best ways to give us our news, and the entertainment and punditry and advertising that go with it, will do us a service and will probably be in demand for a long time to come. ‹

ISRAELIS HIT GAZA WITH 5 ASSAULTS; 11 DEAD, 90 HURT

ARAFAT GETS NEW WARNING

In Speech to Parliament, Sharon Affirms Plan to Remove Palestinian

By JAMES BENNET

GAZA, Oct. 20 — Israeli warplanes and helicopter gunships struck Gaza five times Monday, killing at least 11 people and wounding more than 90, Palestinian hospital authorities said, as Prime Minister Ariel Sharon affirmed Israel's threat to remove Yasir Arafat.

Sirens wailed through Gaza City late Monday night while Israeli fighter jets continued to tear through the darkness overhead, after one of the most intensive, lethal air barrages of the conflict, now more than three years old.

The deadliest attack of the day came after dark, south of here in the

THE MEDIA BUSINESS

A Face-Lift for The Times, Typographically, That Is

Starting today, the front page and main news sections of The New York Times are receiving a gentle typographical face-lift.

In place of a miscellany of headline typefaces that have accumulated in its columns over the last century, the newspaper is settling on a single family, Cheltenham, in roman and italic versions and various light and bold weights. A narrow variation will be used for The Times's signature one-column headline, which often appears at the top right of Page A1 on the main article of the day. (Before-and-after examples are shown on this page.)

Tom Bodkin, assistant managing editor and design director of The Times, oversaw the changes. "Our

An effort 'to enhance legibility and bring a more orderly look to the pages.'

goals were to enhance legibility and bring a more orderly look to the pages while preserving the ability to convey a clear hierarchy of news values," he said. "We wanted to appear traditional but less old-fashioned. And we felt a need for a more robust, less spindly headline on what is often the biggest story of the day."

The new styles were chosen from day in the Page A1 headline "Sniper Suspect/Is Own Lawyer/As Trial Opens.") All of the other faces were created for The Times — and named for it — by the noted type designer Matthew Carter, who based them on traditional letterforms.

Cheltenham type originated in 1896 designs by Bertram Grosvenor Goodhue and Ingalls Kimball for the Cheltenham Press, a private publisher in New York City.

In the early 1900's the face was refined by Morris Fuller Benton of the American Type Founders Company. It is characterized by lines that are almost uniform in thickness and by serifs, or finishing strokes, that are small and blunt. One of the first uses of Cheltenham in The Times occurred in 1906, in front-page headlines about the great San Francisco earthquake.

Before today's change, at least six headline typefaces commonly appeared on the front page. That kind of variety was customary for newspapers in the early 20th century, possibly because metal type was too costly and scarce for printers to stock full ranges of size within a family.

Victorian-era headlines typically comprised many layers, or "decks," in differing fonts. The Times's one-column signature headline — the "A" head, in newsroom jargon — is an abbreviated holdover of that style, which has otherwise disappeared from the paper.

The compressed type in the top part of the "A" head, before today, was Latin Extra Condensed, a face that originated with many foundries

THE TIMES
DIEU ET MON DROIT

À VOIR
Margie Gillis, la danse de la vie
Comment & Analysis
The new McCarthyites
CULTURA
Arte salvadoreño en el corazón de Manhattan
NZZ am Sonntag
Kultur
Der Herr von Gosford Park
BILL GETS EARLY TEST
Balletrobics
Gazette
DIE ZEIT
Politik im Container
Valor
Crise agravada na Argentina afeta o Brasil
Rocky Mount
Baghdad
America and Islam in a Global World

Contemporary newspaper design

Tomorrow HIP Hotels guide
Don't miss our exclusive offers at some of Europe's most desirable hotels

The Daily Telegraph

www.telegraph.co.uk — Britain's biggest-selling quality daily — Friday, April 5, 2002 50p

Bush tells Israel to withdraw

- President sends Powell to Mid-East
- Sharon lets US envoy meet Arafat

'The storms of violence cannot go on. Enough is enough' — President Bush

'We have to ask why some poor countries are succeeding and others are apparent no-hopers'

Two sightings

Blair's Egyptian 'freebie' attacked

THE Sun

Friday, April 5, 2002 30p www.thesun.co.uk

FREE £1 BET ON GRAND NATIONAL TODAY - PAGE 7 Ladbrokes

GET OUT

Bush's stunning demand

Bush . . . yesterday

£15

THE Mirror

Friday April 5 2002

NEWSPAPER OF THE YEAR x2 32p

Liz has a boy

...AND HE'S CALLED DAMIAN

SEE PAGE 11

£1 BET ON THE GRAND NATIONAL WITH CORAL Voucher Page 31

HYPOCRITE

How dare George Bush preach peace to Israel when he's meeting Blair to plan war on Iraq.. and the deaths of thousands more innocent people?

By JOHN PILGER

ENOUGH IS ENOUGH: PAGES 4 & 5 ● NOT IN OUR NAME: PAGES 6 & 7

Hanif Kureishi — How I face both east and west — Friday Review
Badly Drawn Boy — Going mainstream, in a woolly hat — Friday Review
Jonathan Heaf — Coming out as a handbag carrier — G2
Tariq Ali — Who really killed Daniel Pearl? — Page 20

The Guardian

Enough is enough – Bush

President tells Sharon to end West Bank occupation and blames Arafat for failing to halt wave of suicide bombings

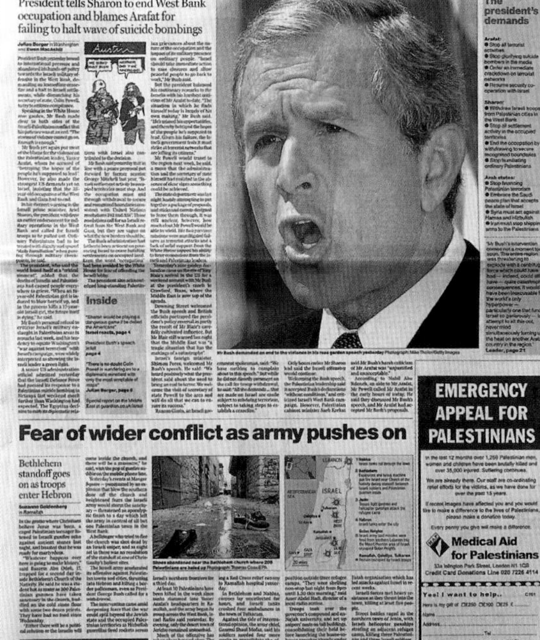

The president's demands

Fear of wider conflict as army pushes on

Bethlehem standoff goes on as troops enter Hebron

EMERGENCY APPEAL FOR PALESTINIANS

Medical Aid for Palestinians

Kit of parts

Simon Esterson

As the news changes, a newspaper's visual vocabulary remains constant

Opposite: Four different British front pages on the same day.

Two contrasting forces shape the design of newspapers. On the one hand, production technologies and the demands of daily or weekly deadlines force them to behave in a similar way; on the other, the need for each title to be different, to have a separate personality and establish a clear position in the market demands that each paper think of itself as unique – and look it.

The way newspapers are made has always had a profound effect on the way they look. Composing, printing, and distributing a newspaper has always been a tightly controlled manufacturing process. Editors want to go to press as late as possible: to get that latest sport result, to update the news story or put in a better picture. Yet once the presses are running, trains and trucks still need time to distribute the papers round the country so they are actually at the newsagents or on the reader's table in the morning. These are absolutes: the pages must go to press. The finer points of language, kerning a headline, or perfect register on press cannot stand in their way. Papers are a perfect example of having to do the best that is achievable in the time available.

Waves of technological change over the past 25 years have rewritten the rules of what is possible in the design of a paper and the way it happens. The machine-age armies of compositors with metal type, assembling pages to the subeditor's instructions, have been reduced and supplanted, first by photosetting; then by direct input by journalists; and now by digital page composition, and transmission of pictures and finished pages. Present-day subeditors lay out their own pages on screen, choose and process the pictures, and send the whole lot directly to press.

Offset litho printing has almost completely replaced rotary letterpress printing, and now the offset plants with limited color facilities are being themselves replaced by machines that will print color on every page and staple the pages together. Increasingly, the production differences between monthly and weekly magazines and multisection daily and weekly newspapers are being narrowed. This has meant that the old ideas about what is possible have changed. Type and rulework had to be very robust in the days of hot metal to stand the crudeness of making the stereoplates and the printing: now fonts don't have to compensate for these pressures. In addition, full color printing and finer screen rulings mean better (and bigger) picture reproduction and the ability to use a full range of color tints and more detailed information graphics.

What is the role of design (and designers) on a newspaper? Because of time and cost pressures, papers are supremely functional objects – "All the News That's Fit to Print" as *The New York Times*'s motto has it. In the newspaper's early form, type was set in narrow columns, with the stories assembled in the order they came into the typesetter's hands, each story beginning with a single-column headline. Even with integrated photographs and display headlines, this is still the essential vernacular of newspaper design, and the person assembling the page today (the subeditor) is in one sense the designer. Yet a paper is also a huge, team-based production: journalists writing stories, editors choosing which to use and assigning their positions within a paper's various sections, while teams of subeditors work in parallel, designing individual pages with pictures and advertisements, writing headlines, and correcting and editing the text to fit. Design is like everything else on a paper: part of the process of editing. A newspaper is a giant kit of parts that gets assembled in different ways each day depending on the emphasis needed for different stories. Contemporary newspaper design is about defining how the kit should look and work. As with a piece of product design, it involves reshaping the parts to take account of a particular newspaper, its audience, its context, and contemporary conditions. Different headline and text typefaces change a paper's appearance, its visual tone of voice, and subtly alter its readability. Multi-section papers mean different content can be given different treatments; sophisticated typesetting systems mean a complex piece of typography, once programmed, can be repeated perfectly on deadline by the subeditor. Just add news and watch the parts assemble.

There has also been a shuffling of roles. With electronic picture desks, the news picture editor's role has changed: anybody with access can choose a picture, and with instant electronic filing by the photographer on location through a laptop there are more pictures available, more quickly, than ever before. The picture editor is struggling to be more than a manager and travel agent for the photographers. As parts of newspapers become more like magazines, and color, information graphics, and typography are given increased emphasis, newspapers now have figures called Design Editors and Creative Directors working alongside the editors and subs.

Why do people read one newspaper in preference to another? Politics? Price? Quality of writing? Better sport or financial news? Easier to read on the train? The choice rests on a complex, largely unspoken equation where design is not apparently the key factor. However, the design of a paper, its visual vocabulary, is integral to its character: from the choice of fonts to its graphics color palette; from the kind and size of pictures it prints to the titlepiece on the front page. In the best papers, these design elements are a perfect match for the journalism: form and content united in expressing a personality. Once established, papers guard these qualities with great care. Newspapers are often afraid to change anything in case they upset their readers, only accepting a dramatic redesign when it has become clear from readers' (and advertisers') responses that the old formulas don't work any more. Television and the Internet have forced papers to be much clearer in how they define themselves: decide what works best for print and learn how you can use the authority of your name to provide linked content for other media, too.

The same models for newspapers – the serious and the sensational, the national, regional, and specialist – can be found all over the world, but they have evolved and been refined by their own national histories and traditions.

In Great Britain the tabloid press, typified by the *Daily Mirror* (until recently *The Mirror*) or *The Sun*, means sensational (and by traditional implication working class). Broadsheet means serious reporting (and not working class). The idea of a serious UK paper produced as a tabloid has been talked about, but none of the existing broadsheets dares change its main news section. Partly, it's about advertising sizes and presses, but in large part (given that the same plant that prints *The Sun* prints *The Times*) it is the sheer weight of British newspaper tradition.

But in Germany, *Bild* is a broadsheet paper with the same tastes (and wonderful bold sans serif typography) as *The Sun*. The other leading German broadsheet, the *Frankfurter Allgemeine Zeitung*, is one of the most austerely designed papers in the world. In Spain most newspapers are tabloid, such as the authoritative left-wing national daily *El País* or *El Periódico*, the Catalan mid-market regional.

The essence of newspaper design is making choices about how to present the news: the news is different every day, but the graphic vocabulary for each paper remains the same. For some papers (and their readers), big sans serif all-capitals headlines, thick rule boxes, and mixed typesetting measures mean urgency and an energetic display of the latest news. For others, restrained headline sizes, stories with background panels, and clear signposting also mean the latest news, but put in a context of commentary, background, and different perspectives. ‹

Design on a daily newspaper is part of the process of editing

One nation, two styles. The leading German broadsheets could not be more different in approach. *Bild* makes the news urgent and vital with a carefully honed vocabulary of tightly fitting type, boxes, reversed-out panels, and other dingbat delights. The *Frankfurter Allgemeine* presents the news with a sense of calm and analytical control: uniformly small headlines, a great deal of text, and no pictures. News, commentary, and an index to the rest of the paper are all contained on the front page.

Herz-Skandal weitet sich aus

Ärzte betrügen ...wir zahlen!

Super-Bingo

Goldene Zahl: 71983494

Entwischen impossible.

Alien Special

Samstag,

Bild

UNABHÄNGIG · ÜBERPARTEILICH

Bundesliga

Völler löst Calmund ab

Superrätsel

12000 Mark gewonnen!

Tic Tac Toe: Der Haß-Auftritt

Böse Worte, viele Tränen

Reisepässe bald länger gültig

Firmen planen mehr Besuche bei Kranken

Energie-Prognose: Verbrauch sinkt

Autofahrer: Spanier wild, Briten brav

„Ein Herz für Kinder" Viele Stars dabei

NACHRICHTEN

Lisa ist topfit für die Disco

Viele Computer ohne Norm

Neue Hoffnung für Krebspatienten

TV-Tip

Weihnachts-Geschenke, die schnell weg sind

Frankfurter Allgemeine

ZEITUNG FÜR DEUTSCHLAND

Verletzte bei Selbstmordanschlag in Haifa

Indiskretionen und Mißtrauen in der CDU bringen die Vorsitzende in Bedrängnis

Amerikanische Luftwaffe bombardiert Tora Bora

Hauen und Stechen

KaDeWe für alle

THE Sun

FREE £1 BET
ON GRAND NATIONAL TODAY - PAGE 7

GET OUT

Bush's stunning demand to Israel

It's a boy for Liz..2 weeks Hurley

£15 SUMMER HOLIDAYS TOKEN 1

As the news changes, a newspaper's visual vocabulary remains constant

April 5, 2002. One day's news as presented by four British newspapers. *The Sun* and *The Mirror* display the same typographic approach, but different news priorities. When you have a tabloid page and you want to shout, bold condensed sans serif is the common option. The broadsheet *Guardian* favours bold sans serif, while *The Daily Telegraph* likes serif fonts and the Queen, but once you have to incorporate barcodes, advertisements, and promotional panels, the disposition of elements becomes remarkably similar.

THE Mirror

Friday April 5 2002

NEWSPAPER OF THE YEAR x2 32p

Liz has a boy

..AND HE'S CALLED DAMIAN

SEE PAGE 11

FREE £1 BET ON THE GRAND NATIONAL WITH CORAL Voucher Page 31

HYPOCRITE

How dare George Bush preach peace to Israel when he's meeting Blair to plan war on Iraq..and the deaths of thousands more innocent people?

By JOHN PILGER

PRESIDENT George W Bush yesterday called on Israel to withdraw from the Palestinian cities occupied by its forces during the last week.

He excused Israel's violence, but lectured the Palestinians and the rest of the Middle East on the need for restraint and a lasting peace.

"The storms of violence cannot go on," said Bush. "Enough is enough."

What he neglected to say was that he needs a lull in the present crisis to lay his own war plans; that while he talks of peace in the Middle East, he is secretly planning a massive attack on Iraq.

This historic display of hypocrisy by Bush will be on show at his ranch in Texas today, with Tony Blair, his collaborator, in admiring attendance.

Yes, enough is enough. It is time Tony Blair came clean with the British people on his part in the coming violence against a nation of innocent people.

● ENOUGH IS ENOUGH: PAGES 4 & 5 ● NOT IN OUR NAME: PAGES 6 & 7

Tomorrow HIP Hotels guide

Don't miss our exclusive offers at some of Europe's most desirable hotels

The Daily Telegraph

FINAL* No 45,663

www.telegraph.co.uk | **Britain's biggest-selling quality daily** | Friday, April 5, 2002 **50p**

Bush tells Israel to withdraw

- President sends Powell to Mid-East
- Sharon lets US envoy meet Arafat

By Toby Harnden in Washington and Andy McSmith

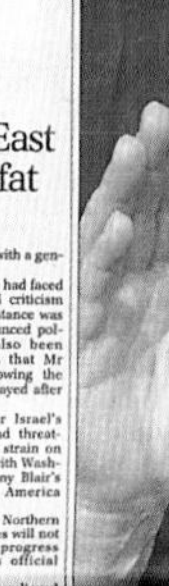

'The storms of violence cannot go on. Enough is enough'

– President Bush

PRESIDENT Bush demanded an Israeli withdrawal from the West Bank last night and ordered his secretary of state, Gen Colin Powell, to the region.

Ariel Sharon, the Israeli prime minister, responded immediately by allowing Gen Anthony Zinni, Mr Bush's special envoy, to meet Yasser Arafat, the Palestinian leader, in his besieged Ramallah headquarters today.

But he insisted that the military siege in Palestinian towns would continue, according to Israeli television reports.

Mr Bush, bowing to intense pressure for greater American engagement, condemned Mr Arafat for helping to foment terrorism and said: "The storms of violence cannot go on. Enough is enough."

He recognised Israel's right to defend itself but added: "Yet, to lay the foundations of future peace, I ask Israel to halt incursions into Palestinian controlled areas and begin the withdrawal from those cities it has recently occupied."

Gen Powell will visit the Middle East next week, but American sources made plain that withdrawal was expected "as soon as possible".

The United Nations Security Council endorsed Mr Bush's initiative to send Gen Powell to the Middle East and demanded that Israel withdraw from Palestinian cities "without delay".

The vote was 15-0, with America for the third time in a month voting for a Middle East resolution after blocking such measures for more than a year.

The US intervention coincided with the collapse of an EU mission on its first day.

Josep Pique, the Spanish foreign minister, and Javier Solana, the EU foreign policy chief, left Israel after Mr Sharon rejected their request to see Mr Arafat.

Fighting raged in the West Bank city of Nablus, where tanks and armoured personnel carriers patrolled the streets in the hunt for Palestinian gunmen.

Israeli soldiers were said to have broken through a gate to the rear garden of the Church of the Nativity in Bethlehem and into the neighbouring Milk Grotto on the third day of the siege of the city.

There were reports that troops had exchanged fire with gunmen in the basilica but did not enter it.

Mr Bush decided to send Gen Powell after advisers conceded that a Middle East conflagration could undermine the American-led war against terrorism.

Washington wants to oust Saddam Hussein and calculates that tolerating continued Israeli military operations against Palestinians will alienate Arab allies.

Mr Bush said that Arab states had to "accept Israel as a nation and as a neighbour". Suicide bombers were "not martyrs – they are murderers", he said.

"No nation can negotiate with terrorists, for there is no way to make peace with those whose only goal is death."

But he placed the immediate onus on Mr Sharon, who must recognise that a Palestinian state "needs to be politically and economically viable" and that "Israeli settlement activity in occupied territories must stop".

Mr Bush said: "I speak as a committed friend of Israel. I speak out of a concern for its long-term security, the security that will come with a genuine peace."

The White House had faced fierce international criticism that its pro-Israel stance was resulting in unbalanced policy. There had also been domestic concern that Mr Bush was not showing the leadership he displayed after September 11.

Controversy over Israel's military actions had threatened to put severe strain on Britain's relations with Washington, spoiling Tony Blair's three-day visit to America starting today.

"As we found in Northern Ireland, the two sides will not be able to make progress alone," Mr Blair's official spokesman said.

Mr Blair will be relieved that once again he and the president are taking a similar approach to a key issue.

He is "appalled" by the Middle East violence and has reason to be grateful that it is going to dominate the weekend summit.

The sight of the Prime Minister taking issue with those on the American Right who equate Mr Sharon's actions against the Palestinians with the campaign against international terrorism will go down well with his critics in Britain and Europe who think that he is too close to Mr Bush.

Mr Blair is under intense pressure from the Labour Left not to involve troops in an American-led ground war in Iraq unless it is conducted under the flag of the UN.

His official spokesman emphasised that "no decisions have been taken or will be taken in a rush", adding that Mr Blair expected to return from America with "a better understanding of the threat we face".

The White House believes that Saddam is offering incentives to the families of Palestinian suicide bombers and issued a warning to him.

"To those who would try to use the current crisis as an opportunity to widen the conflict: Stay out."

Saddam was quoted in the Iraqi press yesterday making a rare public comment on the prospect of an American invasion, saying that his war machine could deal with it.

Reports: Pages 8 & 9
Editorial Comment: Page 27

Picture FIONA HANSON

Smiling despite her grief, the Queen greets about 200 well-wishers in the grounds of Windsor Castle yesterday

Blair's Egyptian 'freebie' attacked

By Benedict Brogan, Political Correspondent

TONY BLAIR was accused of cheapening his office last night after it emerged that his family's Christmas holiday by the Red Sea was paid for by the Egyptian taxpayer.

The arrangements are disclosed in Mr Blair's updated entry in the Commons register of members' interests, in which he confirms that the Egyptian government covered the costs.

In exchange, Mr Blair records that he made "donations" to a charity chosen by his hosts. Downing Street last night failed to say how much or to which organisation.

In 1999 Mr Blair was criticised for accepting hospitality from the regional government of Tuscany for his family's summer break, and tried to ease the controversy with a £3,000 donation to a local children's hospital.

The Blairs wanted to keep their six-day private visit to Egypt secret but were spotted by journalists at Cairo airport on Boxing Day. They were photographed at the Pyramids before flying to the diving resort of Sharm el-Sheikh for their winter break.

Mr Blair, his wife Cherie and children Euan, Nicky, Kathryn and Leo, as well as his mother-in-law and members of his entourage, stayed at two villas.

Although no details were made public, pictures of the Blairs enjoying dinner are now displayed on advertising posters for the local China Garden hotel.

At the time Downing Street said the "entirely private" holiday, during which no official duties were carried out, would be paid for by the Blairs, but did not say that accommodation and flights were provided by President Mubarak. Their

Continued on Page 2

She had a wonderful life, Queen tells well-wishers

By Caroline Davies

THE Queen appeared in public yesterday for the first time since her mother's death and told well-wishers: "She had a wonderful life."

Wearing a black coat adorned with a triple string of pearls, she surveyed the sea of 2,000 bouquets laid on the lawn at St George's Chapel in Windsor Castle.

Speaking to Prince Philip, who accompanied her, she said: "It is an amazing sight, isn't it? People are so kind.

"They are from everywhere, you know: America, Australia, New Zealand and Canada."

About 50,000 e-mails have been sent to the Queen Mother's memorial website since her death last Saturday.

More than 200 people had gathered within the castle walls when the Queen arrived. She smiled at one group who offered condolences and said: "My mother lived to 101, which is a great age. She had a wonderful life."

The Queen spent time reading the tributes. Then she entered St George's Chapel, where preparations for Tuesday's private committal service and interment were well advanced, to look at a book of condolence which about 7,000 people have signed.

Buckingham Palace confirmed that the Princess Royal would break with tradition and march behind her grandmother's coffin in today's procession from St James's Palace to Westminster Hall. Normally only male members of the Royal Family march.

The Queen Mother had agreed to her grand-daughter's request, which was made

Continued on Page 2

Procession: Pages 4 & 5
Alice Thomson: Page 27

He only needs one shot to blow you away...
A JACK REACHER NOVEL
LEE CHILD
ECHO BURNING
Say goodnight
Out now in Bantam paperback

'We have to ask why some poor countries are succeeding and others are apparent no-hopers'

R W Johnson: Page 26

Inside

The Daily Telegraph 5-4-02

14

9 770307 123955

Two sightings of 'crying Milly'

By Stewart Payne

A GIRL seen crying at a roadside may have been Amanda Dowler, the missing schoolgirl, police said yesterday.

The sighting is potentially the most significant development in the hunt for the 13-year-old, known as Milly, since she disappeared two weeks ago while walking home from school.

Two witnesses have told police they saw a girl in school uniform fitting the description of Amanda, who appeared to be in tears.

The sightings were in Rydens Road, which is on the route Amanda would have taken to reach home in Walton-on-Thames, Surrey.

One witness said the girl was at the junction with Sidney Road and the other saw her at the junction with Walton Park, about 10 minutes later. The last confirmed sighting was at 4.05pm as Amanda walked away from Walton railway station.

Det Chief Insp Stuart Gibson, the senior investigating officer, called for the girl to come forward.

"It may well be that it was not Milly but another girl," he said. "In which case, we need to eliminate her from our inquiry."

Police also want to trace the driver of a blue Saab seen in Rydens Road on the afternoon of Thursday March 21, the day Amanda disappeared after phoning her father to say she was on her way home.

A witness has reported seeing a young female talking to the driver, and both are urged to contact police so that they can be eliminated from the inquiry.

Amanda Dowler: river search

Police have said they do not believe that Amanda was forcibly abducted because there have been no witnesses to any suspicious behaviour on a route busy with both pedestrian and motor traffic.

Supt Alan Sharp, who is in overall charge of the investigation, said: "We remain focused on finding her alive and bringing her home."

He said that additional officers had been drafted in to sift through more than 1,000 reports concerning the missing girl.

Metropolitan Police divers searched a river near Malden in south-west London after two 12-year-old boys reported seeing a body as they travelled past in a train.

A police spokesman said: "We did come across a discarded blazer but Surrey Police have told us it had nothing to do with Milly. No body was found and that search has been called off."

In Brief

3,000 flee holiday fire

More than 3,000 holidaymakers were taken to safety yesterday as the main dome complex of the Center Parcs holiday village at Elveden, Suffolk, was destroyed by fire. *Page 3*

Gold cup found

A gold ceremonial cup fashioned by Bronze Age artisans around 1,600 BC has been discovered by an amateur archaeologist using a metal detector in a field in Kent. *Page 7*

Boy for Hurley

Elizabeth Hurley, the actress and model, gave birth to a boy, Damian Charles, yesterday. *Page 11*

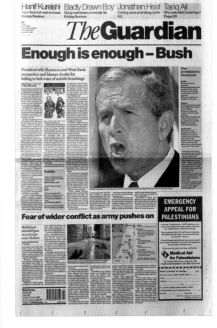

Hanif Kureishi — How I face both east and west — Friday Review
Badly Drawn Boy — Going mainstream, in a woolly hat — Friday Review
Jonathan Heaf — Coming out as a handbag carrier — G2
Tariq Ali — Who really killed Daniel Pearl? — Page 20

The Guardian

Enough is enough – Bush

President tells Sharon to end West Bank occupation and blames Arafat for failing to halt wave of suicide bombings

The president's demands

Inside

Fear of wider conflict as army pushes on

Bethlehem standoff goes on as troops enter Hebron

EMERGENCY APPEAL FOR PALESTINIANS

Medical Aid for Palestinians

EL PAIS

DIARIO INDEPENDIENTE DE LA MAÑANA

DOMINGO 28 DE ABRIL DE 2002
Año XXVII. Número 9.102

EDICIÓN EUROPA
www.elpais.es

EP[S] ESPECIAL BELLEZA

- ▶ Cuerpo a punto para el verano
- ▶ Los bañadores que más brillan
- ▶ Trucos para disfrutar del sol
- ▶ Maquillajes de noche y día
- ▶ Mantener los kilos a raya
- ▶ Ejercicios para estar sanos

George Lucas, el dueño de la galaxia

Los secretos de la nueva película y las imágenes más espectaculares

"Tenemos indicios todos los días de la relación entre ETA y Batasuna"

Entrevista con **Jorge Dezcallar,** director del Centro Nacional de Inteligencia

Jorge Dezcallar, último director del Centro Superior de Información para la Defensa (Cesid) y primero del Centro Nacional de Inteligencia (CNI), el organismo sucesor del anterior, asegura en la primera entrevista que concede desde que accedió al cargo que no le cabe "ninguna duda de la relación de Batasuna con ETA". "Todos los días tengo indicios de ello... Otra cosa son las pruebas judiciales". Dezcallar explica que la creación del CNI no será un cambio "puramente cosmético" con respecto al Cesid, sino que supondrá también "un cambio de mentalidad, de forma de trabajar" de los agentes del servicio secreto. Y así se lo dijo, el pasado viernes, a todos los agentes, tras regresar de un viaje a Canadá: "Lo que hacemos aquí no es nada de deshonroso ni de lo que haya que avergonzarse. Al contrario, podemos sentirnos orgullosos de prestar un servicio a un Estado democrático y satisfechos de que el 95% de los representantes de los ciudadanos nos haya apoyado".

Dezcallar revela cómo en España hay "agentes extranjeros que están operando con mucha agresividad" ante los que la sociedad española "debe defenderse" mediante el contraespionaje. Así, explica que en estos momentos en los que España está ejerciendo la presidencia de la UE, por debajo "de la placidez" aparente "hay mucha actividad". El director del CNI afirma que se recibió información sobre la crisis de Venezuela antes de que estallara ("luego todo se precipitó") y que en algunas mezquitas españolas hay "discursos muy intransigentes que incitan a la violencia". **Páginas 18 y 19**

No hay freno a la violencia doméstica

Ni denuncias ni planes de choque evitan las muertes

Como media, una mujer muere cada semana en España a causa de la violencia doméstica. Un horror que nada parece capaz de frenar, ni las denuncias reiteradas de las víctimas ni los planes de choque del Gobierno, dos desde 1998. El fenómeno crece, además, entre las parejas jóvenes. **Páginas 26 y 27**

DANIEL MORDZINSKI

¡No pasarán!

Más de 200.000 personas se manifestaron ayer en las principales ciudades francesas para mostrar su rechazo al ascenso electoral de la ultraderecha que encabeza Jean-Marie Le Pen, convocadas por asociaciones contra el racismo, sindicatos y partidos políticos democráticos. En la marcha de París, que aparece en la foto, una pancarta recordaba el ¡No pasarán! que popularizaron los republicanos españoles durante la guerra civil.

Páginas 2 y 3 / Editorial en la **página 12**

Cuatro israelíes mueren en un ataque palestino contra una colonia judía en Hebrón

Cuatro personas, entre ellas una niña de cinco años, murieron ayer en las proximidades de la ciudad de Hebrón, en Cisjordania, a manos de un comando palestino. El ataque del *comando* amenaza con bloquear las negociaciones para buscar una solución al asedio de la basílica de la Natividad en Belén y puede complicar la misión de investigación de la ONU destinada a esclarecer la presunta matanza cometida por el Ejército israelí en Yenín. **Página 8**

Un hijo de Pujol hizo de consultor en la mayor privatización de la Generalitat

La firma Europraxis, de la que es fundador y estratega Josep Pujol Ferrusola —hijo del presidente de la Generalitat de Cataluña, Jordi Pujol—, actuó en 1999 como consultora en la mayor privatización realizada por la Generalitat, la de Catalana de Telecomunicacion. **Página 17**

PRECIOS DE EL PAÍS

Alemania	3,20 €	Italia	2,75 €
Austria	3,40 €	Luxemburgo	3,00 €
Bélgica	3,00 €	Marruecos	30 MDH
Dinamarca	28 KRD	Noruega	29,60 KRN
Eslovaquia	135 Sk	Polonia	9,20 ZLT
Estados Unidos	3,25 $	Portugal (Cont.)	2,30 €
Finlandia	2,75 €	Reino Unido	1,80 £
Francia	3,00 €	Rep. Checa	105 Kc
Grecia	2,50 €	Rumania	50.100 LEI
Holanda	3,00 €	Rusia	50 R
Hungría	530 Ft	Suecia	33 KRS
Irlanda	3,00 €	Suiza	5,20 Fs.

En el precio se incluye *El País Semanal*. En Hungría, Finlandia, Polonia, Rumania y Rusia no se distribuye este suplemento.

Muere el barón Thyssen, el gran coleccionista de arte

Ayer, a la una de la madrugada, Hans Heinrich von Thyssen-Bornemisza murió en su residencia de Sant Feliu de Guíxols (Girona) a los 81 años. Dueño de una fortuna valorada en más de 3.100 millones de euros, el barón destacó como un gran coleccionista de arte. Su esposa, Carmen Cervera, lo acompañó hasta el último momento. En 1993, el Estado español compró el núcleo central de su colección, que se expone en Madrid y Barcelona. **Páginas 32 a 34**

Domingo

Estado de alerta en Europa

El filósofo italiano **Paolo Flores d'Arcais** analiza el origen del preocupante ascenso de la derecha radical, que el triunfo de Le Pen en Francia ha puesto de explosiva actualidad en todo el continente

La extrema derecha española está fragmentada y sin líder

El populismo sube en países ricos como Austria, Holanda y Alemania

Negocios

'Eurodeclaración' de la renta

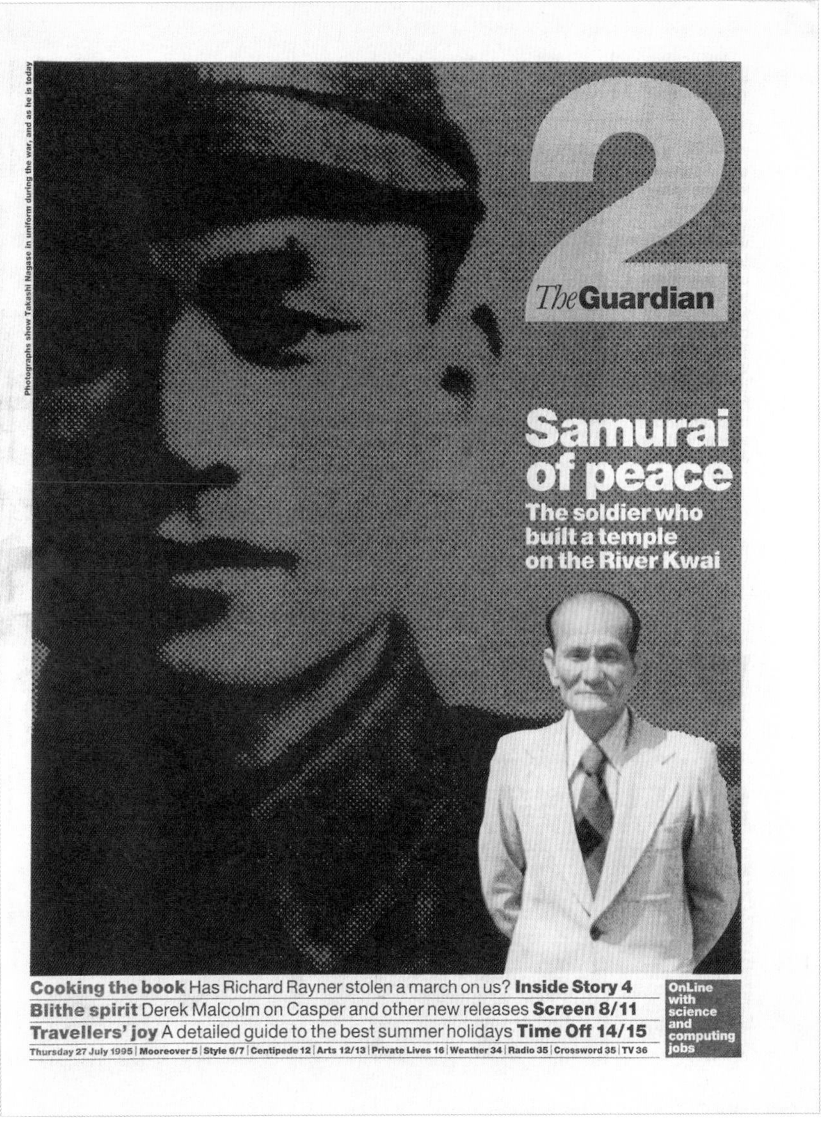

Photographs show Takashi Nagase in uniform during the war, and as he is today

2
The Guardian

Samurai of peace
The soldier who built a temple on the River Kwai

Cooking the book Has Richard Rayner stolen a march on us? **Inside Story 4**
Blithe spirit Derek Malcolm on Casper and other new releases **Screen 8/11**
Travellers' joy A detailed guide to the best summer holidays **Time Off 14/15**
Thursday 27 July 1995 | Mooreover 5 | Style 6/7 | Centipede 12 | Arts 12/13 | Private Lives 16 | Weather 34 | Radio 35 | Crossword 35 | TV 36

OnLine with science and computing jobs

In Spain, most papers are tabloid. The national daily *El País* uses its front page to highlight lots of stories which are covered in more detail inside. Serif fonts and the ubiquitous thin-rule box give typographic structure.

The British paper *The Guardian* has ignored broadsheet prejudices against the tabloid format by making *G2*, its daily second section, into a features-based near-magazine.

In the best papers, design is a perfect match for the journalism

Latin American broadsheet papers bear the stamp of North American newspaper design.

In Brazil, *Agora* uses Font Bureau's recut Bureau Grotesque and colored type to make a bold but organized daily. *O Globo*, based in Rio de Janeiro, collaborated with Milton Glaser and Walter Bernard to create an intelligent mainstream national paper, including working the national colors into the titlepiece.

For Mexico's *Reforma*, Roger Black and Eduardo Danilo used the possibilities of good offset color printing to make a modern paper with fine serif fonts, bold slab serifs for emphasis, and rule elements that appear to have been derived from the Aztecs.

R$0,50

Agora
São Paulo

PAULISTÃO
Saiba quais bancas vendem ingresso barato
Pág. B-4

NOVA PROMOÇÃO
Comece domingo a colecionar o melhor Atlas da História do Mundo

LÍDER DOS AMBULANTES DO VIADUTO SANTA IFIGÊNIA ERA UM HOMEM "MARCADO PARA MORRER"

Assassinado camelô que acusou máfia da propina

PREFEITO SOFRE NOVA DERROTA NA JUSTIÇA

Tribunal cassa mandato, mas Pitta vai continuar no cargo

DENÚNCIA
Notas fiscais do PAS apontam superfaturamento
Pág. A-4

CÂMARA
Governistas já admitem comissão contra o prefeito
Pág. A-7

SUCESSÃO
Erundina ganha com as denúncias feitas por Nicéa
Pág. A-7

REGIÃO
Ministro já mela mínimo de R$ 160
Pág. A-11

OLÁ!
Luana Piovani revela que quer ser mãe
Pág. A-2

JUSTIÇA
Paquistanês condenado a virar picadinho
Pág. A-14

FÓRMULA 1
Chuva atrasa fim das obras em Interlagos
Pág. B-7

AVIÃO

TENSÃO
Rincón manda blindar o carro e Luizão desabafa

QUEDA NAS ALTURAS
Defesa erra demais e Palmeiras perde na Libertadores

PESQUISA
Custo de vida na zona leste é o menor da cidade
Pág. A-10

O GABARITO DA PRIMEIRA PROVA DO VESTIBULAR DA UFF • PÁGINA 21

O GLOBO

IPTU da orla terá desconto reduzido
Página 15

FH critica os políticos ao reagir a ACM
Página 3

Cresce peso de estrangeiros no PIB do país
Página 23

ESPORTES

Flu empata em Manaus e lidera a Terceirona

Atlético vence Corinthians no primeiro jogo da final

Crise na Segurança derruba o chefe de Polícia do Rio

Líder do PDT na Alerj afirma que o projeto Delegacia Legal foi superfaturado

Página 11

Candidato de esquerda sai na frente no Chile

Páginas 28 e 29

TESTE: *Viagem da Praça XV à Barra*

Página 20

— Eu sei que isso é política mas... estão usando contraceptivo?

Paul McCartney en México: Llega a la ciudad (3D) 25,000 lo aclaman (1D)

Viernes 26 de Noviembre de 1993
México, D.F.

74 Páginas
7 Secciones
N$ 2.00

SECCIÓN A

REFORMA

CORAZON DE MEXICO

Año 1, Número 00

Ciudad

Investiga Policía a 10 sospechosos

▸ La Procuraduría del DF informó ayer que la balacera ocurrida el miércoles en la noche en el restaurant Bali Hai tenía como propósito eliminar a Amado Carrillo Fuentes, presunto narcotraficante que logró huir. La PJ investiga a cuando menos 10 sospechosos. (10B)

Iniciará programa anticontaminante

▸ La Comisión Metropolitana para la Prevención y Control de la Contaminación dio a conocer ayer una serie de acciones y recomendaciones para el Invierno 93-94, que se aplicarán del primero de diciembre al 31 de marzo del próximo año. (1B)

Medidas de invierno

▸ Reducir hidrocarburos en gasolina.
▸ Aumentar 50% inspecciones a industria
▸ Se detendrán vehículos contaminantes

Negocios

Establecerían filiales financieras en México

▸ Los intermediarios financieros extranjeros de los países con los que México tiene tratados de liberalización financiera podrían establecer filiales en México, según establece la iniciativa de reforma a la legislación financiera que envió el Presidente de México al Congreso de la Union. (13A)

Alberto Aguilar

▸ La AMB que preside Roberto Hernández solicitó a Hacienda eliminar el impuesto al ahorro de personas físicas, actualmente de 1.7 por ciento. Existen buenas probabilidades de que la autoridad acceda. Femsa-Coca Cola, invertirá cinco millones de dólares en el aeropuerto del D.F.

Alberto Barranco

▸ El paquete de implementación del TLC tiene como propósito dar consistencia a ese tratado internacional, que es ley suprema, con las leyes secundarias. (18A)

Opinión

Granados Chapa

Acción Nacional y el PRI disputarán el próximo domingo la gubernatura, las diputaciones y los ayuntamientos en Yucatán. La redistritación electoral, es una muestra de las dificultades que ponen tensión en el ambiente yucateco. (7A)

Adrián Lajous

En el momento crítico de la batalla interna por el TLC, Clinton empezó a usar con éxito un argumento que sirvió para reanimar a los deprimidos. Les dijo que no deberían escuchar a los negativistas. (8A)

Adolfo Aguilar Zinser

El plan sucesorio que estaría fraguándose ahora mismo en Los Pinos no es para transferir definitivamente las riendas del gobierno y los hilos del poder al preferido, sino la nominación de un regente que gobernaría en nombre de Salinas. (9A)

Propone Salinas cambios a 18 códigos

Ajustan leyes al TLC

Facilitan inversión extranjera y apertura financiera, dando preferencia a Estados Unidos y Canadá

Por Julieta Medina

El Presidente de la República envió ayer al Congreso un paquete de reformas que ajustan 18 leyes y códigos mexicanos al Tratado de Libre Comercio de América del Norte.

Las iniciativas incluyen cambios en materias de inversión extranjera, legislación bancaria, derechos de autor, comercio exterior, ley de profesiones, aduanas, y obras públicas entre otros puntos, se discutirán en las próximas semanas, y de aprobarse, entrarían en vigor el 1 de enero de 1994.

En la propuesta legislativa se liberalizan las condiciones para la entrada de inversión extranjera, se contempla trato preferente para las mercancías estadounidenses y canadienses, se dan facilidades para que profesionistas de esos países ejerzan en México y se abre la puerta para la llegada de bancos y financieras extranjeras a partir de 1994.

También se otorgan facultades al Tribunal Fiscal de la Federación para resolver conflictos por prácticas desleales de comercio y se amplia la protección de derechos de autor de 50 a 75 años para su explotación posterior a la muerte del creador, sea éste nacional o extranjero.

Además, se sujetan las expropiaciones, las prácticas aduaneras y las leyes fiscales a lo marcado en los tratados internacionales que ha firmado México, y se incluyen las bajas en aranceles pactadas en el TLC en los códigos arancelarios correspondientes.

Los cambios planteados por el Presidente Salinas se incluyen en cuatro iniciativas: una que modifica nueve leyes, conocida como "miscelánea TLC", otra que modifica siete leyes, conocida como "paquete financiero", además de iniciativas de cambio a la Ley de Inversiones Extranjeras y a la Ley de Adquisiciones y Obra Pública.

Entre los cambios más importantes que se plantean en las iniciativas presidenciales se cuenta los referente a la inversión extranjera, en la que prácticamente se eliminan requisitos para inversiones menores a 100 millones de dólares ubicadas fuera de las tres mayores zonas metropolitanas.

Les da trato preferente a las empresas estadounidenses y de Canadá sobre las del resto del mundo y abre a la inversión extranjera sectores antes restringidos, tales como el de autopartes.

Se permite que los extranjeros hagan inversiones a través de fideicomisos en la frontera y los litorales, cosa prohibida previamente.

La ley da la categoría de empresa mexicana a toda la que se establezca en el País, aunque su capital sea mayoritariamente extranjero.

Las nuevas leyes
El Presidente Carlos Salinas de Gortari introdujo ayer un paquete legislativo que modifica 18 leyes a fin de ajustarlas a lo acordado con Estados Unidos y Canadá en el Tratado de Libre Comercio de América del Norte.
Estas son las más importantes:
Paquete Financiero
Marca las bases para que a partir del próximo año operen en México bancos e instituciones financieras extranjeras.
Ley de Inversión Extranjera
Elimina requisitos para inversiones medianas, abre nuevos sectores a la inversión foránea y permite inversión extranjera mayoritaria en zonas del País y ramas en las que antes esto estaba restringido.
Ley General de Profesiones.
Se permitirá que profesionistas extranjeros puedan ejercer en México.
Ley de Comercio Exterior
Adapta para México las reglas internacionales en materia de subsidios y dumping.

La silla vacía: ¿De quién es?

Mientras el Presidente Carlos Salinas de Gortari pronunciaba su discurso ante maestros en un acto del SNTE, Luis Donaldo Colosio y Manuel Camacho Solís flanquean el lugar destinado al Primer Mandatario.

Critica Cárdenas a Gobernación

Conversa candidato con sacerdote y empresarios

Por Miguel Pérez y Fabián Muñoz
REFORMA/Enviados

AGUASCALIENTES.- La negativa del secretario de Gobernación a platicar con la dirigencia del PRD es una actitud de cerrazón que no debe sorprender a nadie, afirmó ayer Cuauhtémoc Cárdenas en conferencia de prensa.

"No muestra más que una actitud de cerrazón por parte de las autoridades de la Secretaría, cosa que por otro lado no debe sorprender a nadie", dijo.

El miércoles por la noche la dirigencia perredista y la secretaría de Gobernación iniciarían pláticas sobre el pacto de civilidad, pero la dependencia rechazó dialogar bajo presiones rechazando la concentración de perredistas que se había instalado afuera de esa dependencia.

Cárdenas.

El PRD seguirá buscando la solución de los problemas, pero exige un trato digno de parte de las autoridades, agregó

Interrogado sobre la posibilidad de que priístas renuncien a su partido después de la nominación del candidato a la Presidencia de la República, el perredista señaló que en el PRD no se cobran cuentas.

Postulan a Carrillo Olea

Sectores priístas anuncian su apoyo dos horas después del registro de precandidatos

REFORMA/ Especial

CUERNAVACA.- Jorge Carrillo Olea fue postulado ayer como candidato del PRI a la gubernatura del estado de Morelos.

s

Poco antes del pronunciamiento, la cúpula priísta estatal, encabezada por el coordinador nacional, Eduardo Thomé, el presidente del CDE, Jorge Martínez, y el enviado del CEN, Alejandro Díaz de León, se reunió con el gobernador Antonio Riva Palacio en Casa de Gobierno.

Jorge Carrillo Olea.

A las 11:00 horas de ayer se efectuó una reunión de análisis en la que se eligió la Comisión Dictaminadora para el registro de aspirantes a precandidatos del PRI, integrada por Rubén, Román Sánchez, Vinicio Limón Rivera, Leandro Vique Salazar y Víctor Manuel Saucedo, quienes iniciaron los pronunciamientos a favor del ahora candidato priísta, quien les agradeció el apoyo.

Ayuda Sedesol a la Iglesia

Antes, la colaboración del Gobierno en obras sociales era oculta, ahora es abierta, afirma arzobispo

Por María Elena Medina

La Secretaría de Desarrollo Social colabora con los trabajos de la Iglesia Católica y desde que se hicieron las modificaciones al Artículo 130 de la Constitución, estas cosas no se hacen por debajo de la mesa, dijo Héctor González Martínez, Arzobispo de Oaxaca.

"De una manera simulada, así bajo la mesa, (la Sedesol) habría apoyado antes obras sociales de la Iglesia. Ahora, después de las reformas al 130, yo sé que de una manera más abierta, más clara y sincera, está apoyando también proyectos sociales que lleva a cabo la Iglesia en distintos rumbos de la Nación", dijo el prelado.

Héctor González.

"A mí me consta", aseguró, "que algunos proyectos fuertes, concretos, que se están desarrollando en Oaxaca con el apoyo formal de la Sedesol, que es un organismo del Gobierno".

El también presidente de la Comisión Episcopal de la Pastoral Social, informó que la Secretaría de Desarrollo ha apoyado en Oaxaca la remodelación de un hospital y la construcción de una casa de formación para muchachas indígenas, entre otras obras.

En una rueda de prensa sobre el ciclo "Economía y Desarrollo Integral, Retos y Alternativas para América Latina", organizado por la Comisión Episcopal de Pastoral Social y Cáritas Internacionales, el Arzobispo de Oaxaca aclaró que lo anterior no quiere decir que Iglesia y Estado no tengan su propia identidad.

"No es que nos estemos subiendo al carro del Estado.(Antes de las reformas al 130), distintos gobiernos, de una manera prudente, oculta, apoyaban una iniciativa u otra",dijo.s

Para nosotros, el lector es lo más importante • Nos interesa su opinión • Tel: 628-7100/ Fax: 628-7188

NRC HANDELSBLAD

LUX ET LIBERTAS

www.nrc.nl

ALGEMEEN HANDELSBLAD (1828) EN NIEUWE ROTTERDAMSE COURANT (1844)

DONDERDAG 2 AUGUSTUS 2001
JAARGANG 31 NO. 256

Prijs: ƒ 2,50 (1,13 euro)

Koeler

Vanavond en vannacht enkele (onweers)buien en broeierig. Morgen vooral in het oosten nog een bui. Temperaturen van 20 tot 24 graden. Vooruitzichten tot en met maandag: Af en toe zon, maar ook enkele buien. Temperaturen rond 21 graden.

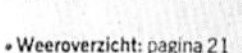

• **Weeroverzicht:** pagina 21

Vinkeveen recreëert pal aan de snelweg A2

• **Binnenland:** pagina 2

Fox belooft veel, maar biedt Mexico weinig of niets

• **Buitenland:** pagina 4

St. Andrews in Schotland: bakermat van golf

• **Agenda:** pagina 15

Doorbraak over status van het Albanees

Overleg Macedonië: akkoord over taal

OHRID, 2 AUG. De Macedonische partijen hebben gisteren in het vredesoverleg in Ohrid een doorbraak geboekt: ze bereikten een deelakkoord over de status van de Albanese taal, een van de gevoeligste punten van het overleg.

De partijen van de Slavische en van de Albanese Macedoniërs spraken af dat het Albanees de status van tweede officiële taal – naast het Macedonisch – krijgt in gebieden waar de Albanezen twintig procent of meer van de bevolking uitmaken. Ook in het parlement zal het Albanees mogen worden gesproken, in plenaire zittingen en in commissievergaderingen. Wetten en wetsvoorstellen worden in twee talen opgesteld. In de ministerraad zal alleen Macedonisch worden gesproken. De Albanezen hebben aanzienlijke concessies gedaan: zij eisten voor het Albanees de status van tweede officiële taal op het hele grondgebied van Macedonië.

Partijwoordvoerders en de internationale bemiddelaars François Léotard en James Pardew onderstreepten gisteren in Ohrid dat het slechts om een voorwaardelijk akkoord gaat, dat pas definitief wordt als over alle resterende problemen ook overeenstemming wordt bereikt. „Het akkoord is voorwaardelijk tot het hele kaderakkoord en alle bijvoegsels zijn goedgekeurd. Dat betekent dat niets is voltooid tenzij alles voltooid is", aldus de Amerikaan Pardew.

Het belangrijkste punt waarover de partijen het nu nog eens moeten worden betreft de politie. De Macedoniërs willen de politie gecentraliseerd houden. De Albanezen eisen dat burgemeesters het recht krijgen de politiechefs in hun gemeenten te benoemen. Volgens de Macedoniërs zou dat de politie kwetsbaar maken voor corruptie. Het zou zelfs kunnen betekenen dat leiders van het Albanese rebellenleger UÇK politiechef in Albanese gemeenten zouden kunnen worden. De Albanezen eisen verder dat de gemeentepolitie in haar samenstelling de etnische verhoudingen in gemeenten weergeeft.

Het overleg in Ohrid wordt vrijdag voortgezet. Vandaag viert Macedonië zijn nationale feestdag.

De Macedonische minister van Defensie, Vlado Bučkovski, een uitgesproken hardliner in het conflict, beloofde gisteren niet meer militair te reageren op kleine provocaties van het UÇK om het overleg in Ohrid een grotere kans van slagen te geven. „De slag om Macedonië wordt in Ohrid uitgevochten", aldus de minister.

Tot dusverre heeft het Macedonische leger elke actie van het UÇK met buitenproportioneel geweld beantwoord, hetgeen de spanning in Macedonië hoog heeft gehouden.

Een andere hardliner, minister van Binnenlandse Zaken Ljube Boškovski, liet zich in geheel andere zin uit. Hij zei gisteren dat de enige oplossing voor Macedonië is gelegen in harde militaire actie tegen het UÇK. „Ze hebben elke grens overschreden. Ze blijven militair geweld gebruiken, ze terroriseren de Macedoniërs en verdrijven hen uit hun woningen. We moeten zelfs de laatste optimist overtuigen dat de enige optimistische variant het verslaan van de terroristen is." (Reuters, AP, AFP)

Ziekenhuizen behandelen meer patiënten

DEN HAAG, 2 AUG. De ziekenhuizen hebben in de eerste helft van dit jaar meer mensen behandeld dan in dezelfde periode in 2000. Het is echter nog onduidelijk of dat invloed heeft op hun wachtlijsten. Bij de thuiszorg, verpleeghuizen en inrichtingen zijn de wachttijden wel aanzienlijk afgenomen. • *Pagina 2*

Politie ontruimt Italiaans consulaat

AMSTERDAM, 2 AUG. De politie heeft gisteren met zachte hand een einde gemaakt aan de bezetting van het Italiaanse consulaat in Amsterdam. Ongeveer dertig activisten hadden gistermorgen de handelsmissie bezet uit protest tegen het politie-optreden tijdens de G8 in Genua. • *Pagina 2*

Buhrmann moet belofte intrekken

AMSTERDAM, 2 AUG. Buhrmann (kantoorartikelen) heeft dit jaar zijn vierde winstwaarschuwing gegeven. Het bedrijf, met op jaarbasis een omzet van meer dan 20 miljard gulden, publiceerde vanochtend een kwartaalbericht dat fors lager uitviel dan verwacht. • *Pagina 9*

Berging Koersk duurt langer

ROTTERDAM, 2 AUG. De voorbereidingen van het Nederlandse consortium Mammoet-Smit voor de berging van de Koersk heeft vertraging opgelopen. Het maken van gaten in de romp heeft meer tijd gekost dan gedacht. • *Pagina 11*

Zwaardere eisen EU aan kip en ei

BRUSSEL, 2 AUG. De Europese Commissie gaat normen opstellen voor salmonella en soortgelijke besmettingen. Over enkele jaren worden de EU-landen verplicht om kip en ei steekproefsgewijs te controleren. • *Pagina 2*

Kritiek Kamer op Ambon-gift RMS

DEN HAAG, 2 AUG. De Tweede Kamer wil opheldering van het kabinet over geld van de Zuid-Molukse regering in ballingschap (RMS) waarmee lokale verzetsgroepen op Ambon vermoedelijk wapens aanschaffen. • *Pagina 3*

Boren in Alaska

WASHINGTON, 2 AUG. Het Amerikaanse Huis van Afgevaardigden heeft gisteren zijn steun gegeven aan een pakket energiemaatregelen dat het boren naar olie en gas in een natuurgebied in Alaska toestaat. • *Pagina 4*

KĘPA GOSTECKA – In Kępa Gostecka, in het zuidoosten van Polen, heeft de buiten haar oevers getreden Wisla het dorpskerkhof onder water gezet. (Foto AP)
Pagina 5: Polen en de Wisla

Recordwinst door zuinigheid Shell

Door onze financiële redactie

DEN HAAG, 2 AUG. Een hogere gasproductie en een forse verlaging van de kosten hebben Koninklijke Olie/Shell een recordwinst in het tweede kwartaal opgeleverd. Het Nederlands-Britse energieconcern zag de nettowinst met 12 procent stijgen tot 3,5 miljard dollar (8,7 miljard gulden).

Dat heeft bestuursvoorzitter J. van der Veer vanochtend bekendgemaakt. De gasprijs is in vergelijking met een jaar geleden met 15 procent gestegen, terwijl de olieprijs in grote lijnen gelijk bleef.

De kostenbesparing is volgens Van der Veer op peil. „In 1998, toen het concern er financieel minder florissant voor stond, hebben we ons voorgenomen om tot 2,5 miljard dollar te besparen. Later hebben we dat bijgesteld tot 4 miljard en uiteindelijk vorig jaar tot 5 miljard. Dat bedrag aan bezuinigingen denken we aan het eind van het jaar te hebben gehaald."

De winstgroei is ook het gevolg van een hoger resultaat bij de divisie Olieproducten. Het resultaat steeg daar met 44 procent tot 1 miljard dollar waarbij vooral in de Verenigde Staten, als gevolg van de krappe benzinemarkt, de marges fors stegen. Shell wilde vanochtend geen prognoses geven voor de korte termijn. Wel benadrukte Van der Veer dat bijvoorbeeld de gasprijzen bijzonder volatiel zijn.

Shell is geïnteresseerd in de oliewinning in Alaska. Het Amerikaanse Huis van Afgevaardigden heeft vannacht ingestemd met het boren naar gas daar. De mogelijk winning in het natuurgebied heeft al tot veel kritiek geleid met het oog op te verwachten milieuschade. „Voordat we daar actief worden zullen we eerst, zoals overal in de wereld, kijken naar de impact op de natuur en alle andere gevolgen. In principe zeggen we nooit dat we niet geïnteresseerd zijn", aldus bestuurder W. van de Vijver vanochtend.

De divisie Exploratie en productie hield de winst grotendeels gelijk op 2,2 miljard dollar. De hogere gasprijzen werden in deze sector grotendeels gecompenseerd door hogere investeringen en exploitatiekosten. De chemiepoot, die al langere tijd te lijden heeft van de slechte marktsituatie, zag het resultaat met ruim de helft dalen tot 127 miljoen dollar. „De productiecapaciteit is wereldwijd gestegen, terwijl de grondstoffen in prijs zijn gestegen", zo verklaarde Van der Veer vanochtend. De totale kwartaalomzet van het concern nam in dollars gemeten iets af tot 35,8 miljard, terwijl de verkopen in euro's met 7 procent stegen.

• ENERGIEPLAN BUSH: pagina 4

'Wereldbevolking piekt rond 2070 op 9 mld zielen'

Door onze redacteur
DIRK VAN DELFT

ROTTERDAM, 2 AUG. Het einde van de groei van de wereldbevolking lijkt in zicht te komen. Rond het jaar 2070, zo wijzen statistische berekeningen uit, zal waarschijnlijk een piek van 9,0 miljard wereldburgers bereikt worden, waarna een daling inzet tot 8,4 miljard aan het einde van de eeuw.

Op dit moment zijn er 6,0 miljard wereldburgers. Tegelijkertijd groeit het aandeel ouderen: in het jaar 2100 maken zestigplussers naar schatting 34 procent van de wereldbevolking uit.

Dit schrijft een internationaal team van demografen, onder wie Sergei Scherbov van de Rijksuniversiteit Groningen, vandaag in het Britse tijdschrift *Nature*. Op basis van een statistische aanpak, uitgaande van gegevens over sterfte, vruchtbaarheid (het aantal kinderen dat een vrouw krijgt) en migratie, is door de onderzoekers gesimuleerd hoe de wereldbevolking zich in de loop van deze eeuw zal ontwikkelen. De uitkomsten zijn, voorzien van statistische marges, uitgesplitst naar dertien regio's, waaronder Noord- en Zuid-Amerika, Afrika (zowel het gebied ten noorden als ten zuiden van de Sahara), China, West- en Oost-Europa en Zuid-Azië.

De kans dat de wereldbevolking deze eeuw haar top bereikt, bedraagt volgens de demografen 85 procent. Per regio lopen de uitkomsten echter sterk uiteen. Zo is voor het Europese deel van de oude Sovjet-Unie, waar de levensverwachting de afgelopen tijd sterk is gedaald, de kans 75 procent dat de bevolkingsomvang nu al daalt. Daarentegen zal die van Afrika ten zuiden van de Sahara, ondanks het grote aantal aidsdoden, voorlopig doorgroeien. Ook in Zuid-Azië is van een krimpende bevolking nog lang geen sprake.

China en Zuid-Azië, regio's die nu elk 1,4 miljard mensen tellen, zullen zich demografisch gezien totaal verschillend ontwikkelen. Halverwege de 21ste eeuw ligt in China, vooral als gevolg van eerder inzettende lagere vruchtbaarheidscijfers, de bevolking zo'n 700 miljoen zielen achter op die van Zuid-Azië (vooral India): 1,58 miljard tegenover 2,25 miljard. Gedurende de tweede helft van deze eeuw, zo wijzen de berekeningen uit, blijft dit verschil bestaan.

Het stabiliseren en zelfs krimpen van de wereldbevolking gaat gepaard met een verschuiving in de leeftijdsopbouw: het aantal ouderen zal drastisch toenewmen. Ligt nu het aandeel zestigplussers wereldwijd op 10 procent, in 2050 zal dat al gestegen zijn tot 22 procent en op het eind van de eeuw ligt het op 34 procent. Vergrijzing speelt in alle regio's, maar de mate waarin kan sterk uiteenlopen. Zo stijgt deze eeuw het aantal zestigplussers in West-Europa van 20 naar 45 procent, en in Japan en omgeving van 22 naar 49 procent. Afrika (beneden de Sahara) komt daarentegen uit op 'slechts' 20 procent zestigplussers in het jaar 2100 – het huidige niveau van West-Europa. [• *Vervolg* DEMOGRAFIE: pagina 5]

ESF-subsidies ten onrechte verstrekt

Door een onzer redacteuren

DEN HAAG, 2 AUG. Ruim 40 procent van de subsidies die Nederland in de periode 1994-1996 heeft gekregen uit het Europees Sociaal Fonds (ESF) is ten onrechte verstrekt. Van alle werkgelegenheidsprojecten die met ESF-geld werden gefinancieerd was nog geen kwart helemaal in orde.

Dat blijkt uit een onderzoek van de Accountantsdienst van het ministerie van Sociale Zaken, dat gisteren naar de Tweede Kamer is gestuurd. Op basis van dit onderzoek vordert de Europese Commissie ruim 440 miljoen gulden, zoals al bekend was, terug wegens de onregelmatigheden met het ESF. Vorige week hebben Eurocommissaris Diamantopoulou en het directoraat-generaal Sociale Zaken en Werkgelegenheid officieel aangekondigd dit geld met een zogeheten artikel-24-procedure terug te vorderen.

Het definitieve bedrag dat terug wordt geëist is 447.184.814 gulden. Daarin zijn voor de periode 45 projecten geselecteerd uit de circa 4.500 projecten die destijds ESF-geld kregen. De onderzochte projecten kregen samen 12,2 miljoen ESF-subsidie. In totaal kwam er tussen 1994 en 1996 ruim één miljard ESF-geld naar Nederland. Over terugvorderingen tijdens de periode 1997-1999 lopen nog onderzoeken.

Slechts bij elf van de 45 projecten is alles volgens de regels verlopen. Bij andere projecten werd de vereiste cofinanciering (Nederland moest zelf 55 procent van de projecten betalen) kunstmatig verhoogd of het aantal opleidingsuren hoger voorgesteld. Ook was bij een groot deel geen (volledige) administratie meer voorhanden.

In bedragen gerekend bleek 41 procent van het ESF-geld onjuist verstrekt of bestaat er grote onzekerheid over. Verder onderzoek zou geen zin hebben. De Europese Commissie heeft in zijn claim aan Nederland die 41 procent geëxtrapoleerd naar het hele ontvangen subsidiebedrag. Eurocommissaris Diamantopoulou schrijft aan minister Vermeend (Sociale Zaken) dat het rapport „de enige informatie is die we tot onze beschikking hebben om de correctie te maken" en dat „wachten niet langer gerechtvaardigd is". Vermeend heeft twee maanden om te reageren. Hij zal het rapport dat oud-Rekenkamer-president H. Koning deze maand zal publiceren, gebruiken bij het verwer. Eerder gaf het ministerie aan het niet eens te zijn met de extrapolatie van Brussel.

• ESF-DEBAT: pagina 3

Chloorthee en lauwe douches

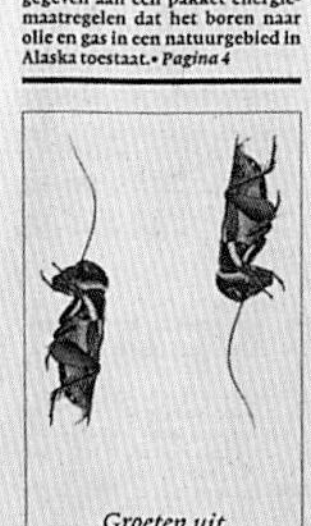

Groeten uit Legionella!

Driehonderd Nederlanders zitten in Italië op een camping waar eerder legionella is aangetroffen. Ze maken zich zorgen.

Door onze redacteur
JOEP DOHMEN

MARINA DI GROSSETO, 2 AUG. „Proef jij ook iets raars aan de thee?" vroeg Erna Gorter gisterochtend aan haar man Jeroen. Al meer dan een week logeert het gezin uit Rolde in een stacaravan van Vacansoleil op camping Le Marze aan de Toscaanse kust. Altijd was de ochtendthee even lekker. „Tot vanmorgen. We hebben de hele boel weggegooid. Chloor!"

Met het chloor kwamen de geruchten, onder de reusachtige parasoldennen van Le Marze. Legionella! Er zouden al een paar Engelse toeristen spoorslags vertrokken zijn. „Eén ding is zeker, ze zijn vanmorgen pas begonnen met chloreren", zegt Herman van Splunter („splinter met een u") uit Harderwijk, die even verderop met zijn gezin in een tent kampeert. Herman geeft graag een rondleiding langs de potentiële gevarenplekken. „Hier de douches, voel zelf maar. Is dát warm?" Zelf had hij al langer zijn bedenkingen, zegt Herman. Het warme water is altijd lauw. „Maar het water is toch pas veilig als het eerst goed verhit is geweest, ja toch?" En dinsdagavond al kwamen zijn Nederlandse buren hem en zijn vrouw Alberdien waarschuwen. Dat zij hun kinderen maar uit het zwembad moesten halen. Er was 'iets' met het water aan de hand.

De driehonderd Nederlandse campinggasten van Le Marze in Marina di Grosseto ontsnapten gisterochtend aan een evacuatie. De touroperators hadden dinsdagavond besloten hun klanten het 'dringende advies' te geven de camping te verlaten. Dat gebeurde nadat de Nederlandse Inspectie voor de Gezondheidszorg besloten had de camping wegens legionellagevaar op de zwarte lijst te plaatsen. Maar de hele operatie ging niet door, omdat de Italiaanse autoriteiten op aandringen van de camping, gisterochtend per e-mail 'Den Haag' alsnog de verzekering gaven dat het allemaal wel goed zit op Le Marze. De e-mail behelsde een éénregelige verklaring van dr. M. Catellani Pastoris, directeur van het *Instituto Superiore di Sanita* in Rome. Die meldt, zonder overigens zelf de camping onderzocht of bezocht te hebben: „Op basis van de informatie van de lokale gezondheidsdienst geloven we dat het legionellarisico geminimaliseerd is."

De Inspectie voor de Gezondheidszorg kon niet anders, zegt een woordvoerder, dan uitgaan van de juistheid van de genomen maatregelen op de camping. Le Marze verscheen niet op de zwarte lijst. De touroperators bliezen hun operatie af en concludeerden dat hun gasten 'veilig' zijn op de camping.

Zes uur woensdagavond staat er een file voor de mannendouches. Aan de andere kant van het gebouwtje staat een file vrouwen. Dit is één van de risicoplekken. Vorige maand nam hier een 66-jarige vrouw uit Zwolle een, naar later bleek, fatale douche. Terug in Nederland was zij doodziek. De artsen constateerden de veteranenziekte, die veroorzaakt wordt door de legionellabacterie.

Een maand eerder nam een 66-jarige inwoner van Leeuwarden de bacterie ook al mee naar huis na een verblijf op de camping. Ook doodziek. En in juli '99 trof dat lot een 44-jarige man uit Wychen. [• *Vervolg* LEGIONELLA: pagina 3]

Nr. 5
25. Januar 2001
56. Jahrgang

JAN PHILIPP REEMTSMA: DER PROZESS EIN ZEIT-GESPRÄCH (S. 11)

DIE ZEIT

www.zeit.de

C 7451 C
Preis 5.00 DM

WOCHENZEITUNG FÜR POLITIK • WIRTSCHAFT • WISSEN UND KULTUR

Stasi-Protokolle

Marianne Birthler, Leiterin der Gauck-Behörde: Kohls Akten sind kein Staatsgeheimnis 7

Rente gut, alles gut?

Das Sozialsystem muss mehr Wahlfreiheit bieten

Von Elisabeth Niejahr

Wer auf Leistungen verzichtet, muss weniger einzahlen

Siehe auch: Zwölf Fragen und Antworten zur Rentenreform, Seite 23

PLÖTZLICH MACHT REGIEREN keinen Spaß mehr: Umweltminister Trittin und Außenminister Fischer

Politik im Container

Fischer, Trittin und die Opposition: Wie der Kampf um die Wählerquote das Politische zum Persönlichen verkommen lässt / Von Josef Joffe

Ewige Vergangenheit

„Runter mit dem Zeigefinger" von Klaus Hartung, Seite 2, und „Ein gefundenes Fressen: Die Mediendemokratie dreht durch" von Gunter Hofmann, Seite 3

Erlaubt das Klonen

Das Embryonenschutzgesetz ist unethisch und verfassungswidrig
Von Reinhard Merkel 37

Unser Los ist Davos

Was die Welt vom Gipfel der Manager lernen kann

Von Uwe Jean Heuser

Siehe auch „Druck auf die Konzerne", Seite 22

The Dutch daily *NRC Handelsblad* now uses Lexicon as its main font, including a specially cut headline version that is slightly condensed to allow longer, bigger headlines.

The German *Die Zeit* plays to its strengths, deliberately classical in typographic style and not trying to disguise that there is a lot to read in this intellectual weekly. Design consultant: Mario Garcia.

Newspapers are often afraid to redesign in case they upset readers

How do you like your news? In Barcelona, *El Periódico* (designed by Cases i Associates) has a clear, contemporary design structure, color palette, and carefully constructed elements.

In Britain, the *News of the World* (published on Sundays) blasts away with big type and lots of white out of black. The main item on the front page becomes the promotional panel for a video and poster that incorporates the title-piece. Inside pages feature photomontages which group pictures into clever narratives.

150 PESETAS

el Periódico ma. 17

EL TRIBUNAL REAFIRMA LAS TESIS POR LAS QUE CONDENÓ A CEPSA

Multa millonaria a Repsol por imponer precios

Defensa de la Competencia sanciona con 500 millones a la empresa por fijar las tarifas a las gasolineras

Las estaciones de servicio aseguran que la medida beneficia a más de 2.000 distribuidores

Rusia y China sellan un pacto contra el escudo antimisiles

Llagostera mantiene el 'no' a la línea eléctrica de Les Gavarres

Más Noticias

Los extranjeros residentes en Barcelona alcanzan el 6,1% del censo

El temor al fracaso marca la apertura de la cumbre de Bonn sobre el clima

Josep Caminal asume la dirección del Fòrum 2004 para reactivar el proyecto

deportes

Samaranch coloca a su favorito

El exmandatario logra también que su hijo sea admitido en el organismo olímpico

JAMAICA

marsans de toda confianza 902 30 60 90

NEWS OF THE WORLD

FREE 1-hour video, sticker album PLUS poster inside

EXCLUSIVE

Becks: I'll be there

BEPPE BLASTS EASTENDERS

• Soap's boss treated me worse than a dog

• I was an outcast.. I'm angry and betrayed

EXCLUSIVE: GRECO LETS RIP

OPINIÓN

MARCADOR SIMULTÁNEO

La UE se queda sola ante el efecto invernadero

Editoriales

La multa a Repsol

El Tribunal de Defensa de la Competencia ha impuesto una multa de 500 millones de pesetas a Repsol por la misma razón por la que hace mes y medio sancionó con 200 millones a Cepsa: ambas imponen los precios finales a parte de sus gasolineras abanderadas, lo que limita la competencia efectiva en la distribución al por menor de carburantes.

Las sanciones a las petroleras son un paso para combatir la perjudicial política de precios actual

Relevo en el COI

Juan Antonio Samaranch ya tiene sucesor en la presidencia del Comité Olímpico Internacional. Al médico belga Jacques Rogge, estrecho colaborador suyo, le corresponderá culminar la lucha iniciada contra la corrupción y el dopaje durante la etapa que acaba de cerrarse.

El sucesor de Samaranch debe seguir la lucha contra la corrupción y el dopaje en los Juegos Olímpicos

Cara a cara ¿Se deben construir más carreteras para evitar colapsos?

Los atascos que se producen en las carreteras catalanas cada domingo del mes de julio evidencian que la red viaria resulta insuficiente. Sin embargo, el Servei de Trànsit cree que la solución está en cambiar los hábitos de circulación.

AUNQUE NO BASTA, DEBEN MEJORARLAS

XAVIER Pérez

A FAVOR

RACIONALIDAD DE LOS CIUDADANOS

JOSEP MARIA Aragay

EN CONTRA

Nando

Opinión

Toros consentidos | La réplica de Altamira | Móviles transparentes | Se acaban los pactos | La línea de Les Gavarres

El billete

FAMILIA INCOMUNICADA

SALAH Jamal*

LOS NIÑOS DE LA INMUNDICIA

CARLOS Fanlo*

El artículo del día

COACCIONES POLICIALES CONTRA LA INFORMACIÓN

Hay una tendencia a poner dificultades a los informadores gráficos, hasta el punto de delinquir cuando se les retiran vídeos o carretes

LLUÍS De Carreras*

COMUNICAR

SUSTRAER

No se trata de defender un interés gremial, sino el derecho ciudadano a estar informado

Opus Mei

JOSEP Pernau

UN BORBÓN EN EL ANIVERSARIO DE LA BASTILLA

Ni las monarquías parecen monarquías, ni las repúblicas parecen repúblicas

EXCLUSIVE

BY PHIL TAYLOR

MICHAEL GRECO LETS RIP... THE MOST EXPLOSIVE SOAP INTERVIEW OF THE YEAR

Wellard the dog got better storylines than me

ALBERT SQUARE favourite Michael Greco put his BBC career on the line last night and launched a blistering onslaught against the man he accuses of wrecking his life on EastEnders.

'Work was affecting my health, even my personality changed'

'I'd much rather be happy and poorer than sad and wealthy'

'They gave Beppe a disease. I thought, 'I really don't need this''

© News of the World 2002

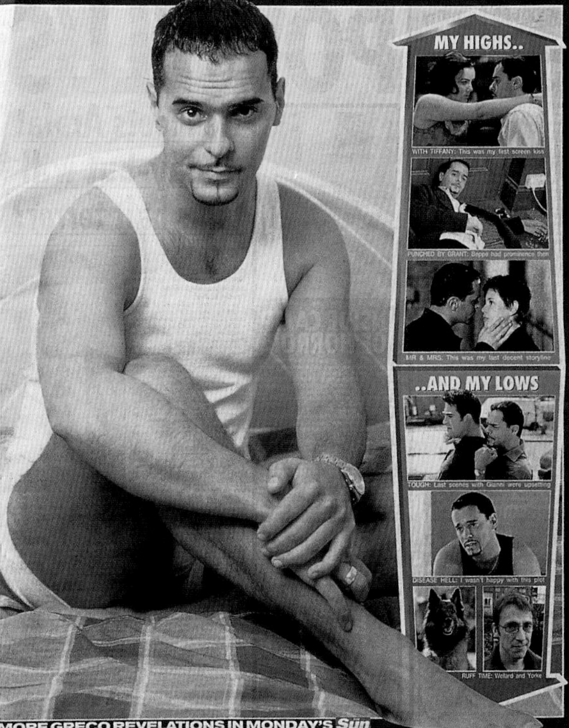

MY HIGHS..

WITH TIFFANY: This was my first screen kiss

PUNCHED BY GRANT: Beppe had prominence then

MR & MRS: This was my last decent storyline

..AND MY LOWS

TOUGH: Last scenes with Gianni were upsetting

DISEASE HELL: I wasn't happy with this plot

RUFF TIME: Wellard and Yorke

MORE GRECO REVELATIONS IN MONDAY'S Sun

Clarín

UN TOQUE DE ATENCION PARA LA SOLUCION ARGENTINA DE LOS PROBLEMAS ARGENTINOS

Lunes 28 de febrero de 2000

Buenos Aires República Argentina Año LV N° 19.430

Precio en Capital Federal y GBA: $ 1,00 • Recargo envío al interior: $ 0,20 Uruguay: $ 23 • Brasil: R$ 4,00 • Paraguay: G$ 6.000 • Chile: $ 1.200

Precios de opcionales, en el índice de la página 2

COMPRA OPCIONAL genios

INTERNACIONALES PAGS. 24 Y 25
Ni el Papa se salva del espionaje
Afirman que con el sistema Echelon espiaron a Juan Pablo II, a la Madre Teresa y a Lady Di.

SUPLEMENTO ESPECTACULOS
Fiebre del sábado a la noche
Luis Miguel y Ricky Martin presentaron a la vez shows en México, a sala llena.

INFORMACION GENERAL PAG. 32
Denuncian que hay racismo en Internet
La Liga Antidifamación, de Nueva York, acusa a Yahoo! de dar cabida hasta al Ku Klux Klan.

PARA LAS ELECCIONES DEL 7 DE MAYO EN LA CAPITAL

Después de tanto pelear, ahora Beliz y Cavallo van juntos

Lo anunciaron en un documento • Habrá internas para elegir quién encabezará la fórmula para jefe de Gobierno porteño • Estos dos ex ministros de Menem se cruzaban duras críticas hasta hace poco • En las encuestas Cavallo iba segundo y Beliz tercero, detrás de la Alianza. **PAGS. 3 A 5**

LA EMBAJADA REPARTE UN MANUAL

Brasil busca llevarse más empresas argentinas

La "Guía para el inversor" cuenta qué ventajas ofrece el socio del Mercosur • Entre otras, subsidios y menores costos • El Gobierno argentino está preocupado y prepara medidas para frenar el éxodo de empresas. **PAGS. 16 Y 17**

LAS GRANDES QUE SE MUDARON

En el último año se fueron parcial o totalmente:

28 empresas	5 nacionales	23 multinacionales

Los sectores más afectados: **Autopartistas, alimentación, neumáticos y textil**

PABLO CEROLINI/Enviado especial

CON ALMA Y VIDA. Cardetti grita el segundo de River. Ya había hecho el primero, al minuto. Los otros dos fueron de Angel y Alvarez.

4-1 A COLON

River saltó a la punta con una goleada en Santa Fe

Su principal virtud fue la eficacia para definir • Hizo un gol en el arranque y otro apenas le empató Colón • Y remató con dos más sobre el final • Así, River alcanzó a San Lorenzo y a Gimnasia La Plata, que igualaron 1-1 en el Nuevo Gasómetro. **SUPL. DEPORTIVO**

Boca dejó escapar una oportunidad: 1-1 con Lanús en la Bombonera

VILLA MINETTI, EN EL NORTE DE SANTA FE

Todo un pueblo en pie de guerra contra los cuatreros

Los vecinos están en asamblea permanente • Dicen que los ladrones se llevan el ganado a Santiago del Estero porque allí los protegen. **PAGS. 30 Y 31**

TIROTEO ENTRE DOS LADRONES Y UN POLICIA EN FLORESTA

Tenía 17 años, fue a comprar al supermercado y la mataron

Llevaba alimentos para donarlos a un comedor comunitario • Los asaltantes la habrían usado de escudo • Estaba con la mamá. **PAG. 44**

FRASE DEL DIA **EAMON MULLEN, FISCAL DEL CASO AMIA: "EL JUICIO ORAL Y PUBLICO ES UNA BUENA NOTICIA. PERMITIRA AVANZAR EN CONDENAS O ABSOLUCIONES". PAG. 12**

SPICE-SEX sjokkerer

Sprekker Bondevik-idyllen?

LEEDS I FLY-DRAMA I NATT

Dagbladet

-Tusener bør få 50 000 mer i lønn

Topp-sjefer: – Flere yrker fortjener kraftige hopp

Tabloid editors and designers talk about the "poster front": it can be a single picture and headline or a front page that is both the main headlines of the day and a graphic table of contents. *Dagbladet* is published in Norway and uses every graphic device to excite. Like *Bild*, it doesn't feel that its titlepiece needs to be at the top of the page. *Clarín* is the leading paper in Argentina and uses a headline plus a few words to announce the stories inside. The *Daily Mirror* in Britain uses powerful type for powerful stories: not every page has to be built around a soap star.

PAGE 6 THE MIRROR, Friday, April 5, 2002

VOICE OF THE Mirror
voice@mirror.co.uk

Show Bush you've got teeth, Tony

THE world again saw the two faces of President Bush last night.

In the White House Rose Garden, he stood forth as the man of peace.

Stop the bombing, he begged of the Palestinians. Get out, he begged Sharon's army.

Thank God, you may think. At last he's coming out and trying to stop the killing.

Yet away from the cameras, we know what the president is doing. He's in the Pentagon playrooms plotting his revenge on Iraq.

Unfinished business with Saddam Hussein, the man his father failed to see off for good.

Prime Minister Tony Blair flies to the US today and he should think how hollow Bush's words sound.

The Mirror has called Mr Blair the president's poodle.

We didn't do so lightly – but the truth is the prime minister has done nothing but play lapdog to the Washington Red Neck.

Whenever Bush has barked, Mr Blair has rolled over with his legs in the air.

As other European leaders held back from jumping at Bush's demands, Britain under Blair has rushed forward with embarrassing haste.

The price we'll pay for dancing to Bush's tune isn't yet clear. Hopefully, it will not be too high.

But there are many of our men now in the frontline whose mission is far from clear.

We pray Mr Blair now realises he has a different role to play. When he sits down with Bush, he must remember just what sort of man the president is.

He's ruthless – a man who has sent hundreds of convicts to the execution chamber. A president determined to take his war wherever he wants.

Mr Blair must be the voice of reason. He must stand up to Bush and, if needs be, say "no".

Don't forget – a poodle has teeth, too.

A royal rock

THE Queen Mother's death has ignited a debate on the role the royal family plays in modern Britain.

But at 11.30am today it is a debate millions will put aside.

For them, the moment will be one of respect.

Thousands will stand in the streets to see her coffin moved to Westminster Hall.

Behind it will walk her family: Two future kings in Prince Charles and his son, William.

We should all take a moment to reflect on what they'll be thinking.

What the Queen Mum really was – the best of Britain and the rock of her family.

Come Moffat!

Sir Brian Moffat/Sat in his turret
Counting his perks and pay
Along came a spider/To deliver a reminder
"Too much and they'll chase you away."

DESERT BATTLE: Royal Navy helicopters over a burning Iraqi oilfield during the Gulf War

THE MIRROR, Friday, April 5, 2002 PAGE 7

NOT IN OUR NAME

JOHN PILGER on why Bush and Blair must not attack Iraq and condemn thousands more to their death

SILENCE: Why has Blair not condemned Israel?

AS THE crisis in Israeli-occupied Palestine deepens, Tony Blair will meet George W Bush today to plan an attack on another country, Iraq.

Their decision may condemn to death more than 10,000 civilians. That is the "medium case scenario" drawn up by the Pentagon. If the Americans implement their current strategy of "total war" and target Iraq's electricity and water, the consequences will be even more horrific.

There is no mandate in any United Nations resolution for this invasion. It will be as lawless as Nazi Germany's invasion of Poland, which triggered the Second World War. Indeed, it may well trigger a Third World War, drawing in nations of the region and beyond.

As Blair arrives at Bush's Texas ranch the question begs: Why does he condemn Iraq, but is silent on Israel's current bloody and illegal rampage through Palestine? Why has he not demanded that the Israeli Prime Minister Ariel Sharon comply with UN Security Council resolutions, to which Britain is a signatory, and withdraw from the Occupied Territories? Why has Blair said nothing as Sharon has sent tanks and gunships and snipers against civilians – a government targeting innocent people, like the deaf old lady shot by an Israeli sniper as she tried to get to hospital? Why has Blair not called at least for military sanctions against Israel, which has 200 nuclear weapons targeted at Arab capitals?

Blair's culpable silence is imposed by the most dangerous American administration for a generation. The Bush administration is determined to attack Iraq and take over a country that is the world's second largest source of oil. The aim is to get rid of America's and Britain's old friend, Saddam Hussein, whom they no longer control, and to install another compliant thug in Baghdad.

THAT is why Bush now tells Israel to withdraw from the Palestinian cities it recently occupied while continuing to replenish the Israeli war machine. The Americans want a rampant Israel guarding their flank as they attack Iraq and expand their control across the Middle East, whose oil is now more critical than ever to US military and economic dominance.

For almost two months, Downing Street, through the discredited system of unattributable briefings that are secret to the public, have spun two deceptions. The first is that the Prime Minister will play a vital role at today's meeting with Bush on his Texas ranch in "counselling caution." The second is that Blair has a "dossier of detailed evidence" that "proves" that Saddam Hussein has "a nuclear capability" and is "investigating a way to launch unsophisticated nuclear bombs" and is also building chemical and biological weapons.

The fiction of Blair as a steadying hand on his Texas buddy is to be read in Blair's unrelenting bellicose statements, and his attempts, against the wishes of his senior military advisers, to send thousands of British troops into the quagmire of Afghanistan, where his "cautionary influence" on Bush saw as many as 5,000 civilians bombed to death while the Taliban and al-Qaeda leaders got away.

While remaining silent on Israel, Blair is alone in Europe in his promotion of an attack on Iraq, a nation of 22 million people with whom the British have no quarrel. Mysteriously, the "dossier of proof" of the dangers posed by the Iraqi regime has now been "shelved." This is because no such proof exists and because, suddenly, more than 130 Labour Members of Parliament are in revolt, including Cabinet and former Cabinet members. It must be dawning on many of them that so much of this government's "spin" during the "war on terrorism" has been a farrago of lies and half-truths provided by an American intelligence apparatus seeking to cover its failure to provide warning of the attacks of September 11.

Lie Number One is the justification for an attack on Iraq — the threat of its "weapons of mass destruction." Few countries have had 93 per cent of their major weapons capability destroyed. This was reported by Rolf Ekeus, the chairman of the United Nations body authorised to inspect and destroy Iraq's arsenal following the Gulf War in 1991. UN inspectors certified that 817 out of the 819 Iraqi long-range missiles were destroyed. In 1999, a special panel of the Security Council recorded that Iraq's main biological weapons facilities (supplied originally by the US and Britain) "have been destroyed and rendered harmless."

As for Saddam Hussein's "nuclear threat," the International Atomic Energy Agency reported that Iraq's nuclear weapons programme had been eliminated "efficiently and effectively". The IAEA inspectors still travel to Iraq and in January reported full Iraqi compliance. Blair and Bush never mention this when they demand that "the weapons inspectors are allowed back". Nor do they remind us that the UN inspectors were never expelled by the Iraqis, but withdrawn only after it was revealed they had been infiltrated by US intelligence.

Lie Number Two is the connection between Iraq and the perpetrators of September 11. There was the rumour that Mohammed Atta, one of the September 11 hijackers, had met an Iraqi intelligence official in the Czech Republic last year. The Czech police say he was not even in the country last year. On February 5, a New York Times investigation concluded: "The Central Intelligence Agency has no evidence that Iraq has engaged in terrorist operations against the United States in nearly a decade, and the agency is convinced that Saddam Hussein has not provided chemical or biological weapons to al-Qaeda or related terrorist groups."

Lie Number Three is that Saddam Hussein, not the US and Britain, "is blocking humanitarian supplies from reaching the people of Iraq." (Foreign Office minister Peter Hain). The opposite is true. The United States, with British compliance, is currently blocking a record $5billion worth of humanitarian supplies from the people of Iraq. These are shipments already approved by the UN Office of Iraq, which is authorised by the Security Council. They include life-saving drugs, painkillers, vaccines, cancer diagnostic equipment.

This wanton denial is rarely reported in Britain. Hundreds of thousands of Iraqis, mostly children, have died as a consequence of an American and British riven embargo on Iraq that resembles a medieval siege. The embargo allows Iraq less than £100 with which to feed and care for one person for a whole year. This a major factor, says the United Nations' Children's Fund, in the death of more than 600,000 infants.

I have seen the appalling state of the children of Iraq. I have sat next to an Iraqi doctor in a modern hospital while she has turned away parents with children suffering from cancers that are part of what they call a "Hiroshima epidemic" — caused, according to several studies, by the depleted uranium that was used by the US and Britain in the Gulf War and is now carried in the dust of the desert. Not only is Iraq denied equipment to clean up its contaminated battlefields, but also cancer drugs and hospital equipment.

I showed a list of barred drugs given to me by Iraqi doctors to Professor Karol Sikora, who as chief of the cancer programme of the World Health Organisation, wrote in the British Medical Journal: "Requested radiotherapy equipment, chemotherapy drugs and analgesics are consistently blocked by United States and British advisers (to the UN Sanctions Committee). There seems to be a rather ludicrous notion that such agents could be converted into chemical and other weapons." He told me: "Nearly all these drugs are available in every British hospital. It seems crazy they couldn't have morphine. When I was in Iraq, in one hospital they had a little bottle of aspirin pills to go around 200 patients in pain." No one doubts that if the murderous Saddam Hussein saw advantage in deliberately denying his people humanitarian supplies, he would do so; but the UN, from the Secretary General himself, has said that, while the regime could do more, it has not withheld supplies.

THREAT: Saddam has been rendered harmless

Denis Halliday, the assistant Secretary General of the United Nations, resigned in protest at the embargo which he described as "genocidal". Halliday was responsible for the UN's humanitarian programme in Iraq. His successor, Hans Von Sponeck, also resigned in disgust. Last November, they wrote: "The death of 5-6,000 children a month is mostly due to contaminated water, lack of medicines and malnutrition. The US and UK governments' delayed clearance of equipment and materials is responsible for this tragedy, not Baghdad."

Those who speak these facts are abused by Blair ministers as apologists for Saddam Hussein — so embroiled is the government with the Bush administration's exploitation of America's own tragedy on September 11. This has prevented public discussion of the crime of an embargo that has hurt only the most vulnerable Iraqis and which is to be compounded by the crime of attacking the stricken nation. Unknown to most of the British public, RAF and American aircraft have been bombing Iraq, week after week, for more than two years. The cost to the British taxpayer is £800million a year. The Wall Street Journal reported that the US and Britain faced a "dilemma" because "few targets remain". "We're down to the last outhouse," said a Pentagon official.

IN any attack on Iraq, Saddam Hussein's escape route is virtually assured – just as Osama bin Laden's was. The US and Britain have no wish to free the Iraqi people from a tyranny the CIA once described as its "greatest triumph". The last thing they want is a separate Kurdish state and another allied to the Shi'ite majority in neighbouring Iran. They want another Saddam Hussein: one who will do as he is told.

On March 13, the Foreign Office entertained Brigadier-General Najib Salihi, a former commander of Saddam Hussein's Republican Guard and chief of the dreaded military intelligence who took part in the invasion of Kuwait in 1990. Now funded by the CIA, the general "denies any war crimes". Not that he would ever face arrest in the West. At the Foreign Office, he is known as a "rapidly rising star". He is their man, and Washington's man.

The British soldiers who take part in an invasion have every right to know the dirty secrets that will underpin their action, and extend the suffering of a people held hostage to a dictatorship and to international power games over which they have no control. Two weeks ago, the Americans made clear they were prepared to use "low yield" nuclear weapons, a threat echoed here by Defence Secretary Geoffrey Hoon.

When will Europe stand up? If the leaders of the European Union fall silent, too, in the face of such danger, what is Europe for? In this country, there is an honourable rallying cry: Not In Our Name. Bush and Blair must be restrained from killing large numbers of innocents in our name — a view, according to the polls, shared by a majority of the British people. An arms and military equipment embargo must be enforced throughout the region, from Saddam Hussein's Iraq to Ariel Sharon's Israel. Above all, the siege of both the Iraqi and Palestinian peoples must end now.

PAUL ROUTLEDGE IS AWAY

Scotland's Business, Financial & Political Daily

Friday 22 September 2000

business a.m.

SPORT

Spread betting Make a killing on Killie with the most extensive guide to beating the bookies

COMMENT

'Extra-terrestrial real estate may not be risk-free ... but it's a great selling point'

Michelle Rodger

CLOSING PRICES

Macfarlane's £92m bid for Scots packaging rival rejected as 'opportunist'

BPI shares end 24% up on the day as market signals higher offer will be needed

Full story: Page 3

Summary

Cash worries for Tories and Labour

Transfer fee row goes into extra time

SCOTTISH COMPANIES

MARKETS AND ECONOMY

EUROPE AND WORLD

Microsoft chief tops the rich list

TODAY'S AGENDA

p.m.

Sweet revenge

Looking the business

Investor

Merger speculation gives Bank shares a big lift

British Airways ditches deal with Dutch carrier

PRICE 60p

International: 13 Investor: 17 Due Diligence: 33 Opinion: 34 TV & Weather: 47 Diary: 48

Some of the best design is in the specialist press. The Scottish business daily *Business a.m.* (designed by Ally Palmer and Terry Watson) uses Matthew Carter's Miller and Jonathan Hoefler's Knockout range to make the news look bold but distinguished.

Daily sports papers combine the drama of action photography and the detailed statistics that fans expect from this type of reporting. In Brazil, *Lance!* turns its tabloid front and back around to make a single poster front page with bravely scaled and finely detailed type. (Design consultant: Cases i Associates.) In Spain, *El Mundo Deportivo* and *Marca* battle it out in the market: *Marca* uses traditional tabloid techniques such as boxes and panels reinterpreted in a "designed" way.

LANCE!

FUTSAL

São Paulo é bicampeão!

Tricolor vence Barueri e conquista o título paulista **Pág. 30**

AMANHÃ

Super Raio-x do Brasileirão

SÉRIE B

Santa Cruz volta à elite após 6 anos Pág. 19

São Paulo, segunda-feira 13 de dezembro de 1999. Número 456. R$ 0,75

o diário dos esportes LANCENET! http://www.lancenet.com.br

SANTOS

Marcelo Teixeira é o presidente

Oposição vence eleição no Peixe. Pelé diz que vai embora do clube **Pág. 12**

PALMEIRAS

Júnior Baiano e Cléber vão jogar juntos outra vez, contra o Flamengo, pela final da Copa Mercosul **Pág. 15**

PORTUGUESA

O goleiro Ronaldo pode acertar com a Lusa. Diretor de futebol confirma a negociação **Pág. 20**

BASQUETE

Santo André conquista o título sul-americano feminino, em casa. Vence o Paraná na final **Pág. 25**

NAS MÃOS DA FIEL

Timão sai com derrota por 3 a 2, do Mineirão, mas pode ser tricampeão brasileiro com um empate e uma vitória simples.

Título pode vir com os gritos da Fiel, histórico 12º jogador do Timão. Mas Oswaldo saiu criticado do Mineirão Págs. 3 a 10

3 ATLÉTICO MG 2 CORINTHIANS

VAMPETA COMEMORA O PRIMEIRO GOL, COM CÉSAR PRATES E LUCIANO

L! o diário dos esportes

Atendimento ao leitor RJ (021) 5020786 SP (011) 856 1310

Ligue e assine: 0800 990 991

SÃO PAULO

LEVIR, VEM AÍ

DIRETORIA TRICOLOR DEMITE PAULO CÉSAR CARPEGIANI POR TELEFONE. LEVIR CULPI CONFIRMA QUE PODE VIR PARA O MORUMBI. Pág. 14

LEVIR CONFIRMA NEGOCIAÇÃO COM TRICOLOR

El Mundo Deportivo

Huracán Muster

Pulverizó a Chang en la final de Roland Garros: 7-5, 6-2, 6-4

Arantxa también perdió la final femenina de dobles

Guerra por la UEFA

El Barça pasará una prueba de fuego en San Mamés, aunque le basta un empate y su porcentaje de clasificación es alto

El Espanyol puntuó en Tenerife (1-1) y también tiene opciones, pero más complicadas

El doble sevillano fue Betis (2-1) y los verdiblancos ya tienen un pie en Europa

Stoichkov: "Yo me quedo"

Segunda A — Lleida promociona y desciende Palamós

Motor / GP de Italia — Puig 3° en Mugello. Crivillé fue quinto y Alzamora se cayó

Ciclismo — Indurain gana su primer Dauphiné Liberé

Cursa El Corte Inglés — Extraordinario éxito ciudadano

MARCA

TODA ESPAÑA PODRÁ VER LA F-1

Barça, es tu final

Esta noche ante el Rayo se juega sus opciones para conseguir la Liga

UN GUARDARRAIL AMPUTA EL PIE A UN CICLISTA

El accidente del Roberto Alcaide se produjo en la Vuelta a Extremadura

Roberto Palomar

Perdonadme, pero he subido a 7.000 metros

Nuestro compañero Roberto, tras realizar la proeza, nos cuenta que al comunicárselo a su familia recibió una respuesta tajante: "bronca y silencio"

CAMACHO: "SI FRACASO EN LA EUROCOPA, ME IRÉ"

MARCA acompañó al seleccionador a Israel para seguir a la selección Sub 16

2 MARCA 06MAY2000 LA PREVIA

La Previa

¡Qué grande es el fútbol!

JUGADORES A SEGUIR — Anelka — Angulo

El Barça se juega el año en 5 días

Necesita ganar al Rayo para meter presión al Depor y soñar con París

Se echan de menos sus goles

OJO CON LOS MALETINES VIAJEROS

ATENCIÓN A LAS FORMAS — Cañizares

EL ENTRENADOR — Héctor Cúper — Tiene a Van Gaal al borde de un ataque de nervios

JORNADA 36 LA PREVIA 3

PARTIDOS

CLASIFICACIÓN

EL MADRID NO PUEDE CEDER NI UN PUNTO

Luis puede mandar a 'su' Atlético a Segunda

Según los números, los rojiblancos sólo tiene un 5 por ciento a su favor

EL DEPOR ANTE EL PARTIDO DE SU VIDA

El Betis no depende de sí mismo

Soria sueña con la permanencia

LUNDI 25 AOUT 2003

Libération

Danger, baisse d'impôt

Dans un contexte économique difficile, Raffarin rend cette semaine les derniers arbitrages budgétaires pour une réduction de 1% à 3% du barème de l'impôt sur le revenu. Page 2

Le rêve inachevé de Luther King

Quarante ans après le discours du pasteur noir américain, ils n'étaient que quelques milliers à célébrer son message, samedi. Pourtant, le sort de la communauté noire des Etats-Unis est loin d'égaler celui des Blancs. **Page 7**

Deux socialistes en précampagne

A l'université des Verts à Marseille, Laurent Fabius a séduit et s'est offert une belle tribune, alors que Bertrand Delanoë était l'invité vedette à la fête de la rose chez Arnaud Montebourg. **Pages 11 et 12**

Cours de soutien chez Attac

A Arles, où elle réunit ses adhérents, l'association altermondialiste s'est consacrée à la formation économique de ses militants lors d'une centaine d'ateliers et de tables rondes. Reportage. **Pages 16 et 17**

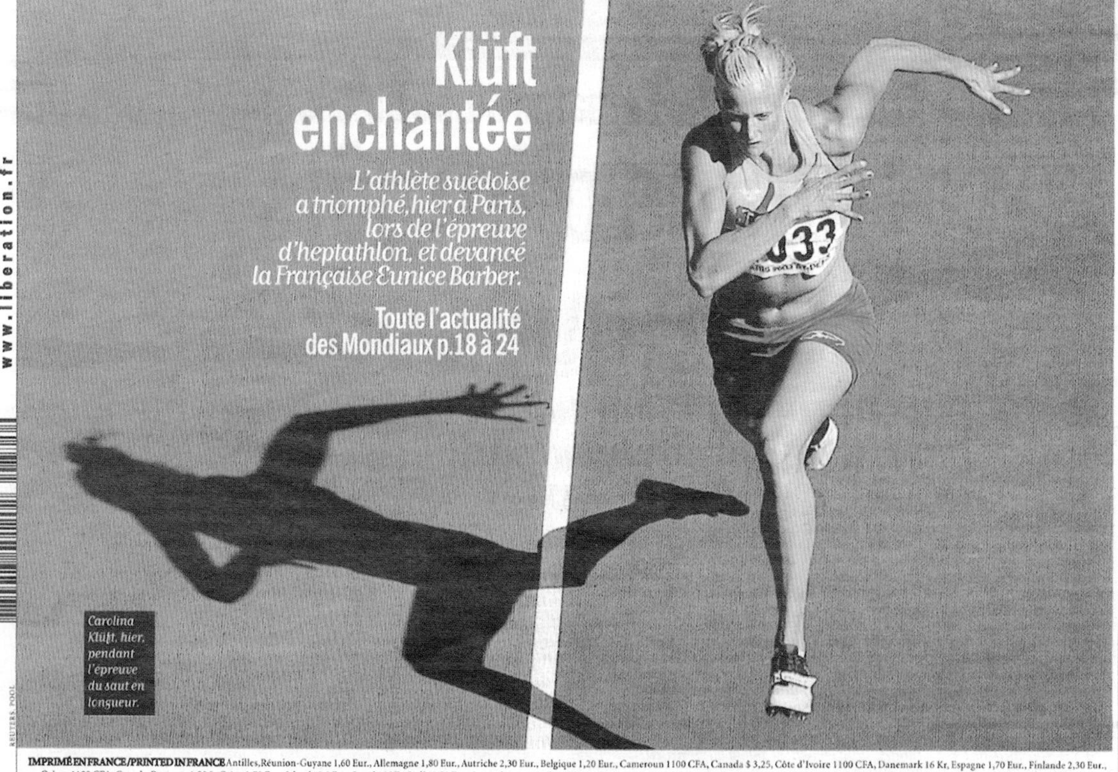

Klüft enchantée

L'athlète suédoise a triomphé, hier à Paris, lors de l'épreuve d'heptathlon, et devancé la Française Eunice Barber.

Toute l'actualité des Mondiaux p.18 à 24

Carolina Klüft, hier, pendant l'épreuve du saut en longueur.

REUTERS POOL

www.liberation.fr

M 00135 - 825 - F: 1,20 €

IMPRIMÉ EN FRANCE/PRINTED IN FRANCE Antilles,Réunion-Guyane 1,60 Eur., Allemagne 1,80 Eur., Autriche 2,30 Eur., Belgique 1,20 Eur., Cameroun 1100 CFA, Canada $ 3,25, Côte d'Ivoire 1100 CFA, Danemark 16 Kr, Espagne 1,70 Eur., Finlande 2,30 Eur., Gabon 1100 CFA, Grande-Bretagne 1,20 L, Grèce 1,70 Eur., Irlande 2,0 Eur., Israël 12 Nis, Italie 1,70 Eur., Luxembourg 1,20 Eur., Maroc 12 Dh, Norvège 22 Kr, Pays Bas 1,80 Eur., Portugal Cont 1,70 Eur., Sénégal 1100 CFA, Suède 22 Kr, Suisse 2,5 F, USA $ 3 .

DEUXIEME EDITION NUMERO 6930

Libération, a tabloid that runs long text, defies categorization

Libération, the Paris daily, happily defies categorization. It's a tabloid, but runs long text as if it were the most austere German daily. It's a newspaper, but it loves writing about books and film. Its front page can feature a cartoon, a single image, or a table of contents. It has wit and style, and yet throughout these different incarnations it always looks like *Libération*.

Rebonds

A l'image du monde sportif, il faut réintroduire l'idée de compétitivité et de réussite dans le système éducatif français.

Remettons l'école en piste

par YVES LASZLO

QUOTIDIENNE

par PIERRE MARCELLE

D'un été meurtrier

Jaargang 44 - nr. 7 - 19 februari 1983 - prijs: drie gulden vijfentwintig - raamgracht 4, 1011 kk amsterdam, tel. 020-26 22 75

De geslaagde lobby van de Saoedi's en de werkgevers tegen de boycotmeldingswet

'De overheid gaat toch niet turven: honderd boycots Israël, dertig gas Sovjetunie. Men wil er wel iets meer over weten'

Het bedrijfsleven komt in de internationale handel veel boycotbepalingen tegen. De overheid weet niet hoe vaak dat gebeurt en wat voor boycots dat zijn. De wet die daar inzicht in moet gaan verschaffen – de wet melding buitenlandse boycotmaatregelen – is door het kabinet-Lubbers voorlopig ingetrokken. In dit artikel: de lobby van Saoedi's, en de Nederlandse werkgevers.

Lex Runderkamp

F. Bolkestein (Foto: Ger Dijkstra)

R. Lubbers (Foto: Bas van den Bogaard)

Onaangenaam

De academische wereld speelt grimmig kwartet met studierichtingen

Ooit waren de universiteiten de paradijselijkste werkgevers van Nederland: vaste banen, hoge salarissen, veel vrijheid. Dat is snel aan het veranderen. Ook de academische wereld ontkomt niet aan gedwongen ontslagen. Maar in hoeverre is dat echt erg? Dit zou ook de kans zijn om het vele dorre hout in het universitaire bos te kappen. De vraag is of dat inderdaad gebeurt.

Hugo Arlman en Gerard Mulder

Vervolg op pagina 2

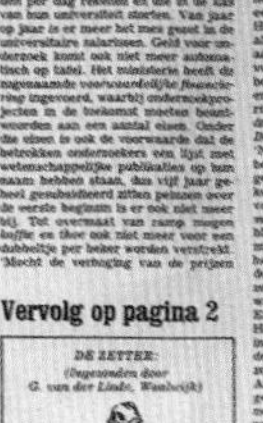

DE ZETTER (Ingezonden door G. van der Linde, Woubrugge)

Vervolg op pagina 2

KISSINGER

en Nixon probeerden te verhinderen dat Allende aan de macht kwam

IN HET KLEURKATERN: onthutsende feiten, nu onthuld

De 'onverzettelijkheid' van **SJARON** pagina 6

Cabaretier **Youp van 't Hek** over zijn plotselinge succes, de reclame, en 'het systeem'/3

KINDEREN IN ZIEKENHUIZEN

Duizenden overbodige opnamen en operaties/5

Aurore Clément Een gesprek over huwelijk, huishouding en actrice zijn/17

De Smeulende Kwestie van **RUDY KOUSBROEK** pagina 15

Steekpenningen van woonwagenbouwers voor gemeente-ambtenaren/7

Willem Jan Otten over zijn toneelstuk 'Een sneeuw'/19

En verder:

De kunst-academies/21

8 710857 000017

The Guardian
Alliance woe helps Labour poll surge
Thatcher in new confrontation
'No' for Clough
Vorsprung durch strike
Bus Stop top just the ticket

LE MATIN

DE PARIS

VENDREDI 15 AVRIL 1977

SANS NOUVELLES DU PDG DE FIAT

p. 11 et 24 nos informations et enquêtes

Consultants introduce grids, space, and hierarchies of information

Newspapers made with design consultants share the use of grids, white space, modular pages, and a consideration about the hierarchies of information: the weekly *Vrij Nederland* from Holland, titlepiece designed by Kart L. Swart; *Il manifesto*, the Italian communist paper; *The Guardian* from Britain and *Le Matin* from France, both by David Hillman; *Basler Zeitung* from Switzerland, by Romano Hanni; *Die Woche* from Germany; and *Tages Anzeiger* from Switzerland, by Roger Black. (Not all of these papers are still published in these forms.)

Seite 3: Osttimors beschwerlicher Weg in die staatliche Eigenständigkeit

Basler Zeitung

BaZ online: www.baz.ch

Mittwoch, 29. August 2001

Französische Ermittler bezweifeln Notwehr

Israel besetzt Stadt bei Bethlehem

Akademie sagt ja zu Embryo-Stammzellen

Ein «Stapi besonderer Art» für Basel-Stadt?

Wieder Panne bei Swisscom

«Uni Möhlin» immer dubioser

DIE WOCHE

GEGRÜNDET 1993

Deutschland vor der Wende

Helmut Kohl im Keller, Rudolf Scharping triumphiert. Der Machtwechsel rückt näher

WOCHENSCHAU

INHALT

UMFRAGE DER WOCHE

INTERVIEW

„Die Russen gehen ihren eigenen Weg"

Freitag, 28. September 2001

Tages-Anzeiger

Blutbad im Zuger Kantonsrat

Blutiges Ende des Sonderfalls

Leuenberger zutiefst schockiert

Andrew Lloyd Webber Gala zum Spezialpreis

Los Angeles Times

CALENDAR

E
Arts
Entertainment
Style
Culture

Friday, March 14, 2003 calendarlive.com

GARY FRIEDMAN *Los Angeles Times*

WATER-COOLER WIT: *Steven Cojocaru is West Coast style editor for People and has a weekly spot on the "Today" show.*

Red-carpetbagger

Fashion 'heckler' Steven Cojocaru has come in from the fringe.

By MIMI AVINS
Times Staff Writer

IT isn't Steven Cojocaru's fault if an actress nominated for a major award steps onto the red carpet wearing a dress she might have borrowed from a crack whore, or stages a homage to the big-hair '80s, a ghastly goof sure to be captured by paparazzi and beamed around the world. There's no point in blaming Cojocaru for calling a train wreck of a look a disaster. He's just the messenger, honey.

"It's all about water-cooler talk," says Cojocaru, People magazine's West Coast style editor and reigning fashion pundit. "I'm my mother and my Aunt Mitzi, and my Aunt Rhoda, all these yentas who the day after an awards show are ripping everybody to shreds. What I say has a tenth of the vitriol that women spout with their girl- [*See Cojocaru, Page E36*]

MOVIE REVIEW

Unsentimental journey to Africa

'Nowhere in Africa' tells tale of a German Jewish family in Kenya with clear-eyed complexity.

By KENNETH TURAN
Times Staff Writer

On the surface, "Nowhere in Africa's" story of a German Jewish family that fled to Kenya in 1938 to escape the Holocaust sounds familiar and uplifting, a safe and predictable piece of inescapably heartwarming cinema. But "Nowhere in Africa" is not the film you may be expecting. It's better. A whole lot better.

The first hint that there is more going on here is the film's success, both critical and popular, thus far. It won five German Film Awards, including best feature, best director and best cinematography, and it was that country's top-grossing German-language film. "Nowhere in Africa" is not only one of the five films vying for the best foreign language Oscar, but it is the likely winner as well.

That's because director Caroline Link (who previously directed the Oscar-nominated "Beyond Silence") has taken a story that could have drowned in sentiment and turned it into an emotionally complex scenario laced with poignancy and conflict, urgency and compassion. This is an intelligent epic told without special pleading, a film able to cut deep enough to reveal a keen specificity of experience.

Not surprisingly, "Nowhere in Africa" does have a strong basis in fact. It's taken from Stefanie Zweig's autobiographical novel, a bestseller in Germany, about her life as the child of the couple who fled with her to Kenya before the war.

Though the daughter, Regina (played at different ages by Karoline Eckertz and Lea Kurka), remains a key character, Link, who also wrote the adapted screenplay, chose to focus on the troubled, complicated but always passionate relationship between husband and wife. It's a textured, realistic story that has the nerve to risk having not one but both partners lose our sympathy at different junctures of the film, just as they might do in life.

Helped by the nuanced yet powerful performance of Juliane Köhler as wife Jettel Redlich, "Nowhere in Africa" is striking in that one of its key focuses is the indomitability of women. Köhler, memorable as the military wife in "Aimée & Jaguar," shows Jettel in a variety of psychological states: angry, despairing, coping, fearlessly wrestling with compelling conflicts and difficulties with both her husband and her daughter.

"Nowhere in Africa's" other great asset was its decision to have director of photography Gernot Roll shoot the film in logistics-challenged Kenya, where it took place, rather than the cozier but more generic environs of South Africa. Link believes that [*See 'Nowhere,' Page E4*]

More Movie Reviews

Avatar Films

MIDDLE EAST: *Elia Suleiman, a Palestinian, wrote, directed and stars; his film's cast and crew is largely Israeli.*

'Divine Intervention'
He's from Ramallah, she's from Jerusalem. **Page 4**

'Le Cercle Rouge'
"The Red Circle" (1970) is still a dazzling epic of love, guns and gangsters. **Page 10**

'The Hunted'
Tommy Lee Jones and Benicio Del Toro grunt their way through William Friedkin's thriller. **Page 14**

AROUND THE DIAL

Taking up battle stations

Both sides in the war debate have their outspoken outposts in Los Angeles radio.

By STEVE CARNEY
Special to The Times

With developments cropping up hourly on the world stage, the arguments for and against attacking Iraq are swirling into a cacophony that Southland radio listeners can cut through, if they want to, by tuning in to direct lines for each of the polar opposites of the war debate.

Whether it's the time and location of the latest peace march in Alhambra, or tips on how to boycott French products, listeners can flip among commercial talk stations on the right, such as KFI-AM (640) and KABC-AM (790), and the left-wing Pacifica affiliate, KPFK-FM (90.7). Each offers the point of view regular listeners would expect, but they also hope to make the most of the Iraq crisis by attracting more [*See Radio, Page 41*]

CRITIC'S NOTEBOOK

Musical currents that carry both East and West

By MARK SWED
Times Staff Writer

NEW YORK — When Madame Mao banned Western music in China during the 1970s, she certainly didn't intend to make America an extraordinary musical gift. She halted all education in Western music and sent young cosmopolitan musicians into the fields, where they would be exposed only to folk music and patriotic ballet and opera.

What she inadvertently produced was a group of budding composers who never lost their thirst for knowledge of the West but also gained an appreciation for their own musical roots.

During the 1980s, following the Cultural Revolution, several of those composers immigrated to New York to study at Columbia University with Chou Wen-Chung, who combined traditional Chinese music with the experimental techniques of Edgar Varèse.

In their 40s, these composers are now prominent. The best known are Bright Sheng and Tan Dun, and coincidentally both have written brilliant, innovative concertos for cellist Yo-Yo Ma in which they make penetrating quests for cultural identity.

Sheng's "The Song and Dance of Tears" was commissioned by the New York Philharmonic and had its premiere in Avery Fisher Hall last week. The composer describes it as a tone poem for *pipa*, *sheng*, cello, piano and orchestra. It was writ- [*See Notebook, Page E31*]

In Calendar

ROBERT GAUTHIER *Los Angeles Times*

LEGUIZAMO LOVE

In "Sexaholix . . . a love story," at the Ahmanson Theatre, John Leguizamo uses raunch, humor and love to energetically re-create his journey from wild child to sexual neophyte to parent, imitating family, girlfriends and lamebrained buddies along the way. **PAGE 26**

Gradual big bang at the *L.A. Times*

Roger Black

Because of editorial changes, a major American paper's new design happens incrementally rather than suddenly

There are generally two ways to introduce a new design to a newspaper's readers. All at once (the big bang). Or gradually.

The big bang can startle readers, but the reasoning is, "They get over it." There can also be great production and training hurdles, so that managing a big bang is not easy.

The slower approach, which Mario Garcia has called the "Grecian Formula," may be easier on everyone, and it has the advantage of allowing experimentation in real time – and strategic withdrawals that are not as noticeable. But it has its own risks. Unless there is a clear roadmap, a heading charted with key waypoints, the design may wander off course, into the shallows and aground.

With the *Los Angeles Times*, we had the opportunity to work on both approaches with two different sets of editors. The first group, led by Michael Parks and John Lindsay, were ready to make some big changes in the newspaper, which had not been completely redesigned since the 1970s, when Sheila Levrant de Bretteville, now dean of the Yale design school, introduced a new headline type based on Times Roman.

Designers at the paper had lamented the fact that over 20 years this great newspaper typeface had become as common as a Starbucks Grande. Quite a good cup of coffee, but generic. It had been installed on every PC and laser printer on the planet. Tom Trapnell, a senior designer at the *Los Angeles Times*, had created a new design with elegant new typefaces such as Adobe's Minion. Calendar, Southern California Living, and the other feature sections appeared in the new format in 1998. However, hardened opponents in the newsroom prevented the design from being implemented in the news section, and the paper took on a split personality, still unresolved when Roger Black, Inc., was hired in 1998.

Jackie Goldberg, an L.A. native, spent months with the *Times* team in a lavish old Chandler reception hall on the top of the *Times* complex in downtown Los Angeles, developing a whole new prototype. Two big changes: an entirely new typeface, based on the Dutch predecessors of Times Roman; and a strong new logotype that was condensed slightly so that it would work better in brand extensions like the web site.

This prototype, featuring a daily sports tab and a handy news summary, envisioned as a piece of the paper readers might grab and take with them even if they didn't have time to read the whole paper before work, was approved and heading for implementation when the entire newsroom came apart in the "Staples scandal." The

Opposite: front page of the daily Calendar section, with a "newsy" approach.

newspaper became a co-sponsor of the opening festivities of a sports arena (named for its sponsor, the office supply chain), and the publisher unwittingly agreed to a publish a special issue of the Sunday magazine, as a quid-pro-quo. The editor was unable to stop this deal, but when the details leaked out to the newsroom all hell broke loose. The retired publisher, Otis Chandler, whose family had always owned the *Los Angeles Times*, weighed in with a testy e-mail message criticizing the management. And before we knew it, our main contact, John Lindsay, was fired, presumably for throwing up the first red flag about the Staples quid-pro-quo. Then the publisher; her boss, a controversial CEO from General Mills (nicknamed "Cap'n Crunch"); and the editor-in-chief, were gone. And immediately thereafter the Chandlers, evidently furious with the whole debacle, sold the family newspaper off to the *Chicago Tribune* company.

It was like a tornado had gone through the newsroom, and we retired back to New York, figuring that was the last we would see of the new design for the *Los Angeles Times*. But, when the debris had been cleared, the *Tribune* announced that the new editor was an old friend, John Carroll, editor of the *Baltimore Sun*. We'd worked together on a successful redesign in the early '90s. Carroll quickly brought in his art director, Joe Hutchinson, whom I'd worked with in Baltimore on the *Sunday* redesign in 1998.

Nevertheless I was surprised when Joe called soon after his arrival in L.A., in December 2000, and proposed that we work together again. John Carroll was thinking about a a gradual redesign, starting with a clean-up of the existing news sections. As Heraclitus said, you can never step into the same stream twice. This was a redesign of the *Los Angeles Times*, but this time there was no "big bang": just a careful reconsideration of the what the newspaper is and what it should look like. It would send the wrong signal to make a radical move in the design of the paper so soon after ownership changed to Chicago.

And this time we would work as we did in the *Baltimore Sunday* redesign. Hutchinson and his team would do the heavy lifting, and Danilo Black designers and I would coach from the sidelines.

If the chief art director of the paper can be sprung from daily duties enough to do a redesign this way, it is often the best way to proceed. It comes from within, rather than from the outside. There is more "ownership" at the paper. And the logic of the design, based on a newspaper's history, its readers, its business plan, and its editorial direction, are better known inside than out. The consultant can still add new ideas, a special kind of spin.

The down-side to this approach is that the staffers are often caught by the local barriers: "We don't do it this way because..." A chief designer like Joe Hutchinson, the deputy managing editor at the *Times*, has to be able to ignore these obstacles and try some radical ideas and escape from the inertia. Newsrooms tend to be self-defining; reporters write for other reporters. As has been noticed before, newspaper people are quick to recommend changes for others, but are startled when they are told newspapers have to change.

Fortunately, Hutchinson is that special kind of newspaper art director who looks at the paper every day as though it's the first time he has seen it. He is an excellent designer, and a very good manager – a combination almost never found. So we were able to proceed with real certainty through

Los Angeles Times

Health

CONSUMER NEWS, MEDICINE AND FITNESS

Free Screenings at Kids Care Fair

In Crashes, Legs Often Take a Hit

'Once you find out it's Alzheimer's, you can trace it back and look at all the things you blamed [a parent] for in the past. There's a lot of forgiveness that can happen.'

A FAMILY HOLDS ON

When Alzheimer's strikes early, life turns upside down as children and spouse begin a slow farewell

Signs Go Beyond Loss of Memory

Meals Program Falls Short

Health Matters

INSIDE

Got Game, Got Sore Muscles

Fitness Bound

Snapshot: Basketball

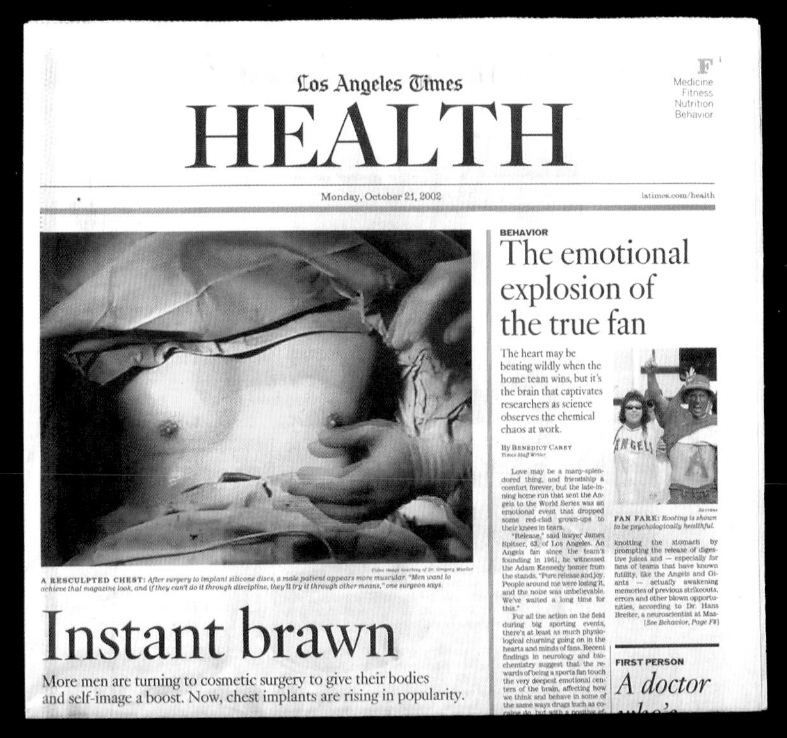

Los Angeles Times

HEALTH

F

Medicine
Fitness
Nutrition
Behavior

Monday, October 21, 2002

latimes.com/health

A RESCULPTED CHEST: *After surgery to implant silicone discs, a male patient appears more muscular. "Men want to achieve that magazine look, and if they can't do it through discipline, they'll try it through other means," one surgeon says.*

Instant brawn

More men are turning to cosmetic surgery to give their bodies and self-image a boost. Now, chest implants are rising in popularity.

BEHAVIOR

The emotional explosion of the true fan

The heart may be beating wildly when the home team wins, but it's the brain that captivates researchers as science observes the chemical chaos at work.

By Benedict Carey
Times Staff Writer

Love may be a many-splendored thing, and friendship a comfort forever, but the late-inning home run that sent the Angels to the World Series was an emotional event that dropped some red-clad grown-ups to their knees in tears.

"Release," said lawyer James Spitser, 43, of Los Angeles. An Angels fan since the team's founding in 1961, he witnessed the Adam Kennedy homer from the stands. "Pure release and joy. People around me were losing it, and the noise was unbelievable. We've waited a long time for this."

For all the action on the field during big sporting events, there's at least as much physiological churning going on in the hearts and minds of fans. Recent findings in neurology and biochemistry suggest that the rewards of being a sports fan touch the very deepest emotional centers of the brain, affecting how we think and behave in some of the same ways drugs such as co-

FAN FARE: *Rooting is shown to be psychologically healthful.*

knotting the stomach by prompting the release of digestive juices and — especially for fans of teams that have known futility, like the Angels and Giants — actually awakening memories of previous strikeouts, errors and other blown opportunities, according to Dr. Hans Breiter, a neuroscientist at Mas-

(See Behavior, Page F8)

FIRST PERSON

A doctor

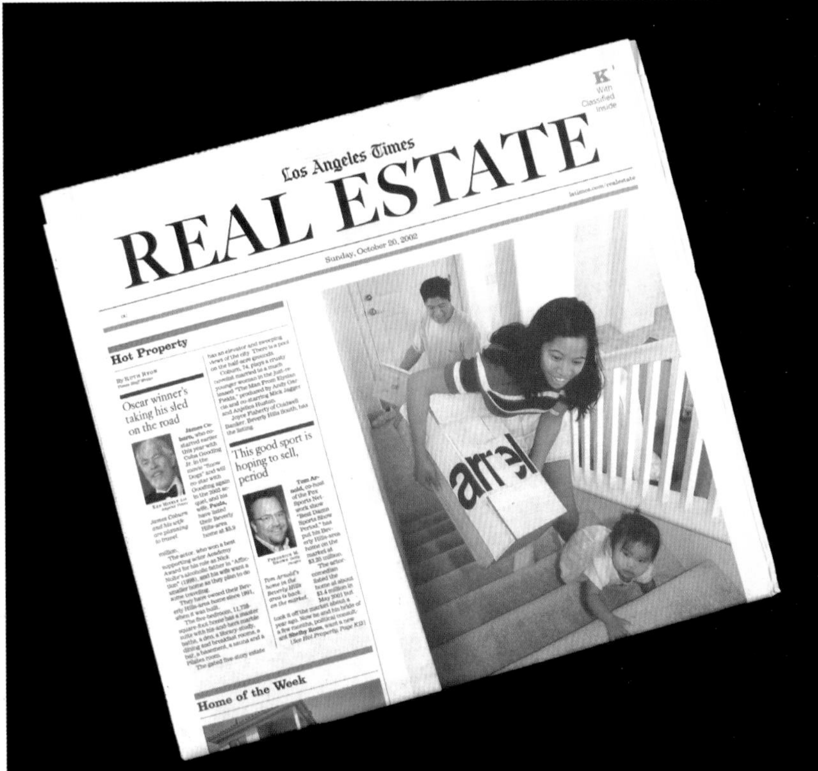

Los Angeles Times

REAL ESTATE

K

With Classified Inside

Sunday, October 20, 2002

Hot Property

Oscar winner's taking his sled on the road

This good sport is hoping to sell, period

Home of the Week

The old design of the Health section (above) and redesigned Health and Real Estate sections of the paper.

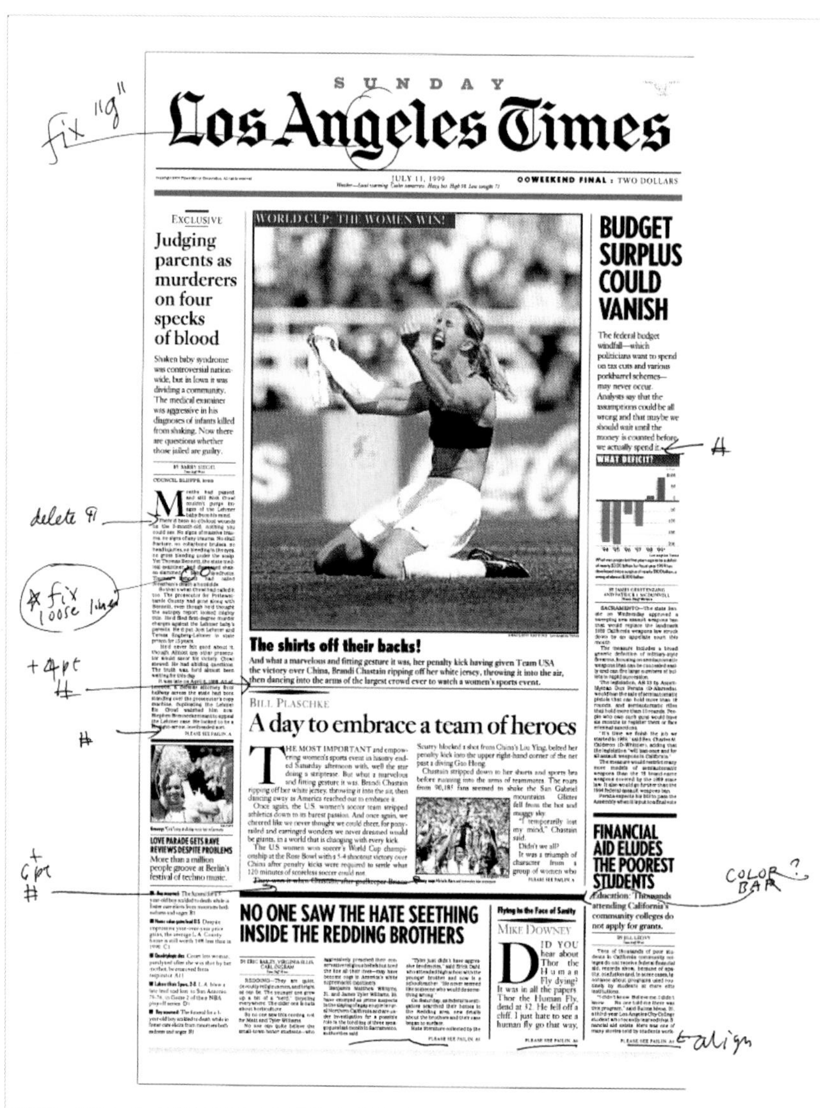

SUNDAY

Los Angeles Times

JULY 11, 1999

WEEKEND FINAL : TWO DOLLARS

EXCLUSIVE

Judging parents as murderers on four specks of blood

Shaken baby syndrome was controversial nationwide, but in Iowa it was dividing a community. The medical examiner was aggressive in his diagnoses of infants killed from shaking. Now there are questions whether those jailed are guilty.

WORLD CUP: THE WOMEN WIN!

The shirts off their backs!

And what a marvelous and fitting gesture it was, her penalty kick having given Team USA the victory over China, Brandi Chastain ripping off her white jersey, throwing it into the air, then dancing into the arms of the largest crowd ever to watch a women's sports event.

BILL PLASCHKE

A day to embrace a team of heroes

THE MOST IMPORTANT and empowering women's sports event in history ended Saturday afternoon with, well the star doing a striptease. But what a marvelous and fitting gesture it was. Brandi Chastain ripping off her white jersey, throwing it into the air, then dancing away as America reached out to embrace it.

Once again, the U.S. women's soccer team stripped athletics down to its barest passion. And once again, we cheered like we never thought we could cheer, for ponytailed and earringed wonders we never dreamed would be giants, in a world that is changing with every kick.

The U.S. women won soccer's World Cup championship at the Rose Bowl with a 5-4 shootout victory over China after penalty kicks were required to settle what 120 minutes of scoreless soccer could not.

Scurry blocked a shot from China's Liu Ying, belted her penalty kick into the upper right-hand corner of the net past a diving Gao Hong.

Chastain stripped down to her shorts and sports bra before running into the arms of teammates. The roars from 90,185 fans seemed to shake the San Gabriel mountains. Glitter fell from the hot and muggy sky.

"I temporarily lost my mind," Chastain said.

Didn't we all?

It was a triumph of character from a group of women who

BUDGET SURPLUS COULD VANISH

The federal budget windfall—which politicians want to spend on tax cuts and various porkbarrel schemes—may never occur. Analysts say that the assumptions could be all wrong and that maybe we should wait until the money is counted before we actually spend it.

WHAT DEFICIT?

'94 '95 '96 '97 '98 '99

LOVE PARADE GETS RAVE REVIEWS DESPITE PROBLEMS

More than a million people groove at Berlin's festival of techno music.

FINANCIAL AID ELUDES THE POOREST STUDENTS

Education: Thousands attending California's community colleges do not apply for grants.

NO ONE SAW THE HATE SEETHING INSIDE THE REDDING BROTHERS

Flying in the Face of Sanity

MIKE DOWNEY

DID YOU hear about Thor the Human Fly dying? It was in all the papers. Thor the Human Fly, dead at 32. He fell off a cliff. I just hate to see a human fly go that way.

A mark-up of the front page (above) to indicate what should change, and proposed changes (opposite) from the 1999 redesign effort.

a careful, staged redesign.

First we took on the initial organization and typography. The title of Metro was changed to California, and regional branding was made secondary to the *Los Angeles Times* brand.

All the typefaces had been squished in the move to the narrow 50-inch web; so we uncondensed all the fonts, and added space back in the gutters to the let the paper breathe a little.

In 2002 we started on a more complete redesign. A general typographical master plan was created, using refined versions of the Kis typefaces from the Michael Parks redesign of 1999.

Layouts were done for both news sections and feature sections, and it was decided to start with the feature sections, in a gradual introduction over the next two years. Of course, this could set up the same split personality that existed in the *L.A. Times* from the last half-successful redesign. The look of the feature sections, Calendar and the rest, differed remarkably from the news sections – emphasizing the classic problem contemporary newspapers have in defining what is news today.

But we believed that we knew what we were doing, and the reason for starting with features is that there was a new team in place, and new ideas, and there was still a lot of rethinking to be done in the news sections. The key in this kind of approach is to have the course, the way-points, and the ultimate goal agreed upon before any sections are launched.

Carroll decided, wisely, to introduce a new body type ahead of the rest of the design changes, so that readers had a chance to get used to it and didn't couple that decision with the other changes. This strategem worked. The new typeface, Ionic No. 5, was really just the original newspaper type that the old body type,

Los Angeles Times

Calendar

Amok in Toyland

Gadgets and gizmos dominate the screen in Wild Wild West.

By Ken Turan

LIKE THE CURIOUS children they often resemble, filmmakers can be fatally distracted by toys. Big, expensive toys that are no doubt enormous fun to play with in person, but don't register quite the same way on screen. Toys like the ones that dominate and finally destroy "Wild Wild West."

With a kiss, Kirov awakens Petipa's 'Sleeping Beauty'

Los Angeles Times

L.A.

SOUTHERN CALIFORNIA

SOUTHEAST L.A. DAWN IS RATTLED BY 3.8 QUAKE

VERNON POLICE KILL WOMAN AFTER THREE-HOUR STANDOFF

2 SUPERVISORS CALL FOR PANEL TO SCRUTINIZE FOSTER CARE

Finally, a sense of justice

2 MEN GUILTY IN WOMAN'S DEATH

BOARD ACCEPTS FEDERAL OFFER FOR QUAKE REPAIRS

PLANE THAT CLIPPED BUSES FOUND LOW ON SPARE FUEL

COUNCIL OKS CENTRALIZED SYSTEM TO MONITOR BADGES

EX-BOYFRIEND SOUGHT FOR QUESTIONING IN SLAYINGS

SHERIFF VOWS TO CRUSH SEX BIAS IN DEPARTMENT

Clerk sues state drug agency over allegations in cocaine case

Where lions roam free

Los Angeles Times

FOOD

Picnics, fireworks, baseball, country fairs—most of all the Fourth is a time to eat!

An American Icon

Four solid salads for your picnic

There's life beyond deli coleslaw

The hot dog can't get any respect, but millions of Americans don't care.

Details of the earlier design, using Minion (left) and a typeface based on Times Roman (below left) for headlines; and the new design (opposite), using Kis for headlines throughout.

Pregnant, With Unexpected Grief

Technological advances bring much knowledge but can make unforeseen loss even harder

By ANN MARSH
SPECIAL TO THE TIMES

A short generation ago, mothers weren't privy to the goings-on in their own wombs. Pregnancies often arose and miscarried, undetected. Women felt, but didn't see, the movement of their future progeny. They guessed at their genders and talked to dreamed-of children through the skin of their bellies. They drank and smoked. They prayed for the best, and they got what they got. In a way, they were lucky.

"I think people were much happier then," says Carol Archie, a doctor of maternal fetal health at UCLA. When they lost an unborn child—one they never had a chance to meet through sophisticated probes and shadowy pictures—it was so much easier. But, she says, advances in medical science "give women today a whole lot more to grieve than their mothers had. That, in some ways, is not a good thing."

The same technology and testing that offer a new window into the health of a fetus may also lead doctors to give mothers an array of dire predictions about their future baby's health. And when test data are ambiguous, doctors may or may not confess their own uncertainty about what they've seen. This year, one defiant Los Angeles mother gave birth to a healthy child although multiple doctors had advised her to abort, based on early ultrasound information.

The parental psyche reels with the information presented by ultrasounds, MRIs, CT scans and over-the-counter pregnancy kits. Couples who used to bond with their children when they were first placed in their arms now carry fetal ultrasound images in their wallets. They attach their imaginations and dreams to life at its most tentative—the eggs in the petri dish, the just-confirmed conception. And if prenatal testing suggests disorders, they're asked to make decisions for which even an advanced course in medical ethics

Please see Pregnancy, E3

ELAINE SKYLAR / For The Times

'If I live to be 80, those extra months weren't much to give my baby. If I hadn't had the routine ultrasound, I couldn't have planned everything I did.'

JANE LEBAK

With husband James. After learning of fetus' fatal condition, she carried it to term and delivered the baby with family present.

t, Charles Garcia, David Norris and Michael Thoennes pass the time with "Conflict: Desert Storm" game.

NEWS ANALYSIS

Chirac Seals Role as U.S. Critic

The French president says 'a problem of principles' led him to brandish U.N. veto option after months of delicate diplomacy.

By SEBASTIAN ROTELLA
Times Staff Writer

PARIS — With the Elysee presidential palace as an elegant stage, French President Jacques Chirac on Monday delivered a dramatic message that had been rehearsed and refined for weeks: France will go to the limit in its opposition to a U.S. war on Iraq.

Chirac used a hastily organ-

Reuters

OPPOSED: *French President Jacques Chirac said U.S. friendship would survive.*

gard their veto power as the dip-

gue with the Americans," said Chirac, looking resolute but relaxed during a half-hour conversation with two journalists. "But here we have a problem of principles. We are not in a conflict with the United States . . . but we have a problem of principles, I would say a moral problem. Are we going to go to war if we have perhaps a means of avoiding it? That's where France, following its traditions, says if there is a means of avoiding it, we must do all we can."

On Monday, Chirac completed the journey from reluctant ally to hard-line critic and in the process iced any lingering hopes in Washington that France would relent in a last-

E28 SUNDAY, OCTOBER 27, 2002 LOS ANGELES TIMES

Back to the days of subversive innocence

'Far From Heaven' is pure homage to those '50s 'women's pictures.'

By David Thomson
Special to The Times

PREPARE yourself for an unashamed beauty such as modern movies seldom yield to. Float on a swooning score by Elmer Bernstein, that essential movie composer of the 1950s. Be ready for a wide-screen composition of four women on a suburban lawn of Kelly green, and the gorgeous clash of their billowing skirts, in rose pink, vermilion, amber and scarlet. Or Scarlett?

Yes, these are attributions of color that might serve as emblematic names in melodrama. I'm talking about the new Todd Haynes movie, "Far From Heaven," one of the headiest experiences of the fall — a picture that could as easily have been titled "All That Heaven Allows," "Written on the Wind" or even "Gone With the Wind." For here we are in Hartford, Conn., in 1957 (where you are entitled to read "heartland" for Hartford, meaning not just the core of Eisenhower's America, but a promise of heartfelt feeling). I don't think any major American picture since "Pulp Fiction" has been so brazen, so radiant even, about saying, "Here's a story (if you like), but more important, here's a certain type of movie."

There's the rub. "Pulp Fiction" is a commonly recognized genre, a stew of noir, sex, violence and intrigue, done with flat-out speed and hard-boiled idioms. Kids and their parents were hip to the riffs Quentin Tarantino was playing off Bogart or Mitchum tunes. But surely in 2002 there are going to be some people who wonder why they're being asked to dwell on this sad story of people from 1957, antiques of desire and repression who seem unable to solve their problems. Fifty years of television and its 12-step dramas have instilled the ridiculous American orthodoxy that we can all make ourselves whole and wholesome. (It's only in life that people do 20 years with a shrink, clinging onto their condition.

Typography of the news

After the previous redesign, feature pages used different display typefaces than news pages: Minion for features, and a face based on Times Roman for news. In the new design, headlines are set in a specially designed version of Kis.

Home (above and opposite), a hyper-visual, content-driven section of the paper that functions as a sub-brand.

a thinned-out version of Linotype Opticon, was based on. Several fonts were tested, along with many variations of point size, leading, and tracking.

Then we turned to the big one, Sunday Calendar, with its big movie ads – a section that brings in an estimated $100 million in annual revenue to the paper. For 40 years it had been a tabloid, but we redesigned it as a broadsheet. This would allow the *L.A. Times* to compete directly with *The New York Times*'s Arts & Leisure section, with its giant color movie ads.

In focus groups, we found that readers could get over the change, but that they really relied on the section's listings. They used them. This came as a bit of a surprise to some editors who spent much of their time working on the Calendar feature stories. So we put more energy into the design of the listings, and beefed up the remaining Calendar tabloid, the Thursday Weekend section.

With the idea of Sunday Calendar approved, we turned to the daily Calendar and the other feature section, Southern California Living. This section had become an orphan of the newspaper, and rather than pour more resources into it, the editors decided to kill it, use that money elsewhere, and then slowly introduce more focused weekly sections to replace it. Meanwhile, general lifestyle features were to be put into the Calendar section.

Food, and then Health, were introduced with the first round of the new design, along with Sunday Travel, and Real Estate. In 2003 we designed Home, Outdoors. At this writing we're starting on Image, a fashion section, and at last turning to the details of the front page.

And so, after five years, the complete redesign should appear

LOS ANGELES TIMES
HOME
WANTED
A desire for everything red
— Barbara King

LOS ANGELES TIMES
The Eye by Barbara King
When you sit upon a star
This may be as close as you get to having Cruz or Russo in your home.
The seats of power
closetfactory
YOUR CLOSET. ONLY BETTER.
FREE
CALL
800.692.5673
Change Your PERSPECTIVE in 28 days
Elizabeth Taylor Shutters
800.748.8377
Girari
AZCAST
NEW FOR 2003
AZCAST DESIGN
SPRING SALE
Savings Up to 50% Off
Bedroom Set, Solid Wood With Cherry Veneer
Living Room Set, Solid Wood With Leather Weave
310/378-8854
310/719-8446
MORE ON SUNDAY
IRA

How to find the right framer
They never speak
SALE

LOWEST
FREE
In Wright's treehouse

Los Angeles Times

Now with 8 days of listings

weekend

Los Angeles Times
Thursday, February 13, 2003
calendarlive.com/weekend

To live and to love in L.A.

Romance may not be easy in the land of Bogey and Bacall, but that doesn't keep most of us from trying.
Page 36

Plus, just in time for Valentine's Day:

- Rating movie heartthrobs
- A look at chocolate history
- Internet love connections
- Singles' bashes, parties and more

in 2004. Of course by that time, we'll be working on improving Calendar and the 2002 sections. A big newspaper is like a great ocean liner. Crews are always working on maintenance, refits, and upgrades. And every day, someone is adding another coat of paint. ‹

COVER STORY

Love in La La Land

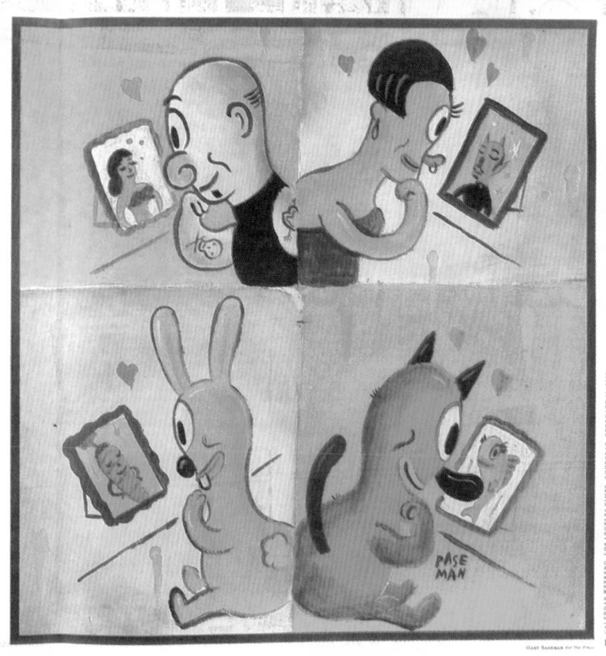

Romance is almost never easy and it can be especially difficult in spacey, sprawled-out L.A., which thrives on images of amour.

By James Verini
Special to The Times

LOVE in Los Angeles? You want to know about love in Los Angeles? It's still like the man said, some 70 jaded years ago: *"It's a Barnum and Bailey world/ Just as phony as it can be/ But it wouldn't be make believe/ If you believed in me."*

Granted, when the Broadway lyricists E.Y. Harburg and Billy Rose wrote "Paper Moon" with Harold Arlen in 1933, hoping the song would find its way west and into a movie and make them MGM-style rich, they may not have mentioned L.A. outright. But then they didn't mention love outright, either, did they? Outright is not how things are done, in jazz or here. But make no mistake, they were looking west. Even back then they knew, just as we know now, that America's dreams of love — the world's dreams of love, really — come from one place. Right here. Los Angeles, the city of illusion, a Barnum and Bailey town, yes, but — if you believe in it — a city of romance too.

But therein lies the rub: to make love in the romance factory. To find and maintain the real thing in a city whose very currency is impossible images of love, a place where stunning young women and men — and they seem to get younger every day — sprout from the pavement like Whack-a-Moles. To be a workaday craftsman in the city ruled by Ares and Aphrodite, in the land of Bogey and Bacall, Pitt and Aniston.

"You'll notice that no romantic comedies are set here," says Jon Lucas, 27, a screenwriter who's sold romantic comedy scripts by setting them in other cities. "The notion is that everybody falls in love in New York. It's always autumn in New York. But we don't associate this town with that. We're willing to watch L.A. get blown up by aliens but not to watch people fall in love here." He's right, Paris this is not. We're in the city that invented noir, not amour.

Steve Martin, probably our most clear-sighted ambassador, found love in "L.A. Story" (1990). But only through embracing the city's crackpot-mystical side for a last-minute miracle: He had to cause a rainstorm with his mind, you'll remember. And Mirabelle, the sensitive heroine of his novella "Shopgirl," falls for a millionaire with a house in the hills but finds true love only when she moves to San Francisco. And yes, young men, of course there's "Swingers." But really — Heather Graham, alone, having a drink at the Derby? *Come on.*

"It's a stereotype, but people do tend to judge *[See Romance, Page 38]*

E36

The Weekend section (opposite, and this page), which comes out on Thursdays and takes over the tabloid mantle of the old Calendar.

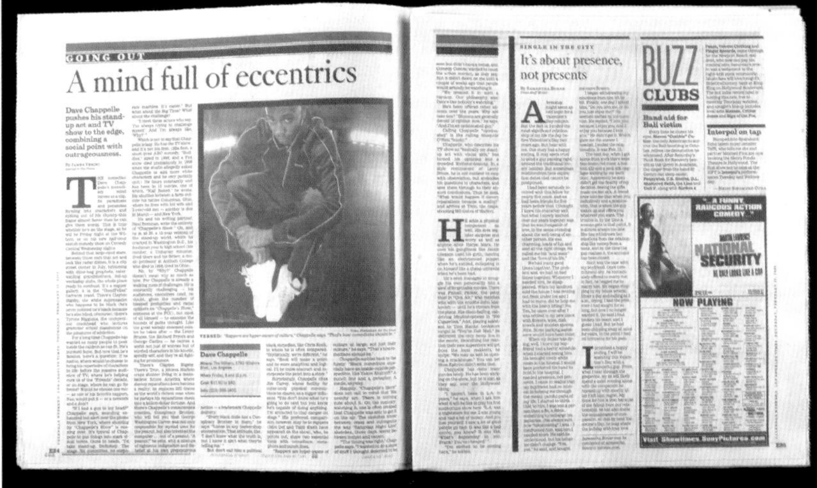

GOING OUT

A mind full of eccentrics

Dave Chappelle pushes his stand-up act and TV show to the edge, combining a social point with outrageousness.

SINGLE IN THE CITY

It's about presence, not presents

BUZZ CLUBS

NOW PLAYING

NATIONAL SECURITY

TUNED IN

Crime, crisis get too close for comfort

Today's Highlights

Today's Talk Shows

PARTING SHOT

Will Call

POP

LAST CHANCE

Theater

My Favorite Weekend: Lydia Lunch

IN THE QUEST FOR WHITER TEETH, A BRAVE SMALL BAND...

Colgate

Los Angeles Times

SUNDAY

Travel

DESTINATIONS, TIPS AND TOURS

WEEKEND ESCAPE

A Sierra Soak

AUSTRALIA

Island of Animal Magnetism

Off the southern coast of the land Down Under, Kangaroo Island is a haven for creatures great and small that delight the human visitors who encounter them

INSIDE

Pages from the Travel section, in the older design (above) and the new design (right and opposite).

Los Angeles Times

TRAVEL

Sunday, October 20, 2002

latimes.com/travel

FRANCE

ANCIENT GUARDIANS: *The Tour St. Nicolas and Tour de la Chaîne have protected La Rochelle's Vieux Port since the 14th century.*

Savoring a fine old port

With its quaint harbor and Franco-American links, La Rochelle delivers history (and seafood) on a platter.

By Peter Wortsman
Special to The Times

La Rochelle, France

WE didn't take long to RSVP when friends who are renovating a 200-year-old farmhouse near La Rochelle invited us to visit in August. "It'll be good for the children's sense of history," said my French wife, Claudie, a college professor. I readily agreed, noting the proximity to Cognac, where the world's most famous brandy was born, and to Marennes-Oléron, France's finest oyster bed. And there was La Rochelle's new aquarium, a tantalizing lure for the kids.

Of course, there was also the setting and the scenery.

La Rochelle has one of the best — and most picturesque — harbors along the Atlantic Coast, as well as western France's largest yachting basin. The entrance to the Vieux (Old) Port is guarded by two 14th century towers, the Tour St. Nicolas and the Tour de la Chaîne, from which links of the chain that once blocked the harbor at night still dangle. The view toward town is also impressive: An outsize clock tower rears its domed head above the town gate, dwarfing all other dwellings. Arcades and stately mansions grace medieval byways that play hide-and-seek in the folds of time.

We arrived at our friends' house on a Wednesday night and enjoyed their hospitality the [*See La Rochelle, Page L13*]

THE SEA'S BOUNTY: *Oysters are shucked for a seafood platter under the arcades of the colorful bistro Chez André, a beloved institution since 1947.*

BRAZIL

Rolling along the wild river

A bare-bones Amazon trip means hammocks, not beds, but the memories are priceless. Page 8

WEEKEND ESCAPE

Shop and stay up Ventura way

Outlet stores, Camarillo Ranch (right) and a beachfront hotel await. Page 4

FLORIDA

Oils and water on Cedar Key

Gallery hopping and bird-watching mix peacefully on a Gulf isle. Page 11

Not starting with the front page

The new design was implemented first in the paper's key franchise, the Sunday entertainment sections, which include the Sunday Calendar and feature sections like Travel.

TRAVEL LOS ANGELES TIMES SUNDAY, OCTOBER 20, 2002 L11

DESTINATION: FLORIDA

Unlocking the charm of Gulf's Cedar Key

Vast, wild marshlands and an island of indolence prove to be fine nesting grounds for waterfowl and artists — and tourists who appreciate both.

By Michal Strutin
Special to The Times

Winging to the key

GETTING THERE:

WHERE TO STAY:

WHERE TO EAT:

TO LEARN MORE:

RICH PICKINGS: *American white pelicans scope out the catch off Cedar Key, whose salt marshes are a fish nursery teeming with life.*

Wowed by the roost

AN AVIAN REFUGE: *At the island's Dock Street pier, gulls and brown pelicans crowd around feeder Owen Freeman, who works with a Cedar Key rescue group that examines the animals for injuries.*

DESTINATION: BRAZIL

An Amazon for adventurers

A budget cruise on the Amazon

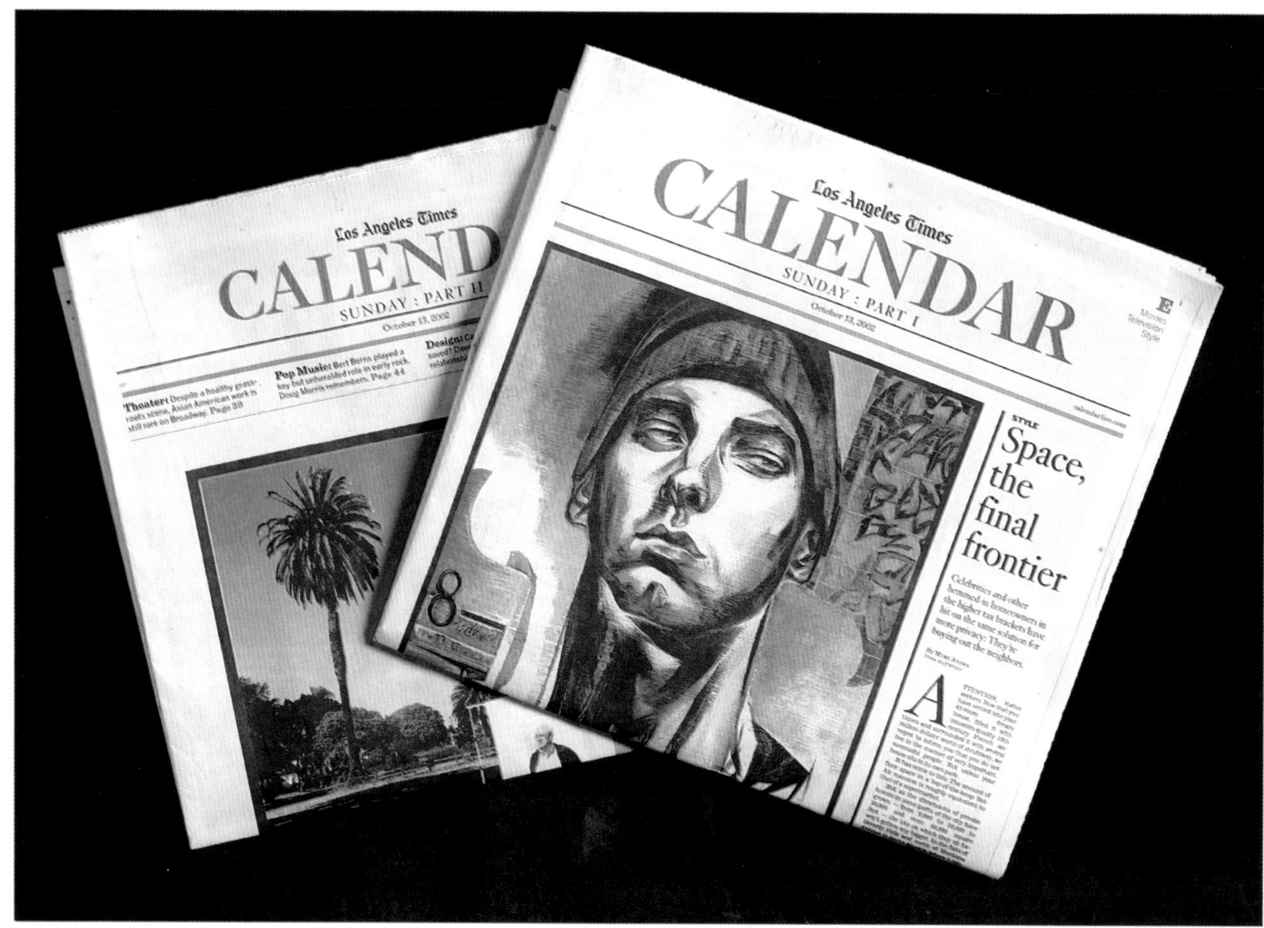

Dropping the tab

Giving up the long-standing tabloid format for the entertainment section was a big risk, but also an opportunity. The change created a bigger, general feature section.

Los Angeles Times

CALENDAR

SUNDAY : PART I

E

November 3, 2002

calendarlive.com

Holiday
SNEAKS

Easy does it

Steven Spielberg emerges from a decade in the dark with "Catch Me if You Can," a lighter-hearted caper set in the go-go '60s starring Leonardo DiCaprio and Tom Hanks. At work with the director on the film he calls his "ray of sunshine." By Rachel Abramowitz. Page 24

A lion in late autumn
Jack Nicholson on Hollywood's failure to honestly portray the aging male and why director Alexander Payne's "About Schmidt" is different.
Page 4

Its time has finally come
For 25 years, devotees struggled to make a film of Kander and Ebb's acerbic '70s musical "Chicago." A single-minded director finally got it on track.
Page 6

What 'The Hours' bring
A film of the acclaimed novel drew three top actresses to the roles of author Virginia Woolf and two women who found echoes of her life in theirs.
Page 13

None dare call them sequels
The second Harry Potter and "Lord of the Rings" films must bear comparison with the books and last year's franchise-launching movies.
Page 18

Examples of the redesigned Sunday Calendar (opposite and left), and the old tabloid format (above).

Los Angeles Times

CALENDAR

SUNDAY : PART I

March 23, 2003

calendarlive.com

E

Movies
Television
Style
Media

THE 75TH ANNUAL ACADEMY AWARDS

The OSCARS

Why they matter

By Kenneth Turan
Times Staff Writer

IT takes a lot to postpone the Academy Awards. Though this year might prove an exception, historically, having a war on has never been a good enough reason to cancel or even put off the annual event. ★ The Oscars have been postponed — for an L.A. flood, for Martin Luther King Jr.'s assassination and for the attempt on Ronald Reagan's life. But though the 1942 Oscar ceremony took place less than three months after Pearl Harbor, neither World War II nor subsequent conflagrations in Korea and Vietnam were considered big enough deals to put a stop to the proceedings. ★ Which is not to say that war hasn't had its effects. According to Mason Wiley and Damien Bona's book "Inside Oscar," the academy board decreed that women were not to wear orchids in 1942 "but donate the money they would have spent for them to the Red Cross." There was some discussion of either canceling the event or holding it in an auditorium instead of a banquet hall (at the suggestion of academy president Bette Davis), but those ideas were shelved, according to Robert Osborne, author of "70 Years of the Oscar." The board also considered serving food "similar to that served soldiers and other servicemen," but that idea was also voted down, though formal attire was discouraged and there were no searchlights in the skies above the Biltmore Hotel in downtown L.A., where the event was held. ★ The following year, the proud gold-plated bronze Oscar [*See Turan, Page E22*]

Unsung heroes, heralded at last

A dance step, a key casting choice, a striking visual detail — they brought something special to the big five films. **Page 4**

Jaded? Not these two

They each played the roles of their lives — now Diane Lane and Adrien Brody dish the charmed existence of a first-time nominee. **Page 6**

Predictably, they have opinions

Manohla Dargis, Kenneth Turan and Kevin Thomas make some strikingly consistent picks. **Page 10**

How TV made Oscar what he is today

But what's worse, a show that starts at 10:30 and lasts an hour (the first radio broadcast) or today's marathons? **Page 20**

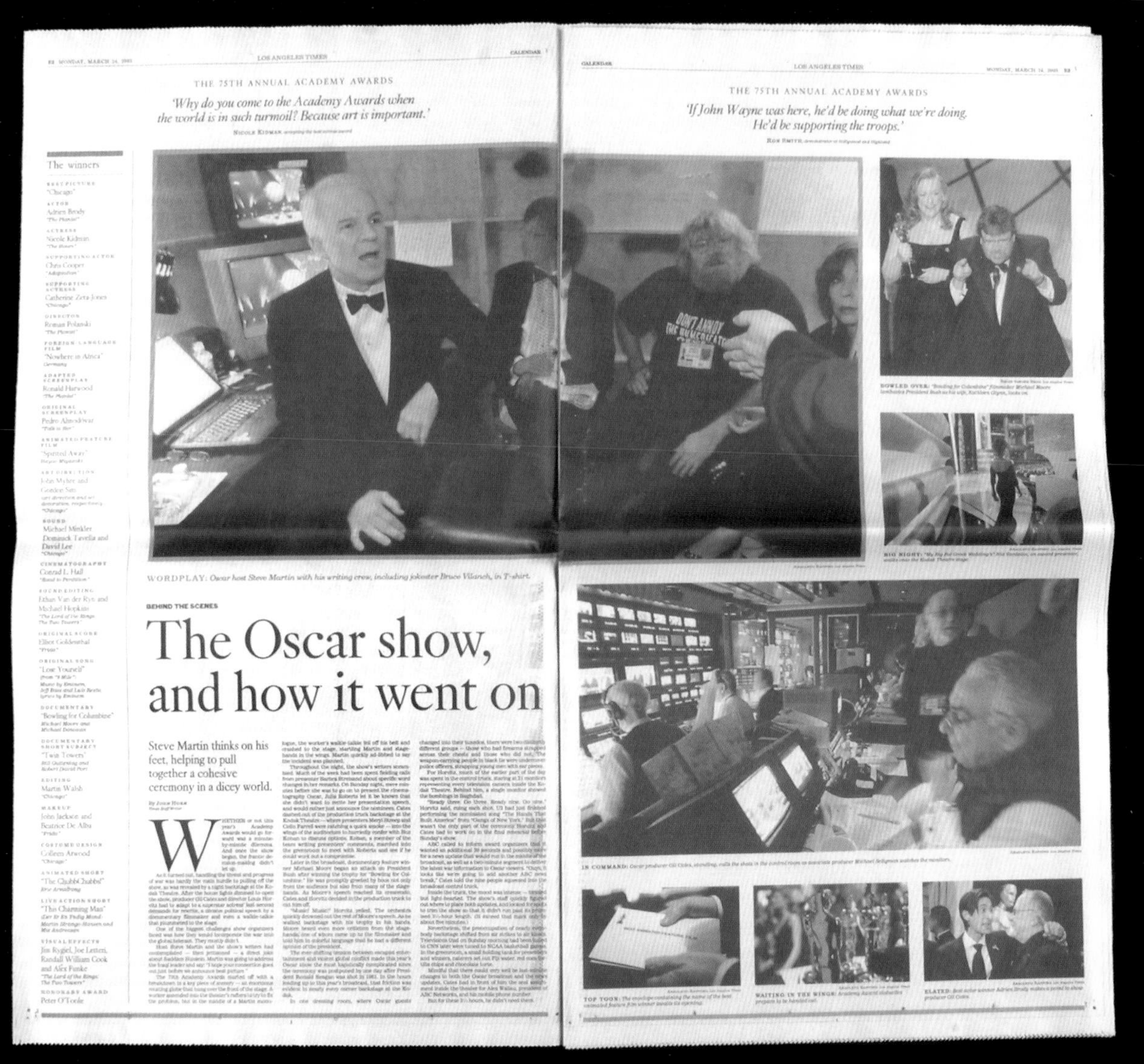

L.A. & the Oscars

The new design of the Sunday Calendar gives the *L.A. Times* room to deal with the the kind of big entertainment story that characterizes Los Angeles.

The Gipper's long run to end communism

LEGACY: *Ronald Reagan took on "Red Menace."*

By Jacob Heilbrunn

Reagan's War

The Epic Story of His 40-Year Struggle and Final Triumph Over Communism

Peter Schweizer

Doubleday: 288 pp., $26

THE president has largely discredited the United States with his wild rhetoric about an evil foreign enemy. Bombing raids in the Middle East have incurred the ire of the Arab world. When he visits Italy, demonstrators throng the streets with placards calling him a warmonger and an executioner. At home, the country is embroiled in a debate about whether the White House's recklessly provocative unilateralism is going to lead to world war.

This might sound like George W. Bush on the eve of war with Iraq, but it also describes the popular view of Ronald Reagan during the Cold War. The parallels are anything but accidental. Bush has staffed his foreign

Cold War provides the model for American foreign policy. Just as Reagan's confrontational policies destroyed the Soviet empire, so Bush's tough-minded actions will defeat terrorism and permanently ensure American global dominance.

But will they? In drawing on the Reagan era, are Bush administration officials following a sure-fire guideline for success or a roadmap to disaster? Was Reagan really a visionary or merely a bumbling dunderhead who happened to be president when the Soviet Union imploded simply because of its own weaknesses? Or are the doves opposed to the Bush administration the true fossils of the Cold War era? The end of the Cold War has not stilled the debates about the merits of militancy abroad but rather given them a new lease on life.

Peter Schweizer's "Reagan's War" thus arrives at an opportune moment. Schweizer, a fellow at the Hoover Institution, makes a rousing and compelling case that Reagan's personal and political odyssey, beginning with his days in Hollywood and concluding with his presidency, was central to bringing down the "evil empire." Indeed, Schweizer argues that Reagan had it right from the beginning. He broke with the passivity of his predecessors to change America's goal from containment to the outright overthrow of the Soviet Union.

Schweizer has conducted numerous interviews with former Soviet and American officials and drawn on archives in the former Warsaw Pact countries. He confines himself to Reagan's role in the Cold War, which makes for a coherent and gripping narrative. But he may have stumbled upon an even bigger story: the transformation of the GOP from being dominated by Wall Street internationalists to being taken over by hawkish Sunbelt conservatives.

As Schweizer reminds us, Reagan cut his anti-Communist teeth in Hollywood after World War II. As an admirer of Franklin D. Roosevelt and Harry S. Truman, Reagan was a Cold War liberal who saw Stalinist aggression as a fundamental threat to the United States and Western Europe. Confronted in 1946 with the specter of Communists trying to take over Hollywood's major labor unions, including the Screen Actors Guild, Schweizer says, Reagan began what would be a lifetime crusade against the "Red Menace": "He was passionate about it, attending meetings, reading up on the subject of communism, talking endlessly about it with friends." His wife, Jane Wyman, thought he had lost it. She divorced Reagan and married pacifist movie actor Lew Ayres, who had sat out World War II in a conscientious objectors' camp in Oregon.

Reagan was undaunted. He became president of the Screen Actors Guild and campaigned full time against Communist influence. But Schweizer takes pains to show that Reagan was not a Red-baiter: He opposed Truman's loyalty oath program for all federal employees and viewed Sen. Joseph McCarthy (R-Wis.) as a loose cannon, although he never attacked him publicly. Reagan's belief was that communism was weak and would crumble as long as the West confronted it and did not become fearful.

As Schweizer tells it, Reagan became progressively dismayed with U.S. presidents for their timidity in con-

Book Review

The *Los Angeles Times Book Review*, a weekly tabloid section, is the most substantial book supplement on the West Coast; it measures itself against competing book publications like the *New York Times Book Review*.

R8 · LOS ANGELES TIMES BOOK REVIEW

Their lives, her camera, full of passion

By Linda Gordon

Dorothea Lange

The Heart and Mind of a Photographer

Edited by Pierre Borhan

Aperture Press, 254 pp., $75

DOROTHEA Lange's Depression photographs — a worried, pensive Okie mother with her children, discouraged farmers squatting in the dust, black and white sharecroppers, Mexican and Filipino lettuce workers — are familiar even to those who don't know her name.

Because Lange was a photographer of unusual emotional power, a few of her pictures were reproduced so often that they became virtual clichés. They served as 1930s icons of "the deserving poor." They built support for Franklin D. Roosevelt and the New Deal and inspired "The Grapes of Wrath." But thousands of never-published Lange masterpieces hide in folders and on microfilm in the Library of Congress, the National Archives and the Oakland Museum of California. Her work also includes exotic portraits of elegant women, imperious portraits of powerful men, romantic portraits of Pueblo Indians, shimmering abstractions, glimpses of tender and painful intimate moments, and a series that denounced the Japanese American internment during World War II as explicitly as a legal brief.

French photo curator Pierre Borhan's new book, "Dorothea Lange: The Heart and Mind of a Photographer," demonstrates Lange's breadth by joining some of her most famous images with some little-known facets of her work. (An exhibit of Lange's work called "About Life: The Photographs of Dorothea Lange" is now at the Getty Center through Feb. 2, 2003.)

Lange, born in Hoboken, N.J., in 1895, went to the Bay Area in 1918 and never left. She constructed a life with mystical edges, as when at age 14, having never held a camera, she told her mother that she wanted to be a photographer, believing that a disability from childhood polio gave her an almost telepathic connection with those who suffered. But mainly she constructed a life through discipline and patient work. First married to Western painter Maynard Dixon, she supported their family with her photography studio in San Francisco. Her insightful and slightly eccentric portraits made her the favored portraitist of the city's elite — the Fleishhackers, Zellerbachs, Strausses — as well as the artistic elite, such as Yehudi Menuhin, Mischa Elman, Ernst Bloch.

In these San Francisco years, lasting until 1935, she lived a bohemian life, socializing with her husband's artist friends in cheap Italian restaurants, venturing on her own to San Quentin to photograph framed union organizer Tom Mooney, hosting Diego Rivera and Frida Kahlo when they visited.

As the Depression hit, her rich clients and her marriage began to seem confining beyond her endurance. She started to move around San Francisco, photographing darker, poorer, more intense scenes. These pictures came to the attention of Berkeley economist/reformer Paul Schuster Taylor, who hired her to illustrate his exposés of the brutal working and living conditions of migrant farm workers. Lange fell doubly in love, with Taylor and with the challenges and rewards of this so-called documentary photography (a phrase she hated).

From 1935 to 1945, she did most of her work for the U.S. Farm Security Administration, documenting — along with Walker Evans, Arthur Rothstein, Ben Shahn and others — the Dust Bowl, agricultural poverty, and, later, wartime defense workers. She slowed her pace considerably for the next 20 years, fighting illness, but she turned out superb, lasting work until her death in 1965.

Borhan has made a beautiful book. The heavyweight production, with thick, creamy paper and 260 elegantly printed photographs, presents both the complexity and the unity of Lange's work. Including some of her slightly eccentric studio portraits allows us to see that her "documentary" work trained on the poor the same respect and insight that she had afforded the rich. Snapshots she took of her children running around naked hint at her bohemian sensibility and, as critic Sally Stein has argued, her extraordinary sensitivity to bodies — some of her most revealing images show only people's backs.

Her first street pictures, from 1933 and 1934, merged this uncanny feel for the language of face, body and gesture with classic composition and concise communication of social content. Always a portraitist, she never sought to capture her subjects unaware, as a photojournalist might. She felt that her subjects needed time to relax into their natural body language; she often recorded their histories in a notebook. She required their collaboration to make photographs, she said.

This collection will not challenge the judgment that she did her strongest work from 1935 to 1945. Far from bureaucratizing her pictures, a government salary gave her freedom to dig ever deeper into her genius. In a twist on gender patterns, she first married a man dependent on her, financially and otherwise; her second husband supported her in every way. Indeed, the Lange-Taylor collaboration was one of the great romantic-intellectual-artistic-political partnerships (think O'Keeffe and Stieglitz, De Beauvoir and Sartre). Taylor's commitment to social justice and expertise on California agriculture helped Lange interpret what she saw.

Borhan provides a selection of fine photos Lange took while accompanying Taylor as he studied agriculture in underdeveloped countries. Despite the foreignness of these cultures, Lange's eye for expressive gesture and composition remained keen. Perhaps the best of her late work was her series on a public defender, part of a project she campaigned for but never got funded: documenting urban America as the Farm Security Administration had documented the countryside.

The book includes brief essays, several translated from the French, that offer glimpses of Lange's charisma, generosity, stubbornness and willfulness. Critic A.D. Coleman praises Lange and Taylor's nearly forgotten book on the Dust Bowl migration, "An American Exodus." A Borhan essay encapsulates the technology, art and politics at the time, but he misses the personal passion of Lange's politics. She was not a Red, although she was in complete sympathy with some of the Communist-led causes of the period, such as the farm workers' struggles, the San Francisco general strike of 1934 and the defense of the Scottsboro Boys. Borhan's assertion that "It is not really in the nature of Americans to want to transform the world" is an example of his failure to grasp the political context that shaped her. In general, the essays offer little that is original — the essays in Elizabeth Partridge's 1994 "Restless Spirit: The Life and Work of Dorothea Lange" are better. But Lange's photographs have bodies and voice enough. ■

Linda Gordon is writing a biography of Dorothea Lange. Her most recent book is "The Great Arizona Orphan Abduction." She teaches history at NYU.

SAN FRANCISCO, 1934: *May Day rally*

1930s AMERICA: *Social Security office lines*

SUNDAY, OCTOBER 20, 2002 · LOS ANGELES TIMES BOOK REVIEW · R9

Photographs by Dorothea Lange

EXECUTIVE ORDER 9066: *Children wearing internment camp ID tags in Hayward, May 8, 1942*

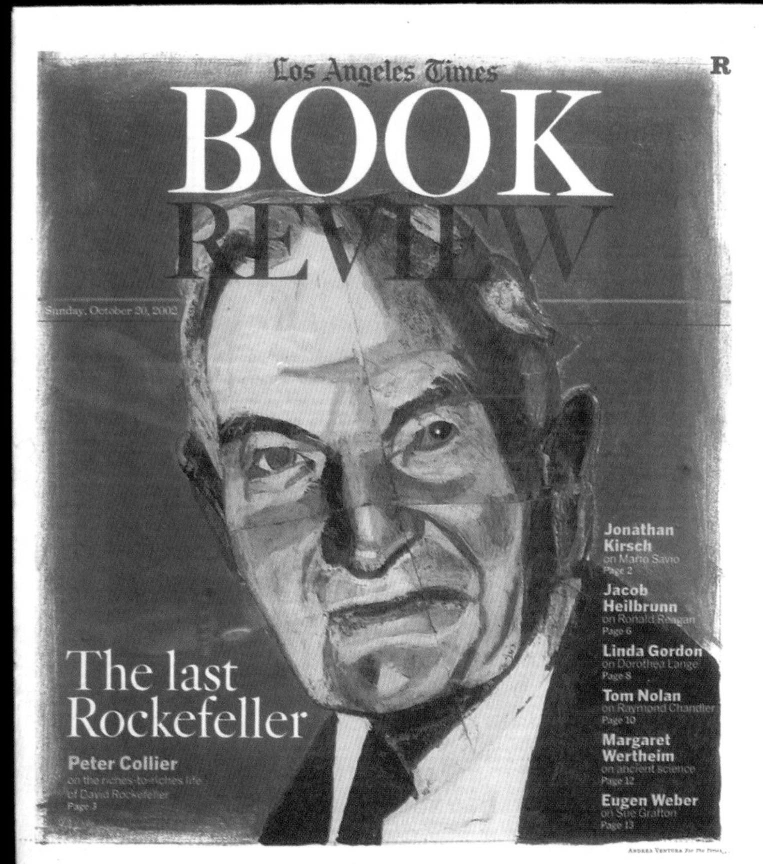

Teens move to Grandma's, then she takes parents to court. *A13*

Eves not sorry as PCs call Liberal rival 'reptilian kitten eater.' *A7*

Designer mania has gone a toilet brush too far. *Kingston SP1*

NATIONAL POST

VOL.5 NO.269 SATURDAY, SEPTEMBER 13, 2003 www.nationalpost.com

Music world mourns Johnny Cash, the voice of dignity. *A3, A19*

Whaddaya mean I can't be in beer ads? Whatta sissy rule! *FP1*

LIBERALS WANT SAUDI PROBE

SPECIAL REPORT

Deported Iranian admits he lied

By Stewart Bell

The deportation of Mansour Ahani was, in the end, remarkably swift. On the night of June 18, 2002, immigration officers escorted the Iranian, deemed a security threat to Canada, from his jail cell in Hamilton, Ont., to a chartered plane for the flight home to Tehran.

But it had taken nine years of epic legal battles to get him on that jet. Backed by refugee and human-rights lobby groups, Ahani fought his deportation in appeal after appeal, eventually before the Supreme Court of Canada.

Describing himself as a defector from the Iranian intelligence service, he argued he knew secrets the Islamic republic would not want divulged. In his refugee claim, he wrote: "I am dead if I return." His Toronto lawyer said he faced "summary execution." The rallying cry of his supporters became Deportation Equals Death Sentence. Since returning to Iran, activists assert, Ahani has disappeared.

They are wrong.

See AHANI on Page A16

INDEX

Published by the proprietor, The National Post Company, a CanWest publication, 300 - 1450 Don Mills Road, Don Mills, Ontario M3B 3R5

0 58778 00100 2

Publication Mail Agreement Number 40089573

Post begins week-long series on Art Deco style and ethos

CENTRE GEORGES POMPIDOU

"As it slowly established itself, just before and just after the First World War, Art Deco signalled a change in sensibility. It succeeded Art Nouveau, and the difference was striking. If Art Nouveau drew its images from flowers and trees, Deco borrowed the style of machines," Robert Fulford writes in an essay starting on Page A14. The Post's Art Deco series will continue in Monday's newspaper on the Avenue page. Shown above is Polish-American painter Tamara de Lempicka's Jeune Fille en Vert, circa 1927.

FOLLOWS RESISTANCE FROM FOREIGN AFFAIRS, BOUDRIA

Government reverses course after citizens voice their outrage over Sampson's torture

By Michael Friscolanti and Mike Blanchfield

The Liberal government reversed its stance in the William Sampson affair yesterday, demanding for the first time that Saudi Arabia formally investigate his allegations of torture and abuse.

The surprising about-face came after the Department of Foreign Affairs repeatedly insisted that Mr. Sampson, who recounted his months of torture in a series of *National Post* articles, had to file a formal complaint with Ottawa before any action could be taken against the Saudis.

The department had even said that until the 44-year-old came forward, it had little choice but to consider Saudi Arabia's denial as being equally credible as his "media noise."

But yesterday, amid the outrage of many Canadians – and just hours after a Liberal Cabinet Minister praised the efforts of Saudi Arabia's Ambassador to Canada – Bill Graham, the Minister of Foreign Affairs, ordered his officials to question the ambassador about Mr. Sampson's accusations.

"In their meeting, [John McNee, the Assistant Deputy Minister responsible for the Middle East] stressed the very serious nature of the allegations of torture made by Mr. Sampson, allegations which are taken very seriously by the government of Canada," said Reynald Doiron, a department spokesman. "Mr. McNee underlined to the ambassador that it is essential for the government of Saudi Arabia to conduct an open and transparent investigation into these allegations."

Mr. Doiron, reading from a prepared statement, would not answer any subsequent questions or provide an explanation for the change of heart.

Reached on his cellphone yesterday, Mohammed R. Al-Hussaini, the Saudi ambassador, would not say whether the kingdom will answer Canada's demand.

"You have to call me through the secretary and we'll see what we can do about it," he said before hanging up.

See TORTURE on Page A5

Leaders' positions, Page A5
A page of letters including one from Sampson's father and one from a cousin, Page A19

FINANCIAL POST

WTO IN CANCUN

Negotiators make progress in resolving deadlock on farm subsidies. **Page FP3**

LUNCH MONEY

With a New York brokerage exec who says it's time to be picky on stocks. **Page IN1**

Elite couples plentiful on Governor-General's trip

By Adrian Humphreys and Heather Sokoloff

The Governor-General's planned circumpolar tour came under new fire yesterday as it emerged that eight married couples were on the list of "exceptional" Canadians joining the vice-regal couple on the tour of Russia, Iceland and Finland.

The inclusion of so many couples raised the ire of critics who call the trip an exercise in extravagance for the pleasure of establishment figures and glitterati.

"The optics are all wrong. This is a junket. Everybody is going to have a good time on this trip so why not bring a spouse? The taxpayer is paying the bill, so why worry about it?" said John Williams, the Canadian Alliance MP who chairs the House of Commons public accounts committee.

See VOYAGE on Page A8

Profile: the *National Post*

Lucie Lacava

Going against the grain in designing a new national newspaper for Canada

The *National Post* was launched in October 1998. The challenge for this new national paper was to infiltrate every Canadian city without cannibalizing its sister papers – eighteen of them at the time owned by the Southam chain. I worked very closely with the *National Post*'s editor-in-chief, Kenneth Whyte. We had to come up with a look that was completely different from every other paper in Canada, including the Toronto-based *Globe and Mail*, which was also undergoing a redesign that was due to launch only two months before us.

Most North American papers were using serif type for headlines. When I initially proposed that we use a sans serif font, the notion was met with skepticism at the corporate level – how can a paper look upscale using a font fit for a tabloid? I reassured them that it would look dignified, and set out to search for the right font. The inspiration came from looking through typography books: I found Vogue, a font originally designed for the magazine, but no longer in use. I commissioned an entire custom-designed font family from Jim Parkinson, using Vogue as inspiration.

We set out to go against what everyone else was doing. The design became non-modular, with a strong vertical stress; briefs were displayed horizontally across the top of pages; and the Dutch wrap (a headline that runs the width of the first leg or two of a multiple-column story) became a strong design component on a consistent six-column grid.

Sans heads seemed to work best displayed vertically, while Miller – the complementary serif font used for features and secondary stories – worked best when used horizontally.

Another challenge was the absence of a final nameplate. Literally over a hundred variations were tested. The final name was adopted three weeks before the launch, following the acquisition of another title, *The Financial Post*, which became the business section of the *National Post*. I sketched the final logo, condensing Miller and giving it elongated Latin serifs; the final version was designed by Jim Parkinson. The section flags were finalized, and approved, and the final fonts were designed by Font Bureau, just a week before the launch.

The unique thing about the *Post* was that every employee in the newsroom was hand-picked by the editor-in-chief. They came from different papers around the world, and we could implement the new design without resistance. ‹

Opposite: a front page of the *National Post*

Gunman on the run after killing five • French and German authorities launched a cross-border manhunt yesterday for a gunman on the run after killing five people in a pre-dawn rampage that began outside a disco in Germany, French police said. The suspect is known to police and was "heavily armed and would not hesitate to use his weapons," said a German police spokesman. The gunman shot two people outside the bar and another two in an apartment building in Dillingen, before entering France and killing a fifth person in Sierck-les-Bains, French police said.

OFF THE TOP

Guatemalans vote on reforms • Guatemalans went to the polls yesterday for the first time since the end of the country's bloody civil war in 1996, in a national referendum on constitutional reforms. If approved, the 50 constitutional reforms would recognize the rights of the Mayan Indian majority for the first time since Europeans arrived in the 16th century.

Four charged with planning school killing spree • Four boys have been charged with plotting a shooting at their Port Huron, Mich., school similar to the rampage at Colorado's Columbine High School. Justin Schnepp and Jedaiah Zinzo, both 14, were charged as adults Thursday with conspiracy to commit murder for allegedly planning to kill classmates at their 560-student Holland Woods Middle School. The two others, ages 12 and 13, were charged as juveniles. Their plans were discovered after a girl overheard them talking about a killing spree.

Since 1913, Thomas Jefferson's descendants have gathered at their ancestral home in Virginia. This year, the family bad boy invited 35 progeny of the president's slave mistress, welcoming them as 'members of our family'

A tangled tale of kinship and race

By Jan Cienski

CHARLOTTESVILLE, VA. • Thomas Jefferson – author of the Declaration of Independence, the third U.S. president, noted scholar, and the owner of more than 200 slaves – has become a symbol of America's centuries-old fixation on race.

He had a white wife, Martha, with whom he fathered two daughters, and a mulatto slave mistress, Sally Hemings. Even during Jefferson's life, rumours circulated that he had fathered several children with his slave.

Most historians dismissed the claims and Jefferson's official descendants scoffed at the notion that the father of their country could also have been the father of illegitimate slave children.

But Hemings' descendants insisted that Jefferson was their ancestor. Last year, DNA tests indicated that at least one of her seven children had been fathered by a Jefferson – although it's still not clear if that male is Thomas or another relative.

Over the weekend at Monticello, Jefferson's Italianate hilltop estate in the rolling green countryside of central Virginia, the descendants of both Hemings and Jefferson finally met and tried to figure out if they are family.

Every year since 1913, Jefferson's acknowledged descendants have gathered at their ancestral home. The family's Monticello Association administers the Jefferson family graveyard located on the estate. All 700 members – and hundreds more acknowledged Jefferson descendants who don't belong to the group – have the right to be buried alongside their forefather and 100 other relatives in the sun-dappled cemetery.

The mostly black descendants of Sally Hemings are not members of the association and have no right to be buried in the graveyard that their slave ancestors helped build.

But this year for the first time, a family rebel invited 35 Hemings' descendants to the Monticello reunion.

"I welcome them to this place and on to this land as members of our family," Lucian Truscott IV, a Los Angeles author and screenwriter, said Saturday during the opening ceremony at Monticello.

As he spoke, dozens of well-dressed people, both black and white, strolled the lush lawns of Monticello sipping glasses of wine.

Mr. Truscott, a sixth-generation grandson of Thomas Jefferson whose mother is buried in the graveyard, wants the Monticello Association to extend membership to the Hemings' branch, granting them the same rights and privileges that the white family enjoys.

Michele Cooley-Quille says it's about time that her family is accepted by the larger clan. Ever since she was a small girl, she remembers hearing family tales of her ancestry.

LESLIE CLOSE / THE ASSOCIATED PRESS

Descendants of Thomas Jefferson and descendants of his slave Sally Hemings pose for a group shot at Jefferson's plantation during the Monticello Association's annual meeting in Charlottesville, Va., on Saturday.

"When I first told my friends at school, I could see their surprise at how someone who is black could be related to someone who is white," said Ms. Cooley-Quille, 33, a clinical psychologist at the Johns Hopkins School of Public Health in Baltimore.

Her father, Robert Cooley III, a Vietnam veteran and a judge, died last summer and his last wish was to be buried at the plantation. He was turned down because the association could not trace him definitively to Jefferson.

Now his daughter insists she wants to be buried at Monticello.

"Half my ancestors were enslaved here and the other half of half my ancestors created this place," she said.

But there is no rushing tradition and genealogy. The association plans to put the matter of accepting Hemings' descendants to a vote of all its members over the next year. The concern is that the Hemings' oral histories and DNA tests are inconclusive, said Robert Gillespie, the association's president.

"We are looking at what criteria could be adopted that would bring them into the association," said Mr. Gillespie, an attorney who works in the state capital, Richmond. "Heretofore we used the genealogy from Jefferson's two daughters. That genealogy doesn't pick up any descendants from Sally Hemings."

Jefferson's affair with his slave has caught the popular imagination in America. After being a taboo subject for many years, it has become widely accepted that he had an affair with Hemings.

"The general public probably does think that the affair happened, but from the family's perspective we had our own oral tradition that the [Hemings] children were fathered by his nephew," said Mr. Gillespie.

As early as 1802, a political rival published a newspaper account of a liaison between the president and his slave – a scandalous accusation in those years.

Jefferson never made any public response to the charges and Sally Hemings left no known account of the matter. But at least two of her children claimed Jefferson was their father.

Historians slowly began chipping away at the story and last year, a DNA test found that a descendant of Eston Hemings, Sally's youngest son, had the same Y-chromosome as the male line of the Jefferson family. Although the test showed a relationship, it could not pinpoint exactly which Jefferson had fathered Eston.

A similar test on the descendants of Thomas Woodson failed to find a genetic link, although a new blood sample is now being tested. The descendants of Hemings' other children can't be tested because DNA tests for paternity can only be determined on the male line.

The irony is that the same genetic tests couldn't prove paternity for the blue-blooded acknowledged family because they are descended from Jefferson's two daughters – Martha Randolph and Maria Eppes. What the acknowledged family does have is birth certificates showing parentage, which weren't issued to slaves.

That leaves any question of admitting the descendants of a slave up in the air, said David Works, 42, a past membership committee chairman and a descendant of Martha Randolph.

"A descendant has to be declared by the father or by blood," he said. "I can't make them an heir."

That's a double standard, said Ms. Cooley-Quille. "I am willing to provide my blood when the Monticello Association provides theirs," she said.

For Mr. Truscott, the family bad boy, all this talk of proof is simply a way for the association to avoid acknowledging that they have black cousins and that the great man used his slaves for sex.

"In this family, the word genealogy has become a code word for race," he said angrily, insisting that he will continue to personally invite the Hemings' descendants every year – even if the association fails to grant them membership.

REED SAXON / THE ASSOCIATED PRESS

Lucian Truscott IV a sixth-generation white grandson of Thomas Jefferson, says the Jefferson family association should admit the black descendants of Sally Hemings, one of Jefferson's slaves.

Mr. Truscott says it is simple justice to welcome the descendants of the slaves who fired every brick, forged every nail, and cut every board used to build Monticello.

"On the morning that Mr. Jefferson wrote the Declaration of Independence, someone woke him up, someone got him dressed, someone fried him an egg, someone prepared his pen. They were slaves," he said. Without those slaves, Jefferson would never have found the time to write, "We hold these truths to be self-evident: that all men are created equal ..."

Just down the slope from the graceful, neoclassical Monticello lie the outlines of the dirt-floored huts that had housed the plantation's slaves.

The tangled tale of kinship, blood, and race shows that America's racial roots are a lot more complex than many acknowledge.

Those DNA tests linking the Hemings' descendants to the Jeffersons were done on a family from Staten Island, N.Y. The family is white.

Estes Hemings was one of only a handful of slaves freed by Jefferson in his will. He eventually made his way to Wisconsin, changed his name to Jefferson and, taking advantage of his light skin, slipped across the colour line to live as a white man.

His mother, Sally Hemings, was very light-coloured. That's because she was the slave half-sister of Jefferson's beloved wife, Martha. Her father, like many other slave owners, had unacknowledged children that were kept in bondage.

Martha died after only 10 years of marriage and it is said that a distraught Jefferson turned to Hemings, who resembled her free, white sister.

That kind of racial fuzziness makes a lot of white Americans uncomfortable, said Russell Adams, chairman of the Department of Afro-American Studies at Howard University in Washington.

"The larger society represented by the Jefferson family association does not wish to admit biological and social relationship to the black community, whose ancestral members were property along with horses, cows, and pigs," he said.

At the family reunion, a young, black Hemings' descendant, with a baseball cap perched sideways on his head, called for all members of the family, both black and white, to gather on the steps of Monticello for a photo. About 80 people crowded together but dozens more stayed on the lawn, looking on.

"I think it's inappropriate," to jump to the conclusion everyone is related, said Mr. Works, as he watched the crowd on the stairs. "If it doesn't work out, you're going to have a lot of people with hurt feelings."

National Post

U.S. Army recognizes witchcraft as religion

WICCANS GET CHAPLAINS

By Ben Fenton

WASHINGTON • The United States Army has recognized white witchcraft as a religion and has appointed chaplains to oversee pagan ceremonies on at least five bases.

A Pentagon spokesman said Thursday there were believed to be at least 100 witches attending covens at Fort Hood, Tex., the army's largest base with more than 42,000 troops.

So respectful has the army become of the pagan rites that security was increased at Fort Hood's Boy Scout camp, where covens are held.

The move is to deter members of Christian groups from intimidating the group.

The pagans, called Wiccans, are accorded the same privileges as practitioners of Christianity, Judaism, and Islam.

They are encouraged to have their religious preference stamped on the metal dog tags each soldier wears.

Lieutenant-Colonel Donald Troyer, the Seventh Day Adventist army chaplain who has been given responsibility for Fort Hood's coven, admitted he was not overjoyed with his job because fellow Christian pastors disapproved and had been "cool" toward him.

"It's such a volatile subject," he said. "It just sparks a fury."

The Pentagon says it has received several requests for a posting to Fort Hood because it has such a large pagan congregation.

"We are obliged by the Constitution to respect and make provisions for the religious needs of members of the military and not to pass judgments on their beliefs," a spokesman said.

The Covenant of the Goddess, which claims to represent most American Wiccans from its base in Berkeley, Calif., says there are about 50,000 followers of the faith in the United States.

They celebrate earth-spirits such as the "great goddess Freya" and on their altars give blessings to water, bread, and salt, the three essentials of life, while the congregation holds hands in a circle around a large bonfire.

Their main festivals are at the vernal and autumnal equinox and at midsummer.

However, sacrifices, either human or animal, are not tolerated. "It is not something we do," said one Wiccan.

The Daily Telegraph

American museum exposes phoney glamour of drugs

Exhibits tell story of U.S.'s century-long battle for and against narcotics

By Hugo Gurdon

PENTAGON CITY, MD. • The most telling exhibits in the U.S.'s newest museum are burnt and bent teaspoons, stained rags, used soda bottles, and a diamond-encrusted Colt 45.

They expose the sordid, deadly reality and phoney glamour of their subject, which is drugs.

Gathered in glass display cases are the paraphernalia of the U.S.'s century-long battle for and against the right to "get high" – bongs (water pipes), psychedelic posters, licorice rolling papers, Tommy guns and grenades.

The Drug Enforcement Agency museum, which opened its doors to the public last week, lays bare the wilful self-delusion of the 1960s and 1970s, when baby boomers swept aside a mass of historical evidence and argued drugs were intrinsic to life, liberty, and the pursuit of happiness, rather than the low road to ruin.

One of the exhibits is a 1937 poster, captioned "The Devil's Roost," in which the vultures of "vice," "want," "insanity," "misery," and "crime" perch on a reaper-like figure marked "Dope." A few feet away is a 1908 *New York Times* front page taken up with a story under the headline "The growing menace of the use of cocaine."

Dominating one wall is a black and white picture of the actress Dorothy Davenport, "shooting up" with a syringe in the 1923 film *Human Wreckage*. More than 100 feature films were made in the silent era focusing on the perils of drugs.

In 1900, one in every 200 Americans was a drug addict. Many of them swigged laudanum.

By the Second World War, though, drug addiction was a marginal, statistically negligible vice in the U.S. Decades of evidence, and policing by federal agents armed with a Tommy gun and two grenades each as standard issue, had worked.

Then came the 1960s and gurus such as Allen Ginsberg, demonstrating in New York with a poster bearing the legend "Pot is a reality kick." The drug culture was born again.

Traditional corner stores, which sold everything from ice cream to toothpaste, gave way to "head shops" that peddled drug paraphernalia, such as hookahs and roach clips (tweezers to hold a marijuana cigarette when it was too small and hot for bare fingers).

Redolent of the drug culture's seediness are the opium-stained rags, pipes made from old 7-Up bottles, and elasticated armbands to make a junkie's veins bulge to make injections easier. So, too, are the photographs of dealers shot dead, and addicts in the final contortions of a fatal overdose.

Perhaps the most telling artifact in the museum is the gleaming, silver Colt 45 handgun, with the diamond-studded grip.

It was owned by Rafael Caro-Quintero, a Mexican drug dealer. It is the quintessence of the phoney heroism and deceptive glitter at the heart of the drug culture.

Mr. Caro-Quintero glares out from a photograph nearby, dishevelled and dressed in nothing but dirty jeans at the time of his arrest. He murdered a DEA agent and is now behind bars.

The Daily Telegraph

STEPHEN CROWLEY / THE NEW YORK TIMES

Among the drug paraphernalia used in 1970 is this homemade bong on display at the Drug Enforcement Administration's new museum. The bong, a water pipe for smoking marijuana, was seized by agents in the field.

WORLD

ORTHODOX STUDENTS NOT EXEMPT FROM ARMY

Clinton leaves for Mideast to repair unravelling deal

Arafat buoyant as he welcomes 'new partner'

A10 CANADA • NATIONAL POST, WEDNESDAY, MARCH 31, 1999

TRENDS: **JOB SEEKING**

Forget about scouring the want ads for a job — most employers are more likely to hire people who make direct contact with them. A Statistics Canada study on obtaining a job has found that nearly half of all job placements came about through the job seeker's direct contact with an employer, either in person or by phone. The study, released this month in a report called *Perspectives on Labour and Income*, scrutinized 8.4 million job hirings which took place in 1994 and 1995 and statistically broke down how they came about. Direct contact was the most common method of looking for work and for obtaining a job, at 46%. Networking resulted in about one-quarter of all hirings. Want ads drew 8% of the hirings. Larger firms are more likely than smaller firms to hire people who contact them directly, but less likely to use personal contacts, said Lee Grenon, the author of the study. One in four jobs with private firms came about through family and friends; in the public sector, the figure was one in 10. Referrals are most common in managerial and professional jobs, and in construction. *Anne Marie Owens, National Post.*

MISSING HALIFAX WOMAN RESURFACES

ABDUCTION ALLEGED

Internet encounter evolves into what she describes as a ride from hell at gunpoint

By Gloria Galloway

A Halifax woman who had been missing since mid-February turned up at a mall in Niagara Falls, Ont., earlier this week saying she had been abducted by a man she met through the Internet.

Michelle Lawrence told police she had been held at gunpoint and taken on a terrifying two-week ride by a man she knew as Joe Kast, a heavily tattooed American with a fascination for the U.S. military.

The 27-year-old woman vanished on Feb. 16 and was reported missing by her family a day later. They apparently suspected that her disappearance had something to do with the stranger, who had suddenly entered her life — a man with whom she had developed a cyberspace relationship.

It wasn't until 13 days later that Ms. Lawrence resurfaced in Niagara Falls.

Emotionally shaken but apparently unharmed, "she walked up to a clerk at the Hudson's Bay Store in the Niagara Square and told this story," said Sergeant Marty Kalagian, of the Niagara Region police.

After meeting Ms. Lawrence through the Internet and corresponding with her via computer, Mr. Kast arrived in Halifax in early February.

"They got to know each other over a week or two," said Staff-Sergeant Paul White, who is also with the Niagara force. "One day, when he was supposed to be taking her to work, and he was supposed to turn left, he turned right. And away they went."

According to Ms. Lawrence, it was Mr. Kast's gun that convinced her not to escape.

They drove to Ontario in his black Ford pickup truck, but eventually he tired of the game.

"She was dumped," said Staff-Sgt. White. "He said 'get out, I'm finished with you.'"

Ms. Lawrence did not complain to police of being assaulted by Mr. Kast.

"There is absolutely no claim of any kind of sexual abuse," said Staff-Sgt. White. "But this girl is mentally traumatized."

The staff-sergeant would not divulge where Ms. Lawrence is staying.

"She is very, very safe," he said, "and I'm not discussing any part of what else may be planned or what went on. Don't forget we are looking for a man who is armed and dangerous."

When Ms. Lawrence recounted her story to police, they immediately called officials at the four local border crossings. "So far, we've had no feedback to suggest

'THIS GIRL IS MENTALLY TRAUMATIZED'

Staff-Sgt. Paul White

that this individual has tried to enter the United States from our bridge points," said Staff-Sgt. White.

Although he told Ms. Lawrence his name was Kast, the man police are looking for also goes by the aliases of James Gunter, Patrick McLain, Scott Bernard, and David Tribby; and he has documents to match each one of those identities.

Police believe the man is 31 years old and comes from Florida. He stands about 6 feet tall and weighs about 200 pounds.

Mr. Kast is easy to identify when not wearing a shirt because of the many tattoos on his upper body — one bicep says Rangers 33, the other AA Airborne, and a set of paratrooper wings adorn his chest. Staff-Sgt. White said the man sometimes wears a patch on his left eye.

National Post

Cleanliness is next to godliness

KEVIN VAN PAASSEN / MEDICINE HAT NEWS

Caretaker Adriano Ciannavei is bathed in colour as he cleans the stained-glass windows at St. Patrick's Roman Catholic Church in Medicine Hat, Alta., yesterday in preparation for Easter services.

Alberta shedding boom-bust reputation

ECONOMY STABLE: REPORT

By Luiza Chwialkowska

The province of Alberta has outgrown its reputation as a volatile, boom-bust economy whose fortunes follow the roller-coaster rides of wheat and oil prices, a new study shows.

The employment rate in Alberta has moved from the most volatile to the most stable of Canada's three western-most resource-dependent provinces, according to Ted Chambers, a business economist at the University of Alberta.

Prof. Chambers found that over the past 10 years, employment rates in B.C. and Saskatchewan were as erratic as they were in the period from 1976–1988, while the Alberta rate stabilized substantially over that period. In fact, Alberta's employment rate was 40% more stable in the years following 1988 than over the 12 years before. In Canada as a whole, employment rates were 16% to 18% more stable in the second period.

The boom-bust cycle is well-known to Albertans who lived through oil booms and shocks of the 1970s ad 1980s. While drops in employment can throw an economy into a tailspin, booms can also be damaging because they lead to speculation in real estate, he said.

"Reduced variability in the employment rate is important to the average person and average business because it reduces risk," Prof. Chambers explained. "[Low variability] makes planning for the household and business firm easier and more reliable."

In recent years, the Alberta economy seemed to perform at odds with its erratic reputation, attracting the interest of researchers.

"We became interested in this because the Alberta economy continued to do very well after 1988 despite the fact that commodity prices had fallen sharply," explains Prof. Chambers.

Prof. Chambers analyzed employment rates in various economic sectors of Alberta, B.C., and Saskatchewan, using the same methodology that financial analysts use to evaluate the risk in a stock portfolio. Instead of rates of return on stocks, however, he analyzed the changes in employment rates.

The turning point for Alberta seems to have been the adoption of the 1988 Free Trade Agreement. In the post 1988 period, volatility declined in both service and goods-producing sectors, by 50% and 30% respectively.

"The free-trade agreement has been instrumental. Alberta is a case of export-led growth," Prof. Chambers said.

Prof. Chambers said Alberta's agriculture sector diversified from wheat, with livestock, specialty crops, and oilseeds diluting the prominence of traditional grains. The energy industry also diversified, as free trade opened markets to Canadian natural gas, the price of which is more stable than crude oil.

The growing dependence of the energy sector on high-technology also fuelled "spectacular growth" in the manufacture of electrical and telecommunications equipment, Prof. Chambers said.

Highly educated energy workers also created a software sector in Alberta, Prof. Chambers said.

In contrast, B.C. did not take full advantage of the U.S. market, and depended on Asian markets for exports, while Saskatchewan did not diversify and stayed with its core industry, agriculture.

National Post

N.B. psychiatrist's licence revoked

FOLLOWING BRITAIN'S LEAD

Sexual contact with patients alleged

SAINT JOHN, N.B. • A psychiatrist who fled New Brunswick amid accusations he sexually abused his patients has had his licence to practice in the province revoked.

The New Brunswick College of Physicians and Surgeons followed the lead of its British counterpart by pulling the licence of Kwabena Akuffo-Akoto, after authorities in England found the psychiatrist guilty of professional misconduct based on the allegations that surfaced in Canada.

He had been accused of sexually preying on female patients in St. Stephen, N.B., a small, coastal town near New Brunswick-Maine border, but fled to Britain before the college could investigate the allegations two years ago.

Dr. Ed Schollenberg of the college of physicians says it had been a long road reaching the point where they could pull Akuffo-Akoto's credentials. The college will now alert other licensing authorities in North America as to their decision.

Akuffo-Akoto had practised in Britain for 10 years before coming to the Maritimes in 1992. But it was the New Brunswick college which first tipped off authorities in Britain about allegations against him.

So popular was Akuffo-Akoto in St. Stephen that town councillors rallied to his defence when the accusations first surfaced in the summer of 1997.

But the British medical council accepted testimony that he'd had sexual contact with at least three of his female patients — in one case plying an alcoholic patient with liquor.

The Canadian Press

Speaker's office sought wholesale changes to NFB film

ENTIRE SCENES QUESTIONED

Director, producer fixed factual errors without changing work substantially

By Anne Marie Owens

The National Film Board got the first whiff of trouble over its documentary about Gilbert Parent, the Speaker of the House of Commons, at a meeting in Ottawa more than two months ago when the Speaker's office outlined a long list of concerns.

The film, *Le Guardien de la Colline* or *The Guardian of the Hill*, was yanked from what was to be its showcase screening at a festival last weekend to appease the Speaker's office.

Sandra Macdonald, the government-appointment commissioner, will not reveal the complaints which led her to pull the film. She said it will likely be at least 10 days before she has completed her investigation into the complaints.

But in January, when Jacques Menard, an NFB producer, met with Heather Bradley, the spokeswoman for the Speaker, he received an earful.

Although many of the complaints were minor quibbles over dates and translations, some of the concerns focused on entire scenes which, if removed, would have substantially reduced interest in the one-hour film.

These are the scenes to which the Speaker's office objected:

▮ A golf scene, which shows Mr. Parent on the grounds of Kingsmere Estate, the historic manor once occupied by Mackenzie King, the prime minister, and now the official Speaker's residence. The voiceover has a journalist talking about what a lovely life it is for the Speaker, with a chauffeur-driven car, a house in the country, and then, "Thwack!" the next image cuts to Mr. Parent teeing off on a golf ball on the estate grounds;

▮ Scenes showing Mr. Parent at a parliamentary conference in Barbados. As a guest of the Speaker in Barbados, he stays at a luxury hotel and gets a polite flutter of applause when he talks about how Cuba should be included in such gatherings. His remarks on Cuba at other times have caused a stir in Canadian politics, when he likened Cuba's dictatorship to a landslide democratic win in New Brunswick. The scenes also show Joan, his wife of many years, who has multiple sclerosis, left alone at the hotel. The couple separated a short time later.

Other scenes which caused concern include one where Mr. Parent, in his acceptance speech, refers to the 35th parliament, instead of the 36th and is corrected in his gaffe by the gentle heckles of his fellow parliamentarians, and one which shows him barking, "bullshit."

The Speaker's office also suggested that former speakers could be interviewed and added to the film to give it weight and make up for the scenes to be cut.

And there was a complaint that there was not enough in the documentary to show Mr. Parent's love of country and Parliament.

The documentary begins with a statement about Mr. Parent's "reputation preceding him" and how "he'd given impassioned speeches declaring his love for Canada that could move audiences to tears..."

Another controversial scene shows the filmmaker being cut off by the Speaker. On this day, the director and her cameraman were in the Speaker's office when he was to sort out a controversy over the office of John Nunziata, the former Liberal and now Independent MP whom Mr. Parent beat out for the Speaker's job. Mr. Parent and his assistant were to discuss how to go about moving Mr. Nunziata out of the Liberal office wing. The scene shows the Speaker shrugging at the camera crew to shut down, followed by a dramatic clicking of the camera, and a voiceover of the director saying, "It looks like a lot of doors are closing on me."

The documentary project, which began in 1996 and has cost about $300,000, had the full approval of Mr. Parent at the outset, who told Claudette Jaiko, the director, of his apparently contradictory desire "to demystify his role while preserving its mystery."

The opening scene shows him talking to a group of school children about how his father was the custodian of the Park Theatre in Welland and now he is custodian of the Hill. Interestingly, it is from that anecdote that the film got its original title, *Custodien de la Colline*, which was altered because of concerns that custodien could be translated as janitor and be pejorative.

When the first list of concerns were reported back to Ms. Jaiko and Yves Bisaillon, the producer, they corrected the few factual problems, but left the film pretty much as it was. They had heard "verbal mutterings" of the other concerns throughout the fall, and have still yet to see any formal roster of complaints.

The contract between the NFB and the Speaker's office does not provide for the Speaker's approval of the final cut; the only detail in the contract is an agreement "that nothing in the film would dishonour the House of Commons or the role of the Speaker."

National Post

Quebec report may call for end to Catholic public schools

By Yvonne Zacharias

MONTREAL • Girding for a new round of holy wars in the province's education system, the Quebec government will release a far-reaching report today that is widely expected to recommend a gradual end to Catholic public schools in Quebec.

The report by former *Le Devoir* education reporter Jean-Pierre Proulx will likely picture the crosses and photos of the Pope coming down, one by one, in elementary and high schools across the province, ending a long era of church-run public schools.

"It's going to be a bombshell," said Spencer Boudreau, a member of the Catholic committee of the Quebec Superior Council on Education. "Groups are gearing up on both sides."

François Legault, the Education Minister, is expected to rise in the National Assembly and announce public hearings to take place toward the end of the school year and extending into the fall.

Last July, the province ushered in new linguistic school boards, scrapping the old confessional ones, but the government stopped short of secularizing the education system down to the school level. Instead, it left a system of Catholic and Protestant schools in place, promising to pronounce itself on this question at a later date.

Mr. Proulx will make recommendations on whether God still has a place in Quebec classrooms through continued moral and religious instruction.

While schools are likely to lose their religious identities and all outward appurtenances of the faith, they could continue religion classes, either as part of the regular curriculum or as part of extra-curricular activities offered by non-teaching staff after school.

Since last July, school boards have been scrambling to comply with a slight change in the wording of the Education Act that spelled big changes in schools. It required that each school, regardless of its confessional status, provide a choice between Catholic, Protestant or the generic moral instruction for two hours every week, even if only a handful of parents request one of the three options.

The change has forced schools to look at rejigging timetables and hiring new staff to teach the courses when they are hard-pressed to teach core subjects.

The Gazette

A practical metaphor

The horizontal "attic" across the top of the page anchors the vertical, non-modular page design. It can also be thought of as echoing the breadth of the Canadian landscape.

OBITUARIES

MOUNA AGUIGUI

'Street surrealist' something of a folk hero

He could lead hundreds yet once mused: 'But where to? And what for?

Mouna Aguigui, a self-proclaimed "street surrealist" and something of a folkloric figure in Paris, where he combined the roles of philosopher, prankster, and anarchist, has died aged 88.

His bushy beard often dotted with flowers and his coat bedecked with medals, Mr. Aguigui was usually to be found in the Latin Quarter, in the open spaces of Beaubourg, or on the streets of Montmartre. Perched on his ramshackle, garlanded bicycle, he would harangue, advise, exhort, and enthuse, employing such slogans as "Don't take power, take the Metro" and "Bicycles, not cars – lawns, not asphalt – sheep, not guns."

He was well known to the police, who regularly arrested him for acts of public disorder. These included leading a crowd through the city streets, shouting "We are happy, we are very happy."

On another occasion, he proclaimed the rallying cry "Retirement at the age of 15" outside a movie theatre one evening. The bored crowd rapidly fell in behind him, building up to a mob of 150-strong by the time they had reached St-Germain-des-Prés.

As the founder of the Aguiguiste Club, "an association devoted to the promotion of joy, gaiety, and optimism," he recruited Albert Einstein as its president of honour, receiving an approving letter in reply. The Aguiguiste manifesto, launched in 1963, advocated "the spirit of tolerance and the rejection of all social, racial, and religious discrimination."

Mr. Aguigui delighted in the absurd, and was seen by many as an heir to the Surrealists; but he was only half in jest, and was an ecologist before ecology was modish, a pacifist, and a *soixante-huitard* long before 1968.

He "could lead hundreds of people," he once said. "But where to?" he pondered. "And what for?"

He was born André Dupont in 1911 at Meythet, near Lyons. By the age of nine he and his brother had been orphaned.

He went to work in a factory at 13, joined the navy at 16, and after being thrown out for "lack of discipline" went on to be sacked from a succession of menial jobs. During the Second World War, he ran a restaurant in Paris until it was closed by the German occupying forces.

By the early 1950s he was in Antibes running a bistro, the walls of which he daubed with his favourite slogans. But the establishment was next to a funeral parlour, which depressed him, and set him thinking, until in 1951 he had what he later termed his "Aguiguiste revelation."

Electrified by a self-devised doctrine based on pacifism and the principle that "only laughter can change the world," Mr. Dupont reinvented himself as Mouna Aguigui and moved to Paris to open another café. In 1955 the business failed. At this point, Mr. Aguigui gave up cooking and set himself to talking, guided by the axiom "It is by speaking that one becomes a loudspeaker."

Mr. Aguigui's political career was enthusiastic but largely unsuccessful. He tried three times to run in the French presidential elections and won 722 votes in the 1993 legislative elections.

He was appointed Chevalier dans l'Ordre des arts et lettres in 1981.

The Daily Telegraph

AGENCE FRANCE-PRESSE

Mouna Aguigui was well known to police, who regularly arrested him for acts of public disorder. He is shown in 1987.

YVONNE ALEXANDER

Credited with husband's successful political career

PUT HIM THROUGH SCHOOL

She was a private person whose life became public

Yvonne Alexander, who has died in Hamilton, was a descendant of escaped American slaves who came to Canada on the Underground Railway, and who forbore discrimination against black people in her early life to rise to the pinnacle of Ontario society as wife of the lieutenant-governor, Lincoln Alexander.

When the vice-regal couple went to Buckingham Palace to meet the Queen in 1986, Mrs. Alexander was calm and remembered every detail, including what she described as the Queen's elegant outfit. Mr. Alexander said he remembered the Queen putting him at ease, by asking them both to sit down as she led the conversation. But he had to be told later that the audience lasted 25 minutes, a record, according to his aide-de-camp.

Yvonne Alexander was, in many ways, responsible for her husband's success, having worked to put him through law school, and standing by him in his career as a politician and then as the Queen's representative in Ontario.

Yvonne Phyllis Harrison was born in Hamilton, the daughter of a railway porter. She attended a local grade school and then graduated from the High School of Commerce in Hamilton. The black community in Hamilton was small then, perhaps only a couple hundred people. There was overt discrimination and despite her secretarial training, the only job Yvonne Harrison could find was as an elevator operator at the Lister Building.

Social life in Hamilton's black community centred around the Stewart Memorial Church, which

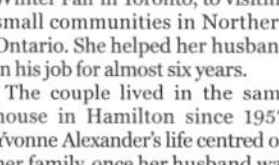

LINCOLN ALEXANDER DECIDED TO MARRY YVONNE THE DAY HE FIRST SET EYES ON HER

was African Methodist Episcopalian. During this period Yvonne lived at home on Victoria Avenue with her parents and three sisters. In the early 1940s she went to a dance in Toronto, where she met the young Lincoln Alexander.

Mr. Alexander recalled he was struck by her beauty, and decided on the spot he would marry the tall, slender Yvonne Harrison. After the dance, he decided to take a job in Hamilton, working in the Otis-Fenson munitions plant.

Later he joined the air force, and the couple were not married until well after the war. After graduating from McMaster University, Lincoln Alexander went on to Osgoode Hall Law School. His wife worked in a laundry to support their young family.

Yvonne Alexander was a private person, though her husband led a public life, being elected for the Progressive Conservative Party for Hamilton West in the elections of 1968, '72, '74, '79 and '80. Even when he became a minister in the government of Joe Clark, Yvonne stayed in Hamilton, only joining her husband on occasion in Ottawa.

When Brian Mulroney named Lincoln Alexander lieutenant-governor of Ontario in 1985, Yvonne Alexander's life took on a more public role. She did her duty, and enjoyed it, accompanying her husband on many of his official tours, from opening the Royal Winter Fair in Toronto, to visiting small communities in Northern Ontario. She helped her husband in his job for almost six years.

The couple lived in the same house in Hamilton since 1957. Yvonne Alexander's life centred on her family, once her husband was established in his law practice.

She had eclectic taste in music, ranging from opera to jazz.

Yvonne Harrison married Lincoln Alexander in 1948. They had one son, Keith, and two granddaughters.

National Post

THE SPECTATOR

Lincoln Alexander, the former lieutenant-governor, with his wife, Yvonne, in 1991. Yvonne Alexander died in hospital on Saturday after a lengthy illness.

WILLIAM NEUDORF

Former Tory MLA at ease with parry, thrust of politics

ACQUITTED IN SCANDAL

Known for 'dugout rescue caper' and 'water-bomber caper'

William Neudorf, a former Progressive Conservative MLA who was acquitted of fraud in the scandals that rocked the Saskatchewan government, has died aged 59.

In 1995, Mr. Neudorf became enmeshed in the years-long investigation of expense-account corruption – a scandal that saw 21 Tories, including 18 former MLAs, charged with fraud or breach of trust – when he was charged with filing a false expense claim for some promotional baseball caps and T-shirts. A provincial court judge later concluded that Mr. Neudorf had simply been "naive and unsophisticated."

The minister of social services following his first election win in 1986, Mr. Neudorf won re-election in 1991 but retired as the MLA for Rosthern before the 1995 NDP sweep to power that reduced the PCs to a rump representation.

A big man – six feet, four inches tall and 250 pounds – Mr. Neudorf's booming voice was a familiar one in the corridors of the legislature. Colleagues from all political parties appreciated his good nature and handshake commitment.

At ease with the parry and thrust of politics, he was a fearless debater who could give as good as he got. When his questioning in the legislature got too pointed, political opponents heckled him back, always referring in the end to the infamous "dugout rescue caper" – which usually brought a hearty Neudorf laugh.

Somehow Mr. Neudorf had managed to run his tractor and manure spreader into a huge dugout on the family pig farm near the town of Hague. Only the exhaust pipe of the tractor was visible above the water. Mr. Neudorf donned his scuba gear and, gingerly, plunged into the murky water to attach cables to the tractor. He finally got it out of the water, but when word of the antics reached the legislature, he was ribbed forever after.

If it wasn't that, it was the "water-bomber caper."

Once, on his way home from the legislature, Mr. Neudorf got a call from his wife, Alma, who shouted that their pig barns were on fire. He immediately rang up his caucus office in Regina and asked that a provincial government water bomber be sent to the site. Then he called his family back and warned them to scatter or they would be doused with fire retardant.

The bomber did its job, saving most of the buildings, but the propriety of using a government aircraft was debated for years.

A native of Saskatchewan, Mr. Neudorf studied at the University of Saskatchewan and then taught school for more than 20 years. He left teaching to start the pig-raising business he operated until his death.

As minister of social services, he was particularly concerned about hungry children. When the plight of Romanian orphans came to his attention in the early '90s, he pledged to take in 1,000 of them in Saskatchewan homes.

A deeply religious man, Mr. Neudorf was a board member and Sunday-school teacher at the Hague Mennonite Conference church. He also acted as the town of Hague's fire chief, as a municipal councillor, and as vice-chairman of the Saskatchewan Pork Producers Marketing Board.

After nine years in politics, he retired to spend more time with his family. Near the end of his life, he confessed that he missed being on the floor of the legislature, telling his opponents how it should be run.

He is survived by his wife and four children.

Edward Keen, National Post

DON HEALY / REGINA LEADER POST

William Neudorf

EDITORIALS

Kenneth Whyte Editor-in-Chief
Martin Newland Deputy Editor | Hugo Gordon Managing Editor
Alison Uncles Associate Editor | Douglas Kelly Executive Editor
Martin Zivitz Deputy Managing Editor
Paul Waldie National Editor | David Walmsley Political Editor

Air deracination

Savour it/Breathe it in ... Experience Roots Air. So reads the meaningless chunk of blank verse that welcomes travellers to the Web site for Roots Air, Canada's newest airline. Anyone interested in savouring "it" had better act fast, since Roots Air is also Canada's shortest-lived airline – ceasing operation today after just a month of flights. And along with the Roots Air experience dies Transportation Minister David Collenette's claim that a regulated near-monopoly will provide a viable solution to Canada's airline competition problem.

Yesterday Air Canada, the country's dominant airline with an estimated 80% market share, announced it had bought half the voting shares of Skyservice Airlines, the parent company of Roots Air. Roots, which focused on business-class service, will shut down but the specialty and discount leisure flights offered by Skyservice will become part of Air Canada's offerings. And while Air Canada has gone to great lengths to stress that Skyservice sought them out as a purchaser, the details of who asked whom are immaterial. What is important is that this will result in even greater market share for Air Canada at a time when real competition is constrained by federal regulations that prevent foreign airlines from providing domestic flights in Canada, which is known as cabotage.

As recently as this January, Mr. Collenette was repeating his claim that there is no need to open Canada's skies to foreign competitors since a panoply of new airlines was already chipping away at Air Canada's position. "We're convinced that we won't need to open up and have cabotage because we will have that competition domestically," he remarked, pointing to the range of options available to Canadian travellers: WestJet, Royal Airlines, Canada 3000, CanJet and the then-anticipated Roots Air. Since he made those comments Royal Airlines, Canada 3000 and CanJet have merged and Roots Air has been bought and closed by Air Canada. While WestJet and the beefed-up Canada 3000 provide credible competition on a limited number of routes, this alone is not enough to keep Air Canada honest.

What the recent round of flame-outs clearly demonstrates is that the airline business is one characterized by substantial entry costs, particularly given Air Canada's dominance. It should now be obvious, even to Mr. Collenette, that the only practical way to check Air Canada's near-monopoly is to invite established foreign carriers to compete on domestic routes since they will have the resources to survive the start-up period. To savour and breathe in the experience of real competition, Canadians require cabotage.

Justice for some

Osgoode Hall is one of this country's most prestigious law schools. But a discriminatory policy applied by its community legal aid clinic is besmirching its reputation.

For 13 years, Parkdale Community Legal Services has provided free assistance to low-income residents of Toronto's West end. The clinic's services are open to anyone, male or female, even if they have been accused of serious crimes such as breaking and entering or armed robbery. Yet where domestic abuse is alleged, the clinic refuses to help men. Glenn Stuart, the director, says the clinic believes in "the inherent ability of the law to effect social change," and is therefore entitled to pick and choose its clients based on how their *alleged* crimes play in legal theory symposia.

If the clinic were raising its own money, from private sources, it would be free to impose policies as it sees fit. But most of its funding, $618,000 this year alone, comes from the province of Ontario. Tens of thousands of dollars more are provided each year by York University, another publicly funded body. The clinic also receives funding from a mandatory student levy (imposed, we might add, on both male and female students) and has also been the recipient of provincial lottery proceeds. That an organization receiving public funds should be permitted to practise bald-faced sexual discrimination is a disgrace to itself and to the law school that funds it.

But a second perversion is at work here. The presumption of innocence is the bedrock principle of our criminal justice system, and the whole idea of legal aid is to permit poor people accused of crimes to vindicate that presumption. The Parkdale community clinic's policy sends the message that men accused of domestic abuse, merely by having been *accused* of the crime, are legal lepers and, therefore, as good as guilty. What an edifying lesson to be teaching to Osgoode Hall law students.

Sack Hedy Fry, II

So now we know she is a liar.

On March 21, Hedy Fry, the Minister of Multiculturalism, told the House of Commons: "We only have to look around the world today ... to know that people are still discriminated against ... because of their race, their religion and their culture. We do not have to go too far. We can just go to British Columbia in Prince George where crosses are burning on lawns as we speak."

Crosses were not burning in Prince George or anywhere else in Canada. Yet the Minister told reporters who asked for evidence that she had a letter from the Mayor of Prince George confirming her claim. She would give a copy of the letter to the media, she said, but did not do so. Instead, her staff contacted the RCMP and the Minister herself called the Anti-racism Education and Research Society desperately seeking evidence to support her claim. None was available, which did not surprise Colin Kinsley, the Mayor of Prince George, who revealed that Ms. Fry's tale of his letter was an "outright lie." Now, CBC Radio, which filed an access to information request with the federal government's Information Commissioner, reports that the commissioner has searched for the letter Ms. Fry claimed to have. He found nothing.

So far, Ms. Fry has done nothing to make amends but deliver a half-baked statement of regret to the House of Commons. By stretching credulity almost to the breaking point, it is possible to believe, as Prime Minister Jean Chrétien told the House of Commons, that Ms. Fry's original cross-burning comment was a mistake. But her efforts after the fact to hunt down evidence to support her claim and, worse, her follow-up lie about the letter, are utterly disgraceful. An administration more easily embarrassed than the one in power would have dismissed Ms. Fry long ago, when it was only her manifest incompetence that showed how unsuitable she was for high office. Now that she has added flat-out lying to the list, surely even this government will tell her to clear her desk.

LETTERS

Tyrants

Re: Tyrants Don't Make Peace, May 1.

While I agree with your editorial analysis of Yasser Arafat's complete disregard for the rule of law, I take issue with your conclusions.

First, tyrants can make peace. Mr. Sadat and the late King of Jordan, dictators both, were willing and able to make peace with Israel. Syria, though, is not willing to make peace with Tel Aviv, not so much because the Assad regime needs an external threat to legitimize itself (it doesn't), but rather because it insists on the complete, unconditional return of the (illegally occupied) Golan Heights. This is something Israel has been unwilling to agree to.

Secondly, you make the statement that things have changed partly in Egypt and Jordan over the decades. While this is true, things have yet to change in Israel. Palestinian lands are still being illegally confiscated, Palestinian houses and orchards illegally destroyed, torture is still commonplace in Israeli jails, and Israeli settlements are still being constructed on illegally occupied land. Pretty sad for the "only democratic state" in the region.

Patrick Page, Kingston, Ont.

Free speech

Two recent letters to the Editor have raised concerns about freedom of speech at the Osgoode Hall Law School of York University.

I fully agree with your readers that the best defence to offensive speech is more speech, allowing people to form their own views of the validity of each point of view. However, in a university with a diverse student body, members of religious and racial minorities are entitled to be treated respect. That is why York University requires its students to refrain from speech that amounts to harassment or discrimination contrary to the principles of the Ontario Human Rights Code.

In the case of the anti-Islamic articles that appeared in the Osgoode Hall Law School's student newspaper, a student has filed a complaint that the article offended the York University standard of conduct. Under the rules, Osgoode's Associate Dean is obliged to investigate the complaint, and, if she believes that it is one to which the University's regulations apply, to refer it to a University body for an informal resolution or a formal determination. The Associate Dean is now conducting that investigation. Neither I nor the President of the University have any control or influence over the proceedings, but I am confident that a result will be reached that is properly respectful of freedom of speech and is fair to both sides.

Peter W. Hogg, Dean, Osgoode Hall Law School, York University, Toronto.

Restaurateur

Re: Smoking by-law confuses restaurant owners, May 1.

I am annoyed by restaurateurs' complaints about the financial impact on restaurants of smoking bans. I used to live in Montreal, where smoking is endemic. I rarely went to restaurants because of the stench of cigarette smoke spoiling my dining experience.

After moving to Toronto, I go to restaurants frequently as I can now find smoke-free dining. As the majority of people are non-smokers, it follows that catering to the non-smoking population would benefit restaurateurs financially. Non-smokers eat, smokers smoke. What is it that restaurants sell? Restaurateurs can now stop their schizophrenic existence and decide whether they are food establishments or bars.

John M. Thompson, Toronto.

Breaking rank

Re: We're All in This Together, May 3.

Stockwell Day's op-ed was his biggest blunder yet, and proves beyond a doubt that he's unfit to lead a principled opposition against the tax-and-spend Liberals. Given a golden opportunity to tell Canadians what he stands for, he offered nothing but empty verbiage: "discipline," "a culture of victory," "common message of hope, opportunity and growth," etc.

But the most damning aspect was his one criticism of the Liberals: "The Liberal legacy of broken promises, incompetence and waste is sapping our potential as a nation." In other words: If only the Liberals would keep all their socialistic promises, and spent our money on them efficiently – we'd realize our "potential." A total concession to destructive Liberal policies. With enemies like Day, who needs friends?

Glenn Woiceshyn, Calgary.

Stockwell Day told his caucus that he has a strategic plan to put the Alliance back on track to winning the next federal election. Why should I believe it? Why should I give my time, effort and money to support something I have not seen, and will likely not see until sometime in June? Why should I trust Mr. Day? What has he done to inspire my confidence? Why should I follow him any longer? The plan, if there is one, should be made public to the Alliance membership.

Jonathan Hook, past vice-president of the Oxford Canadian Alliance riding association, Woodstock, Ont.

Re: Day Suspends MP for Breaking Ranks, May 3.

Mr. Day is quoted as saying, "There are hard lessons in life and our mistakes are our teachers."

Could it be that our mistakes are our leaders?

Mike Vaydik, Yellowknife.

Arrest them all

So big, brave Mark Steyn thinks that because he's "a warmonger" this gives moral credence to his rant against Bob Kerrey (Even War Must have its Codes and Courtesies, May 3).

What self-serving hypocrisy. Instead of applying standards of justice to Kerrey that were applied to Serb troops, Mr. Steyn might consider applying his noble "standards" to the Canadian CF-18 pilots that blew up civilians in Belgrade. Or how about Mr. Steyn applying his brand of justice to the Allied air crews who levelled Dresden or Hiroshima? Or better yet, let's just charge Canada's Defence Minister with war crimes.

Steve d'Apollonia, Dartmouth, N.S.

National Post welcomes letters to the editor by mail, fax or e-mail. Please include name, home address and daytime telephone number. We reserve the right to edit, condense or reject letters. 300-1450 Don Mills Road, Don Mills, Ontario M3B 3R5, Canada. Telephone: (416) 383-2300; fax: (416) 383-2439; e-mail: letters@nationalpost.com

When a leader becomes repugnant

ANDREW COYNE

So Stockwell Day stumbles on, white mice eating out his innards.

The mice in question are to be found among his critics in the Alliance caucus, aghast at his leadership yet too timid to force him out. Instead, they will eat away at his support within the party at large, one riding at a time, until either one quarter of the riding associations have called for a vote on his tenure or next April's mandatory leadership review, whichever comes first.

Get used to it, Alliance supporters. The party has landed itself in the worst possible fix, with a leader who won't quit and rebels who won't give in: war without cease, months on end.

In its own way, the crippling of the Alliance leader is as illustrative of the deficiencies of our democracy as the excessive power of his counterpart across the Commons aisle.

As Opposition leader, Mr. Day cannot maintain caucus discipline quite so effortlessly as a prime minister, who has all the delights of power at his disposal. But neither can he be easily removed as leader. Like the prime minister, he was chosen not by the caucus he leads, but by the broad mass of members in his party.

The combination is grotesque: the head of the party grafted on to the body of the caucus; a presidential system of leadership selection superimposed on a parliamentary model. It has been with us since Mackenzie King, but its flaws have been apparent almost as long.

Party leadership elections are a scandal in themselves. Lacking any official register of party affiliation, leadership races have instead turned into massive, unruly recruitment drives, the race going to the candidate who can sell the most memberships. But the chief responsibility of a party leader in our system of government is not to shill membership cards in legion halls; it is to lead his party's delegation in Parliament. The skills required are quite different.

Even at the best of times, the system is inimical to parliamentary government. Armed with the popular mandate conferred upon him by the membership – including teenagers, busloads of old drunks, and other memorable constituencies from past such elections – the leader can more or less tell the caucus to go to Hell. Indeed, he can say much the same to the party. Once elected, he is effectively answerable to no one, until the time, some years hence, when his leadership comes up for "review" – that is to say, when the incumbent runs unopposed, with the threat of electoral oblivion hanging over the party should it turn against him, matched by severe reprisals against any foolish enough to organize such a campaign. Not surprisingly, the leader is commonly confirmed by margins exceeding 90%, the sort of result more often seen in the staged elections of dictatorships. And for the same reason: This is less democracy than Bonapartism.

It is part of the creeping presidentialization of Canadian politics: the inordinate focus on the party leader, rather than its program or the team of ministers who will implement it; the growing marginalization of individual MPs; the overwhelming dominance of the executive over the legislative, and of the prime minister over everyone else.

As I say, this is how the system works at the best of times. But when a leader becomes repugnant to a majority of his caucus – as is arguably the case in both major parties – it is absurd that they should be forced to carry on as if this were not the case.

Many reforms will be necessary if this unfortunate trend is to be reversed. But one of these is surely to return to the system of choosing party leaders in place in the early part of the last century (and still in effect in the British Conservative party): election by caucus.

This will strike many as out of step with our democratic times. But as we have seen, the present system hardly qualifies as democratic: not only in its methods, but in its results. A leader chosen by the caucus, by contrast, would have to be more solicitous of individual MPs' concerns. He would still retain many powers, notably the power of selection to Cabinet or shadow Cabinet positions. But the balance would be righted between the leader and the led; each would have some power over the other.

For a "grassroots" party such as the Alliance, this may be an especially difficult change to swallow. But democracy need not always take the most direct route to be effective. If it can be shown that a leader, by being more accountable to his caucus, would also be more accountable to the membership at large, Alliance members might be persuaded. The present impasse may be the best argument of all.

Make the caucus accountable to the membership, by all means. Leave party policy in the hands of the members. Keep MPs on a short leash. Use referendums, recall, all the rest. But let the caucus choose who will lead them. They're the ones who have to work with him.

National Post

COMMENT

Crossed wires over hydro market

Consumer free to choose under Ontario model

But system would add risk and costs

COUNTERPOINT

Globalization isn't one-size-fits-all

Obituary page (opposite), with the regular news grid; editorial and comment pages (left and above), with grids that vary according to the content.

NATIONAL POST, MONDAY, AUGUST 20, 2001

AVENUE

A WESTERN CANADIAN HERALDRY

No Logo, Naomi Klein's treatise on the "brand bullies," makes no reference to the western practice of what she might term logoizing livestock with a branding iron.

Of course, some ranchers and cowboys may well feel the need to spring into their Birkenstocks and wax lyrical about how their peculiarly western form of livestock identification causes them to "... dream instead of their brands' inner meanings – the way they capture the spirit of individuality, athleticism, wilderness or community." Klein was referring, naturally, to multinationals and their "... need to identify with their earthbound products." But this is exactly what the legions of unapologetic red meat eaters and buckaroos do in the West when tucking into the prime rib.

Having been recently involved in the annual spring roundup and branding on the family allotment, I can assure Klein that cowboys and ranchers feel similar preoccupations insofar as horses and cattle are concerned. In fact, at the Hodgson outfit west of Edmonton, the roundup and branding crews were very connected with the cows, calves and horses. With cattle outfits large or small, similar operations reflect both the rhythm of nature and deeply held attachment to a shared western legacy. Anti-branding activists have had no impact in the last best West. The popularity of this form of branding remains as strong as ever, with more than 100 new brands being registered every month in Alberta alone.

Cattle and horse brands are a tradition and a part of the heritage of the West. Livestock brands have been around in western Canada for more than 125 years, having been registered since January, 1880. In a new land, largely unfettered by European custom and Eastern pretension, a brand was a heraldic symbol as much as a coat of arms or a family crest. Whether one owned a few head or thousands, the brand was a statement of both ownership and independence. Depending on the nature of the brand, it might say something about the fellow who owned it too. In modern brand parlance, many of these brands were "arbitrary." Branding irons depicting crosses, dots, hats, cowboy boots, pistols, spurs, bison heads or birds frequently found favour among early ranchers. These days, a brand must conform to a set of regulations, and for ease of computer recording, most consist of a combination of letters except Q and G (which can be used in the reverse position), numbers (except zero and one), "characters" limited to an anchor, triangle, diamond or a box and "symbols" such as the bar, half-diamond and quarter-circle.

In Alberta, the Livestock Identification Service Brand Recorder acts as the sort of Chief Herald in applying the rules for those wishing to register a cattle or a horse brand. British Columbia and Saskatchewan are the only other provinces that have a livestock brand registry, with 8,000 and 18,000 brands respectively. Alberta has the lion's share of brands – more than 54,000.

Chief Herald Robert Watt, Canada's ultimate heraldic authority, declared that brands are "potentially very appropriate heraldic symbols which are so simple themselves ... they share the drama and history of the owner." There are, however, only three references to brands in heraldic practise, according to Watt. Two belong to former vice-regal representatives of Alberta, the other to a town in B.C.'s cattle country.

A grant of arms given to H.A. "Bud" Olson, then lieutenant-governor of Alberta, incorporates his bar-Z-bar brand (see left) on the pronghorn antelope stags that support the crest. His predecessor, the late Gordon Towers, had his brand, the half-diamond TH on the sinister supporter, a bull flanking the left side of the crest. A complete branding iron figures in the Arms of Oliver, B.C.

The late Frank Lynch-Staunton, lieutenant-governor of Alberta from 1979 to 1985, used one of the oldest brands in the province, the 4H monogram, on the family ranch, uniquely equipped with a tennis court, at Antelope Butte.

There is at least one other brand with a regal connection. In 1921, the Prince of Wales, later Edward VIII, purchased the EP ranch near Pekisko in the foothills of the Rockies. Thought to be the only property owned by a reigning monarch outside of the United Kingdom, the unfortunate Duke of Windsor, as he became after abdicating in 1936, sold the property in 1962. The ducal holding was subsequently bought by the Cartwrights, a prominent and successful ranching family. The original brand, EP, was changed slightly to the quarter-circle EP and is now owned by the Cartwright line. In defence of the practice, John Cartwright said, "Other methods just don't work."

Corporal Ed Truco of the RCMP Livestock Theft Investigation Unit agrees. "Rustling is pretty well under control due to an excellent brand inspection system. Other methods like eartags aren't tamper-proof and tags can be cut off when livestock are stolen."

While a brand does not appear in Alberta's coat of arms, the Legislative Assembly is the only parliamentary body in the Commonwealth known to possess a registered cattle and horse brand, the rafter or half-diamond AB. This brand was among the last to be registered before the Brands Registry was privatized in 1999.

The current Lieutenant-Governor of Alberta, Lois Hole, does not yet have a grant of arms. A spokesperson for her office said that "Her Honour does not plan to have a brand in her family coat of arms, but is considering registering an honorary brand for the Office of the Lieutenant-Governor." Fair enough, as her interests in things agricultural are focused in the horticultural arena. She is a well-known author of several best-selling books on gardening that enjoy a wide readership that includes Charles, The Prince of Wales.

Ernest Gietz's daughter, also an author of fairly wide reputation, has within the last few months registered a brand with Alberta's Livestock Identification Services (ALIS). Born and raised the ranching country at Pincher Creek in the Alberta foothills, she is better known as Beverley McLachlin, Chief Justice of the Supreme Court of Canada. When in her native province, Madame Justice can brand her bovine charges with the quarter-circle reverse G on the right shoulder.

The Calgary Stampede has a brand, of course. The CS brand appears on more belt buckles, drink glasses, coasters and other promotional items than it does on livestock. Bob McKay, ranch manager for the Calgary Stampede ranch, 250 kilometres northeast of Calgary, said, "We run 400 head of horses and try to breed bucking stock. Bred mares foal in April/May and we freeze brand about 70 colts after they're weaned in October. Our horse brand, the CS, is applied on the left shoulder. We've got about 40 bulls as well that are branded with the reversed lazy S or pot hook. There has been a lot of talk about using other methods, but none have found to be anywhere as good."

Hank Pallister, now retired in High River, but for 43 years a brand inspector, and a leading authority on the subject, says, "Brands are a part of Alberta's heritage. In Alberta, you can go into museums, restaurants, hotels and bar rooms and see cattle and horse brands. People are interested in them." Pallister noted, however, that "the purpose for branding livestock on rangeland and pasture is to identify ownership. Once in a while you've got to rope the animal and clip [the hair] over the brand on an animal to get a positive identification, but no one has been able to identify livestock without a hot brand. Eartags, computer chips in the ears and other methods just don't seem to work. Brands are permanent and hard to alter, so it's still the best way."

Brian Hodgson, National Post

Not the Globe and Mail

The design mandate was to look different from any other Canadian newspaper – especially *The Globe and Mail*, which had long been an established national voice.

NATIONAL POST

VOL. 5 NO. 268 FRIDAY, SEPTEMBER 12, 2003

G-G's polar trip
Ralston Saul hopes to sell wine to Iceland, chat among elites. A12

¡Ay Caramba!
Johnny Depp is irresistibly cool in Once Upon a Time in Mexico. B1

'We remember lives lost. We remember the heroic deeds.'

A woman remembers the victims of Sept. 11, 2001, at a monument in Montclair, N.J. Our coverage of the attack's second anniversary appears on Pages A3, B6 and FP3.

Canadians fired upon in Kabul

UP TO FOUR ROCKETS

By Chris Wattie

CAMP JULIEN, AFGHANISTAN • Canadian soldiers in Afghanistan came under fire last night in a pair of attacks aimed at the Canadian base camp and the main base for the International Security Assistance Force (ISAF) in Kabul.

An explosion was heard within a kilometre of Camp Julien, home to the 1,900 Canadians in Afghanistan, a few minutes after three rockets – characterized as "small-calibre" by ISAF spokesmen – were fired at Camp Warehouse, which houses most of the troops of the NATO-led, 31-nation Kabul Multinational Brigade.

The rockets caused only minimal damage, and no casualties have been reported.

See ROCKETS on Page A2

ISRAEL RESOLVES TO 'REMOVE' ARAFAT

No timetable for expulsion of Palestinian leader, who vows, 'No one can kick me out'

By David Blair

JERUSALEM • Israel dramatically increased its onslaught against the Palestinian leadership last night when the government resolved to "remove" Yasser Arafat and ordered the army to come up with a plan for expelling him.

There was no timetable attached to the order.

The long-threatened decision, which flies in the face of American demands for Mr. Arafat to be left in place, came in an emergency session of the Security Cabinet chaired by Ariel Sharon, the Prime Minister, after two Hamas suicide bombings killed 15 people on Tuesday.

"The events of the last few days have again proven that Yasser Arafat is an absolute obstacle to the whole process of peace and compromise between Israel and the Palestinians," the Cabinet said in a statement. "Israel will act to remove this obstacle in a manner, time and way that will be decided separately."

The ominous announcement came after a three-hour meeting of the 11-member Security Cabinet – the most exhaustive discussion yet by Israel on Mr. Arafat's fate. Israeli troops took up positions in buildings overlooking Mr. Arafat's compound in the West Bank city of Ramallah, but officials said there were no immediate plans to move against the Palestinian President.

"That does not mean we are going to expel him tomorrow," said Raanan Gissin, Mr. Sharon's spokesman. "We want to make Arafat worry a bit about what we might do."

Aware of the debate raging over his fate, a defiant Mr. Arafat spoke to journalists ahead of the Israeli decision and said he fully expected to be killed. "No one can kick me out," he said.

See ARAFAT on Page A9

EXCLUSIVE ANALYSIS

The authors of a new Arafat biography write that he prefers chaos to order, never renounces violence for long and is an impediment to the creation of a Palestinian state. Page A12

Writing his story helps Sampson to recover

The Post's Francine Dubé has covered William Sampson's story since his arrest in Riyadh nearly three years ago. Today, she describes a man permanently marked, yet revelling in freedom and trying to get back to normal.

LONDON • Until his angina flared up again, sending shooting pains through his chest and left arm, Bill Sampson walked the streets of London for hours at a time in his stiff new walking boots, trading them, when they hurt his feet, for a pair of well-worn and well-loved cowboy boots. He dresses comfortably, in jeans, a white cotton T-shirt and a beige sports coat, knapsack slung around his back as he walks, reclaiming his city and himself.

He has lost so much weight that his clothes hang off him. He is pale. It is clear, to look at him, that he has recently survived some terrible trauma.

Since his release from prison in Riyadh on Aug. 7, Bill has been leading a quiet life in London.

He lives in a pretty, borrowed flat. He spends large chunks of time attending to legal and medical matters, riding to appointments on the top deck of London's double-decker buses to better admire the architecture of a city he loves.

He underwent two heart operations while imprisoned in Saudi Arabia. Refusing to take medication for two years has not helped his condition. He may need further surgery. Refusing to bathe or brush his teeth for two years left him with a skin infection, which is being treated with antibiotics. His teeth acquired a yellowish hue and need major restoration – three back teeth were broken during beatings he underwent in prison.

He is in counselling, in part to help him deal with the anger he feels over the torture he suffered.

It took him seven days to write the five-part story of his arrest and incarceration in Saudi Arabia. Working alone, he produced 45 dense pages of notes. We sifted through the notes, drawing outlines for the five stories, mercilessly pruning, until he had something he could work with.

The most difficult story for him to write was the second one, which recounted the sadistic beatings he endured in the days following his arrest on Dec. 17, 2000.

See SAMPSON on Page A6

More coverage including reader reaction and whether Sampson can sue, Pages A6, A7, A12, A13

Published by the proprietor, The National Post Company, a CanWest publication, 300 - 1450 Don Mills Road, Don Mills, Ontario M3B 3R5

Publication Mail Agreement Number 40068573

THE FAT FILES

When rich and poor kids eat the same diet, poor ones get fatter

By Brad Evenson

Liz Goodman is part of a growing group of researchers who believe growing up poor, or feeling poor, makes you fat.

"Over the past 20 years, economic and social inequalitites have been rising," says Dr. Goodman, an obesity researcher at Brandeis University in Waltham, Mass.

"And it's interesting that there's this burgeoning epidemic of obesity at the same time."

As another scientist puts it, "Poverty really does get under your skin."

In Canada, kids from poor families are twice as likely to be obese as rich kids. A study published in August in the *International Journal of Obesity* found 6.4% of children in the wealthiest quarter of the Canadian population were obese, compared with 12.8% of those in the poorest quarter. The heaviest children live in single-parent homes, with 46% either overweight or obese.

It's easy to blame obesity on poor diet and lack of exercise. But this is overly simplistic, like blaming high unemployment on the number of people not working. It doesn't explain underlying causes.

See OBESITY on Page A8

FINANCIAL POST

Air Canada says it might not be able to buy jets from Bombardier without federal help. Page FP1

Exclusive Irshad Manji and Alan Dershowitz on Israel. A10, 16
NATIONAL POST
Tellier attacks
It's a myth that Bombardier is at the public trough, CEO says. FP1
Balletrobics
Star athletes swear by a former ballerina's stretching regimen. B3

Parties debate today's non-binding vote on marriage as Commons returns

SAME-SEX BILL GETS EARLY TEST

Cholesterol pills carry risk, UBC group says
He wags the finger but who listens?
Murder, politics collide in California
FINANCIAL POST
Canada finishes well ahead of U.S. as OECD tests teenage students
INDEX

A spread from the cultural section, Avenue (opposite), and two front pages (left and above).

Barometern

DAGENS VÄDER
Vackert vårväder, +8 grader.
Sidan 56

Oskarshamns-Tidningen. Vecka 11. Nr 61. Pris 12 kronor. 0480–591 00. www.barometern.se **FREDAG** **14 mars 2003**

KALMAR LÄN
Färre hyrläkare besparing
Landstinget har sparat mångmiljonbelopp på att skära ned antalet inhyrda läkare. På 1,5 år har man gått från 25 läkare per år till fem.
Sidan 28

KALMAR
Kvällslivet ska sälja Kalmar
Kalmar ska säljas med kvällsliv. När turistmässan hålls i Göteborg kommer Kalmar att representeras av Larmtorget i miniatyr.
Sidan 3

Elever besvikna på skolan
Ett tiotal elever på Stagneliusskolan får kanske inte gå den utbildning de valt. "Vi känner oss jättelurade", säger eleverna.
Sidan 4

TORSÅS

▶▶ Det kom som en överraskning
SIGRID ÖSTERSTRÖM, årets mottagare av priset Dé é guld värt.
Sidan 15

ÖLAND
Rökare vräkt från lägenhet
En hyresgäst på södra Öland har blivit vräkt för att ha rökt i lägenheten trots att det inte stod något om rökförbud i hyreskontraktet.
Sidan 13

Villa i Böda brann ned
Ett hus i Böda brann ned på torsdagen. Ingen person kom till skada. Brandorsaken är okänd.
Sidan 12

EMMABODA
Färre barn men mer idrott
Trots att befolkningen och barnantalet minskar kommunen ökar aktiviteten i idrottsföreningarna.
Sidan 14

HÖGSBY
Ingen Högsbydag i år
Högsbydagen ställs in. Tre idrottsföreningar var beredda att gå in, men krävde ett garantibelopp.
Sidan 10

KLS-utsläpp slog ut reningsverket

KALMAR. KLS misslyckades med ett rörarbete och fyra–fem ton rent glykol läckte ut från slakteriet. Utsläppet var så stort att det slog ut stora delar av Kalmars avloppsrening. Fortfarande, drygt tre veckor senare, släpper reningsverket ut vatten med höga kväve- och fosforshalter. Det kommer att ta ytterligare några veckor innan reningen är fullständig igen. **Sidan 5**

Metall i munnen modefluga. Alltfler unga piercar sig.

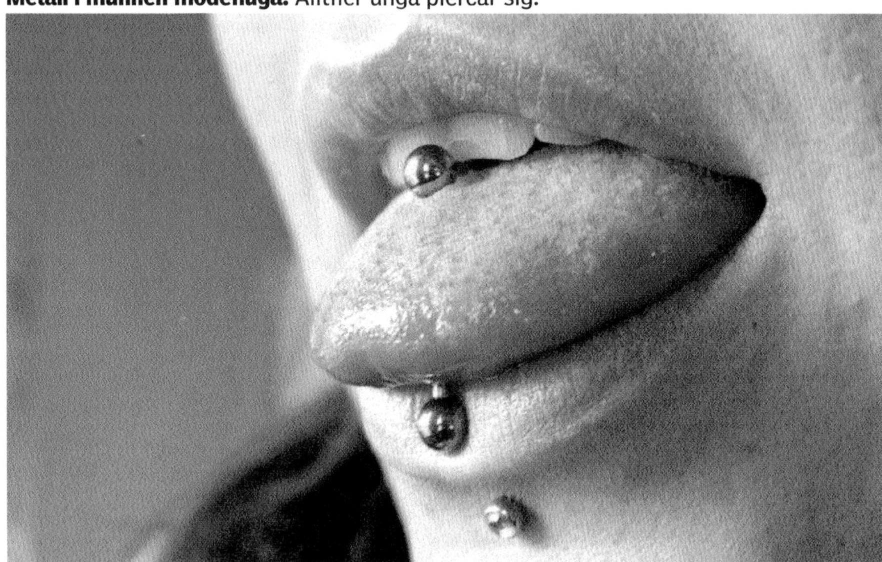

Kalmar sidan 7. Hälsoriskerna med piercing utreds av Socialstyrelsen. Johan Reinel-Lundin hoppas på en lagstadgad minimiålder för den som vill pierca sig. När Barometern-OT besöker hans studio i centrala Kalmar är tillströmningen av ungdomar stor. FOTO: LARS JOHANSSON

Nöjet. Basist till Japan.

FOTO: OLLE NILSSON

Roger Nilsson åker på turné. **Sidan 40**

Sporten. Guld i sim-SM.

ARKIVFOTO: SONJA PALM

Malin Fredriksson vann stort. **Sidan 29**

Ekonomi. Förening firar.

FOTO: SONJA PALM

Björn Lilliehöök vill gynna idéer. **Sidan 22**

Front page from *Barometern*, in southern Sweden, after the redesign.

Redefining the whole process

Ole Munk

Design training paves the way for major change at three papers in Sweden

The visual quality of a newspaper depends upon the skills of those working with the paper on a daily basis, rather than upon whatever guidelines lie behind the design. No matter how good the consultant and how splendid a design job he or she may have done, if the staff does not catch the idea – or if their resources do not match the ambitions of the design concept – the result is bound to fail.

On the other hand, it is my contention that a resourceful art department may take any old combination of typefaces and graphic devices and produce high-quality newspaper design out of it.

The fact that few Scandinavian papers have art departments (instead, copy editors are expected to take care of layout and editing at the same time) makes it even more important to ensure that the level of complexity in a design concept corresponds to the actual manpower available for doing page layout. Moreover, as the design of a newspaper is never static (and never should be) but is constantly evolving, with new editorial ideas and demands calling for constant design innovation, a paper needs to possess resources not only for practicing daily design but for developing it as well. If not, the paper will depend heavily on the consultant who did the original design – quite a comfortable position for the consultant, maybe, but not a very healthy one for the newspaper.

In my early years as a newspaper design consultant (actually not so long ago, hardly more than five or six years), more than once I had the frustrating experience of seeing a newspaper rapidly lose the visual quality it had just gained through an otherwise successful redesign process, for these very reasons.

I began looking for ways to avoid situations like this, and it came as a very pleasant surprise when, in May 1999, I was asked by the Sydostpress newspaper corporation of southern Sweden to arrange a design course for selected members of their staff. The aim was to solve problems exactly like the ones mentioned above. Sydostpress wanted to anchor the future design development of their three papers within the organization.

Two people from each newspaper (*Blekinge Läns Tidning*, *Smålandsposten*, and *Barometern/Oskarshamns-Tidningen*) were picked out and interviewed by me in order to let knowledge about their design skills (all six were editors with a background in journalism) and their expectations for the course influence the syllabus. One thing which became clear was that several of the "students" already had a good sense of shape but relied completely on their intuition in design matters; they had no system of terminology to help them prefer one possible design solution to another.

The first lap of the design course ran in January 2000 in the Media Center of *Blekinge Läns Tidning* in Karlskrona. For a start, we dealt entirely with graphic design basics: typography, composition, color, visual perception, rhythm, etc.

During the first three days of the education, the word "newspaper" was hardly mentioned at all. Instead, I tried to direct the attention of my "students" to the design decisions they were already making all the time, in every part of their lives. As a rule, they made the "right" decisions, too; they just didn't know why. Design theory was, of course, a central part of the education.

Going tabloid

In 1994, *Blekinge Läns Tidning* had changed from broadsheet to tabloid, and circulation had kept going up ever since – quite remarkable in a market moving mainly in the opposite direction. Surveys indicated that readers in both Växjö and Kalmar would prefer a smaller paper, too, and from a corporate point of view the advantages of having one format for all three papers seemed pretty obvious. During the year 2000, the decisions were made. *Smålandsposten* should go tabloid at the beginning of March 2001; *Barometern* was to follow eight weeks later.

Logically enough, both papers appointed their design "students" to head the tabloid projects. At *Smålandsposten*, subeditor Anders Tapola and executive editor Gun-Britt Iderheim became project managers; at *Barometern*, former sports editor Dennis Andersson and subeditor Mikael Larsson Ek got the responsibility.

I was asked to help the processes along as a consultant. But before that, we were to go through a couple more laps of the educational process together. During 2000, a total of ten days were spent

Måndag 17 mars 2003
KULTUR
NÖJET
SPORTEN

Nöje. Lyckliga vinnare i Melodifestivalen

Sidan 40–41

INNEHÅLL I SEKTION B

Sport	26–36
Högsby	37
Kultur	38–39
Nöje	40–42
Annonser	43
Radio	44
TV	45–47
Väder	48

Christian Olsson, Kajsa Bergqvist, Mathias Fredriksson, Carolina Klüft, Anja Pärson, Emma Igelström och Stefan Holm – alla är de bäst i världen. Och svenskar. FOTO: PRESSENS BILD

Världens bästa Sverige

SVERIGE ÄR BÄST I VÄRLDEN.

I höjdhopp (Kajsa Bergqvist, VM-guld).

I höjdhopp (Stefan Holm, VM-guld).

I tresteg (Christian Olsson, VM-guld).

I femkamp (Carolina Klüft, VM-guld).

I simning (Emma Igelström, världsrekord).

I skidåkning (Mathias Fredriksson, världscupetta).

I storslalom (Anja Pärson, världscupetta).

Vilken topp svensk idrott har!

Och vilken bredd det finns på toppen!

När ett par vinteridrotter gjorde bokslut samtidigt som det var inomhus-VM i friidrott fick Sverige, som idrottsnation, ett kvitto på sin storhet.

Det är visserligen inget nytt med svenska världsmästare, svenska världscupvinnare eller svenska världsrekordhållare. Svensk idrott har en stolt historia med massor av guldkorn.

Men varje generation idrottare är unik på sitt sätt – så även den nya svenska generationen, väl representerad av de sju namnen ovan.

SEDAN PENGARNA GJORDE sitt intåg på alla håll i idrotten för ett antal år sedan har kraven på potentiella världsstjärnor bara ökat. Under 1980-talet kunde snälla, träningsvilliga talanger från Sverige slå världen med häpnad. Men i 1990-talets hårdnande konkurrens och det hårdnande mentala klimat blev vi på många håll omsprungna, omsimmade, omkörda och överkörda.

Det tog ett tag för svensk idrottsrörelse att reagera på det. Men reaktionen kom, kunskapen inhämtades, en ny generation växte fram. En generation som förstod och förstår att talang och hård träning bara räcker till en viss gräns.

Det som avgör om man ska lyfta från toppidrottare till världsstjärna är andra egenskaper.

• Kunskap

I en tid där träningsmetoderna och kosthållningen blir alltmer förfinade gäller det att känna sin kropp, veta vad den tål och hur den ska skötas. På Sixten Jernbergs tid var det den som tränade mest som vann. Nuförtiden är det den som tränar smartast och bäst som vinner.

Att känna sin kropp innebär också att man vet hur man ska göra för att få den att fungera som bäst vid ett givet tillfälle.

• Självförtroende

Det har skett en markant förändring i svenska idrottares sätt att se på sig själva. Anja Pärson och Emma Igelström vågar säga att de är bäst, att de tror att de ska vinna utan att det låter som tomma, kaxiga ord. Det allra bästa är att så gott som alla stjärnor – med Stefan Holm och Christian Olsson i spetsen – dessutom har kvar den patenterade svenska ödmjukheten.

• Förmåga att hantera press

Vi har under jag vet inte hur många år levt i villfarelsen att det är lättast att slå underifrån. Svenska favoriter håller aldrig. Men Anja Pärson gör det, precis som Carolina Klüft. Och Stefan Holm och Kajsa Bergqvist som tidigare haft svårt för att klara förväntningarna har nu gjort det till en vana.

DE MENTALA DELARNA av idrotten blir bara mer och mer betonade. Vikten av att kunna vinna, att veta hur det känns, att ha vanan inne är så oerhört viktig.

Det är därför (bland annat) som Norge aldrig slutar vinna i skidspåren, därför som Kajsa Bergqvist, Stefan Holm och Christian Olsson hade ett övertag på sina konkurrenter redan innan de började hoppa i helgens finaler.

Och det är därför som det känns så bra att det är VM i friidrott i sommar.

Där kommer nästa svenska guldfest.

JONAS KANJE
jonas.kanje@barometern.se

▶ **Sporten.** Johanna Nilsson överlägsen i USA. **Sidan 28**

Front page of the B section (above), and spreads from the Entertainment and Culture sections (opposite) of *Barometern*.

Hetaste banden kommer till Skälby

KALMAR

The Ark, The Sounds, The Mo, Charlies Magazine, Timbuktu och Robyn. På samma scen, samma dag. I Kalmar.

Det kan bli verklighet den 31 maj. Nattklubben Palace i Kalmar planerar att bjuda på en riktig avslutningsfest.

Magnus Ohlsson, vd, bekfräftar planerna när Barometern-OT når honom på ett ganska högljutt after ski i Åre.

Först blir han förvånad över att vi känner till uppgifterna. Sen säger han:

– Det stämmer. Vi har sökt tillstånd hos Kalmar kommun för servering av öl och vin.

Planerna på en rejält avslutning har växt fram sedan det visat sig att de artister som Palace bokat under våren kunnat dra en betydligt större publik bara utrymmet funnits.

– Vi hade kunnar sälja 2 500 biljetter till The Arks spelning. Vi har tackat nej till The Sounds, säger Magnus Ohlsson. Det fanns inga som helst möjligheter att arrangera en konsert med Sveriges kanske hetaste band för tillfället. I det sammanhanget räcker inte 1 300 biljetter långt.

Magnus Ohlsson, vd Palace.

Palace har helt enkelt inte fått plats med alla.

– Det finns ett genuint musikintresse i Kalmar. Konserterna har fungerat väldigt bra och när sedan bokningsbolagen Ema och United stage gärna vill placera artister i Kalmar har vi fyllt ett tomrum. Det ska vi bygga vidare på, säger Magnus Ohlsson.

Hetas i landet för tillfället

Artisterna Palaces vd räknat upp tillhör de hetaste i landet för tillfället. Inte i det absoluta toppskiktet, men i kategorin: heta och på väg dit.

– I det skiktet hittar du också artisterna som vi vill satsa på för att bygga en kvalitativ rockscen här i staden. För fem–tio år sedan kunde du inte göra en sådan här satsning utan att hämta artister utanför landets gränser. Nu kan vi göra det med artister där flera har sitt ursprung i Småland.

Kalmar kommun har anvisat Skälby för ändamålet och Ema har inspekterat området och sagt okej.

Palaces ledning har också inlett ett samarbete med Rockparty i Hultsfred som naturligtvis har stor erfarenhet av arrangemang i den här storleken.

– Vi tar del av deras rutin, hämtar in kunskap och i förlängningen ser vi båda möjligheter att kunna boka artister till den här regionen och samtidigt kunna sänka våra kostnader, säger Magnus Ohlsson.

Listan kan bli längre

Sereveringstillståndet är helt nödvändigt för att kunna genomföra konserten. Och beslutet bör komma ganska snabbt. Just nu är de nämnda artisterna tillgängliga – och listan kan bli längre – men väntetiden är givetvis begränsad.

– Logistiken är det stora problemet. Det är mycket som måste klaffa.

Men Magnus Ohlsson är inte orolig.

– Nu är vi på banan. Får vi klartecken finns det möjlighet att ta emot 5 000–10 000 åskådare ute på Skälby. Det här är något vi saknat i Kalmar...

PETER AHLÉN

The Ark.

Robyn.

Charlies Magazine.

▶ FAKTA | **Eric Gadd**

Namn: Eric Gadd.
Ålder: 37 år (fyller 38 den 31 juli).
Bor: På Östermalm i Stockholm.
Familj: Gift med Cornelia, inga barn men en katt.
Läser: Hela tiden, men just nu Elizabeth Georges senaste deckare.
Lyssnar på just nu: Jag lyssnar på väldigt lite musik när jag är på turné, men nu när jag kör bil har jag Queens of the Stone Age på väldigt hög volym.
Äter just nu: Mexikansk mat, alltså inte det vanliga tacos och sånt, utan mer Deep mexican food...
Favoritlåt av sina egna: Wish I. Jag hajar den inte riktigt, förstår inte vad texten handlar om...

För första gången under karriären känner Eric Gadd att han kan slappna av och befinna sig i nuet. På fredag den 21 mars står han på Palace scen i Kalmar. FOTO: STOCKHOLMS RECORDS

Eric Gadd vågar äntligen titta framåt

KALMAR/STOCKHOLM

I juli fyller Eric Gadd 38 år. För 17 år sedan släppte han sin första platta. Men att vara på turné har aldrig varit roligare än just nu.

– Jag tycker jag har roligare än någonsin, säger han. Jag känner mig lugnare på scenen. Jag vågar vara mer närvarande i nuet och det är bara great!!

Har du haft problem med scennerver förr om åren?

– Jag har kanske aldrig varit den som haft jättescenskräck, men ibland... jag vill inte helt dissa mig själv, men i bland har jag varit lite forcerad i öset. Kanske känt mig tvungen att ösa på för att fånga publiken. Men nu kommer det mer naturligt.

Eric Gadd är gotlänningen som flyttade till Stockholm och blev mobbad för sin dialekt som liten. Han började med att göra uppkäftig pop på svenska, mjuknade och bytte till engelska, blev sedan hela Sveriges soulman och nu med det senaste albumet Life Support är han tillbaka vid popen. Ett medvetet val. Men kritikerna har varit ljumma i sina omdömen.

Hur känns det?

– Nej, vad tråkigt. Är det så? Jag visste inte det. Jag läser aldrig vad tidningarna skriver om mig. Jag har hört folk säga att jag har fått både bra och dåligt.

Tar du åt dig av dålig kritik?

– Ja, alltså med flit läser jag inte kritik. Som artist är det farligt att göra det, tror jag. Men det gäller positiv kritik lika mycket. Det spelar ingen roll, en dålig recension eller en bra recension, det som står där stämmer aldrig ändå. Sanningen är alltid någonstans mittemellan.

"Jag hade det skitjobbigt när jag var ung"

Eric Gadd är snart 38 år nu. Det känns som om vi kommer tillbaka till det hela tiden. Inte åldern, men att han har mognat, funnit en större trygghet i sig själv och sin roll i livet såväl som på scenen. Han säger det själv; att närma sig 40-strecket tar han med ro.

– Det känns inte farligt alls. Jag vill inte alls vara ung igen, ungdom är hemskt att vara. Jag hade det skitjobbigt när jag var ung, berättar han.

– Däremot hade jag åldersnoja när jag var i 28–30-årsåldern. Men den släppte när jag passerat 30 år. Nu är det ändå för sent. Jag är inte ung längre och det känns bra.

Men det fanns en tid när Eric Gadd sprang ned och köpte Aftonbladet och Expressen direkt dagen efter han hade släppt en platta.

– Fick jag en bra recension kallade jag det att vara lycklig. Och blev det dåligt kallade jag det att vara olycklig. Men det är inga äkta känslor, säger Eric Gadd.

"Att skriva musik för mig har varit ganska privat"

Själv tycker han att Life Support blev bra. Men han säger samtidigt att den är för ny för att han ska kunna bedöma den ordentligt. Om några månader eller så tror han sig ha tillräcklig distans för att kunna säga om den är bra eller inte.

Life Support är den första plattan där Eric Gadd inte har skrivit alla låtar själv. Han åkte till USA och England på låtskrivarturné.

– Inför varje skiva skaffar jag mig någon sorts ny utmaning. Det här var någonting jag hade funderat på att pröva ganska länge.

– Att skriva musik för mig har varit ganska privat. Jag ville se om det gick att göra på det här sättet också, förklarar han.

Det gick lättare än vad han hade väntat sig. Eric Gadd berättar om möten med ödmjuka musiker som ansträngde sig för att han själv skulle bli nöjd.

– Jag trodde att det fanns en risk för att låtarna skulle komma längre ifrån mig, inte kännas lika nära hjärtat. Men så blev det inte, de känns lika nära mig som de brukar.

Eric Gadd är just nu mitt inne i sin turné. Den 21 mars spelar han på Palace i Kalmar. Då bjuder han på sitt nya material, men en del gammalt hänger också med.

– Ja, spela gamla låtar gör jag gärna. Men jag lyssnar aldrig på min musik. Min musik är inte till för mig, den är till för andra.

LOTTA NYBERG
0480-592 38
lotta.nyberg@barometern.se

▶ NÖJET SPANADE IN | **Anna Brewitz och Jonas Kellander, Agog, på Byteatern**

Naturligt samspelta Agog visade upp dynamisk och levande musik på sopplunch

Anna Brewitz och Jonas Kellander, Agog, spelade på Byteatern.

KALMAR

Två kan bli ett. Det visade Anna Brewitz och Jonas Kellander på Byteaterns sopplunch i går.

Anna har en kraftfullt röst.

Jonas Kellander följer henne som en skugga på en lågmäld elgitarr.

För åhörarna blir det en häftig upplevelse att följa samspelet paret emellan.

Tillsammans har Anna Brewitz och Jonas Kellander en duo, Agog, och de har spelat tillsammans i över tio år nu. De träffades första gången på musikgymnasiet i Oskarshamn. På tisdagen var det Byteaterns tur att få besök under lunchtimmen.

Namnet Agog kommer från ordet agogik som betyder de små temposkiftningar som tillsammans med de dynamiska schatteringarna gör musiken levande och kraftfull.

Programmet Från träsktugg till bubbeljazz kändes både dynamiskt och levande. Musikaliskt var det blandat med bland annat Stina Nordenstams Soon after christmas, Hendrix Little wing, All by myself som många känner igen från filmen Bridget Jones dagbok men också Strayhorns Lush life och Lullaby of birdland av Forester och Shear.

Duon drog ned tempot och Anna Bewitz röst fick utrymme att briljera. Hon visade vägen och Jonas Kellander följde tätt i hasorna. Ibland var det som om Annas röst och Jonas gitarrspel smälte ihop och blev till ett. Som om de båda helt naturligt hör ihop.

Men de erkänner att det inte alltid är så naturligt som det låter.

– Ibland är vi helt borta, har ingen aning om var den andra är. Men det är också det som är spännande. När det händer nåt musikaliskt, säger Anna Brewitz.

– Och vi hittar alltid tillbaka till varandra till slut, tillägger Jonas.

Läckert ihopsmält var också All by myself och Calling you när Agog valde att varva de båda låtarna på ett mycket lyckat sätt.

Som en smårolig avslutning på lunchen bjöd de på Brels Begravningstango.

LOTTA NYBERG

"**Han kunde allt**. Provade det mesta. Alltid med stor respekt för hantverkarnas skicklighet. Det var en fröjd att arbeta tillsammans med honom."
Gravören **Hasse Linus Andersson**, Kosta, är bestämd. **Vicke Lindstrand** var en av de bästa. Lagom till 100-årsjubileet av konstnärens födelse 2004 lyfter Lindstrand-Stiftelsen fram hans gärning på en hemsida, i en ny bok och i en stor utställning.

En hyllning till glasblåsarna. Skulpturen står utanför utställningshallen i Kosta.

En pionjär i glasriket

KOSTA

– Vicke Lindstrand var en verklig konstnär. Tecknare, illustratör, skulptör, målare och industriformgivare. En nydanare som vågade utmana materialet och förnyade det svenska glaset.

Det säger Lars Thor, ordförande i Lindstrand-Stiftelsen.

– Visst har det skrivits mycket om Vicke Lindstrand genom åren och visst har hans verk visats på olika utställningar men ännu finns massor att upptäcka, fortsätter Lars Thor.

Ett drygt år har Lindstrand-Stiftelsen på sig att gå igenom det rika arkivmaterialet och sätta in Lindstrand i ett 1900-talsperspektiv. I november 2004 på konstnärens födelsedag öppnar en stor utställning på Röhsska museet i Göteborg.

– Vicke Lindstrand var en spännande konstnär med internationella utblickar. Han var fylld av experimentlusta. Närmast en forskare när det gällde glaset, säger Margareta Artéus Thor, projektledare för jubileumsåret.

Mycket är känt om Vicke Lindstrand, mer finns att upptäcka.

– Han är del av designlandet Sveriges utveckling. Kunskapen om honom och hans verk är en viktig grund för den som arbetar med design idag, påpekar Margareta Artéus Thor.

Gate lockade Lindstrand

Ändå var det en tillfällighet att han hamnade i glasriket. Unge Vicke Lindstrand som envist kämpat sig till en konstnärlig utbildning i födelsestaden Göteborg – föräldrarna hade hoppats att han skulle bli bokbindare, eller i alla fall litograf – engagerades som dekoratör vid en utställning i Jönköping. Så mötte han Simon Gate från Orrefors som bad ynglingen komma till bruket och prova på glaset. Så kunde det gå till på den tiden.

Vicke Lindstrand tvekade faktiskt. Vad skulle han kunna tillföra?

Drygt femtio år senare kunde han se tillbaka på en av de längsta och märkligaste gärningarna inom glasindustrin. Tolv år på Orrefors och dryga tjugo år på Kosta. Däremellan tio år som konstnärlig ledare på Upsala-Ekeby.

– Lindstrand-Stiftelsen har ett rikt material att ösa ur, berättar Lars Thor. I dag finns ett hundratal målningar, mer än 150 glasobjekt och ett femtiotal keramiska objekt hos Hanne Dreutler och Arthur Zirnsack som grundade och driver sin studioglashytta i Åhus. Hanne Dreutler lärde känna Vicke Lindstrand i Kosta. Han kom att betyda mycket för hennes utveckling till glaskonstnär. I Åhus finns också en permanent men föränderlig utställning kring Vicke Lindstrands konstnärliga gärning.

– Det finns många objekt och nytt material även på andra håll, berättar Börje Åkerblom som just nu går igenom alla glas- och keramikarkiv i Sverige för att få överblick över Vicke Lindstrands hela rika konstnärskap.

"Monumentalmålningen är Vicke Lindstrands", säger ordförande i Lindstrand-Stiftelsen Lars Thor på besök i museet i Kosta tillsammans med glasskännaren Börje Åkerblom och gravören Hasse Linus Andersson. FOTO: MATS HOLMERTZ

Vicke Lindstrand blev snabbt, trots att han bara var 24 år när han kom till Orrefors, ett namn på bruket. Tecknaren Lindstrand som drygade ut kassan under studietiden i Göteborg med att teckna för göteborgstidningarna, nämns som en nydanare, frisk och djärv, ett komplement till radarparet Gate och Hald. Han syns redan på Stockholmsutställningen 1930 och kom sedan att arbeta med de nya teknikerna ariel och mykene. Han var också en förnyare av det graverade glaset.

– Jag minns när vi arbetade med de stora glasskulpturerna Ikaros nål i Stuttgart, Prisma i Norrköping, Grön Eld i Umeå och Legend i glas i Växjö, berättar Hasse Linus. Skulpturerna som vägde mellan 20 och 45 ton, limmades samman av tusentals slipade glasskivor från Emmaboda.

Smått och monumentalt

Vicke Lindstrand växlade ständigt mellan bruksglaset, de små objekten och de monumentala utsmyckningarna. Tecknaren Lindstrand lämnade inte heller pennan och ynglingen som älskat att måla fortsatte att måla hela livet.

Såväl naturstudier med småländska björkdungar som expressivt prismatiska verk med stark rörelse. Han ger och tar inom sitt eget konstnärskap. Pennteckningarnas linjestyrka kommer igen i gravyrer. De keramiska djuren graverades på stora glasvaser, textiltryckens livfulla mönsterikedom finns i glas och keramik. Vicke Lindstrand tog och gav av sin egen kreativitet. De olika uttrycken korsbefruktade ständigt varandra.

GUNILLA PETRI

Den 20 och 21 mars ordnar Lindstrand-Stiftelsen och Orrefors Kosta Boda ett tvådagarsseminarium kring Vicke Lindstrand – modernist med utsökt materialkänsla! i Kosta och Orrefors.

I drygt trettio år arbetade Vicke Lindstrand med glas. Först tolv år på Orrefors och med tiden också dryga tjugo år på Kosta.

▶ FAKTA | **Viktor Lindstrand**

- Viktor Emanuel Lindstrand föddes den 27 november 1904 i Göteborg.
- Papper och penna var det enda som gällde under barndomen. Som fjortonåring började han på kontorsbokfabriken för att bli bokbindare.
- Ganska snart bytte han bana och blev litograflärling istället. Samtidigt gick han på Slöjdföreningens kurser.
- Som sextonåring hoppade Vicke Lindstrand av även litografutbildningen och började studera konst på heltid.
- Under studietiden försörjde han sig som tecknare i göteborgstidningarna.
- Kom 1928 som 24-åring till Orrefors och stannade till 1940.
- 1940–1950 konstnärlig ledare för Upsala-Ekeby.
- 1950–1973 konstnärlig ledare på Kosta.
- 1973–1983 egna gravyrer på glas tillverkat i Åhus.
- 1983 avled Vicke Lindstrand.
- 1986 bildades Stiftelsen Marianne och Vicke Lindstrands Stiftelse. Stiftelsen har sitt säte i Åhus. Lars Thor som skrev boken Legend i glas 1982 är ordförande i stiftelsen.
- I Studio Glashyttans lokaler i Åhus finns en permanent utställning av Vicke Lindstrand som bygger på stiftelsens material.

Astrids litteraturpris delas ut i dag

VIMMERBY

Vem får det första litteraturpriset på fem miljoner kronor till Astrid Lindgrens minne? Världens största barn- och ungdomslitteraturpris.

Prick klockan 14 i dag stiger tolvmannajuryn upp på en liten scen i Astrid Lindgrengården i Vimmerby för att tillkännage sitt val. Den fjärde juni delas priset ut på Skansen i Stockholm av kronprinsessan Victoria.

Detta internationella pris instiftades 2002 av regeringen.

Det skall ses som hela svenska folkets barn- och ungdomslitteraturpris.

I november i fjol sammanträdde juryn för första gången. Tolv personer, sex män och sex kvinnor, med särskild anknytning till barn- och ungdomslitteratur.

Litteraturpriset till Astrid Lindgrens minne som kan gå till författarskap, illustratörskap och läsfrämjande insatser i Astrid Lindgrens anda, skall tilldelas en författare vars litterära verk är av allra högsta konstnärliga värde och präglas av humanistisk anda. Författaren belönas för hela sitt författarskap, inte för ett enskilt verk.

Priset som kan ges till en eller flera nu levande personer är internationellt och tilldelas mottagare oavsett språk och nationalitet. Målet är att stärka intresset för barn- och ungdomslitteratur och på global nivå främja barns rättigheter.

I år nominerar juryn själv pristagare. I framtiden skall mellan 400 och 600 organisationer och institutioner i hela världen föreslå kandidater.

I juryn sitter Janne Lundström som är ordförande och barn- och ungdomsförfattare, Ulla Rhedin, litteraturvetare och bilderboksforskare, Maria Nikolajeva, litteraturvetare, Ulla Lundqvist, barnlitteraturforskare, ungdoms- och fackboksförfattare, Fibben Hald, tecknare och barnboksillustratör, Lars H Gustafsson, docent i socialmedicin och författare, Birgitta Fransson, litteraturkritiker, Larry Lempert, bibliotikarie, Mats Berggren, ungdoms- och vuxenboksförfattare, Ulf Boethius, professor emeritus i litteraturvetenskap, Agneta Edwars, litteraturvetare, och Annika Lindgren redaktör på Prisma bokförlag och barnbarn till Astrid Lindgren.

GUNILLA PETRI
gunilla.petri@barometern.se

Nr 236 ONSDAG 11 oktober 2000 • Vecka 41 • Pris 12 Telefon 0470 - 77 05 00

SMÅLANDSPOSTEN

Mulet och regn

http://www.smp.se

Lungläkare saknas

Avtal och finansiering inte löst

Satsar på fler vuxna i skolan

Ledare

Sverige

Världen

Älmhult

Ljungby

Flanören

Reportage

Konsult granskar ekonomin

Sidan 10

Träkunniga flyktingar sökes

Sidan 10

Förre teaterchefen Henning Mankell

Teatern – en gränslös mötesplats

Stora framgångar för småföretagen

Äppelpaus.

Sidorna 18–21

Biskopen vädjar för flyktingar

Sidan 11

I DAG ONSDAG

Del 1		Del 2	
Växjö	3-5	Lessebo	18-21
Sverige	6	Sport	22-25
Världen	7	ZickZack	30
Familje	8	Radio/tv	30, 31
Tingsryd	9	Ljungby	32
Röster	9	Älmhult	32
Uppvidinge	10		
Allmänt	11		
Börs	12		
Ekonomi	13		
Kultur	14		
Nöje	15		
Alvesta	16		

Annonsmarknader	
Arbeten	25, 26
Meddelanden	26
Varor	26, 27
Motor	27, 28
Bostäder	28, 29
Resor	29
Evenemang	29

Taif-ledare som inte kan hockey

Sporten

Årets skörd av äpplen förlorad

Sidan 9

Sidan 17

Ljungby · Alvesta

Resecentrum i Alvesta dröjer

Ljungby

Alvesta

Föräldrar besvikna när planer ändrats

Oroar sig för effekt av bergtäkt

Total förvandling av Garvaren föreslås

Lärarna hoppar av gymnasieprojekt

Passa på kanonbilligt

SÖNDAGSÖPPET

STORCKENS

Before the redesign

As broadsheets, the two papers looked very different. *Smålandsposten* was extremely calm, disciplined, some would say boring, whereas *Barometern*'s look was rather messy, although it was in certain ways quite dynamic. The confusing presentation of local material, however, was one thing they had in common, partly because of the format.

A
TORSDAG
21 december 2000

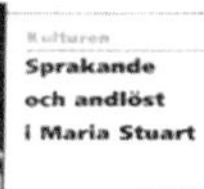

Kulturen
Sprakande och andlöst i Maria Stuart
SIDAN 16

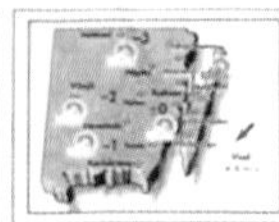

Väder
Dis och kyligt
Efter en del dis på förmiddagen blir det växlande molnighet. Måttlig nordostlig vind. Temperaturen håller sig mellan 0 och 3 minusgrader.
BAKSIDAN

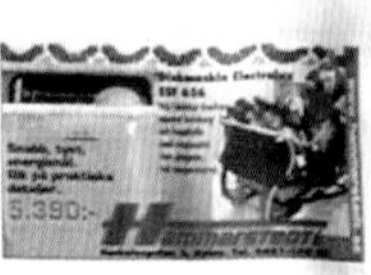

Småland största dagstidning

Barometern

Oskarshamns-Tidningen

Ny njure till Fitnete Limani

Insamling ska gå till transplantation • Idén får starkt bifall

KALMAR
En insamling är nu på gång för att ge Fitnete Limani en ny njure.

SIDAN 4

Kritiken stoppar fallskärm

Det blir ingen fallskärm för landstingets personalchef Håkan Petersson. Efter kritiken väljer han själv att inte skriva under det.

SIDAN 10

Dan-Åke Olsson är inne i en fin avslutning på 2000.

Mannen som kan trava med hästar

KALMAR

SIDAN 26

"Mordet" kan vara läkarslarv

KALMAR LÄN
Det har kommit fram nya uppgifter i fallet med den 55-årige företagare från en ort i Kalmar län som sitter häktad i Dominikanska republiken.

SIDAN 10

Mer brott efter östs frigörelse

KALMAR
Östeuropas frigörelse leder till att kriminaliteten i Sverige ökar. Bara de senaste månaderna har Kalmarpolisen gripit ett 30-tal balter, ryssar och polacker för stölder.

SIDAN 8

Nu framförs krav på sänkt hastighet vid Funkaboskolan på Norra vägen.

Skolan vill sänka farten

KALMAR
– Sänk hastigheten på Norra Vägen vid Östra och Västra Funkaboskolan innan det händer en olycka.

SIDAN 7

Läs kändisars listor och gör din egen
SIDAN 19

Julhelgens fettfällor
SIDAN 1, sektion B

Katt beskjuten med luftgevär
SIDAN 29

Allmännyttan är avskaffad?
SIDAN 2

Torsdag 21 december. Vinnare för årskurs 3 blev Frida Lembke, klass 3B, Transtorpsskolan i Nybro.

EMMABODA
Satsning på nya bussar
SIDAN 21

MÖNSTERÅS
"Tårtan inget hån"
SIDAN 14

KALMAR
Mörk framtid för Östersjön
SIDAN 9

KUNSTEN
Eleverna vann rikstävling
SIDAN 30

KALMAR LÄN
Hör av dig om Barometern-OT
0480-59 111
0480-592 05
SIDAN 10

Har du en NYHET – Ring 0480-180 18

Tre dagar återstår

Träffsäkerhet av vikt

M vill ha program för privatisering

Kalla handen för kulturskola

Välbesökt träff

Populärt lopp för många barn

Sporthall kan bli upprustad

Forum

Provtryck B

onsdag

SMÅLANDSPOSTEN

Tingsryd redo höja skatten 25 öre

Allians. Inte socialdemokraterna, inte vänsterpartiet, utan centern lade överraskande förslaget vid kommunstyrelsens budgetmöte att Tingsryds kommun ska höja skatten med 25 öre nästa år.

SIDAN 50

Hanna berättar om sitt FN-jobb

SIDAN 26

Ljungbybor går före kön till ortopedisk operation

Väntelista. Ljungbypatienter som behöver ortopedisk operation får gå före patienter från östra länsdelen.

– Vi måste begränsa oss för att klara tre månaders väntetid för patienter inom vårt upptagningsområde, säger klinikchefen Claus Jörgensen.

SIDAN 15

Kvinna omkom vid krock på E4

E4. En 49-årig kvinna omkom vid en frontalkollision på E4 strax söder om Strömsnäsbruk på tisdagsmorgonen. En man i en mindre paketbil, på väg söderut, kom plötsligt över på mötande körbanan.

SIDAN 58

Onsdag 1 november 2000 • vecka 41

Hem till Växjö med silver och brons i bagaget

Endast guldet fattas. Håkan Ericsson kom hem med två nya medaljer. Nu har han fem silver och två brons i sin ägo.

Nu saknar Håkan bara OS-guld

Nöjd. Håkan Ericsson, 32-årig rullstolsåkare, åkte till Sydney för att ta sin första guldmedalj.

I går kom han, och coachande hustrun Elin, hem till Växjö med en silver- och en bronsmedalj i bagaget. Guldet, på 100 meter i paralympics, hade Håkan missat med fem hundradelar av en sekund.

– Jag är nöjd ändå. Kommer man fem hundradelar efter har man visat att ambitionen att vinna funnits där, säger Håkan.

Nu dröjer det fyra år innan Håkan får nästa chans att ta det efterlängtade guldet.

– Ännu har jag inte bestämt mig för om jag ska fortsätta som rullstolsåkare eller inte, förklarar han.

SPORTEN, SIDAN 37

” I kväll arrangerar kyrkor i Lagan ett fackeltåg mot halloweenfirandet. Det har väckt mycket uppmärksamhet och nog finns det anledning att nyktert diskutera inslag i den kommersiella amerikanska trend som växt sig stark i Sverige.

LEDARE, SIDAN 2

Halvklart till mulet

VÄDRET, SIDAN 36

Främling är Helenas favorit

Helena Bergström spelar kvinnan som avgudar Carola i Livet är en schlager.

NÖJE, SIDAN 35

Test issues

A number of test issues were produced along the way, some of which were also presented to readers at open-house arrangements. This early *Smålandsposten* test issue shows the typography we believed in for a long time, based on the use of Swift for body text as well as for headlines.

in the BLT Media Center, moving gradually from general graphic design to a more newspaper-oriented syllabus, and emphasizing the crucial relationship between writing, editing, and design – between form and function.

The fourth lap of the education course, running in late August, contained (among other things) a revision in which the "students" were to sum up what they had learned. These were their conclusions:

- You cannot discuss form isolated from content, and vice versa; the two are inseparately connected.
- Aesthetics are about more than just beauty; creating unity and consistency.
- The importance of details – and of cutting away details.
- Respect towards, and knowledge about, typography.
- Color theory; combining colors with both harmony and contrast.
- Rhythm.
- Grids and modules.
- International variations on the newspaper theme (successful and less successful).
- Relations between different components of a newspaper; showing function through form.
- Flexibility; how to break rules without ruining the concept.
- To know why you are doing as you do.
- Theoretical knowledge about design; how to motivate your choices.
- Courage.
- The importance of entry points – and how to handle them.
- The maestro concept.
- It takes time to change a newspaper!

The design process

Design work on the *Smålandsposten* tabloid began in October 2000. One month later, *Barometern* started a similar process. For six months, traffic was heavy between Växjö, Kalmar, and Espergærde – both physically, as we were frequently seeing each other, and in cyberspace. E-mail gave us the opportunity to practise "virtual teamwork" to such an extent that we sometimes forgot we were not sitting at the same desk.

The fact that we knew each other through the education course made cooperation easy, even when we disagreed. We spoke the same language. Also, the project managers' newly developed skills made it easier for them to promote new design ideas to their colleagues. Decisions and motivations were not based on fashion or personal taste so much as on actual knowledge and explicit editorial intentions.

On March 1, 2001, *Smålandsposten* became a tabloid newspaper. On April 24, *Barometern* followed.

The three Sydostpress tabloids do not look the same. They didn't when they were all broadsheets, either – nor should they, since they have significant editorial differences, and they operate in markets quite unlike each other's, especially in terms of competition. Nevertheless, there are similarities among the new tabloids, some of which can be traced back to the design education which the project managers had in common.

The systematization of entry points is one example. Our aim was to maximize the number of optical signals inviting readers into the pages. By using narrow headline faces, we give editors a way to put lots of information into the top layer of the text. And as a supplement to standard entry points such as headlines, subheads, captions,

10 KALMAR | BONUS

Lördag 1 februari 2003 | BAROMETERN-OT

Tre människor och tre olika livsöden. Det är vad vi får följa genom Jan Nordströms bilder.
Tre människor som vårdas och tas om hand av människor i vitt. Det är nära bilder, nakna och utlämnande.
Men de är tagna med stor respekt och en oändlig värme.

Det kostar så lite att glädja en människa. Att visa ett leende.

Ny kraft. Fika. Erik gillar pepparkakor.

Kärleksfull resa genom livet i ny landstingskatalog

KALMAR LÄN

Landstingets nya katalog är ett register med viktiga telefonnumer och adresser inom sjukvården.
Den förklarar utförligt hur man ska bete sig som patient och vad man har för rättigheter.

Men den har också ett helt annat liv genom att frilansfotografen Jan Nordström har fått lov att följa tre olika personer genom vården.

Det är Ruben Johansson, 80 år, som snart ska få åka hem igen efter en operation.

Det är Erik Karlsson, tio år, som haft blodcancer och som nu går på efterbehandling.

Och det är Mona Iveby, 59 år, och hennes älskade Bengt Ohlsson, 64 år. Mona har cancer som inte längre går att behandla men hon lever så mycket hon kan. I varje ögonblick.

Dessa tre människors berättelser går som en röd tråd genom hela landstingskatalogen som plötsligt blir något mer än ett register med viktig information och nödvändiga telefonnummer.

Den blir en odyssé över det sköra ömtåliga livet men också en viljestark kamp för att inte ge upp, en kamp för kärleken och det ljusa.

Annika Billberg, informatör på landstinget är glad över satsningen på en annorlunda landstingskatalog.

– Tidigare har vi haft fina genrebilder men det här är något fullständigt annorlunda. Vi är unika i Sverige med att satsa på en bildberättelse med tillhörande bildtexter. Och det är så fina bilder. Jan Nordström har gjort ett fantastiskt arbete. Liksom Ia Johannesson som har gjort layouten.

Jan Nordström säger att det är en ynnest att ha fått följa dessa tre människor i situationer där de är som mest utlämnade och har det svårt.

– Man har ett väldigt ansvar när man får lov att komma andra så nära. De vågar visa all sin glädje och sorg vilket gör dem väldigt utsatta. Jag känner en väldig ödmjukhet och respekt inför deras mod.

▶▶ Att få ta del av en annan människas liv på det här sättet berör en på djupet. De är så utsatta och ändå så otroligt modiga.

JAN NORDSTRÖM

Katalogen ligger i brevlådan hos alla i Kalmar län runt den 9–10 februari. Titta på bilderna och följ dessa modiga människor under några ögonblick av deras liv. Följ dem i vitt som med hjärtat vårdar andra.

Jan Nordströms bilder kommer även att ställas ut i entrén på länssjukhuset med vernissage den 8 februari och därefter kommer utställningen att turnera runt i länet.

Många, många borde se den.

PIA ANDERSSON HOBERT
pia.andersson.hobert@barometern.se
0480-59227

Vardagsrummet en tisdag. Dansar en stund. Älskar varandra.

FOTO: JAN NORDSTRÖM

28 SPORTEN | VASALOPPET

Måndag 3 mars 2003 | BAROMETERN-OT

VASALOPPET | SPORTEN 29

BAROMETERN-OT | Måndag 3 mars 2003

79:E VASALOPPET AVKLARAT

”Jag kör ju lite på rutin numera”

MORA
(Barometern-OT:s utsända)

För två år sedan halkade Erik Pettersson på vägen till starten och fick tillbringa dagen på sjukhuset i stället för i skidspåren.
I går genomförde ölänningen sitt 33:e Vasalopp.
– Det kändes ovanligt bra. Jag kör ju lite på rutin numera, man förtar sig inte precis.

Dramatisk start för Joakim Åleheim

Svärd i guldtårar efter klassisk spurt

Nummer 6635, Leif Rydholm från Nybro Ski, går i mål för 13:e gången. Han är nöjd men tillägger: ”De bästa killarna har varit i mål sedan länge nu”.

From *Barometern*: a spread from the “bonus” section (above) with a local story, and a spread from the Sports section (left).

Advertising campaign

The *Smålandsposten* tabloid was launched with a campaign produced by the advertising agency Ahlqvist & Co, exploiting the fact that in Swedish the word for "smaller" is the same as for "less." The words of the posters, therefore, are promising *less stress*, *smaller opponents*, *smaller wolves*, *less grey*, *smaller cars*, etc., promoting the newspaper's change to a smaller format.

3
Mindre stress
FGM 563
LÄNSTRAFIKEN KRONOBERG
Smålandsposten - i mindre format den 1 mars

smart
ROA 262
Mindre bilar
Smålandsposten
- i mindre format den 1 mars
Mindre bilar

Logotypes

The redesigns of the two nameplates were two very different tasks. In *Smålandsposten*'s case, I had to look for identity where it could hardly be found; this newspaper had never used anything but a plain sans serif logotype. In a way, the simpleness reflects how people in this part of Sweden see themselves; nevertheless, I think a logotype should always be more than just typing the name of the paper. Finally, I stumbled upon an old advertisement where, perhaps by coincidence, the letter Å looked awkward, thus emphazising the most characteristic sound when you pronounce the name: "Smoalandsposten." This became my clue to designing a nameplate with more personality and, at the same time, getting in tune with the new typography of the paper.

Barometern's logotype was quite the opposite: it had lots of personality and signaled one of the strongest brands of the Swedish provincial press. We agreed, however, that it needed a redesign; as a piece of graphic design, the execution had been rather amateurish right from the beginning, and years of reproduction and auto-tracing had not made things any better. The result, you might say, is an attempt to make a design that looks both old and new at the same time.

The ad that inspired the new *Smålandsposten* nameplate (right); and the before (top) and after (bottom) versions of the nameplate.

SMÅLANDSPOSTENS
ANNONS- OCH TRYCKERIKONTOR
SAMT REDAKTION
äro fr. o. m. fredagen den 22 sept. inflyttade i fastigheten
STORGATAN 1

TELEFONER:
Annons- och tryckerikontor: 103, 1090.
Redaktion: 182, 397, 1016.

SMÅLANDSPOSTEN

SMÅLANDSPOSTEN

Before (top) and after (bottom) nameplates for *Barometern*.

Barometern

Barometern

SPORTEN

Kalmargolfare tvåa på Europatouren

Kalmarhäst felade bort segerchansen

Stefan Holm visade nyfunnen hoppform

Guld – trots usel målgång

Jennie Lindh tog Kalmars första JSM-seger i simning i Sundsvall.

Elitfyran. Två sena mål satte punkt

Ölands fotbollsunder fortsätter imponera

Real Madrid vill värva drömelva

Barcelona kan få tysk landslagsmålvakt

Sverige vann ödesmatchen

Besviken Johansson ute ur Wimbledon

Entry points

As our original aim was to maximize the number of optical signals inviting readers into the pages, we introduced two new kinds of entry points: at *Smålandsposten*, the "fast lane" – an attempt to summarize the information of an entire page or double truck in one text box; at *Barometern*, the "window" – not a pullout quote, not a subhead, but a way to extract a particularly interesting piece of information from the article and place it, like a quote, in the middle of the body text. However, with the 2003 simplification of the *Barometern* design, the number of entry points was reduced. The "briefs shelf" topping each page had to go, too, as it turned out to be too time-consuming to produce the briefs.

Älmhult

Illegal handel allvarligt hot mot vilda fåglar

Sökes: Ensam berguvshanne

Kommunekologen hoppas att Selma hittar häckningspartner

En av världens största ugglor

175 berguvar har släppts fria i Småland

KONST I HALLEN

Sara Ljungblad och Johanna Weberg

Utställningen pågår 5-30 november 2001.

SMÅLANDSPOSTEN

Lessebo

Karateklubb på gång

Ungdomar kan prova på under påsklovet

Bejublad rollfigur på plats vid Kul Kultur

Lions stöttar kolloverksamhet

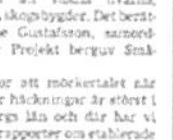

Uppvidinge

Fler spelningar lösningen på pengaproblem för blåsorkester

Bilist förd till sjukhus efter krock med buss

Hockeycoach fick ta emot ungdomsledarpris

SMÅLANDSPOSTEN B

Karl är kung i vattnet – älskar att dyka

Babysim ger barnet trygghet och vana vid vatten

William Shakespeares

Pages from *Barometern* (opposite) and *Smålandsposten* (above), showing a variety of entry points to the information on the pages.

pullout quotes, etc., we have introduced a couple of more unusual tools: at *Smålandsposten*, the "fast lane" summary; at *Barometern*, the "window," a particularly interesting piece of information placed in the middle of the body text.

At both *Smålandsposten* and *Barometern*, typographical simplicity has been an objective, to allow staffers to use as little time as possible on graphic design in order to concentrate on communication instead. As I said before, these newspapers are being laid out not by an art department, but by a rather small group of copyeditors, having neither the time nor the graphic skills for executing complicated layout rules and typeface combinations.

Barometern's typography is based on one sans serif for headlines (Poynter Agate) and one serif for body text (Utopia). David Berlow's Poynter Agate, originally designed for miniature type (as the name suggests), had proved to work astonishingly well as a headline face in the Spanish sports daily *Marca*. I showed the typeface to my client, who immediately fell in love with it. It seems to reflect a boldness which had, for years, been characterizing *Barometern*'s reporting without ever shining clearly through in the visual appearance of the newspaper.

The choice of Utopia for body text went smoothly, too; in *Barometern*'s rather poor printing, the new typeface appeared more readable than the old Gazette. We agreed, however, that as a headline face Utopia would not provide the desired contrast to Poynter Agate – and therefore decided to include Sabon as a slightly more sophisticated serif face for larger type, limiting the use of Utopia to sizes below 12 point.

Smålandsposten makes use of two sans serif typefaces and one serif face. The serif, Nimrod,

2 **LEDARE | OPINION**

Måndag 24 mars 2003 | **BAROMETERN-OT** | Politisk chefredaktör: Per Dahl 0480–592 11 | Politisk redaktör: Sylvia Asklöf 0480–591 44 | E-post: opinion@barometern.se | Fax: 0480-864 06

Att vinna freden

Konflikten avgörs inte i Irak utan i arabvärldens kåkstäder

Utgången av den första fasen av Irakkonflikten är given: en ny regim kommer att ta över efter Saddam Husseins skräckvälde. Men vilken roll kommer USA och Storbritannien att spela i bakgrunden? Det som beslutas här kommer att ha stor påverkan på västs framtida relationer med den islamska världen.

Vissa grupper i USA för nu fram en ny term: "nationsbyggande". Skulle inte USA kunna få demokratin att gro i Irak likaväl som man fick den att ta sig igen i Tyskland och Japan åren efter 1945? I viss retorik framställs till och med detta som USA:s nya uppgift i världen: att säkra demokratin varhelst denna är hotad.

Resonemanget bortser från ett viktigt faktum, den besegrade regimens ställning i världen. Både Tyskland och Japan hade under år underkuvat sina grannar och terroriserat folken i ett vitt område runt det egna landet. Icke någon folkgrupp någonstans såg 1945 upp till Berlin eller Tokyo. Den samhällsomvandling som skedde hade omvärldens fulla stöd.

Västs relationer till den arabvärlden avgörs dock inte av meningen bland Iraks under lång tid förtryckta shiamuslimer, sunnimuslimer, kristna eller kurder. De vet mer än väl vad Saddam gick för. De som lidit av hans krig mot Iran och Kuwait vet det också. Men för miljontals fattiga i läger och kåkstäder från Kairo till Karachi har Saddam inte varit förtryckaren utan hoppet, den som förde arabvärldens talan. De har nåtts av hans propaganda, inte av hans terror.

De grupperna kan utöva ett starkt tryck på sina regimer och omgivande samhällen. Inte inom respektive lands etablerade politik, men ideologiskt och propagandamässigt, med den fattiges moraliska auktoritet. Och det är i dessa hopplöshetens miljöer terrorceller växer och förökar sig.

I helgens Dagens Industri varnar en debattör för följderna av den lösning som Tony Blair nu förespråkar: att Iraks oljeinkomster läggs i en FN-fond, som får bekosta återuppbyggnaden. FN är i sig inte fel. Men, förmodar skribenten, det finns risk att resurserna huvudsakligen går till amerikanska och brittiska företag. Och att fonden också får bekosta USA:s och Storbritanniens fortsatta övervakning av landet.

Om denna farhåga är berättigad eller ej är svårt att säga. Men skribenten pekar på den stora fara som ligger i att ett enskilt land, då i synnerhet USA, dröjer kvar med sitt engagemang i Irak. Ansvaret för återuppbyggnad och den reella makten över Iraks resurser måste lämnas över till irakier. Och det internationella stödet gå via FN utan slagsida för enskilda länder, eller favoriserande av de stater som nu deltar i kriget. Det kommer annars att bli mycket svårt att undvika bilden av att de segrande staterna också är de som tar befälet över Iraks ekonomi och oljeresurser.

Kanske kommer då de ytliga demokratiseringstecknen att ta längre tid. Irak kommer kanske inte att gå i Japans och Tysklands fotspår. Men landet kommer heller inte att ses som en marionettstat av den övriga arabvärlden. Och det kan finnas chans att övertyga om att befrielsen från hot och förtryck var ett tyngre skäl än Saddams försök att utmana en västlig världsordning.

Barometern

Grundad av Jon Engström 1841
Södra Långgatan 33
Postadress: 391 88 Kalmar
0480–591 00
Internet: http://www.barometern.se
Efter växelns stängning

Nattchef	0480–592 31
Sport	0480–592 52
Fax	0480–864 06
Radiotidning	0480–592 59

CHEFREDAKTÖR och TIDNINGSCHEF
ansvarig utgivare
GUNILLA ANDREASSON
chefred@barometern.se

Redaktionschef, stf ansvarig utgivare
PÅR ARGUS
palle.argus@barometern.se

Politisk chefredaktör
PER DAHL
per.dahl@barometern.se

Vd Sydostpress AB
BENNIE OHLSSON
bennie.ohlsson@sydostpress.se

Oskarshamns-Tidningen

Grundad av Mauritz Linder 1880
Trädgårdsgatan 1 Postadress: Box 922, 572 29 Oskarshamn
0491–872 50
Internet: http://www.barometern.se
Efter växelns stängning

Nyhetsredaktion	0491–872 69
Sport	0491–872 68
Nattchef	0480–592 31
Fax	0491–872 66

▶ För insänt ej beställt material ansvaras ej
▶ Allt material i Barometern och Oskarshamns-Tidningen lagras digitalt och publiceras och tillhandahålls i digitala medier liksom i arkivdatabas. Den som sänder material till tidningen anses medge sådan digital lagring och publicering samt sådant tillhandahållande.

Pressombudsmannen, adress:
PO, Allmänhetens Pressombudsman, Box 12708, 112 21 Stockholm

Vid utebliven tidning
Ring 020–22 33 10
(må–lö 7–10, sö stängt)
E-post tidning.sydost@predist.se

Prenumeration 020-22 33 00
(må–fr 8–17, lö–sö stängt)
E-post kundcenter@barometern.se

Prenumerationspriser
Helår 1 795:- Halvår 999:- Tre mån 579:- Månadskonto 152:- (from 1/9 2002)
Alla priser inkl moms

Annonsavdelningen: 0480–59 100
Öppen helgfri mån–fre 08–17
Rubrik- och familjeannonser:
020–22 33 00 fax: 0480–297 63

Skatt på vinster i Barometern-OT:s tävlingar betalas av vinnaren

▶ ORDET ÄR MITT | **Per Dahl, politisk chefredaktör**

Svegfors och Sverigebilden – en ny historia

▶ Jag läser en skrift om EMU av Mats Svegfors, tidigare inflytelserik i moderat, nu landshövding i Västmanland. Det är en egenartad upplevelse, för häftet handlar om det mesta utom EMU. Mest av allt om Sverige och dess plats i världen.

Jag menar inte att vara elak när jag skriver att Mats Svegfors argument tycks mig slående lika de lundaprofessorn Fredrik Böök en gång förde fram om Sverige, och Historiens utveckling. Sverige borde inse, sade Böök, att Historien nu ändras. Antingen tar man smyghuvat avstånd från det som formar Framtiden. Eller så accepterar man Förändringen och Historiens Nödvändighet. Det mest kända tysklandsvänliga talet hölls under något av 1940-talets första år.

Det vore mig fjärran att utmåla Svegfors som arvtagare till de sympatierna. Men i synen på det historiska skeendet som tvingande kraft finns likheter. Vad som erbjuds, är att acceptera det nödvändiga, menar Svegfors. Moderniseringsprocessen mot det förenade Europa rullar på. De bäst anpassade vinner.

Svegfors citerar Marquis Childs om "Sweden – the middle way". Han talar sig varm om det moderniseringsprojekt som socialdemokratin startade. Det som ger det svenska innebörd är sådant som rationalitet, framtidsinriktning, värderingsfrihet, objektivt handlande.

Här ligger Svegfors storhet och begränsning. Få kan som han och identifierar sig som han med den svenska modernismen. Från Stockholmsutställningen och tidskriften "acceptera" till det sena nittonhundratalets uppbrott. Det är hans Folkhem och han försvarar dess värde. Men ska inte vår identitet och självkänsla brytas måste vi vidare med nästa stora moderniseringsprojekt, Det förenade Europa. Och vi är sent anlända i Europa!

Är vi? Undrar jag. Någon mil österut från mitt arbetsrum ligger Ölands gamla centralpunkt under järnåldern. De romerska importfynden ingår i dag i vårt kulturarv. 50 meter ifrån mig står en av Sveriges finaste italienska barockkatedraler, ritad av en Tessin hemkommen från Rom. Nere på Stensö kan jag betrakta Ludvig XVIII:s minnessten. Tre minuter från tidningen ligger hotell Witt, där en från Ryssland hemkommen löjtnant rörde ihop den första biff Lindström. I stort sett i varje kvarter, hörn och gata ser vi lämningarna av sekel av kontakter med Baltikum, Polen, Tyskland, Frankrike... "Nykomlingar i Europa?"

▶▶ **"Och mörkret skildes från ljuset, landet från staden, fritiden från arbetet, skatten från lönen"**

Men däremot tycks Mats Svegfors präglas av en historiesyn värdig en nykomling till världen. Allt var öde och mörker. Men Hjalmar Branting sade "Varde socialdemokrati". Och det vart socialdemokrati. Och mörkret skildes från ljuset, landet från staden, fritiden från arbetet, skatten från lönen. Och människan sattes i socialdemokratin och fick uppdraget att genom arbetarrörelsen behärska samhället. Och på sjunde dagen kunde efterträdaren Hansson betrakta det skapade och säga sig att det var gott.

Svegfors kan tycka till om euron. Men bevare det samhälle som präglas av hans inskränkta Sverigebild!

▶ CITATET

"Respekten för människoliv behöver förstärkas, inte försvagas. Därför var det rätt att döma 22-åringen till fängelse, även om det är fullt möjligt att förstå den förtvivlan som ligger bakom hans handling" DAGEN

Ett ben mer eller mindre...

▶ Åter ett fall med vanvård av en gammal kvinna. Denna gång hade hon brutit foten. I fem månader låg hon på sjukhem utan att få rätt behandling. Nu är hennes underben amputerat.

Den läkare som ansvarade för sjukhemmets boende hade ansvar för 210 människor. Man läkaren saknade relevant specialistkompetens för sin uppgift.

Kvinnan remitterades till sjukhus. Där mötte hon en AT-läkare på akuten, alltså en läkare som ännu inte är fullärd. Läkaren hade bara varit på akuten i fem dagar. Det var meningen att kvinnans fot skulle röntgas. Men ett missförstånd gjorde att undersökningen glömdes bort. På sjukhemmet hann man sedan med att göra tolv (12!) journalanteckningar om att kvinnan kände smärtor i foten och benet. Ett sår som varade sig medförde slutligen att hon sändes till Sahlgrenska sjukhuset i Göteborg, där ett ben fick kapas.

Vi hör då och då anklagelser om att de som vill förändra vården skulle hota dess kvalitet. Vilken kvalitet, undrar man när man läser telegram som dessa. Just det, "dessa"! Inte bara ett, inte bara två, utan en jämn ström av rapporter om vanvård av gamla människor.

Svensk sjukvård är ofta mycket bra, i synnerhet för den som råkar ut för en akut åkomma. Men den som är beroende av fungerande vårdkedjor och samarbete mellan sjukhus och långvård och primärvård har andra villkor i vårdens vardag. Här har alla reformers svallvågor slagit sönder många av de kontakter och den personkunskap som är absolut nödvändig.

Borde mindre politisering och ökad möjlighet för vården att själv finna fungerande former vara ett av alla accepterat grundkrav?

Page two of *Barometern* (above), with opinion pieces; page spreads of local news from *Smålandsposten* (opposite).

4 Smålandsposten | Fredag 10 januari 2003

Växjö

Byggfråga snabbutreds

Växjös kommunledning vill inte ge tummen ner till tre åttavåningshus vid järnvägsbranten på Södra Järnvägsgatan.

I stället ska man snabbutreda om det går att lösa alla intressefrågor i sammanhanget.

Det beslöt kommunstyrelsens arbetsutskott på torsdagen och gav kommunledningskontorets tjänstemän uppdraget att göra en förstudie med redovisning i april.

Förstudien ska ge politikerna en översiktlig bedömning över huruvida det går att förena nya bostäder med parkeringsbehoven på bangården samtidigt som man säkrar järnvägens framtida markbehov.

– Det är vår förhoppning att vi ska kunna tillgodose alla intressen, säger kommunstyrelsens ordförande, Carl-Olof Bengtsson (s).

Växjöbo klagar på skogsarbete

Arbeten med skog och äng måste göras på vintern, den lämpligaste tiden för många arbeten.

Så förklarar kommunekolog Lars Andersson varför skogsarbetare är ute på skilda håll i kommunens marker.

En Växjöbo har klagat över att det huggs och röjs vid Växjö golfbana vid Araby.

Han kommer inte fram så bra i spåren då ris och träd ligger i vägen.

– Man måste då och då gallra lövträd och man måste öppna vissa slåtterytor. Allt detta görs bäst vid kyla då marken är hård och inte så sårbar, säger Lars Andersson.

Vi väntar tills gymnasiekommittén presenterat sitt betänkande. Så har Växjös skolpolitiker resonerat och de är inte ensamma. Statliga beslut har stor betydelse för kommunala framtidsfrågor. Men nu kan gymnasiepolitikerna sluta vänta. I dag ska allt avslöjas.

Gymnasieelevernas framtida studievägar presenteras i dag

Den parlamentariska kommittén lämnar betänkandet till Thomas Östros • Nu återstår den långa vägen till beslut

Den 4 maj år 2000 beslöt regeringen låta en parlamentarisk kommitté utreda vilka studievägar den framtida gymnasieskolan skulle erbjuda. I dag, den 10 januari år 2003, lämnar kommittén sitt betänkande till utbildningsminister Thomas Östros. Men det kan dröja många år innan förslagen förverkligas, och kritiker har redan hört av sig.

Av Elisabeth Cederholm
elisabeth.cederholm@smp.se
0470-77 06 19

Det betänkande som läggs fram i eftermiddag är en rejäl pappersbunta som många väntat på och spekulerat kring de senaste åren. Inte en skolkonferens har hållits utan att gymnasiekommittén nämnts i ett eller annat sammanhang.

På Växjös två senaste rikskonferenser har kommitténs ordförande Jan Björkman berättat – om än i försiktiga ordalag – om hur arbetet fortskridit.

Nya direktiv kom

Kommittén skulle ha jobbat färdigt för länge sedan, men när de trodde de var klara kom nya tilläggsdirektiv.

Förutom förslaget till struktur för den nya gymnasieskolan ville regeringen i februari 2001 också …

Många förslag redan kända

Alla är med – utom folkpartiet

Vad hade du föreslagit om du hade suttit med i gymnasiekommittén? Vi frågade några elever och anställda vid Växjös gymnasieskolor

Växjö | 5 Fredag 10 januari 2003 | Smålandsposten

Sensus söker bidrag för studier

4 Smålandsposten | Onsdag 19 mars 2003

Växjö

Anställd vid polisen bluffade med kuvert

Är det rätt av USA och Storbritannien att börja ett krig mot Irak? Vilka är de egentliga motiven till det? Och vad händer med FN om världssamfundet nu blir marginaliserat? Vi ställde frågan till några slumpvis utvalda personer i Växjö i går.

Payman och Fathi Karim framför sin jourbutik på Öster i Växjö, en lugn vrå av världen långt från krigshot, övergrepp och svält. Fathi kom till Sverige som desertör från Saddam Husseins armé i Irak.

Payman och Fathi från Irak vill återvända för gott efter kriget

"Man undrar vilket land de ska gå i krig mot härnäst"

"Det känns som det mera handlar om ekonomin än om kamp mot terrorism"

Protester planeras

Växjö | 5 Onsdag 19 mars 2003 | Smålandsposten

Befrielsen har börjat

Desinformation om biblioteken

Krönika

Castro passar på

Citat ur pressen

SMÅLANDSPOSTEN

---

* VECKA 4 · NR 16 · 21 JANUARI 2003 tisdag

SMÅLANDSPOSTEN

Flicklego irriterar politiker

Foto: STEFAN NILSSON

Leksakstillverkaren Legos nya flicklego behöver inte byggas. Barnen kan gå direkt på rolleken – som oftast innebär att leka prinsessa.

Det har retat upp Kristina Knöös-Franzén, moderat ledamot i jämställdhetskommittén som nu kräver att Växjö kommun agerar.

– I och med att lego används på kommunens förskolor så måste vi reagera. Flickor är faktiskt precis lika kluriga som pojkar.

Men Cornelia Nyman, 9 (bilden) skulle inte tacka nej till ett, nästan färdigbyggt sagoslott.

DEL A, SIDAN 5

Studenter utan engagemang

Utbildning utan bildning. Så verkar vardagen och verkligheten se ut för de flesta av Växjös studenter visar en ny rapport från Växjö universitet. Studenterna engagerar sig varken politiskt eller kulturellt, utan ägnar sig åt träning, öl och video på vägen mot ett välbetalt jobb. Kulturiksidan undrar vart bildningen, poesiaftnarna och det kritiska ifrågasättandet tog vägen.

DEL A, SIDORNA 22 OCH 23

GRUNDAD 1866 www.smp.se håller dig ständigt uppdaterad · Telefon 0470-77 05 00 · Vardag 12:- Lördag 15:-

Projekt läggs ner – konsult försvann

Vårdsektorn behöver rekrytera mycket personal de närmaste åren. För att underlätta arbetet satsade Landstinget Kronoberg på projektet Män och kvinnor i vården. 180 ungdomar intervjuades om sin syn på vårdyrket. Men konsulten som skulle analysera svaren försvann. Nu har projektet avbrutits och landstinget måste betala tillbaka 100 000 kronor av EU-medel.

DEL A, SIDAN 4

Försäkringskassan nerringd

Informationen om det nya pensionssystemet svår att förstå

Försäkringskassan i Kronoberg upplever sin värsta telefonanstormning någonsin. Sedan mitten av december har 20 pensionsutbetalare i genomsnitt tagit emot mellan 300 och 400 samtal per dag om det nya pensionssystemet.

– Vi har aldrig upplevt något liknande. Även om vi var förberedda trodde vi inte att behovet av information var så stort, säger Lennart Emriksson, chef på Försäkringskassan i Växjö.

Han håller med om att den information som gått ut till länets 33 000 berörda pensionärer är svår att förstå.

– Det hade varit en fördel om insättningsbeskeden från försäkringskassan, statliga SPV och kommunala KPA hade gått ut samtidigt. Dessutom kom beskeden från försäkringskassan tidigt medan beskeden från SPV och KPA kom betydligt senare. Detta ökade osäkerheten, säger Lennart Emriksson.

DEL A, SIDAN 4

Prisad: Carolina Klüft störst vid idrottsgalan

Foto: PRESSENS BILD

Svensk friidrott är större än någonsin. Det blev måndagskvällen ännu ett bevis på. Och störst är Carolina Klüft. Hon vann tre priser vid idrottsgalan i Globen – bland annat Jerringpriset.

–Det är ett fantastiskt pris att få när svenska folket får rösta. Jag ska verkligen försöka förvalta ert förtroende, sade Klüft i sitt tacktal.

Förra gången hon var på plats vid idrottsgalan fick hon ta emot priset som årets nykomling. Den här kvällen blev det mer – mycket mer – för sjukamperskan från Växjö. På bilden också prisutdelaren Pernilla Wiberg.

SPORTEN

Trensums slapp konkurs

En hotande konkurs avvärjdes när Växjö tingsrätt i går medgav fortsatt rekonstruktionsarbete av Trensums Food AB i Tingsryd. Antalet anställda uppges till drygt 130.

Någon andhämtningspaus är det inte frågan om. Den av Växjö tingsrätt redan tidigare utsedda rekonstruktören, advokat Erik Fock från Linköping, lovar ett stålbad.

DEL B, SIDAN 5

Boss Media nyanställer

Boss Media har fått sin finaste order. Tillsammans med kasinot i Monte Carlo ska det Växjöbaserade företaget utveckla och lansera ett Internetbaserat system som kommer att drivas från furstendömet Monaco.

Eftersom orderingången även i övrigt ökar ska Boss Media under våren nyanställa tiotalet tekniker, vilket innebär att antalet anställda på huvudkontoret ökar från nuvarande 80 till cirka 90.

– Just nu pekar det mesta uppåt, säger Peter Bertilsson, vd för Boss Media.

DEL A, SIDAN 16

”Säg nej till EMU, det ger ändå ingen fred men väl en rad ekonomiskt negativa effekter. Säg i stället ja till Nato, som nu mer än någonsin står som garant för freden.

DEBATT – DEL B, SIDAN 18

VÄDRET
Regn

DEL B, SIDAN 20

was already used as the body face in the broadsheet version. In the early stages of the redesign, Anders Tapola and I worked on the assumption that Gerard Unger's Swift would form *Smålands-posten*'s new typographical identity, to be used for body type as well as (in a condensed display version) headlines. Poynter Gothic was introduced as a complementary sans serif for subheads, captions, etc. However, despite numerous attempts, we did not manage to convince Anders's colleagues that Swift was as legible as their good old Nimrod. The final rejection of Swift left us with neither body nor headline face. I spent a number of weeks in the search for a typeface having as much legibility and character as Swift, and at the same time getting along with Nimrod and Poynter Gothic, with which we had now come quite a long way.

Finally, a colleague drew my attention to a brand new condensed sans serif out of Lucas de Groot's Thesis family: TheSans Condensed. The response in Växjö was similar to the way my client in Kalmar had reacted to Poynter Agate one month earlier: they simply adored it. Moreover, TheSans Condensed appeared to go surprisingly well along with Poynter Gothic, the latter being used only in small point sizes and the former exclusively for headlines. Not having to change the entire setup saved us precious time at this rather late stage of the design process.

The troika of Nimrod, Poynter Gothic, and TheSans Condensed appeared to offer solutions to all our typographical problems except one: the 20-point subhead, floating in the grey area between micro and macro typography. In a size like this, Poynter Gothic would not suit a headline set in TheSans Condensed. We decided to include a regular-width version of TheSans to solve the problem.

6 | SPORTEN
Måndag 3 mars 2003

IFK Växjö tog tio medaljer

IFK Växjö är tveklöst en av landets bästa friidrottsklubbar. I inomhus-SM tog man tio medaljer – tre guld och sju silver.

Medaljerna
Carolina Klüft: guld – längd, silver – höjd, silver – 60 m häck, silver – 200 m.
Camilla Johansson: guld – tresteg, silver – längd.
Malin Öhrn: guld – 3 000 m.
Per Karlsson: silver – vikt.
Erica Mårtensson: silver – 400 m.
Linda Persson: silver – stav.

Ett guld och tre silver till Carolina Klüft

Förbundskaptenen tycker att

Växjö har bra friidrottsklimat

SPORTEN | 7
Måndag 3 mars 2003

Stark inledning av SM-helgen

Camilla Johansson guld. Malin Öhrn Guld. Carolina Klüft silver.

Kajsa Bergqvist satte rekordsvit

Till publikens stora glädje bestämde sig till slut Kajsa Bergqvist för ställa upp i SM. Vilket slutade med rekordsvit.

Page two and front page from *Smålands-posten* (opposite), and a spread from the sports section (above).

The continuation

The two new tabloids were introduced right on schedule, in the spring of 2001. Two years later, the publishers seem satisfied with the result even though circulation has not gone up; in the current situation of the Swedish newspaper market, a status quo is considered a success.

Layout appears to be easier with the new format, according to the editors. As a rule, the papers are laid out in spreads rather than single pages, and many stories are visually planned at early stages.

Then what about identity? Have *Barometern* and *Smålandsposten* lost their soul, given the fact that virtually everything changed with the redesign?

Apparently not. To quote *Smålandsposten* editor-in-chief Ulf Johansson: "The tabloid clearly appears more modern and more alert. Still, readers feel familiar with it and are content and confident with the new *Smålandsposten*." At the 2002 Newspaper Design of the Year contest arranged by the Society for News Design/ Scandinavia, *Smålandsposten* was awarded silver in the redesign category and *Barometern* received an award of excellence.

In keeping with the original intentions, the design development at the Sydostpress papers continues. In November–December 2002, adjustments were made in the *Barometern* design in order to make the pages less noisy and easier to lay out. Cutbacks in staff were among the reasons for these adjustments, which were executed by Herbert Tinz, the paper's new picture and layout editor, with me as consultant. Most of the pages shown in this book are from 2003 issues, produced after these adjustments had been implemented.

Despite spending cuts, the design education is being continued, too – now more in the form of a workshop. As might be expected in a changing industry, a couple of replacements have been necessary in our group; nevertheless, we believe our goal is within reach. Soon, the design future of the Sydostpress papers will no longer be dependent on outside assistance. ‹

34 Smålandsposten | Torsdag 20 mars 2003

KULTUR | 35 Torsdag 20 mars 2003 | Smålandsposten

Kultur

FOTOGRAFEN MALICK SIDIBÉ från Bamako, Mali blir 2003 års Hasselbladspristagare. "Malick Sidibé har dokumenterat en viktig period i Västafrikas historia med stark inlevelse, värme och entusiasm" skriver juryn. Priset delas ut 25 oktober och då öppnas samtidigt en utställning med Sidibés bilder i Hasselblad center i Göteborgs konstmuseum.

Kulturredaktör Camilla Carnmo
E-post camilla.carnmo@smp.se
Tel 0470-77 06 14

När nu USA på nytt riktar vapen mot Irak råder ännu hårdare restriktioner. Så om medierna upplevde att Pentagon hade "total kontroll" över Gulfkriget – hur blir då rapporteringen från denna konflikt, där informationsflödet strypts ännu mer?

Medierna rapporterar

KARYN BOSNAK tänkte efter. Hade hon festat för mycket? Hade hon köpt för många skor? Antagligen. Hur som helst ville banken ha 170 000 kronor – pengar som hon gjort slut på för länge sedan.

Lösningen blev att be om hjälp på internet. 23 juni förra året lanserade hon sin kampanj "Save Karyn", där hon bad de som besökte hennes sajt att skicka pengar. Ett halvår senare kunde hon betala sina skulder.

Makalöst. Men värt en tanke. För om folk är villiga att betala okända människors shoppingräkningar kanske de också är beredda att göra vettiga saker. Som att till exempel skicka en oberoende reporter till Irak.

Christopher Allbritton sitter just nu i New Yorks East Village och håller tummarna för just detta. Medan reportrarna från de stora mediebolagen forslas längs säkra rutter under beskydd av amerikanska soldater, planerar Allbritton, tidigare reporter på *New York Daily News*, att lifta och muta sig fram till norra Irak för att där bevaka humanitära frågor snarare än krigsstrategiska.

Allbritton är utrustad med mobiltelefon och bärbar dator. Han tänker publicera texterna på sin web-log, "Back to Iraq 2.0".

OM HANS LÄSARE skickar iväg honom (det ser lovande ut, hittills har han fått in drygt 45 000 kronor) kommer Allbritton att bli den förste oberoende krigskorrespondenten på internet.

Den förste oberoende internetjournalisten är han dock inte. Sedan vågen med web-logs startade för något år sedan har nätet fyllts av amatörjournalistik.

Web-logs eller "blogs" är sajter med ett slags snabba dagboksanteckningar som alla kan klara av att skapa.

Detta dagboksskrivande fick sitt stora genombrott den 11 september, då hundratusentals amerikaner började bearbeta sina upplevelser.

Utan att de själva hade en aning om det, levererade de just den sortens texter som de stora tidningarna letade efter: personliga skildringar, fulla av liv och närvaro.

SAMTIDIGT SOM web-logs-skrivandet sköt i höjden (i dag är långt över en miljon människor aktiva) skapades en ny sorts amatörjournalistik som i ett slag plötsligt fanns överallt. För när en miljon människor dagligen skildrar sin verklighet är det dags för elitjournalisterna att se upp. Inte ens den samlade mediekåren i världen kan nämligen uppbringa en miljon reportrar.

För ett tag sedan köpte dessutom sökmotorn Google det ledande weblogsförtaget Pyra, vilket med stor sannolikhet betyder att amatörernas texter kommer att dyka upp som träffar när man letar efter information på Google.com. För första gången likställda med elitjournalisternas.

Göteborgskravallerna visade tydligt vilken betydelse amatörjournalistiken kan ha. De vanliga mediernas reportrar gav till en början endast ett polisperspektiv på händelserna, men bara efter några dagar ändrades allt – tack vare demonstranternas egna filmer och berättelser som fanns utlagda på nätet.

MEN TILLBAKA till Irak för ett ögonblick. För vad är det för perspektiv som förmedlas från denna konflikt, som ju trots allt har hela världens ögon på sig?

Ja, det är inte så allsidigt som man skulle kunna förmoda. Eller ha rätt att kräva.

Två månader efter Gulfkriget skickade 15 amerikanska chefredaktörer en skarp protest till dåvarande försvarsministern **Dick Cheney**.

Chefredaktörerna, som företrädde några av de största nyhetsorganisationerna i USA, slog fast att Pentagon hade haft i det närmaste total kontroll över krigsrapporteringen, vilket omöjliggjort varje form av kritisk granskning.

När nu USA på nytt riktar vapen mot Irak råder ännu hårdare restriktioner. Så om medierna upplevde att Pentagon hade "total kontroll" över Gulfkriget – hur blir då rapporteringen från denna konflikt, där informationsflödet strypts ännu mer?

Det hade varit fullt förståeligt om ledande medier riktat starka protester mot varje försök att krympa de redan små bevakningsmöjligheterna. Men situationen har faktiskt varit den omvända.

Ända sedan den 11 september har de amerikanska medieföretagen helhjärtat ställt upp på en rad eftergifter (till exempel gick ABC, CBS, NBC, Fox och CNN genast med på att stämma av med regeringen innan de visade bandupptagningar från **Usama bin Ladin**). Man är med på noterna, helt enkelt. Och det är från dessa källor som svenska medier hämtar sitt stoff.

I ETT ÖPPET brev till de amerikanska medierna gick en rad journalister, forskare och politiker (bland annat **Studs Terkel** och **Ralph Nader**) nyligen till angrepp mot vad de anser vara en bristande rapportering.

Undertecknarna hävdar att medierna nu gör om samma misstag som under Gulfkriget: de väljer att betona militära strategier snarare än att göra politiska analyser och de varken klagar på eller rapporterar om regeringens kontroll över informationen.

Intressant nog har internettrafiken till oberoende och radikala nyhetssajter ökat markant den senaste tiden. Folk söker sig till nätet för att få en annan version av verkligheten än den som serveras i de breda massmedierna.

REPORTERN Christopher Allbrittons enmansexpedition är ur det perspektivet talande för tiden. Den pekar på milsvida skillnader från Gulfkriget – då fanns ju inte ens en debatt om mediernas trovärdighet, den kom först då kriget var avslutat och forskare sakta började ifrågasätta CNN:s vinklingar.

Nu, år 2003, tar människor i stället själv tag i saken för att förändra mediernas bild av verkligheten. En tröst så god som någon, i tider som dessa.

Anders Mildner

Illustration: SUSANNE SVENSSON

Tranströmers transatlantiska tvivel

Inlåst i ett hörn av alla tvärsäkra ledarskribenter och talskrivare, krigshetsare och motdemonstranter plockar jag fram mitt sönderfallande exemplar av **Tomas Tranströmers** samlade dikter. Plötsligt slås fönstren upp! Poesin talar om världen, resten är bara verklighetsflykt.

Också i *Airmail*, den publicerade brevväxlingen mellan Tranströmer och den amerikanske poeten **Robert Bly**, finns rader som bryter sig loss ur samtidens monotona textmassa och låter tvivlet, tveksamheten, förvirringen lysa i eldskrift.

Det handlar om Vietnam men kunde lika gärna vara det planerade kriget i Irak. Bly engagerar sig mot kriget från sitt amerikanska perspektiv.

Tranströmer är lika kritisk och personligt berörd. Samtidigt känner han sig kvävd i det svenska kulturklimat som kräver mangrann och reflektionslös uppslutning bakom en antiamerikansk retorik.

"I detta klimatet gäller allt eller intet. Den som inte är 100% för är, i själva verket, 100% emot", skriver han vintern 1968. Och lite längre fram: "Det enda man kan göra är att följa sitt eget krokiga samvete, vänta på the moment of truth och hoppas att man inte ska behöva skämmas en gång för hur man genomlevde de här åren".

Bly i sin tur levererar en teori om kriget, dess förespråkare och motståndare, som låter skrämmande aktuell: "Vi [amerikaner] är fast beslutna att skämma ut oss och tänker inte låta någonting hejda oss. Vi gör det i stället för européerna, åt dem. Européerna har skämt ut sig så mycket att det har fått nog nu".

David Björklund

Foto: PRESSENS BILD

Tomas Tranströmer.

Den tredje ståndpunkten

I skuggan av det krig som i skrivande stund står och skramlar i kulisserna (och i läsande kanske redan gjort entré), har den ryktbara/beryktade "tredje ståndpunkten" ånyo bildat ett fruktbart/fruktlöst diskussionsunderlag, bland annat på *DN*:s kultursidor.

Det rör sig alltså om den moraliska hållning som vill markera en politiskt obändig neutralitet mellan två stormakter, ursprungligen initierad i den ideologiska konflikten mellan öst och väst under kalla kriget.

Bland svenska författare hörde som bekant **Karl Vennberg** till de mest hängivna förespråkarna för tredje ståndpunkten, medan **Eyvind Johnson** – åtminstone i detta avseende övertygad pro-amerikan – var en av dess ivrigaste kritiker.

Söker man efter ett slags poetologisk och transcendental motsvarighet till denna tredje ståndpunkt, hamnar vi omedelbart hos **Gunnar Ekelöf** och hans existentiellt "objektiva" position och närmast orakelmässiga upphävning av dialektiska element som liv–död (Demokrati–Diktatur), vitt–svart (USA–Irak), riddare–drake (**Bush–Saddam**). "Liv är varken ett ont eller ett gott, det är mälden mellan stenarna", står det att läsa i den epokbildande diktsamlingen *Färjesång* (som för övrigt skrevs när andra världskriget rasade som värst).

Men frågan är om inte vår käre **Gustaf Fröding** klår sin diktarbroder vad gäller framsynta anmärkningar till världspolitiska konflikter, åtminstone att döma av ungdomsdikten *Hök och duva* (uppenbarligen tillägnad vår tids mäktiga och minst sagt handlingsdugliga första-och-andra-ståndpunkts-ivrare:

"Giv höken svag och mjölig mat,
den djärve jägarn skall bli lugn och lat
/---/ Och se, och se, hur duvonäbben kröks, den spetsas till, förlängs, det är en höks!"

Martin Lagerholm

Frågan är om inte Gustaf Fröding slår sin diktarbroder Gunnar Ekelöf i framsynta kommentarer.

A page spread from the Culture section of *Smålandsposten*.

guidewednesday Eight pages of the best TV, cinema and entertainment listings in G2

45p
Wednesday
December 22 1999
Published in London
and Manchester
www.guardian.co.uk
Newspaper
of the Year

The Guardian

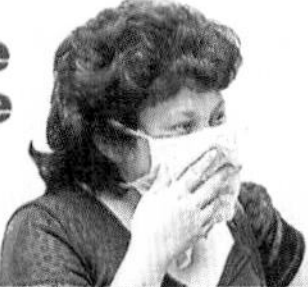

1999 — the year of the disaster In G2

Polly Toynbee — hands off the NHS Page 16

Snow White and the Dwarf shortage In G2

and in society The mother of mothers

A greedy, corrupt liar

Hamilton faces ruin after jury unanimously finds he took cash for questions

Matt Wells, Jamie Wilson and **David Pallister**

Neil Hamilton's five-year fight to clear his name ended in ignominious defeat and financial ruin last night when a high court jury unanimously declared the former Conservative MP corrupt.

The result ended any hopes he may have harboured of resuming his political career, condemning him as a greedy man who had been "on the make and on the take" during his time in parliament.

The verdict, delivered in the highly charged atmosphere of a crowded court 13 at the high court in London, was a dramatic finale to the bruising five-week libel trial brought by the former minister against the owner of Harrods, Mohamed Al Fayed. It brought to an end his protracted battle to clear his name of the cash-for-questions controversy first reported by the Guardian in 1994.

After almost nine hours of deliberation, the jury returned to court yesterday to deliver its verdict. Asked whether members had found "on the balance of probabilities" that Mr Fayed had established corruption by Mr Hamilton "on highly convincing evidence", their forewoman replied: "Yes."

Sitting in the front of the court, Mr Hamilton and his distraught wife, Christine, looked on in disbelief. She held her face in her hands and he repeatedly shook his head. As the jury filed out, the couple stared intensely at them and then retreated through the corridors of the court to consult with their lawyers.

As the Hamiltons continued to protest their innocence of corruption, outside the court Mr Fayed — who had been accused of being "the biggest crook in town" and a Jekyll and Hyde character — arrived jubilant. Bowing on the steps of the court, he wished everyone a merry Christmas. Of Mr Hamilton, he said: "He knows he is corrupt. People like that should never be in power."

Mr Hamilton sued Mr Fayed over claims he made in a Dispatches documentary broadcast on Channel 4 in 1997 that the former MP had demanded and received thousands of pounds in cash, Harrods gift vouchers and hospitality at the Ritz hotel in Paris, in return for parliamentary services.

Mr Fayed pleaded justification —that the allegations were true.

The clinching piece of evidence in the case — introduced on subpoena only days before the trial began — concerned Mr Hamilton's claim that he had a legitimate consultancy with Mobil Oil in 1989.

It later emerged that he had done little more for the company than to table an amendment to that year's finance bill, for which he later demanded payment. Under ancient parliamentary rules taking cash solely for parliamentary action is corrupt.

Minutes before the jury said it was ready to deliver the verdict, its members were still divided: in a note to the judge, they asked whether they could disregard the adjective "highly" in the question put to them about convincing evidence. Mr Justice Morland refused their request.

Emerging from the court, Mr Hamilton faced journalists with a grim smile.

With his wife beside him, he said: "I would never have embarked on this action had I been guilty of the charges against me. I do not regret bringing the case, of course, because I could not have gone through life without straining every sinew to do everything that was possible to bring the truth out. Sadly the jury were not convinced.

"The waters were muddied at the very beginning of the trial when, on to Mr Fayed's allegations were clamped entirely unrelated ones connected to a consultancy I had with Mobil Oil. It may well be from the questions the jury asked the judge during the trial, that that is what has secured this verdict."

Asked about the future, he simply said: "It is the beginning of a new road. I'm not sure where it leads but I will find out."

For the first time his formidable wife, who has fiercely protected him since the allegations broke, had no ready riposte. Asked how she had felt throughout the epic trial, she said: "I can't tell you that now, but I will."

Any hopes that Mr Hamilton may have harboured about a return to the political scene have now been utterly dashed.

The Conservative party chairman, Michael Ancram, was among the first to comment. "I have noted the verdict of the jury and I hope that this is the end of a sad and unpleasant episode which has been damaging to our party," he said.

"I trust that the personalities involved will now retire from the scene. They certainly can expect little understanding from this party if they do not."

Alan Rusbridger, the editor of the Guardian, called for Mr Hamilton to make an apology to the newspaper over accusations that he made against Guardian journalists.

"Neil Hamilton has now been found guilty by both parliament and the courts," he said. "Today's verdict vindicates the Guardian's reporting of this case. The jury has found that Neil Hamilton is corrupt.

"The Guardian's reporting exposed the mire of MPs on the take in the mid to late 80s and led to the setting up of the Nolan commission into standards in public life. Our original reporting has never been shaken, despite the slurs of Mr Hamilton, his friends and his legal team.

"The Guardian never doubted the integrity of its journalists, who deserve an apology from Neil Hamilton."

The end of the road for Hamilton, pages 2–5

Alan Rusbridger and Peter Preston, page 15

Guardian editor Alan Rusbridger will be online on the Guardian network at 2.30pm today to discuss the Hamilton case. Post your questions and messages at www.newsunlimited.co.uk/hamilton

Christine and Neil Hamilton face the media outside the high court after yesterday's verdict ended their five-year fight Photograph: Haydn West

The catalogue of offences

- Between 1985 and 1989 Hamilton received up to £110,000 in cash from Fayed or through political lobbyist Ian Greer for parliamentary work for Fayed
- The Hamiltons took undeclared hospitality from Fayed at the Ritz hotel in Paris, at Fayed's Scottish castle and at Dodi Fayed's apartment in Paris
- From Greer, Hamilton took undeclared fees of $10,000 (about £6,250) for introducing two companies to Greer's organisation — National Nuclear Corporation and US Tobacco.
- Part of the £4,000 NNC fee was paid in kind to reduce tax liability: paintings, value £700; garden furniture, value £959.95; and air fares, value £1,594.
- Hamilton had two separate hotel stays in London and New York, paid for by UST
- In 1989 he moved an amendment to the finance bill on behalf of Mobil Oil and demanded £10,000, which he corruptly and dishonestly disguised
- He lied about his work for Mobil to his then boss Michael Heseltine, Sir Gordon Downey and to the select committee on standards and privileges. He also failed to disclose the information to the Guardian when he sued in 1994

Backers may pay price as costs hit £2m

Kevin Maguire and **Jamie Wilson**

Neil Hamilton faces bankruptcy and his wealthy right-wing sympathisers could be forced to pick up a massive legal bill after yesterday's £2m-plus libel defeat.

Mr Justice Morland ordered the disgraced ex-minister to pay all the costs and to name within 28 days an estimated six backers who donated more than £5,000 to fund his case. This was to enable Mohamed Al Fayed to recover his costs.

Mr Hamilton's own costs, thought to be more than £1m, may force him to sell a London flat and the Old Rectory, his beloved Tatton home worth an estimated £700,000.

Mr Fayed's costs were also thought to be more than £1m. The judge has discretion to force those who funded the ex-MP's action to pick up the bill if Mr Hamilton fails to pay. This will be decided next month.

The ex-minister's list of supporters included free market champion Lord Harris of High Cross, Spectator columnist Taki Theodoracopulous, Freedom Association chairman Norris McWhirter and Enoch Powell's biographer Simon Heffer.

Lord Harris, a long-time friend and mentor of Mr Hamilton and founder of a £400,000 fighting fund to defend the ex-minister, yesterday vowed not to disclose any names.

He maintained his contribution was under £5,000 and mainly "in kind" as he declared: "I am the only one who has any names of donors and I have not even told Hamilton so it would come to me.

"I am highly disinclined to reveal any names. All my correspondence has been strictly confidential. It would be a grotesque thing to name the people who have tried to help him out of a hole."

He said that the ▸ **Page 2**

Racist killers of black musician convicted after family campaign

Nick Hopkins
Crime Correspondent

A family won belated justice for the murder of the black musician Michael Menson yesterday, when an Old Bailey jury convicted two men of killing him in a horrific racist attack three years ago, after an investigation that had striking parallels to the bungled Stephen Lawrence case.

Mr Menson's brothers and sisters sat in silence as Mario Pereira, 26, was found guilty of murder, and Harry Charalambous Constantinou, 26, was found guilty of manslaughter.

Ozgay Cevat, 24, who fled the country after the attack, was found guilty of manslaughter by a court in northern Cyprus last month, but there was a news blackout on the proceedings until yesterday's verdicts.

The three men were accused of taunting, robbing and abusing Mr Menson, before throwing petrol or white spirit on his anorak and setting it alight. Mr Menson died 16 days later, on February 13 1997.

For almost two years, detectives maintained Mr Menson had tried to commit suicide, ignoring the pleas of his family who were convinced he had been set upon by thugs.

After the verdicts Kwesi Menson, Michael's brother, said: "Michael didn't deserve to be burned to death and he didn't deserve his murder not to be taken seriously and it is that that has kept us strong in our drive to get these convictions."

Dr Essie Menson, Michael's sister, added: "An innocent person was attacked and killed and on multiple occasions in multiple places by multiple agencies we met resistance.

"We had to ensure that the people who killed Michael were brought to justice."

Pereira, a former student, and Constantinou, unemployed, both of Edmonton, north London, had denied killing Mr Menson.

Along with Husseyin Abdullah, 50, unemployed of Edmonton, they were also found guilty of perverting the course of justice by obstructing the police investigation. All three men will be sentenced today by Mr Justice Gage.

John Grieve, the deputy assistant commissioner of the Metropolitan police and head of the race and violent crimes task force, paid tribute to the Menson family after the verdicts. "Michael's family were utterly steadfast in their determination in bringing those responsible to justice. Their campaign really was pivotal, a model of keeping an investigation in the public mind."

Long road to justice, page 7

Menson: belated justice

Profile: *The Guardian*

Simon Esterson

High design and sharp politics on the Left

The Guardian, the left-wing British broadsheet (daily circulation 400,000 copies), is a good example of the way in which broadsheet papers have embraced design in an attempt to react to a shrinking and extremely competitive market. The paper underwent a radical redesign by David Hillman of Pentagram in 1988. Ranged-left Helvetica Bold headlines and the use of column rules, white space, and a strict eight-column grid upset newspaper pundits at the time, but they provided a very strong visual foundation for the development of the paper in recent years.

As printing has changed from rotary letterpress to offset and page make-up to QuarkXPress, improved typography could be implemented. Matthew Carter's Miller family was introduced for text, and for some display typography, alongside Helvetica.

The paper also created a range of daily and weekly sections, beginning ten years ago with a daily tabloid-format features section, G2. With its bold front pages and spread-based layouts, G2 reflects the influence of magazine design as much as newspaper traditions.

Over a week, *The Guardian* produces broadsheet, tabloid, and heatset offset sections, as well as a gravure magazine on Saturdays. All the sections use the paper's basic typographic vocabulary of Helvetica, Miller, and Griffith fonts, but vary the weights, proportions, and relationships to create a flexible typographic language.

Editor:
Alan Rusbridger
Consulting Art Director (1995-2000):
Simon Esterson
Art Director:
Mark Porter
Deputy Art Director:
Roger Browning

Opposite: A recent front page of *The Guardian*.

The Guardian

Sport

Watson case sinks boxing board

Athletics seeks a venue as Wembley stops at football

Blades cut Diamonds so fine

Guardian Crossword No 21,775 Set by Mercury

Paul Weaver

Where you always have to take guard

The Guardian Wednesday December 22 1999 7

Michael Menson murder

A long and tortuous road to justice

Family Detectives condemned for their attitudes and inept handling of inquiry

Vikram Dodd and **Nick Hopkins**

On January 28 1997, the members of the Menson family were a world apart from each other. Essie Menson, who had gone to Australia to work as a doctor, celebrated giving birth. Her sister, Chris, was holidaying with their mother in Ghana. And in north London their brother, Kwesi, was getting the news that would change all their lives for the next three years.

Their brother, Michael, had been found alight on the North Circular Road in Edmonton, north London.

Police said Michael, who had suffered horrific burns, had tried to kill himself, but when Kwesi saw his brother in hospital he told a different story, that he had been attacked by four white youths. On February 13, 1997, Michael died.

All the family wanted was to be left in peace to grieve for the talented musician while the police hunted the killers. Instead, Michael became another victim of a serious racist crime that Scotland Yard did not initially take seriously.

Looking back the Menson family are struck by the juxtaposition of events.

The day after Michael died an inquest jury decided that black teenager Stephen Lawrence was unlawfully killed. As one chapter of disgrace over race and crime for the Met was gathering pace, another was opening.

Michael's elder brother, Kwesi, said: "I don't have any doubt that had a white man been set on fire in a street in north London that there would have been an active and vigorous investigation. My view is that a set of conditions were seen which were considered to be able to be written off as unworthy of full and proper investigation and a systematic approach was undertaken to write it off."

Statement

In the hours after the attack Kwesi was astonished that no police officer came to the hospital to take a statement from Michael. It was the first sign that things were going wrong. An officer, Detective Chief Inspector Roger Williams, turned up two days after the attack. He failed to take a statement from Michael, but took one from Kwesi who had written down details his brother had told him.

Michael would die with no officer having taken a formal statement from him.

In hospital he told at least six people he had been set ablaze by white youths. A policewoman he told at the scene did not mention it to anyone for a fortnight.

Kwesi, and sisters Essie and Chris, recounted that their grief was compounded because of police unwillingness to hunt Michael's murderers. Essie said: "During the first few weeks we were floundering, realising things were going wrong. The things they failed to do were so wilful and so blatant that it just has to be wilfully deciding not to take appropriate action."

The family had had no dealings with the police or justice system until they tried to get justice for their brother. At first they doubted their own instincts that the police were bungling the case.

"We went through feeling disbelief at what we were going through. We wondered whether we were being paranoid, or taking things too far," said Essie. "Letting them get away with it – the people who did it and the people whose duty it is to investigate and haven't done so is worse than the option of pressing on with this stressful and arduous task, and that's the bottom line."

Essie said that at the time of the attack on her brother, with the Stephen Lawrence case entering mainstream consciousness, she believed that police attitudes on race were under so much scrutiny that the police would have to investigate the death properly.

The Mensons say officers refused to give them basic information about what happened to Michael nor news of how their investigations were progressing. As in the Lawrence case they dismiss family liaison as little more than "tea and sympathy".

Shortly before the inquest at Hornsey coroner's court, north London, in September 1998, senior officers from the local investigation pool, which was in charge of the inquiry, were still telling the family that their brother, who had a history of mental illness, had tried to commit suicide.

The position became unsustainable when the inquest jury ruled that Michael had been unlawfully killed.

The verdict triggered a meeting with the home secretary, Jack Straw, and a fresh investigation headed by deputy assistant commissioner John Grieve, head of the race and violent crimes task force.

His vigorous and determined approach was all the family had wanted all along. Grieve treated the case as murder, an approach that led to the three arrests.

The pain of the ordeal is visible in the eyes of the three of Michael's eleven siblings who have agreed to talk.

Their criticism of the police is strong, but measured. Their diction is ungilded; adjectives kept to a minimum. "You don't cope," said Kwesi. "There's no book to tell you how to feel or what to do. If we did nothing then the people who murdered Michael would be laughing in the face of justice."

Essie said: "We also felt that by not investigating it, the police were almost sending a message to these people that that's fine, you go and burn a black man in the street to death and nothing is going to be done about it."

Complaints

Now the criminal case is over, formal complaints from the family against officers in the first two investigations will begin. Ben Gunn, the chief constable of Cambridgeshire police, has been put in charge of the inquiry by the police complaints authority.

Essie added: "It felt like they [the police] were saying you don't matter, Michael doesn't matter and that is what drove us on. By wilfully failing to investigate it properly we felt there was a taint of Michael doesn't matter, shut up and be quiet. We weren't prepared to stand for that. There was no way we were going to let Michael down. The point was to show that Michael's life and death mattered."

'It felt like police were saying you don't matter and Michael doesn't matter. That's what drove us on'

Michael Menson's sister, Essie, after the conviction yesterday of two of his killers and Michael (below) performing with his group Double Trouble Photograph (top): Martin Godwin

Diary of a race killing

January 28 1997: Michael Menson found by police in flames in street in Edmonton, north London.

February 13: He dies of multiple organ failure in hospital.

September 16 1998: Inquest returns verdict of unlawful killing.

September 29: Police complaints authority begins inquiry. Home secretary Jack Straw meets family.

November 4: Police announce new murder investigation.

December 1: Met apologises to family for mistakes.

January 24 1999: Police admit murder "racially motivated".

March 11: Two men charged with murder.

August 5: Third man charged in Northern Cyprus.

September 27: Trial of Ozgay Cevat begins in Cyprus.

November 15: Trial of Mario Pereira and Harry Constantinou begins at Old Bailey.

November 25: Cevat found guilty of manslaughter and sentenced to 14 years imprisonment.

December 21: Constantinou found guilty of manslaughter and Pereira of murder.

New broom turned investigation on its head

Police £1.2m inquiry a small price to pay for credibility

Nick Hopkins

Within a few days of taking over the case in December last year, John Grieve turned the investigation on its head.

The deputy assistant commissioner of the Metropolitan police read through the 300 witness statements, spoke at length to Michael Menson's family and conferred with senior detectives on his newly formed race and violent crimes task force.

"I didn't like it at all," said Mr Grieve. "It read like murder to me."

That assessment was borne out yesterday when Mario Pereira, 26, was found guilty of Mr Menson's murder. Harry Charalambous Constantinou, 27, was found guilty of manslaughter.

Both men, together with Husseyin Abdullah, 50, were found guilty of perverting the course of justice. They will be sentenced today.

Mr Grieve's analysis, which came amid intense criticism of the force following the inquest ruling, contradicted the assessment made by two previous investigations.

This third inquiry cost Scotland Yard £1.2m and also involved the prosecution for manslaughter in the case of a man, Ozgay Cevat, in northern Cyprus for a crime committed in Britain – a legal first.

Sir Paul Condon, the commissioner, and his deputy, John Stevens, realised it was a small price to pay to salvage what remained of the force's credibility with the black community.

The 12-strong murder squad did not have to start from scratch. They knew the names and addresses of the key suspects – most of them had been identified by the police within weeks of Mr Menson's murder – and they used the second anniversary of the attack in January to launch a publicity blitz.

Members of Mr Menson's family appeared on Crimewatch on January 26. The north London suburb of Edmonton, where the killers lived, was leafleted the day before.

Mr Grieve knew that if the men were involved in the murder, they would start talking about it. And if they did, the police would be listening.

Late in January, a bug was placed covertly in Charalambous Constantinou's flat. It recorded conversations between the defendants which showed they were deeply racist and unquestionably involved in the murder.

"The intrusive surveillance proved extremely productive very quickly," said Detective Chief Superintendent Kevin Davis. "On February 8, Pereira discussed the murder. On the 14th, they mentioned the car that had been used in the murder."

Although the recordings were imperfect – the conversations were fractured by noise from the television – the men chatted about what happened the night Mr Menson was attacked.

During another taped conversation on March 2, Constantinou said: "Basically they approached him, I got out the car and I goes to them 'leave him alone', know what I mean, 'leave the geezer alone'.

"Mario started going on about shit, started saying 'Oh, he's a black cunt' and shit, 'let's burn him', and all that. I mean what could I do?"

The prosecution case was supported by evidence from former friends of the defendants who gave fresh statements after the police asked them to reflect on the horrific nature of the attack.

Pereira, Constantinou and Abdullah were arrested on March 8, when one of them found a video camera which had been secretly placed in Constantinou's flat.

To begin with, Scotland Yard did not give much hope of bringing Cevat to justice. The government does not recognise the Turkish republic and there is no extradition treaty.

The breakthrough came in April, when a senior legal officer from northern Cyprus visited Britain and explained there was a law which gave them the right to prosecute someone accused of an offence in another country where the likely prison sentence would be more than two years.

The preliminary hearings took place in front of a judge in September and the trial began in late October. Thirty-two witnesses, including members of the Menson family and 13 others who travelled from Britain, gave evidence before three judges – there is no jury system in northern Cyprus.

The attorney general's office sent repeated reminders to the press in Britain not to report the proceedings to ensure the defendants at the Old Bailey received a fair trial. Cevat was found guilty of manslaughter on November 25 and sentenced to 14 years.

Outside the Old Bailey yesterday, Essie Menson asked for a few moments silence to remember her brother, saying that he was a "a man who stood for peace and for love".

Born in Moscow in July 1966, Michael Menson was the seventh of 11 children and lived in several countries before settling in Britain in the late 1960s. After studying A-levels at Brent college in London, he become involved in the music industry and formed the group Rebel MC and Double Trouble, which had two hit singles in Britain.

He was described in court as a "gentle, natural, quiet, caring man with a strong faith and high values".

However, Mr Menson had a nervous breakdown when his recording studio business, Noise Gate, went bust. Nigel Sweeney, prosecuting, said he was diagnosed as suffering paranoid schizophrenia.

Mr Menson had talked about taking his own life, saying ghosts had suggested he commit suicide but he was also adamant he would not harm himself. "I have not got it in me," he told one doctor. "I could not do it. I want to live."

When Michael was stressed, he fell into a catatonic state.

Pereira, Cevat and Constantinou probably found him in a similar condition on the night they attacked him. Mr Menson had got lost on his way to hospital from his supported accommodation flat in Arnos Grove, north London.

The police believe he would have been powerless to defend himself. It would also help to explain why Mr Menson did not seem aware of the flames on his anorak.

Mr Grieve said Mr Menson was abused, bullied and robbed. The three men only left him to find an accellerant, probably petrol or white spirit, and returned to drench the back of his clothes before setting him alight.

He added: "Michael was the wrong person in the wrong place at the wrong time. He was the victim of an unprovoked racist attack. They were determined to kill him. Mr Menson was black and that is why they attacked him."

Ms Menson said: "We have had to fight against resistance to get to the truth and we think it is inappropriate that families are put in a position where the only way they can be relying on the truth coming is to do the work themselves."

Mario Pereira: guilty of murdering Michael Menson

Harry Constantinou: convicted of manslaughter

Ozgay Cevat: serving 14 years in Cyprus for part in murder

Guardian editor online
Alan Rusbridger will discuss the implications of the Neil Hamilton case on the Guardian network today at 2.30pm
www.newsunlimited.co.uk

Lawrences to sue 42 police including Condon

Paul Kelso

The parents of Stephen Lawrence are suing 42 police officers involved in the failed investigation of their son's murder, including Sir Paul Condon, the outgoing Metropolitan police commissioner and the highest ranked officer named in the action.

The case is being brought under section 20 of the race relations act, which permits legal action against discrimination on the grounds of colour. The Metropolitan police confirmed that proceedings had been lodged on behalf of Doreen and Neville Lawrence and yesterday moved to back the officers, who were each served with writs on December 14.

New Scotland Yard confirmed that the force would meet the officers' costs in defending the action and any damages made against them. They had been "reassured of the continuing support of the commissioner in defending the civil claims," said a spokeswoman.

The Lawrences' intention to sue was revealed by the Guardian in February, when the couple consulted lawyers after seeing an advance copy of the public inquiry report on their son's death.

The action, for which the family will receive legal aid, raises the possibility that some officers will be called to upon to explain their actions during the bungled inquiry into Stephen Lawrence's death, and that for the first time senior officers will be called to account.

Stephen Lawrence special report on the Guardian network at www.newsunlimited.co.uk/lawrence

Eat, drink and be merrier

Win a Christmas hamper

Shopping Unlimited has teamed up with lastminute.com to offer one lucky winner a traditional Christmas hamper packed with goodies. Pol Roger champagne, Belgian pralines, stollen cake, sugar mice – there's more grub in this hamper than you could shake a spoon at. To take your fill, simply come to www.shoppingunlimited.co.uk

www.shoppingUnlimited.co.uk

in association with lastminute.com

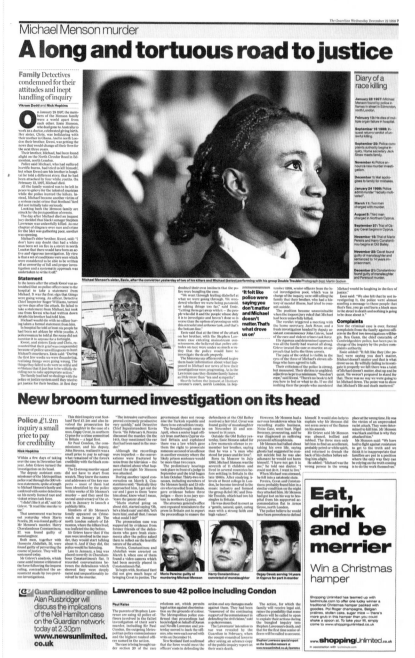

Bringing order to chaos

Contrast and organization characterize the *The Guardian*'s design. The news pages are densely packed, but they seldom seem cluttered. Comment & Analysis has a slightly looser look, though still on a strict grid.

'Yet more rolling news and inane phone-ins instead of great music' Letters, page 17

Comment & Analysis

David Brindle The child support agency is more than a fiasco — it has turned into a national tragedy

To hell in a handbag

The disaster in public policy making that was the child support agency has been a tragedy for hundreds of thousands of people. Their lives have been blighted by the agency's ineptitude and what turned out to be its politically driven mission to raise cash for the treasury.

Anyone working in the Blair government today should regard as required viewing a Channel 4 television documentary series which reveals just what fiascos can occur under a moralising prime minister.

Michelle Counley was one of those who, as she now puts it, "very naively" thought the agency was going to be her saviour. Michelle had separated from her first husband, but his maintenance payments for their daughter, Victoria, had dried up. The CSA said it was on the case, but never seemed to be getting anywhere. "I actually used to phone every Tuesday, every week for a lengthy period of time," says Michelle, from Dudley in the West Midlands. "I once threatened to actually go to the CSA offices, complete with my daughter, and not move from their doorstep until someone provided me with either money or food."

Eventually, the agency assessed her ex's liability at just under £52 a week. But for the 18 months that had passed in the process, it succeeded in extracting from him a grand total of £280. "That was when I told them that was it: they could stick it where the sun don't shine and I would manage as best I could."

Through a newly introduced complaints system Michelle has now succeeded in getting £700 compensation for the way her case was handled. But she wants nothing more to do with the agency, even though her new husband, Mark Betteridge, pays maintenance through it for his two daughters from his first marriage.

The complexity of family life in modern Britain was something the policymakers seemed to miss when they set about constructing the CSA in 1989 and its notorious maintenance assessment formula. Mavis Maclean, a policy adviser at the time, now admits: "We didn't look at what happens after a family splits." If the niceties of balancing the interests of a first and second family were never properly addressed by officials, they were unlikely to cut any ice with ministers

Mrs Thatcher, then prime minister, was in overdrive. She had learned that more than 1m lone mothers were living on income support, in 80% of cases without any money being recouped from the fathers . Her zeal had been fired by Labour MP Frank Field, who had told her of a case in his Birkenhead constituency where a child had begged her father not to attend the school nativity play because she would feel the odd one out if both her mum and dad were there.

"She came to cabinet one day and said: 'Lone parents are a problem, what are you going to do about it?'" says Mike Whippman, former department of social security policy director. "'Come back next week with all your answers.'"

Maclean reports that there was "no enthusiasm" for the project among officials, who foresaw difficulties. Sir Michael Partridge, then DSS permanent secretary, says he was "not very keen". Yet nobody piped up. As Maclean puts it: "This was a government led from the front, with the handbag, and [it] was not really very interested in hearing about the difficulties."

Tony Newton, then social security secretary, insists he did voice reservations. "If Margaret Thatcher saw me as hostile, I think that simply reflected my recognition that this was a much more difficult problem than some of my colleagues appreciated."

It was Newton, nevertheless, who went to the American state of Wisconsin in 1990 to see the agency that was to be the model for the British CSA. There he met Irwin Garfinkel, the man who had masterminded the idea, who taught him two golden rules: do not make budget savings the primary goal of the policy; and do not make the system retrospective. Once back in London, Newton was forced to break both.

Partridge says the DSS thought it "pretty essential" that lone mothers on benefit should be able to keep up to half of any cash obtained from their former partners by the CSA, rather than all of it go straight into government coffers. Newton's bottom line, says Partridge, was 20% of the money for mothers.

In a cabinet committee, however, Thatcher sided with the treasury and vetoed the idea of any so-called "disregard": all maintenance was to be charged, penny for penny, against benefit. That decision was to undermine fatally the chances of lone mothers cooperating with the agency.

The second decision, to empower the agency to reopen cases where maintenance settlements had been reached, correspondingly undermined the chances of fathers cooperating.

Again, the treasury would give no ground. Partridge says the decision was "largely financial", seeking to maximise the treasury's take straight off, and it had "a big effect on the public acceptability and willingness of people to cooperate with the scheme".

Newton says: "I do recall expressing the view that what I regarded as a worthwhile social reform in principle would be made much more difficult — I'm choosing my words carefully — by an attempt to push it too far, too fast."

As if all this was not enough to scupper the CSA from the outset, it was saddled with a maintenance formula of mind boggling obscurity. Maclean showed it to her brother-in-law, an econometrician. "I mean, this man can do numbers and squiggles and formulae and all the rest of it. And I remember showing it to him, and he sat there for an hour, sort of tearing his hair out and saying: 'I can't make head nor tail of this.'" It was also a formula that would produce maintenance bills of up to four times what many county courts had been setting.

Thatcher said: 'Lone parents, what are you going to do about them?'

Yet nobody in government, and precious few in opposition, appeared to realise what impact this would have on fathers — especially those whose cases were reopened, often because they worked in the public services and the CSA could easily dock their pay to notch up what became known as a "quick win".

Peter Kemp, a former permanent secretary at the cabinet office, says the policy "ignored one of the major rules of change, which is 'nurture the losers'." He recalls: "I don't think it got the proper scrutiny."

Frank Field says: "The real danger is when politicians start agreeing, taxpayers and voters ought to watch out beause that's usually the basis of pretty bad legislation."

The pretty bad CSA legislation has led to a pretty bad six years for both Tory and Labour governments, saddled with a useless and detested institution.

Changes, including a small £10 a week disregard and a simpler and less punitive formula, are in the pipeline, but will not take effect until at least late 2001.

For Michelle Counley, the system is beyond tinkering. Earlier this month she was elected to chair the National Association for Child Support Action, the main anti-CSA campaign group.

There is a lesson in this sad saga. When a dominant prime minister, appalled by a single case study of moral decline, orders radical action from colleagues, the result can be a political catastrophe.

Can't Pay, Won't Pay, narrated by Guardian columnist Polly Toynbee, continues on Channel 4 next Sunday

ILLUSTRATION: DANIEL PUDLES

Andrew Roth

The new McCarthyites

So they have again dug up deceased old friends Ray Fletcher and Tom Driberg as Soviet "agents" as well as Labour MPs! As a former US intelligence officer myself, I would have balked at recruiting a manic-depressive like Ray, who would get so drunk he woke up in gutters. Or Tom, the most blatant homosexual in politics, who could be compromised in any gay urinal from Leicester Square to Moscow.

As sources of information and insights, of course, at best both were superlative. I still recall my first 1946 interview with Tom on the Commons terrace as a young foreign correspondent. There were lots of stimulating exchanges with Ray too, when he featured in Tribune, before he became an MP and lost his brilliance through the electric shock treatment recommended by his doctor, David (later Lord) Pitt.

This distinction between "sources" — deliberate or inadvertent — and conscious "agents" is crucial to make any sense of information sold by defecting Soviet intelligence men trying to buy their way to comfortable retirements in the west. All agents try to exaggerate the value of their sources, like journalists trying to justify heavy expense accounts. When pushed by demanding spymasters to set up a network, they even convert inadvertent sources into agents.

I have never doubted the existence of genuine communist agents, including those for whom communism was a revealed religion and Stalin its "pope". Julius Rosenberg, who was electrocuted with his wife, sat opposite me, always silent, for years in an alcove in the basement lunchroom of New York's City College, where I munched my peanut-butter-and-jam sandwiches. The brother-in-law who shopped him was a classmate. Two other classmates, Irving Kristol and Melvin Laski, were Trotskyists later picked by the CIA as the first editors of Encounter.

As the "depression generation" we were intensely political because we did not think we would get jobs. Those of us whose parents had left Jewish families in Hitler's path had a special foreboding about their fates. In 1936 I was temporarily converted into a fellow-traveller when the Young Communist sitting next to me in history class told me he was off to fight Franco in Spain. Only communists seemed willing to fight fascists. My naivety was cured by the 1939 Nazi-Soviet pact. For others, Stalin remained infallible.

A problem with the belated disclosures of old treacheries is the re-energising of the new McCarthyites. Writers like former Tory MP Rupert Allason and a half-dozen US counterparts have already used the CIA's release of the Soviets' Venona spy-traffic — decrypted communications —to loose charges against mostly-dead people who may have been inadvertent sources. The late Sir Rudolf Peierls FRS was one target, (although Allason's allegations have now been challenged). Accusations against Laughlin Currie, a liberal, Galbraith-type Canadian-American, who was President Roosevelt's adviser, have also been exploded.

As virtually the only survivor of those attacked by J Edgar Hoover in 1945 and Senator McCarthy in 1950, I have sued Allason for defamation in his Venona book. He has sought to use a reference in the traffic to an alleged Soviet agent, Joseph Bernstein, to make a renewed false case against me.

In May 1945, the European war was ending and the world was jubilant about the allied forces' meeting with the Soviet Red Army, ending the Nazi threat. There were discordant voices. A cable crossed my desk in US naval intelligence from Ambassador William Bullitt. This urged that the Polish forces being released from Siberia by Stalin for service in Italy, be held back for an early attack on the war-weakened Russians!

A friend, Philip Jaffe, the wartime editor of Amerasia magazine, was also a fellow-traveller who became obsessed by the danger of an attack on the USSR. He thought he might get advance word of this from a source in the state department.

I spelled out the dangers of his contacting Joe Bernstein, who, Jaffe said, had "contacts" at the Soviet embassy. "I don't like it! I don't like it!" I repeated. Unfortunately for us, we had the FBI listening. I was arrested with five others. Justice decided there was no case against me and all-too-quietly dropped the charges. The rest of the case fell apart when the remaining defendants discovered that the raids on their premises had been illegal.

J Edgar Hoover never forgave us for the black eye he suffered. And Hoover's ghost still lives on among the new McCarthyites. From my 54 years of experience, all spy stories need swallowing with buckets of salt.

Andrew Roth edits Parliamentary Profiles

Hugo Young, page 16

Australia's courtship of Indonesia has underpinned its foreign policy. Now it has a difficult path to tread

Advance Australia fair

Martin Woollacott

No country is more important to Australia than Indonesia, Paul Keating declared after he became prime minister in 1992. High-level visits, military cooperation and increased trade have underpinned the rhetoric since, with the result that Australia is now leading the attempt to manage the East Timor crisis. It also has more to lose than anyone else if it fails.

The intimate relationship created in the 90s between the two nations is the capstone of the foreign policy Australia first began to shape some 30 years ago when it broke away from dependence on American power. But was it a moral and practical error to have put so much effort into cultivating what some see as an irretrievably corrupt and oppressive regime?

East Timor dramatises the moral issues underlying Australian foreign policy. The country went from killing Asians (Japanese in the second world war and then, in the name of anti-communism, Koreans, Vietnamese, and Chinese Malaysians) to embracing them. It is preferable to enmity, but how much appeasement and careful looking in the other direction when shameful things happen does it involve? This is the broader dilemma which East Timor makes so clear.

Australia's changing relationship with Asia over the near century since it became a federation can be illustrated by imagining a map being manoeuvred around on a desktop. The first map was the familiar north-south projection in which gravity appeared to be about to dump Asia's masses into an empty continent — those were the days of the yellow peril. In the post-war period, the focus changed back to China again after the communist takeover but the sense of threat was just as keen. Australia, supposedly, was the last domino, which would fall once the struggle for south-east Asia had been won by the communists.

Although his predecessors had begun a limited retreat from these policies, it was Gough Whitlam in the 70s who really punctured this paranoia and put Australian foreign policy on a new basis. He withdrew the troops from Vietnam, dismissed the anti-communist South East Asian Treaty Organisation as "defunct", made overtures to China and confirmed the shift in immigration policy which had begun to allow Asians to enter Australia in large numbers.

Since the Vietnam war was winding down and America had already begun its own rapprochement with China, Whitlam's moves were not quite as brave as they appeared to be, but they were welcome nevertheless. Yet, when Whitlam went, Australian policy still retained a cold war dimension, now directed at containing the Soviet Union and its Asian allies and friends, especially Vietnam. Shifting the old map onto its side illuminates the crescent of countries, from Beijing to Canberra via Tokyo and Washington, involved in this unofficial anti-Soviet coalition.

When the cold war faded in the late 80s, the map changed again, to something like the one which the former Australian foreign minister Gareth Evans used to illustrate his concept of an "east Asian hemisphere community", in which, he hoped, Australia would not be "an outsider or bit player but an accepted, involved and participating partner". On this map, troops, planes, and naval task forces are less important than growth indices and trade figures.

As Australia's military security policy underwent these changes over the years, a revolution took place in its economic situation. British markets dwindled and trade with Japan and then also with South Korea, Hong Kong, Taiwan, Singapore, and China grew ever more important. Australia became more and more concerned to be a full member of the Asian economic club, hence its keen interest in regional bodies like the Association of South East Asian Nations (Asean), of which it is not a member but with which it aspires to be closely involved, and Asia-Pacific Economic Cooperation (Apec). Hence also Australian dismay when excluded by Asians, and irritation whenever the Malaysian prime minister, Dr Mahathir, makes it clear that Australia is not and never will be an Asian country.

The lucky country

Population: 18,613,000
GDP per capita: A$21,400 (UK=A$21,200)
Exports: Japan 20%, Asean 16%, South Korea 9%, US 9%, NZ 8%
Imports: US 22%, Japan 17%, UK 6%, China 5%, NZ 5%
Military expenditure: $8.2bn = 1.9% GDP

Signposts on the road from a defence-oriented foreign policy to one preoccupied with economic security within Asia came with two important reports commissioned by the Labour governments, the Dibb on Australian defence and Garnaut on economic relations.

The Garnaut inquiry identified north-east Asia as the most important centre in the new world economy and thus the key region to which Australia had to relate if it was to achieve economic security. Dibb flew in the face of Australia's continuing obsession with threats by declaring it one of the most secure countries in the world. It effectively discarded forward defence. Forward defence meant fighting, or being ready to fight, in the countries of south-east Asia or beyond so as to deal with threats before they even reached Australia's shores. Dibb declared this expeditionary era to be over.

But Australia's special relationship with Indonesia was in a way a continuation of forward defence by other means. Australia's interest in a stable Indonesia could best be served, it was decided, by a close embrace of the New Order regime, an embrace which went as far as a security treaty with Jakarta. Indonesian troops exercised in Australia and Australian training missions went to Indonesia. Cultural exchanges were encouraged by the foundation of an Australia-Indonesia institute. Australia became the country of choice for Indonesian students looking for education abroad, and Australian tourists continued to flock to Bali.

Begun under Bob Hawke, this policy was taken even further by the Keating government, and the Liberal coalition government of John Howard has retreated from it only a little. Those who argued for a policy which made Australia Indonesia's closest western partner defended it against critics charging that the people of East Timor and Irian Jaya were being sold out on the grounds that it would give Canberra real influence in Jakarta when it mattered. That time has now come, and with it an unprecedented test for Australia's foreign policy.

Find useful links on the Guardian network at www.newsunlimited.co.uk/analysis

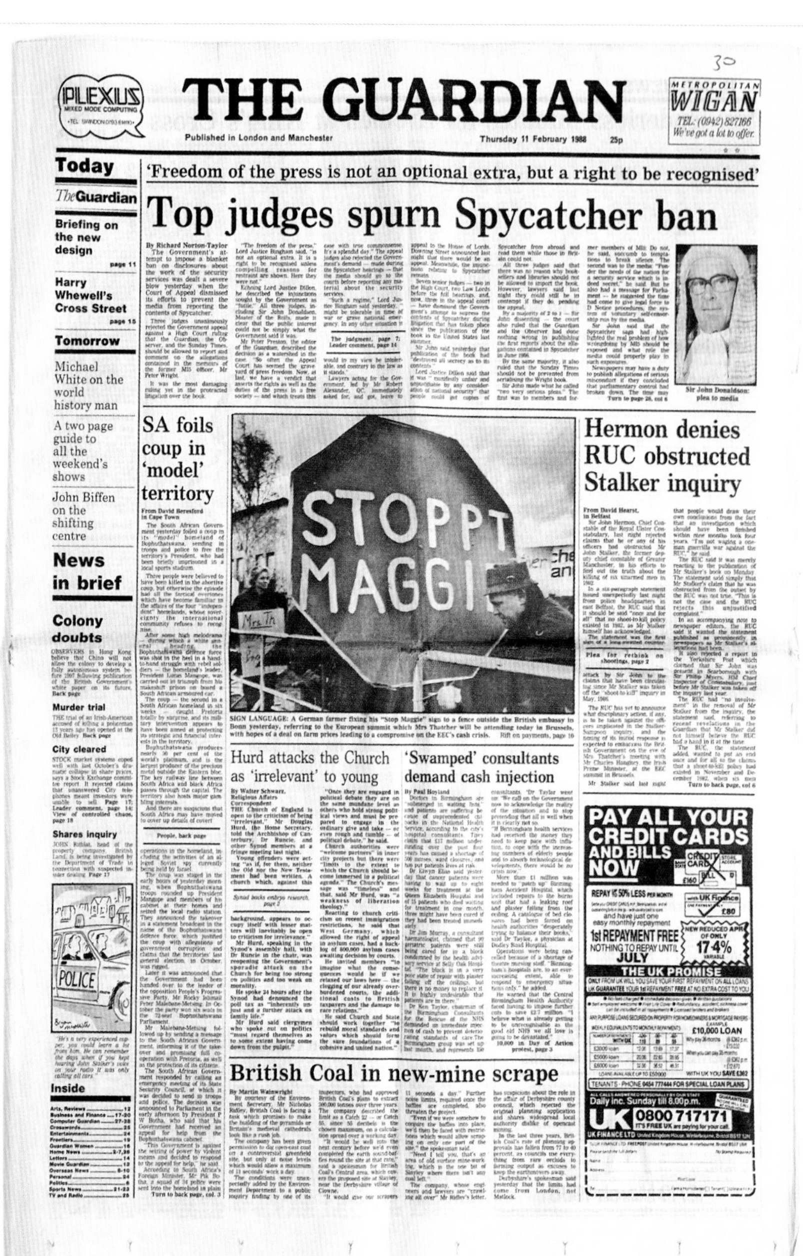

PLEXUS MIXED MODE COMPUTING

THE GUARDIAN

Published in London and Manchester — Thursday 11 February 1988 — 25p

METROPOLITAN WIGAN TEL: (0942) 827166 We've got a lot to offer.

Today — The Guardian — Briefing on the new design page 11 — Harry Whewell's Cross Street page 15

Tomorrow — Michael White on the world history man — A two page guide to all the weekend's shows — John Biffen on the shifting centre

News in brief — Colony doubts — Murder trial — City cleared — Shares inquiry

Inside

'Freedom of the press is not an optional extra, but a right to be recognised'

Top judges spurn Spycatcher ban

By Richard Norton-Taylor

Sir John Donaldson: plea to media

SA foils coup in 'model' territory

From David Beresford in Cape Town

SIGN LANGUAGE: A German farmer fixing his "Stop Maggie" sign to a fence outside the British embassy in Bonn yesterday, referring to the European summit which Mrs Thatcher will be attending today in Brussels, with hopes of a deal on farm prices leading to a compromise on the EEC's cash crisis.

Hermon denies RUC obstructed Stalker inquiry

From David Hearst, in Belfast

Hurd attacks the Church as 'irrelevant' to young

By Walter Schwarz, Religious Affairs Correspondent

'Swamped' consultants demand cash injection

By Paul Hoyland

British Coal in new-mine scrape

By Martin Wainwright

The front page of *The Guardian* on the day before (left) and the day after (opposite) the introduction of the new design in 1988.

Before & after

The change was dramatic from one day to the next – not least in the nameplate. A triple contrast of weight, form, and style made it possible to close up the two words, turning them into a single visual unit. This style was echoed elsewhere in the paper, and it was soon imitated widely.

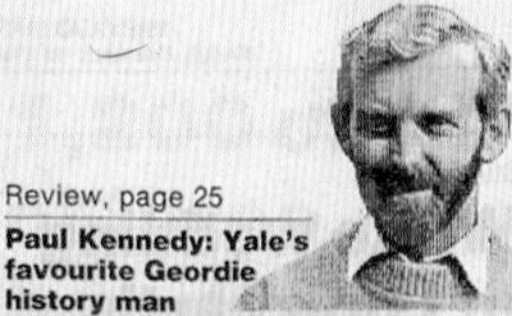

Review, page 25

Paul Kennedy: Yale's favourite Geordie history man

People, page 2

Marion Serravalli's prison wedding

Opinion, page 23

John Biffen looks in vain for the opposition

Arts, page 28

Clint Eastwood conducts Charlie 'Bird' Parker

25p

Friday
12 February
1988

Published in London and Manchester

The Guardian

Alliance woe helps Labour poll surge

Guardian Marplan

Martin Linton

LABOUR has reached a six-year high in the Guardian Marplan Index with a February rating of 42 per cent, one point behind the Government at 43 per cent.

The rise in Labour's support, putting it through the 40 per cent "barrier" for the first time since the Marplan index started its monthly record of public opinion in 1982, appears to be a result of the crisis in the National Health Service. Polling started two days after the nurses' day of action.

But the Government has not suffered yet from the chorus of criticism it has faced from the nurses and the opposition. Its support has, in fact, gone up by one per cent in the last month and is at exactly the same level as its vote in last summer's general election.

It is the Alliance parties that have suffered, dropping from 17 to 14 per cent after the fiasco of their merger negotiations and the divisions revealed by their conferences at Blackpool and Sheffield over the last month.

That will do nothing to spoil Mr Neil Kinnock's relief that his party has cleared the 40 per cent hurdle which Labour leaders began to feel was an invisible barrier before the election.

Other polls have occasionally put Labour above 40 per cent, and Labour has twice reached 40 per cent in Marplan. But on both the earlier occasions — in February 1984 and September 1986 — its support has immediately started to recede again.

It could easily do the same again since public opinion has been more than usually volatile over the last few months and the polls have recorded rapid fluctuations. Last month's Marplan Index in the Guardian put the Conservatives just 2 per cent ahead, but a week later Gallup gave them a lead of 7½ per cent.

They put the Conservatives at 45½, Labour at 37 and the Alliance, then in the middle of its merger negotiations row, down at 15. But at the end of January, Mori gave the Government a commanding 14 point lead with the Conservatives at 50, with Labour at 36 and the Alliance at 12.

"If an election were to be held tomorrow, which party would you vote for: Conservative, Labour or Alliance? A. . .L. . .L. . . I. . .A. . .N. . ."

	Now	Jan	Dec	Nov	Elec
Con	43	42	47	(46)	43
Lab	42	40	37	(33)	32
Lib/SDP	14	17	13	(17)	23
Other	1	2	3	(3)	2
Con lead	+1	+2	+10	+13	+11

What the Marplan poll appears to show is that disillusioned Alliance supporters, who have been drifting away since the merger negotiations and the ill-feeling and public acrimony which came in its wake, are moving in greater numbers to Labour.

These are the very voters that Mr Kinnock has made it his job to attract to Labour. But he will be only too aware that their support is likely to be highly volatile. It could be lost as easily as it is gained if internal divisions in the Labour Party match those in the Alliance.

Many of these voters may have suspended judgment on the Alliance until March when the new merged party, the Social and Liberal Democrats, is finally launched and Dr Owen's continuing SDP is relaunched and will decide then where to put their support.

But the Government will be worried by Labour's showing. Many Conservatives had begun to believe after the January polls that they could come through the NHS crisis unscathed.

● Marplan interviewed 1,276 adults aged 18-plus in 103 randomly selected constituencies countrywide. Interviews were conducted face-to-face between February 5 and 9.

Leader comment, page 22;

COMPETITORS at Cruft's Dog Show, which opened yesterday, *pictured by Martin Argles* waiting to show their paces in the gundog section. Hundreds of setters, spaniels and pointers arrived at the Earls Court exhibition centre in London with owners and full make up in tow. Some even had lucky rabbit mascots in their pens. All have won at least one champion's certificate this year to qualify for Cruft's, where success can be worth a small fortune in stud fees and dog food commercials. The highlights of the show are the working dog demonstration tomorrow and the judging of best-in-show on Sunday. Meanwhile, visitors to the competitions were given the chance to enrol their pets for the British Airways Flying Pets Club — 'The Animal World's Favourite Airline' — or indulge them with special formula bones, biscuits and balls. The show, 92 years old this year, runs for the next four days.

Report, page 3

Thatcher in new confrontation

John Palmer in Brussels and James Naughtie

MRS THATCHER and the Irish Prime Minister, Mr Charles Haughey, are to meet today in Brussels in a highly charged atmosphere as the row over the Stalker affair continues unabated. Both governments were last night making desperate attempts to play down the seriousness of the talks, but privately officials were not disguising the deepening rift in Anglo-Irish relations.

The meeting had been planned for last night but was postponed until later today. And although both governments insisted that the only reason for the postponement was lack of time during the first day of the European Community summit, there were indications that the Mr Haughey was pressing for a more extended exchange with Mrs Thatcher than expected in London.

The announcement in London yesterday by the Attorney General, Sir Patrick Mayhew, that Mr John Stalker is not to be prosecuted under the Official Secrets Act for publishing his story, has not lessened the tensions in Brussels.

Irish Government officials did not hide their unhappiness yesterday with the UK government on the handling of the "Stalker-Sampson" inquiry and the refusal of the Attorney-General to prosecute the Royal Ulster Constabulary officers for attempting to pervert the course of justice.

While Irish government officials would not be drawn on the precise demands Mr Haughey wants to put to Mrs Thatcher it seems clear they include at least the partial publication of some of the three separate reports into the "shoot to kill" affair.

The Irish Government will not be satisfied with any outcome which does not go beyond diciplinary action against the RUC officers involved even if this includes their "dismissal with ignominy" from the RUC. But Mr Haughey was anxious not to "talk up" his demands ahead of the meeting with Mrs Thatcher lest any failure to agree was seen as a politicial humiliation at home.

The Attorney General announced yesterday that Mr Stalker would not be prosecuted under the Official Secrets Act for his book Stalker but ministers are still considering a civil action against him aimed at reducing his profits.

A number of ministers are deeply sceptical about the likely value of such an action, but the anger directed at Mr Stalker from Downing Street is such that the possiblity has not yet been ruled out. Sir Patrick is currently advising Mrs Thatcher on the likelihood of success in a court challenge.

Mr Stalker said that he was delighted with Sir Patrick's announcement that he would not be prosecuted.

His book has so far sold some 57,000 copies.

Summit report, page 24

Forest put a stop to Clough's Welsh mission

Ian Ridley

BRIAN Clough, one of soccer's most buoyant figures, was left deflated yesterday when his desire to become part-time manager of Wales was blocked by his full-time employers, Nottingham Forest. The chairman, Maurice Roworth, who met officials of the Football Association of Wales earlier this week and agreed in theory to Clough accepting a two-year, £10,000-per-annum contract provided he was not away from the club for more than 10 three-day periods, said yesterday's board meeting unanimously decided the two jobs were incompatible.

Clough said: "I bitterly regret their decision and quite simply I think they are wrong."

Report, David Lacey, page 20

Dagenham Euro-threat

Stephen Cook reports from Cologne

WE ARE cursing the English all right, says a jovial German car worker as he heads through the driving rain towards the bright blue Ford plant at Cologne to start his morning shift.

"We are cursing the management of Ford of Europe.

This is a highly political company and the strike is a highly political business," he says, declining to give his name.

"I can't blame the workers over there for striking. We had a two week strike here six or seven years ago and there have been hardly any strikes in Britain recently."

Not all of his colleagues at the largest Ford plant in West Germany are so forthright.

"It's not for me to judge whether they're right or wrong," says Bernd Zeller, a thoughtful production worker, who detaches himself from the industrious tide heading towards the factory entrance in and away from the chill Rhine winds. "I don't know the conditions over there."

He himself has settled this year for a 2 per cent rise and a 15-minute reduction in the working day.

But his response was typical of many of his fellow-workers in the land of *Vorsprung durch Technik* to the four-day-old strike by their significantly worse-paid counterparts in Britain: a slightly bemused solidarity, coloured by anxiety that, if the strike does bite, the Cologne end of the production line will have to start worrying.

Cologne would be the last German plant to be affected, since it depends on Britain only for engines for the diesel-powered Fiesta — not a great seller — and for small parts and instruments which the management thinks it can resource in France and Belgium. But it is accepted that Cologne could well shut down if the strike lasts until the end of March.

The formal union view yesterday came from Rudolf Bambach, an IG-Metall representative, who was brought into a management office for the interview.

This was mainly because management won't allow journalists into any Ford factories during the strike, but it spoke volumes about the more comfortable union-management relations in West Germany.

"We were surprised the offer was refused in Britain, and I think a lot of people in Britain were surprised too," said Herr Bambach.

"But the two questions we had to answer in the works council were: what can we do to help and what effects will it have here?

"I'm afraid international solidarity is our biggest problem. But it might be in our interests for the people in Britain to earn as much as us — then the management wouldn't go on about switching production to England all the time".

Doubtless his fellow Ford workers in England would agree. "International solidarity" may not be quite as snappy a slogan as *Vorsprung durch Technik* and the like but it is a one that would certainly attract the attention of the Ford managements throughout Europe.

Europe grinds to halt, page 24

Tax cut warning

Christopher Huhne
Economics Editor

THE BANK of England warned the Chancellor yesterday to go easy on tax cuts in his budget — or face the inflationary consequences.

The Bank's quarterly bulletin takes aim squarely at the budget: "It will also be important . . . that the anti-inflationary burden continues to be shared between monetary and fiscal policy."

This does not rule out tax cuts, but it probably means that the bank would prefer them to be limited to around £2-3 billion — merely compensating for the extra tax revenues coming in as incomes rise — rather than the £4-5 billion widely expected in the City.

The Bank's commentary justifies last week's half point rise in interest rates by arguing that the latest indicators depict a still buoyant economy amply provided with credit.

City Notebook, page 14

Your Guardian comes today in two redesigned sections

In section one, you will find the **Home News, International News, Financial News** and **Sports News,** running on in that order. The two editorial pages of **Comment and Analysis,** clearly separated from the news, appear on the two pages inside the back of this section. The back page itself, like the front page, combines major news from home and abroad. The main **Crossword** is there, too.

Today's second section is **Review Guardian,** with all the books, records and arts events of the week. There are two new pages of entertainments listings. On the back page of the second section, you will find a full page of **Television and Radio** programmes together with a new expanded **Weather** service. Inside the back, there is the new **Personal Page,** with obituaries, appreciations, birthdays, and our legal service. Cartoons — including the new **Bloom County** strip — and the **Quick Crossword** face Personal.

Here is the index to today's paper:

News in brief

Tomorrow

The new 20-page Saturday section, Guardian Choices, with helpful thoughts on how to pass your leisure time

Community crisis hopes

THE leaders of the 12 European Community governments were last night wrestling with a complicated compromise to the EEC budget crisis. Page 24

Under pressure

Speculation grew in Vienna that the two partners in Austria's governing coalition are pressing on President Kurt Waldheim to resign. Page 10

Investor action

THE Stock Exchange is facing the threat of government action over its treatment of small investors. Page 14

College cuts

SEVEN universities are scheduled to have their grants cut in the next two years, according to figures released by the University Grants Committee. Page 2

Seamen fined

THE National Union of Seamen was fined £7,500 in the High court for failing to call off an illegal strike immediately. Page 4

Somme record

A RESEARCH museum, largely hinging on the British role in the battle of the Somme, will be set up in Amiens. Page 10

Divided city

LABOUR-controlled Birmingham council, which is split after spending millions promoting the city for sports events, faces a threatened strike over staff cuts. Page 2

Plutonium row

TWO US Congress committees have objected to British Nuclear Fuels' plan to fly plutonium to Japan. Page 4

Party time

THE Tory Central Office is resigned to a weekend of embarrassment as Young Conservatives gather in Eastbourne. Page 8

Walking out

SOME 1,200 health workers walked out at three Glasgow hospitals. Page 3

Bus Stop top just the ticket

John Ezard

THE skimpy black-laced blouse worn by Marilyn Monroe in the film Bus Stop sold at Sotheby's for £7,150 yesterday, more than twice the forecast price, in an auction full of nostalgia, affection and reminiscent lust.

Although as a film costume it had little inherent rarity value, it was treated as an established historic relic. It fetched £3,000 more than a nightshirt reputedly abandoned by Charles I in mysterious circumstances in a Suffolk mansion — and nearly £7,000 more than a pair of the society photographer Cecil Beaton's monogrammed velvet slippers.

It went to Mr Patrick Mills, a Hertfordshire property developer, who wanted it to launch his 16-year-old daughter Chantelle's show business career.

Jauntily paraded among bidders by a lookalike model, Kay Kent, with photographers shouting like their predessors "Marilyn, look this way" it achieved the same love affair with the camera as when the star wore it 31 years ago.

Yet the filming of Bus Stop began miserably for Monroe. In his recent autobiography, her second husband, the playwright Arthur Miller, records her saying in a desperate phone call that the producers "can't stand women, none of them can, they're afraid of women, the whole gang of them . . . I can't fight for myself any more".

Film historians, however, regard it as the work in which she triumphed after studio quarrels by showing "a new gift for pathos, playing a small time showgirl who ekes out a living by wiggling her hips for cowboys. It was the first time audiences were fully aware of her vulnerability."

The blouse was sold by a woman film buff who won it in a contest run by the magazine Picture Show in the 1950s.

Its new wearer is still at theatre school. Asked if he was worried about the blouse being unlucky, Mr Mills said yesterday: "Marilyn's problem was her family and background, wasn't it? We have a good family and we look after each other and that's the secret."

Picture, page 2

2

The Guardian

VW in reverse

How the German economic miracle has run out of road

Young at heart Brandon Lee and the Peter Pan syndrome **Suzanne Moore 5**
Cancer ward 18-year-old Claire Khan's diary of optimism **Women 6/7**
Dora's dilemma Carrington, Apollo 13 and the rest of the releases **Screen 8/13**

OnLine with science and computing jobs

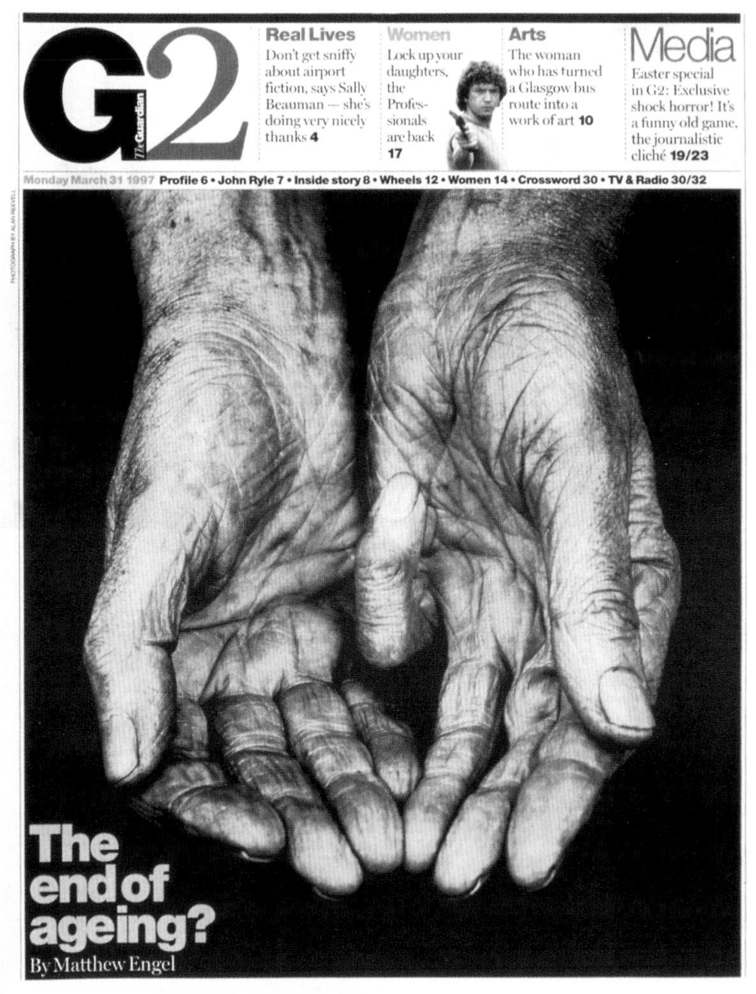

G2 The Guardian

Real Lives Don't get sniffy about airport fiction, says Sally Beauman — she's doing very nicely thanks **4**

Women Lock up your daughters, the Profes-sionals are back **17**

Arts The woman who has turned a Glasgow bus route into a work of art **10**

Media Easter special in G2: Exclusive shock horror! It's a funny old game, the journalistic cliché **19/23**

Monday March 31 1997 **Profile 6 • John Ryle 7 • Inside story 8 • Wheels 12 • Women 14 • Crossword 30 • TV & Radio 30/32**

PHOTOGRAPH BY ALAN REVELL

The end of ageing?

By Matthew Engel

G2

Arts The King and I: Simon Hattenstone remembers his idol Marc Bolan **4**

West Side Stories Swapping the couch for the coach: the latest in Manhattan therapies **8**

Autumn Books Martin Amis, Lee Marvin, Robert Hughes, Ruth Rendell and more in a bumper nine-page section **9**

Plus online The best place for IT jobs

The Guardian Thursday September 11 1997 **Pass Notes 3 • Women 6 • Time off 18 • Crossword 22 • TV and Radio 22-24**

The Guardian

MediaGuardian

What a carve-up!

Breaking up the BBC by Maggie Brown

Q: Why is Earl Spencer at war with this man? A: He's SA's No1 paparazzo 4

Is Dazed And Confused ready to challenge The Face? 6

Mercury takes silver for its ad campaign: the best of British ads 6

Creative, Media and Marketing jobs start on page 12

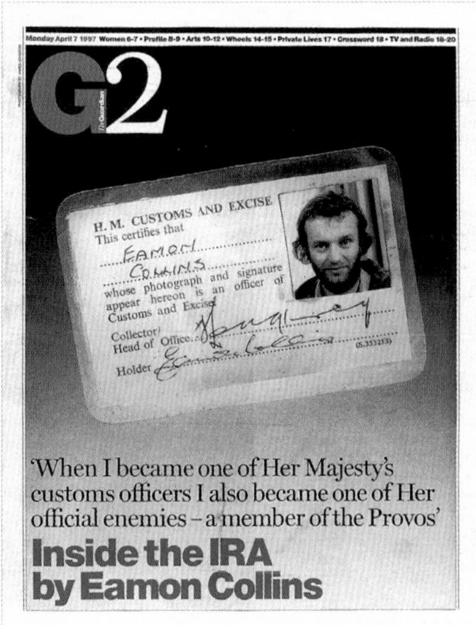

Monday April 7 1997 Women 6-7 • Profile 8-9 • Arts 10-12 • Wheels 14-15 • Private Lives 17 • Crossword 18 • TV and Radio 18-20

G2

'When I became one of Her Majesty's customs officers I also became one of Her official enemies – a member of the Provos'

Inside the IRA by Eamon Collins

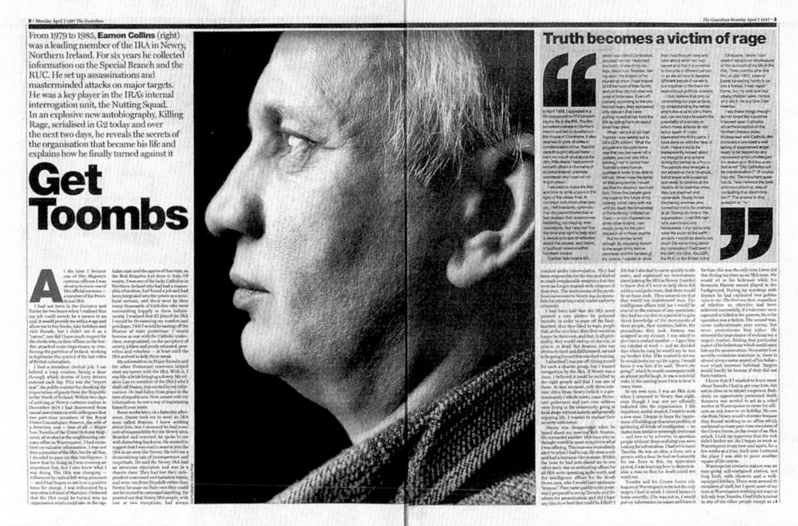

From 1979 to 1985, **Eamon Collins** (right) was a leading member of the IRA in Newry, Northern Ireland. For six years he collected information on the Special Branch and the RUC. He set up assassinations and masterminded attacks on major targets. He was a key player in the IRA's internal interrogation unit, the Nutting Squad. In an explosive new autobiography, Killing Rage, serialised in G2 today and over the next two days, he reveals the secrets of the organisation that became his life and explains how he finally turned against it

Get Toombs

Truth becomes a victim of rage

The Guardian's G2

The tabloid section G2 splits into two categories: the covers with the large "2" are work done initially, then the ones with "G2" are the main redesign. Media Guardian is an additional Monday section.

ENFOQUES

LA PRENSA GRÁFICA DOMINGO 6 DE JULIO DE 2003, SAN SALVADOR, EL SALVADOR, C.A. AÑO 6 N.° 265

LOS PESOS políticos en la CORTE

DIEZ DE LOS 15 MAGISTRADOS TIENEN VÍNCULOS POLÍTICOS EVIDENTES. EL RESTO NECESITÓ DEL EMPUJÓN DE UN PARTIDO PARA LLEGAR AL CARGO.

ILUSTRACIÓN DE LA PRENSA POR AGUSTÍN PALACIOS/ FOTOS DE LA PRENSA POR FÉLIX AMAYA

8 ENTREVISTA: ANTONIO CABRALES 11 ANDRÉS OPPENHEIMER 12 EL DILEMA SOBRE IRÁN

Above: The front page of *La Prensa Gráfica*'s weekly *Focus* supplement.

Three newspapers in one: *La Prensa Gráfica*

Miguel Angel Gómez

El Salvador daily *La Prensa Gráfica* was redesigned to become three papers in one

The goal in the redesign of *La Prensa Gráfica* was to give the readers the information in three big blocks that were totally different from each other, and to toss several "hooks" to the readers in order to capture their attention in one way or another.

The first part contains the hard news, focusing on national, international, and financial information. The second part deals with "soft news," which includes articles about lifestyle, show business, and culture. Last but hardly least is the third part: sports, which has the greatest number of readers in the Salvadoran market.

Each one of these "three papers" has its own identity, while still being part of the whole. The decision to break down the paper this way, made after long conversations with the editorial board, allowed for a better definition of each area's character, creating a major newspaper with variety and dynamism.

The result is a newspaper that is sober but never dull, dynamic but never messy.

The strategy

The redesign was done by Danilo Black. As in all of their work, typographic geography and color played a very important role. Each of the three parts establishes its identity through specific typefaces that give it a unique personality, and colors that organize the information and stress the transition from one space to another.

Typographically, part one (hard news) is based on Benton and Prensa – sober, modern, highly legible, big-impact families. Part two (soft news) stresses the use of Prensa Display, and includes the Stainless family to make contrast and to give a refined, fresh, provocative style. Part three (sports) uses Benton very aggressively and on a big scale.

The constant typographical feature is that the text throughout the publication is in Quiosco Roman, and the sidebars are in Benton.

The use of color similarly varies from part to part. Part one (hard news) uses sober colors, with a distinctive color for each kind of information. Part two (soft news) uses bright colors in different shades, to create different environments. Part three (sports) uses an intense red color to create dynamism.

The constant is the use of the blue color as an institutional color that reinforces the trademark presence.

The different spaces

The front page is a display window that invites readers to read the main articles in each section. It is broken up into several smaller "windows," each of which reflects the design of the section where it belongs, in order to stress the newspaper's variety.

Muerto y heridos en otro atentado en Filipinas › 28

LA PRENSA GRÁFICA

NOTICIAS DE VERDAD

Lunes

70 mil morosos en comercio y banca

› Empresa Dicom, con 8 millones de registros, vigila el comportamiento crediticio de los salvadoreños › 34

FAMA› PAULA HEREDIA

EL MUSEO DE JAMES BOND

Señales de tránsito para peatones.

LA PRENSA GRÁFICA

NOTICIAS DE VERDAD

Viernes

Fiscalía investiga corrupción en hospital del ISSS

Seguro reformará sistema de compra de medicinas ‹2-4›

RADIOGRAFÍA DEL ÁGUILA

FAMA

CARLOS VIVES

CONCIERTO

EL HERALDO DE ORIENTE

Civiles heridos en Colombia.

CÓDIGOS DE GUERRA

ESTRENOS DE CINE

40 DÍAS Y 40 NOCHES

LA PRENSA GRÁFICA

NOTICIAS DE VERDAD

Jueves

Corrupción en hospital de Oncología del ISSS

Tres médicos sindicalistas viciaron licitaciones de medicamentos ‹2-4›

Faltante en Alcaldía de Mejicanos

Corte de Cuentas detecta desórdenes administrativos ‹10-11›

589

Testigos describen al francotirador

FENADESAL para los locomotoras

FAMA

CHICHI PERALTA

Marcha contra reforma de salud.

CIENFUEGOS

LA HORA DE LA GALAXIA

The main headline is solid and legible; its purpose is capture the attention of the reader in the street, the arena where the battle for sales is fought out with rival publications.

The daily paper always features a large image with human content, to give a face to the news and avoid the impression that the design is a thing in itself.

In the Saturday and Sunday papers, which our research shows are sold later in the day and bought by different readers from those on the weekdays, the front page takes on a magazine look, which makes a difference in the reading dynamic. The articles in the Saturday and Sunday papers are longer and more analytical.

Hard news

Through a clean design, with a variety of supporting elements, and through the use of large, well-selected images, *La Prensa Gráfica* presents the news in a complete way, giving the reader information that covers the same issue from several angles.

We also created the Theme of the Day section (Tema del Día), which is, after the cover, the most important space in the newspaper. This is where the main story is presented, with a lot of related elements. The design is very "display"; it asks the reader to plunge into a sea of stories with different depths.

In the Opinion pages, which are devoted to ideas, typography is the master, and the space is employed completely.

The Economy section uses elements such as figures and tables to convey complicated financial information to the reader, clearly and directly.

The area called Summary (Resumen) was created as a place for brief information that got left off the front page; it deals with lighter, everyday issues.

LA PRENSA GRÁFICA

Sábado

NOTICIAS DE VERDAD

Nuevo diseño

Director ejecutivo de LA PRENSA GRÁFICA presenta nueva imagen. <20

NACIÓN

Flores vetará decreto

Presidente contra decisión de Asamblea de firmar plan de salud. <6

ECONOMÍA

Sectores a la baja

Investigan a ex rectores por títulos falsos

CORTE SUPREMA ABRE EXPEDIENTES CONTRA DOCE AUTORIDADES POR DAR TÍTULOS DE ABOGADOS <2-3

MARIPOSA SUBMARINA

INAUGURAN COPA ABIERTA EL SALVADOR

La nadadora guatemalteca Gisela Morales ganó plata ayer en los 100 metros mariposa de la Copa Abierta El Salvador. El oro fue para la boricua Solmari Mojica.

FAMA

JLO

LA AMBICIOSA

Jennifer López se ha convertido en la artista latina más deseada y seguida. <62

DEPORTE

CIEN-FUEGOS

ESTÁ EN LA FINAL

Tres centroamericanos serán protagonistas en la final de la MLS. <78-79

EN ESTA EDICIÓN

La Tribuna

Fútbol modesto

La ficha

Karate do

HOY MOTOR

EL SALÓN DE PARÍS

LA PRENSA GRÁFICA

Domingo

116 páginas

NOTICIAS DE VERDAD

MUNDO

Investigan pistas del francotirador

El casquillo de una bala se ha vuelto el centro de las pesquisas. <34

DEPARTAMENTOS

Festival de bandas de paz

Mil 500 adolescentes y niños de 31 centros educativos se reúnen en El Cafetalón. <16

DEPORTE

Real Madrid y Ronaldo caen

El Racing de Santander derrotó 2 a 0 al que se creía equipo invencible. <49

Cienfuegos listo para final MLS

El Galaxy y el Revolution cierran hoy el campeonato de fútbol de E.U.A. <80

INTERPOL busca a 44 salvadoreños

LA POLICÍA INTERNACIONAL PERSIGUE A 31 POR HOMICIDIO Y A 13 POR SECUESTRO <6-7

Elecciones internas

Miembros de una junta receptora de votos del FMLN revisan en la sede departamental de San Salvador las boletas de elección de los candidatos para diputados y alcaldes. Un total de 230 municipios definió sus postulaciones. <2

VIVIR

LOS SUEÑOS IMPOSIBLES

El insomnio es considerado como un trastorno mental. <24

FAMA

CARLOS VIVES

El colombiano estrenació las instalaciones de la Feria. <38

EN ESTA EDICIÓN

SUPLEMENTO

Revista Dominical

Los nuevos scouts

SUPLEMENTO

Revista Enfoques

Vida al mínimo

Front pages of the Saturday and Sunday editions (above), and of weekday editions (opposite).

Hard news

The first sections of the paper give the reader serious, complete, precise information. The news headlines are presented in two complementary, high-legibility typefaces: Benton and Prensa. The Mundo section contains stories that expand on the front-page news, and may include subjects like science, health, astronomy, technology, or religion.

LA PRENSA GRÁFICA

MUNDO

44 **Guerra en Washington** La Policía intenta evitar nuevas acciones del francotirador.

48 **Nuevos ataques** E.U.A. confirmó ayer que tropas en Kuwait fueron atacadas nuevamente.

Indonesia y E.U.A. acusan a Al Qaeda por atentado

E.U.A. ya había advertido a sus ciudadanos del riesgo

» Un miembro de la red capturado en junio reveló planes para atentar con bombas en Asia.

DESASTRE. Un policía indonesio custodia el área del atentado terrorista que dejó en ruinas una discoteca repleta el sábado pasado. Indonesia acusa a Al Qaeda de la explosión que dejó al menos 187 muertos.

VÍCTIMAS DEL TERRORISMO

190 muertos al menos dejó el atentado.

300 heridos, muchos de ellos con graves lesiones.

200 desaparecidos, muchos de los cuales se teme estén muertos.

IN MEMORIAM. Mujeres encienden veladoras en una plaza de Bali, en Indonesia, en memoria de las casi 200 muertos en el atentado del sábado pasado.

Bin Laden elogia ataques

ENVÍA MENSAJE. Osama bin Laden, líder de la organización terrorista Al Qaeda.

LA PRENSA GRÁFICA MARTES 15 DE OCTUBRE DE 2002 — MUNDO 43

Europa teme "gran golpe"

TEMOR EN EUROPA. Berlín podría ser uno de los objetivos de un ataque de Al Qaeda, según expertos antiterroristas del viejo continente. Europa teme un ataque terrorista en Alemania, Francia o Bélgica.

Resurge el terrorismo

» Autoridades estadounidenses creen que Al Qaeda se ha reconstruido con la ayuda de grupos más pequeños en Asia.

"Aprendimos una lección esta semana. Nos tomará algún tiempo lograr algo." George W. Bush, presidente de E.U.A.

"El terrorismo global, el extremismo y el fundamentalismo no conocen límites." Tony Blair, Primer Ministro británico.

"El mundo está en problemas. No he visto que las cosas estén tan mal en mucho tiempo." Kofi Annan, Secretario General de la ONU.

Llamado a la coalición

LA PRENSA GRÁFICA

MUNDO

Atentado en Bali

Referéndum por Sadam

"Se que no les hemos dado mucha información, pero créanme, estamos progresando."

Carrera contra la muerte

La Policía busca desesperadamente pistas del francotirador

» Las autoridades confirmaron ayer que el asesinato de una mujer el lunes por la noche fue obra del homicida.

La novena víctima era agente del FBI

» Linda Franklin era analista en el FBI. La Policía descarta que su muerte tenga relación con su empleo.

Linda Franklin, la mujer que cayó muerta de un disparo el lunes por la noche en Falls Church, Virginia, era un agente del FBI que trabajaba en inteligencia antiterrorista.

De hecho, la división en la que Franklin trabajaba es la única del FBI que será integrada pronto a la recién creada Oficina de Seguridad Nacional.

"Trabajaba para nosotros", ha declarado escuetamente la oficina de prensa del FBI, sin dar más detalles.

Franklin, madre de dos niños, llevaba tres años y medio trabajando como analista de la Agencia Federal.

Linda Franklin. Esposa y madre de dos niños.

"The Washington Post" asegura que su esposo, Ted, fue testigo de la muerte de su mujer.

Según el periódico, ella y su esposo pensaban mudarse de casa este viernes, y habían ido a Home Depot, un almacén de productos del hogar, para comprar utensilios necesarios para la mudanza y los arreglos de la casa que ocuparían el fin de semana.

Ambos se encontraban en el estacionamiento del almacén cuando Linda cayó muerta a los pies de su marido.

El FBI confirmó que Franklin trabajaba desde hacía tres años y medio en el Centro de Protección de la Infraestructura Nacional, una división creada el año pasado para investigar crímenes por computadora, electrónicos o con el uso de alta tecnología.

Descartan relación

Sin embargo, el jefe de la Policía a cargo de la investigación sobre el francotirador, Charles Moose, descartó ayer que el asesinato de Franklin haya tenido alguna relación con el trabajo que efectuaba.

La Policía, que intenta establecer algún patrón del esquivo asesino, sostiene que éste elije a sus víctimas al azar, y que no hay ninguna relación entre ellas.

De hecho, entre las 11 víctimas se encuentran hombres, mujeres y niños de diversas razas y estratos económicos y sociales.

Franklin es la novena persona en fallecer por los disparos; dos se encuentran heridas.

Las víctimas del francotirador

La Policía se encuentra en virtual pie de guerra en la zona de Washington, intentando encontrar alguna pista que ayude a la captura inmediata del francotirador. El asesino ya ha terminado con la vida de nueve personas y ha herido a otras dos, sin vínculos entre ellas, y no se ha encontrado el patrón que sigue para seleccionar a sus víctimas.

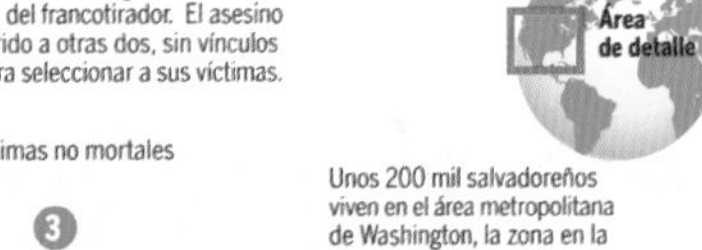

9.- Linda Franklin, de 47 años, analista del FBI, se convirtió en la novena víctima mortal del francotirador el lunes por la noche.

1.-James D. Martin, de 55 años, asesinado el 2 de octubre en el estacionamiento de un centro comercial en Wheaton, Maryland.

2.-James Buchanan, jardinero de 39 años, murió el 3 de octubre al recibir un disparo mientras cortaba el césped en Montgomery, Maryland.

3.-Prem Kumar Walekar, taxista de 54 años, asesinado 31 minutos después mientras cargaba gasolina en Aspen Hill, Maryland.

4.-La salvadoreña Sara Ramos, de 34 años, recibe un impacto de bala el 3 de octubre a las 8:37 a.m. en una banca en Silver Spring.

5.- Lori Ann Lewis, de 25 años, asesinada ese mismo día mientras limpiaba su vehículo en Kensington, Maryland.

6.-Pascal Charlot, un inmigrante haitiano de 72 años, recibe un disparo cuando caminaba por una calle de Washington, D.C., el 3 de octubre por la noche.

7.-Dean Harold Meyers, de 32 años, se detiene a cargar gasolina en Manassas, Virginia, el 9 de octubre, y recibe un disparo en la cabeza.

8.- El 11 de octubre, Keneth H. Bridges, de 53 años, es asesinado en una gasolinera de Fredericksburg, en Virginia.

LAS INVESTIGACIONES

Asrto Van Blanca, vehículo en el que el sujeto se transporta.

Estriado

Campos

Valles

El estriado hace girar la bala y es necesario para lograr precisión. El número, espacio, dirección (derecha o izquierda) y cantidad de vueltas de los "campos" y "valles" del estriado aparecen como marcas características en la bala.

1 2

La bala 1 salió disparada de un arma con un "campo" menor y más vueltas que la bala 2.

Las marcas características pueden aparecer en repetidas ocasiones en las balas que salen disparadas de la misma arma.

Fuente: USA TODAY, Washington Post, Reuters

Ricardo Orellana, LA PRENSA GRÁFICA

CASA DE VÍCTIMA. *Un agente habla con una persona no identificada en la residencia de Linda Franklin.*

Una aguja en un pajar

La Policía está buscando a un asesino que no responde a ninguno de los perfiles criminales contenidos en sus archivos.

Después de nueve muertes y dos personas heridas, la Policía ni siquiera sabe si el homicida actúa solo o cuenta con un cómplice.

Hasta el momento, sabe que es un tirador experto y preciso, probablemente entrenado.

Que utiliza un rifle de largo alcance y munición calibre .223.

Y, dos semanas después del primer ataque, también sabe que no actúa los fines de semana.

Las autoridades creen que se moviliza en una camioneta blanca, de color claro, tipo "van".

Y tiene una pista más: la carta de tarot que el francotirador dejó en el lugar del noveno ataque, en el que hirió a un menor que ingresaba a su escuela.

La carta representaba a la muerte, y llevaba escrito un pequeño mensaje: "Querido policía, soy Dios".

Hasta el momento, se ha detenido a más de cinco personas que han sido interrogadas, y después liberadas porque, mientras estaban bajo custodia policial, afuera las víctimas seguían cayendo.

Sin embargo, dos periódicos estadounidenses, que citan a un testigo, aseguran que la Policía ya tendría imágenes del criminal.

Éstas habrían sido obtenidas por una cámara de vigilancia.

La Policía dijo ayer que tiene más información y que está progresando, pero que no es momento de dar a conocer lo que tienen.

Pero lo recabado hasta ahora no ha servido de mucho.

Las pistas

La Policía dice haber avanzado en las investigaciones. Éstas son las pruebas con las que cuenta.

- El francotirador viaja en una camioneta color claro, con una luz trasera rota.
- **Es un experto tirador, probablemente un ex militar.**
- Utiliza un arma de largo alcance, y munición calibre .223
- **No actúa los fines de semana.**

"Hemos recogido nuevas informaciones gracias a los testimonios de anoche, y confío en que nos lleven a un arresto."

Tom Manger, jefe de Policía de Falls Church.

LA PRENSA GRÁFICA

CULTURA

La nueva Biblioteca de Alejandría

La legendaria biblioteca resurgirá este día en la ciudad del mismo nombre, en el mismo lugar donde fue consumida por el fuego en el año 47 a.C. El edificio costó $220 millones.

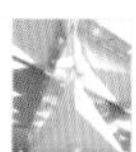

AGENDA CULTURAL

"Naque, o de piojos y actores" Muestra Internacional de Teatro. 6:30 p.m. Teatro Nacional de Santa Ana. $3.

Exposición Muestra de Pintura y Escultura Latinoamericana. Galería Espacio.

"En el jardín de las angustias" Muestra Nacional de Teatro. 4:00 y 8:00 p.m. en el Museo David J. Guzmán. Valor: $3 y $2.

Concierto Sinfónico Teatro Presidente. 7:00 p.m. Entrada gratis.

"Relato de un viaje americano" La pintora boliviana Patricia Mariaca expone una colección de lienzos en el Centro Cultural de España (Col. San Benito, Calle La Reforma, n.º 166, San Salvador). La muestra permanecerá abierta al público hasta el 31 de octubre.

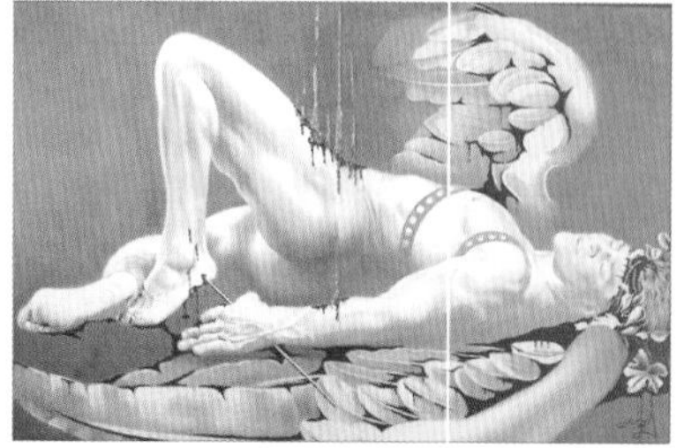

Arte salvadoreño en el corazón de Manhattan

La pintora Sonia Melara se ha afincado en Nueva York. "Es parte de mi desarrollo como artista", afirma. Ahora expone en la gran ciudad una colección que muestra el arte salvadoreño a través de una desgarradora visión del dolor y la figura humana.

Creación salvadoreña

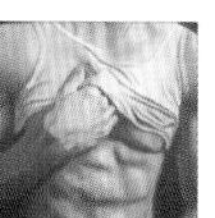

LA FIGURA humana ha sido un tema recurrente en su obra.

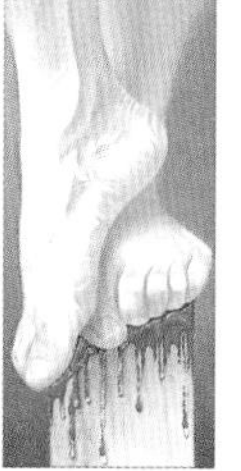

Trayectoria artística

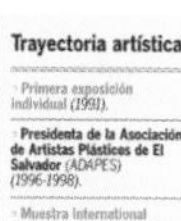

« BREVES »

Feria del Libro en Guadalajara

Murió Jacques Borel

Cuarta mujer en la Academia

BRYCE ECHENIQUE SALTÓ A LA FAMA CON LA OBRA "UN MUNDO PARA JULIUS".

Premio Planeta para Bryce Echenique

» El escritor peruano Alfredo Bryce Echenique se adjudicó el Premio Planeta de Novela por su obra "El huerto de mi amada". El galardón está dotado con 590 mil dólares.

AL MARGEN

Un mundo para Bryce

Santiago Mendive

Jefe de Redacción

LA PRENSA GRÁFICA

CULTURA

Feria del Libro en Francfort

La Feria del Libro de Francfort terminó este lunes con la visita de unos 250 mil lectores. La actividad albergó a unos 6 mil 375 expositores provenientes de 110 países.

AGENDA CULTURAL

"El lazarillo de Tormes" Muestra Nacional de Teatro. 4:00 y 8:00 p.m. en el Museo David J. Guzmán. Valor: $2.

Exposición De la pintora boliviana Patricia Mariaca. Centro Cultural de España.

Hora literaria Recital poético con Ricardo Lindo, Rafael Mendoza, William Alfaro y Pablo Agudelo. 6:30 p.m. El Arbol.

Concierto Sinfónico Teatro Presidente. 7:00 p.m. Entrada gratis.

Imágenes del Japón Exposición de artículos tradicionales elaborados en diferentes regiones del Japón. Abierta hasta el 17 de octubre en el Teatro Nacional de San Miguel. Habrá proyección de cine japonés. Mayor información en los teléfonos 224-4740.

DEL EDITOR

Un espacio para la cultura

José Víctor Huezo

Editor de cultura

KERTÉSZ, NOBEL DE LITERATURA 2002:

"Siempre que pienso en una nueva novela, pienso en Auschwitz"

Testigo, superviviente y fatigado hondo y tranquilo del Holocausto, el escritor húngaro obtuvo el Premio Nobel de Literatura.

IMRE KERTÉSZ ofreció una conferencia de prensa un día después del anuncio del Nobel de Literatura. A la cita acudió junto a su esposa Magda.

Algunos de sus libros

- Sin destino (1975)
- El fracaso (1988)
- Kaddish por el hijo no nacido (1990)
- Diario de la galera (1992)
- The Holocaust as culture (1993)
- Yo, otro (1997)
- Un instante de silencio en el paredón (1998)
- The exiled language (2002)

IMRE KERTÉSZ

Banfield llega a Santa Ana

» El titiritero de Banfield nos ofrece su arte en la Muestra Internacional de Teatro, otra de las actividades de este octubre escénico.

SERGIO MERCURIO presentará su espectáculo en este Muestra Internacional de Teatro.

Muestra internacional

« BREVES »

Récord de visitantes en el Guggenheim

Martin Walser recibe premio en Francfort

Se agotan memorias de García Márquez

Hoy anuncian Premio Planeta de Novela

BRYCE ECHENIQUE.

Two-page spreads from the Culture section of the paper.

Soft news

The Culture section marks the transition from one "newspaper" to another (remember the three-papers-in-one concept). It manages its information more like a magazine.

The Living section (Vivir) provides a change of environment that contrasts with the daily news stories. It approaches different issues every day, counseling and guiding the family. It does this through the use of a very organic, playful design and harmonic color management.

Fame (Fama), in contrast with Living, bombards the reader with a lot of brief show-business items, in a layout that takes advantage of all the space in a more dynamic way. Big photos and typographic games distinguish this section.

Sports (Deporte)

This part of the paper shows passion and movement. It is bold, with big, expressive photos, dramatic editing, provocative headlines, and a wide range of intense colors.

Soccer (Fútbol) is a subsection that takes advantage of Salvadorans' addiction to this sport, offering all the national and international information that a fanatic could possibly want.

The Sports section is so important that on Mondays it wraps the whole newspaper, covering the front page with Sports Monday, a supplement that dynamically presents all the information about the weekend's sports activities.

Weekly supplements

The redesign included a strategy for supplements, whose front pages have more impact and a more maximalist presentation.

The Tribune (*La Tribuna*): Deep sports coverage with analysis and interviews. It has its own design, conceptual photos, and very creative headlines.

Focus (*Enfoques*): Investigative reporting and critical analysis, with photos that reflect social drama and seek to provoke changes in people's attitudes – material that sets an agenda for the week. It uses the typographic range of the hard-news part of the paper.

Sunday Magazine (*Revista Dominical*): Presents deep themes about culture, art, and science in an ingenious way. The relaxed design and inviting typography shape a product meant for quiet reading to enjoy during the week. ‹

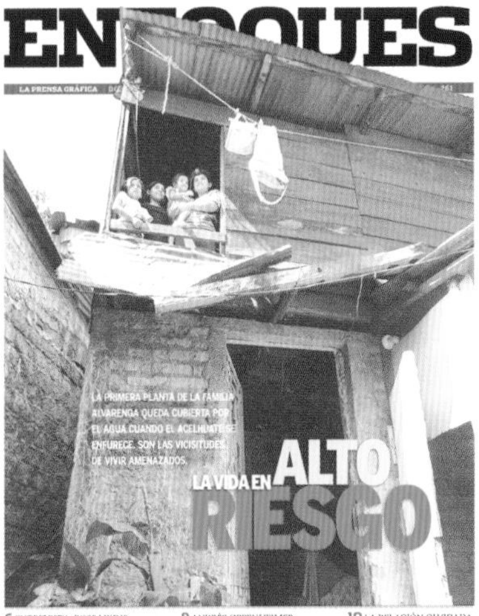

Front pages of the weekly supplements *Focus* and *Sunday Magazine*.

LA PRENSA GRÁFICA

FAMA

CINE › CELEBRIDADES › **ARTISTAS** › MÚSICA

Quieren imponer LA LEY EN DISNEY

El grupo chileno La Ley grabó una canción, en inglés y en español, para la nueva película de dibujos animados de los estudios Disney, llamada "El Planeta del Tesoro". Beto Cuevas, el vocalista, confirmó que también preparan algo para un filme de Jennifer López.

El "derby" del terror: JASON VRS FREDDY

Sangriento y colosal. Así promete ser el choque entre los malvados Freddy Krueger y Jason Vorhees, batalla que tomará lugar en una película producida por New Line Cinema, y que saldrá al público en las próximas semanas.

Freddy contra Jason enfrentará a los villanos de "Nightmare on Elm Street" (Freddy) y "Friday the 13th" (Jason), dos filmes del género de horror que le han quitado el sueño a adultos y adolescentes.

Krueger ha asesinado a múltiples adolescentes. El enmascarado y estrella de "Friday the 13th" también prefiere ultimar a los jovencitos, en especial mientras realizaban actos sexuales en paseos y campamentos de verano.

Robert Englund interpretará a Freddy por octava vez en este proyecto, que también contará con la actuación de Brad Renfro (el pequeño de "The Client"), según reporta "Daily Variety". Aún no se sabe quién estará detrás de la máscara de Jason.

Ally McBeal atrapó al fugitivo

Harrison Ford y su novia, Calista Flockhart, -famosa por el papel de Ally McBeal- dieron vida a un improvisado espectáculo en un restaurante de Nueva York, cuando el protagonista de las aventuras de "Indiana Jones" y de "El Fugitivo" le propuso a su pareja que se casase con él.

Según ha relatado el diario romano "La Repubblica", en un momento dado Ford se puso de rodillas ante Flockhart, le ofreció un anillo con un gran diamante y le pidió que fuera su esposa.

La intérprete de Ally McBeal comenzó a dar saltitos de alegría mientras la gente que se encontraba en el restaurante empezaba a aplaudir. La escena continuó como si se tratase de una película con los dos protagonistas fundidos en un abrazo.

VIENEN MÁS SUSTOS

Cada Halloween surge, al menos, un "cinestreno" que sea fiel al género de horror. Este año la dosis de susto llega, además, a través de dos nuevos filmes, "The Ring" (El anillo) y "Ghost Ship" (El barco fantasma).

OTROS DUELOS A MUERTE

No es la primera vez en la historia del cine que se enfrentan dos protagonistas de franquicias. El morbo por ver a criaturas mounstruosas empezó en a mediados del siglo pasado.

- Frankenstein conoce al Hombre Lobo *(1942)*
- **King Kong vrs. Godzilla** *(1963)*
- Godzilla vrs. Mothra *(1964)*
- **Billy the Kid vrs. Dracula** *(1966)*
- Frankenstein vrs. Dracula *(1971)*.

THE RING

Debutará el 18 de octubre. Es un "remake" del filme japonés Ringu. Naomi Watts interpreta a una reportera que hace cuenta de un video con un pasado misterioso... toda persona que ha visto el video muere en un lapso de siete días.

EL BARCO FANTASMA

Julianna Margulies y sus amigos hallan un barco a la deriva. El crucero italiano Antonia Graza ha estado "desaparecido" durante 40 años, y ahora su pasado resurge como una amenaza. Se estrenará el 25 de este mes.

« EL MUNDO DE LA FAMA »

Le fue mal a Naomi en los juzgados

La supermodelo británica Naomi Campbell tendrá que pagar 5 mil dólares, después de que un diario sensacinalista que había revelado su lucha contra las drogas ganara el lunes una apelación en la corte.

Zeta-Jones espera segundo hijo

Los actores Michael Douglas y Catherine Zeta-Jones están esperando su segundo hijo. Zeta-Jones, de 33 años, dará a luz nuevamente en la primavera boreal del próximo año.

AVRIL LAVIGNE

¡CONÓCELA!

¿Temblará Alanis Morissette al ver a su compatriota Avril Lavigne? Adolescente, talentosa y rockera. Lavigne tiene al mundo de la música en sus manos.

UNA CERVECITA CON VERGARA

La playa, una cerveza y Sofía Vergara. El sueño de muchos. La diva de la televisión y los calendarios anunció que se ha convertido en la nueva portavoz LATINA de la cervecería Miller.

La escultural actriz y modelo colombiana fue contratada por esa compañía como parte de una nueva campaña dirigida a la comunidad hispana en Estados Unidos, informó la página electrónica de la agencia de noticias CNN en español.

Además de un comercial televisivo, Vergara aparece en carteles publicitarios y también hará presentaciones en mercados hispanos a nombre de Miller Lite.

Penélope andará por las nubes

Penélope Cruz encarnará a una gitana, en la cinta "Head In The Clouds" ("Cabeza en las nubes"), la cual se comenzará a rodar en París en diciembre, informó CNN en español.

El drama de la cinta consiste en una historia de amor, con la Segunda Guerra Mundial como trasfondo.

También estará protagonizado por Natalie Portman, quien hará el papel de una fotógrafa. Portman se unirá a esta producción luego de que finalice el rodaje de "Cold Mountain", producción a cargo del director Anthony Minghella.

Penélope Cruz, por su parte, acaba de finalizar el rodaje de "Masked And Anonymous", película protagonizada por el músico Bob Dylan, dijo la CNN.

Baila más sucio que Ricky Martin

Hazte a un lado, Ricky Martin, que aquí está Diego Luna, quien llega con su nuevo aire de bailarín.

El intérprete de "Y tu mamá también" ha desplazado a Ricky Martin como protagonista de Havana Nights, basada en la exitosa Dirty Dancing.

¿Quieres ver los movimientos del Diego? Calma, que para eso hay que esperar, a que se estrene "Havana Nights" el 21 de noviembre de 2003, según informa "Hollywood Reporter". Eso en Estados Unidos, en El Salvador, habrá que esperar.

"Havana Nights", la precuela de "Dirty Dancing", gira alrededor de una chica estadounidense de 17 años que se muda a la Cuba de 1959 junto a sus padres. Allí desafía los deseos de su familia cuando se enamora de un bailarín local, encarnado por el joven y talentoso actor Diego Luna.

LA PRENSA GRÁFICA

FAMA

CINE › CELEBRIDADES › **ARTISTAS** › MÚSICA

Madonna, LA HUMILDE

Madonna dijo que ya no quiere ser tan egocéntrica; al contrario, dijo que quiere preocuparse por las cosas más trascendentales para la humanidad, como la ecología y el hambre entre los pobres. "Estoy en la misión de deshacerme de mi gigantesco ego", dijo la cantante, con mucha humildad.

"VEN A VER" A ODALYS: *además de bella... ¡canta!*

Causante de las más atrevidas fantasías masculinas, la cubana Odalys García quiere que la reconozcan más por su talento artístico y cualidades humanas que por sus atributos físicos. LA PRENSA GRÁFICA habló en exclusiva con la escultural artista.

HENRY MEJÍA

Provocó la pasión de millones de televidentes cuando aparecía en el programa "Lente loco", de la cadena Univisión. Enloqueció a miles cuando lanzó sus calendarios con poses sugerentes. Pero ahora seduce con su voz en "Ven a ver", su primera producción discográfica.

Apadrinada por Abraham Quintanilla, padre de Selena, la recordada cantante de Corpus Christi, Odalys nos muestra su propuesta musical en la línea del pop, baladas y dance.

Cansada por una agotadora jornada de promoción en la ciudad de Los Ángeles, pero con un estado de ánimo envidiable, nos habla sobre su álbum y sobre el amor, mientras se pone cómoda en un acogedor sofá.

Luce el rostro limpísimo, con un mínimo de maquillaje. Viste un "jeans tronconero", una blusa de tela blanca semitransparente, gafas oscuras, para disimular un poco el cansancio, y sandalias, que muestran unos pies delicados y perfectamente arreglados.

Su disco, "Ven a ver", le cierra la boca a quienes creían que su talento se limitaba a la animación en la pantalla chica. A la vez, demuestra que sabe transmitir emociones a través de su voz y los acordes de su música.

¿Desde hace cuánto querías lanzar tu disco?

Yo estoy con esta gana y preparándome desde hace mucho. El proceso inició hace dos años cuando empezamos a hacer los demos con Abraham Quintanilla.

¿Cantar era tu sueño?

Todo comenzó en Cuba cuando tenía cinco años de edad. Iba a una escuela de ballet, me encantaron los escenarios, la música y las luces. Luego vine a Estados Unidos, se dio la oportunidad de hacer televisión y hoy se me da la oportunidad de grabar mi primer disco.

¿Ha sido difícil convencer a la gente de que cantar no es un capricho?

El negocio se ha malogrado porque han salido muchachas famosas que se metieron a cantar y no han funcionado. Por eso costó tanto trabajo que creyeran en mí.

¿Fue difícil la transición?

Difícil, pero no imposible, si crees en lo que estás haciendo. No le puedes gustar a todo el mundo, pero te puedo decir, por lo que he sentido, que la mayoría de la gente está contenta con el trabajo.

¿Qué podemos esperar de ti en este álbum?

A una Odalys más romántica, más apasionada, más ella. Estaban acostumbrados a ver una Odalys que se basa más en un personaje para un programa de televisión y no a la mujer que en realidad soy.

> *"Me he puesto a pensar muchas cosas, ¿qué será, qué sera, qué será? Y yo creo que eso ha sido lo esencial del porqué no ha funcionado bien. Pero yo adoro a los hombres, de todas maneras, aunque diga eso.*
>
> Odalys García

¿Por qué escogiste el pop, si tienes raíces caribeñas?

Como mis influencias son latinas, hay canciones muy sabrosas como "Soy latina" y "Ven a ver". El álbum es un compendio de cosas que hicieron al final un disco muy bonito.

En el programa radial de "El Cucuy de la mañana" (Los Ángeles) presentaste un tema grupero que no está en el disco

Lo que oíste fue la balada "Globo sin gas", que hicimos grupera porque "el Cucuy" lo recomendó, porque abre más las puertas para las estaciones de radio que no tocan pop y balada, pero que sí programan el género grupero.

¿Escribiste alguna de las canciones que aparecen en este primer álbum?

Tengo algunas cosas que he hecho, pero como uno siempre piensa que lo que escribe no es muy bueno, quise que la gente que de verdad sabe de música pusiera las manitos en este disco. Esperaré a un próximo disco -espero que haya un próximo disco- y en ese sí irá material mío.

¿Sobre qué compones?

Compongo sobre el amor, sobre el desamor y sobre el sufrimiento.

¿Te han hecho sufrir en el amor?

Claro. Nos podemos enamorar y nos pueden dejar también...

¿Te ha costado encontrar a alguien que comprenda tu vida tan intensa?

Creo que es difícil encontrar el amor cuando eres una mujer trabajadora, luchadora, independiente y segura de ti misma. Es muy difícil encontrar a un hombre que de verdad esté seguro de sí mismo. Que no parezca ego, pero he tenido relaciones lindas en las que el gran problema ha sido la inseguridad de mi pareja. Creo que algunos hombres aún tienen la mentalidad de que la mujer debe estar encerrada en la casa para cocinar y hacer la limpieza.

¿Te preocupa esa situación?

Me he puesto a pensar muchas cosas, ¿qué será, qué sera, qué será? Y yo creo que eso ha sido lo esencial del porqué no ha funcionado bien. Pero yo adoro a los hombres, de todas maneras, aunque diga eso.

Veo que te gustan los detalles. Un admirador vino y te trajo un sombrero texano durante la entrevista radial...

¿Viste? ¡Me trajeron un sombrero texano! Son detalles que un hombre puede hacer. No es necesario que sea un regalo, basta con una rosa o que te ponga la silla. Son detalles que a los hombres a veces se les olvidan, pero a las mujeres en realidad nos llenan.

NO HAY UN PROTOTIPO DE HOMBRE

Para conquistar a Odalys no es necesario tener ojos azules y ser rubio. Ella dice que se le conquista con pequeños detalles. Y aunque no tiene novio, dice que no se desespera.

"No tengo en la mente la pregunta: '¿Por qué no llega?' Sé que va a llegar. Además, cómo que no va a llegar... si soy tan buena ('estalla' en risas)... ¡estoy bromeando!", dice.

Ni la "principessa"

Más de 200 mil italianos acudieron ya a los más de 900 cines en los que se exhibe la última película de Roberto Benigni, "Pinocchio". Nunca antes un estreno provocó tanto alboroto en Italia.

"Quiero que la gente se sienta identificada, que se besen al salir del cine", expresó el actor y director, quien celebró un éxito internacional sin precedentes con "La vida es bella", famosa por la frase "Buon giorno principessa".

Las primeras críticas a "Pinocchio" no fueron brillantes, pero se trata de un fenómeno que va más allá de la película. Los comentaristas ven en el niño de madera de la nariz larga "la esencia nacional italiana" y toda Italia vive ya, la "fiebre Pinocchio", como le llaman los medios.

ROBERTO *Benigni*

Presentarán "presunto" disco

Presuntos Implicados prepara para el próximo mes su primer disco recopilatorio. Se trata de "Selección natural - Grandes éxitos", que incluirá 36 canciones recogidas en dos CD y, además, un DVD con sus 20 videoclips.

Este retrospectivo tendrá las regrabaciones de "Alma de blues" y, por su puesto, su éxito "Como hemos cambiado".

A probar su "edad de la inocencia"

Winona Ryder consiguió impresionar dos veces a la Academia de Hollywood con su talento interpretativo. La actriz obtuvo una de las dos nominaciones al Oscar por "La edad de la inocencia", de Martin Scorsese, en 1993.

Ahora, Ryder, de 30 años, deberá convencer de su inocencia a un tribunal de Beverly Hills, en el que esta semana comienza el proceso en el que la fiscalía la acusa de varios delitos: robo, vandalismo y posesión de medicamentos sin receta alguna.

En diciembre pasado, la actriz fue detenida en el centro comercial de lujo Saks Fifth Avenue, donde aparentemente robó mercadería valorada en un aproximado de 5 mil dólares.

Ryder se declaró "no culpable", pagó la fianza de 20 mil dólares y quedó en libertad. Pero en caso de ser condenada, podría pasar hasta tres años en la cárcel.

Tras varias negociaciones fracasadas entre sus abogados y la acusación, con el fin de evitar el proceso, la actriz deberá presentarse ante el juez hoy.

WINONA *Ryder*

ALGO EN SU CARRERA LE FASCINA

Elvis Crespo dijo recientemente que llegó a hartarse de su carrera. Fue sólo el AMOR del público lo que le recordó cuánto ama lo que hace.

"Mi carrera me hartó tanto que consideré el retiro, pero en tres meses sin un escenario me di cuenta de que la necesitaba", dijo el autor de Tu sonrisa.

ELVIS *Crespo*

LA PRENSA GRÁFICA

EN SOCIEDAD

NUEVA *Miss Teen* EL SALVADOR 2002

Mayra Muñoz rumbo a concurso en Venezuela

En un vistoso evento, 12 señoritas participaron para conseguir la corona de Miss Teen El Salvador. Un prestigioso jurado nombró como ganadora a Mayra Muñoz.

REINA MARÍA DE ÁLVAREZ
vivir@laprensa.com.sv

Mayra Muñoz no pudo ocultar su felicidad, el pasado sábado por la noche, cuando fue electa Miss Teen El Salvador 2002. El concurso se efectuó el pasado sábado, con una cena y show bailable, en el hotel Terraza.

Esta belleza trigueña, de 17 años, ojos café y 1.71 m de estatura, cautivó al jurado calificador y al público asistente, con la dulzura que irradia su rostro y su simpatía.

Muñoz realiza estudios de secretariado bilingüe en el Centro Cultural Salvadoreño.

Ella, con su belleza y elegancia, representará a los salvadoreños en el concurso Miss Teenager World, que se efectuará en Venezuela, el próximo mes de mayo de 2003, donde competirá con adolescentes de todo el mundo.

Las cinco finalistas representarán al El Salvador en otros concursos como Miss Turismo Internacional, Miss Turish of the World, Miss Expo Mundial, Miss Iberoamérica Internacional y La Modelo Latina del Año.

En la búsqueda de Miss Teen El Salvador participaron 12 jovencitas entre los 17 y los 19 años.

Las concursantes desfilaron en trajes casuales, de baño y de noche, para deleitar al jurado y al público asistente. El jurado calificador estuvo integrado por reconocidas personalidades nacionales como Jonás Herrera, Eduardo Miguel, Jorge Arguett, Carmen María de Salazar, Sergio Hernández y Georgina Machuca.

Mayra tiene 17 años y estudia secretariado bilingüe. Esta belleza adolescente representará al país en Miss Teenager World, en Venezuela.

Después de ser coronada por Luz de María Castro, Miss Teen El Salvador 2001, la nueva reina fue felicitada por sus compañeras. Cinco de ellas también competirán en otros concursos internacionales.

Las concursantes hicieron brillar la pasarela en los diversos desfiles que realizaron durante la elección de Miss Teen El Salvador.

FOTOS DE LA PRENSA GRÁFICA, POR FRANCISCO ALEMÁN

Finalistas del concurso: Liliana Masis, Dora Marriette Martínez, Erika Lau, Karen Quezada, Mayra Muñoz (ganadora) y Verónica Meléndez son las seis bellezas adolescentes finalistas en Miss Teen El Salvador.

LA PRENSA GRÁFICA

EN SOCIEDAD

Fiesta nacional República de China

Soft news

In addition to serious topics of culture, the second part of the paper covers society, lifestyle, and celebrity stories. The color palette, layout, and typography (including lavish use of the typeface Stainless) reflect this looser, livelier subject matter.

LA PRENSA GRÁFICA

DEPORTE

PALERMO: VOLVERÉ AL BOCA

"BATISHIP"

"CAPO DI TUTTI CAPIS"

Las autoridades del automovilismo mundial presentaron las propuestas para recuperar el encanto perdido en la Fórmula 1.

FÓRMULA PARA LA FÓRMULA

"SCHUMIFOBIA"

CASTIGO PARA UN HINCHA

Un carro distinto

JACQUES ROGGE.

Presidente COI estará en San Salvador 2002

Agenda histórica

DOUG MIENTKIEWICZ, DE LOS MELLIZOS, LAMENTA LA DERROTA.

Encontraron su ángel

Los Angelinos de Anaheim acabaron el domingo con 41 años de frustraciones.

LOS REYES DEL BATE

¿Sede olímpica?

Este gráfico de computadora muestra cómo será el Parque Olímpico de Stuttgart, siempre y cuando el Comité Olímpico Internacional otorgue a esta ciudad del suroeste alemán la sede de los Juegos de 2012.

BREVES

GOZO CHILENO

VOELLER DESEA SALIR

SIGUEN BASTOS

Sports

The Sports section gives information, opinion, and analysis on a wide variety of sports subjects. Its design emphasizes the hierarchy of information and the use of space. It includes a final section (Fútbol) devoted solely to national and international soccer.

LA PRENSA GRÁFICA

DEPORTE

¡UN TAILANDÉS VENCIÓ A GUGA!

El tailandés Paradorn Srichaphan dio ayer la gran sorpresa en el Masters Series de Madrid al derrotar en la primera ronda al brasileño Gustavo Kuerten, ex número uno del mundo, por 6-4 y 6-4.

¡GIGANTES!

» Los Gigantes de San Francisco consiguieron su pase a la Serie Mundial tras derrotar a los Cardenales.

SAN FRANCISCO, E.U.A.
agencia ap

Los Gigantes de San Francisco serán los representantes de la Liga Nacional en la Serie Mundial que dará comienzo el sábado en Anaheim, luego de derrotar la noche del lunes por 2-1 a los Cardenales de San Luis.

Un sencillo de Kenny Lofton en la parte baja de la 9ª entrada, con dos "outs", remolcó a David Bell para la carrera del triunfo ante el lanzador relevista Steve Kline, quien recién a esa altura reemplazó a Matt Morris, quien lanzó casi la ruta completa.

Momento decisivo

Bell conectó sencillo después de que Morris dominó a Ramón E. Martínez y a J.T. Snow, y después Shawon Dunston también le conectó sencillo.

El entrenador de los Cardenales, Tony la Russa, decidió relevar a Morris, por lo que envió a la lomita a Steve Kline. Sin embargo, Lofton le conectó el sencillo al jardín derecho para remolcar a Bell y dejar tendidos en la cancha a los Cardenales.

Los Gigantes, que llegaron a los playoffs como el "wild card" de la Nacional, ganaron la serie 4-1 y enfrentarán en la Serie Mundial a los californianos Serafines de la ciudad de Anaheim, quienes también ganaron el gallardete de la Liga Americana en calidad de "wild card".

SERIE MUNDIAL

Juego 1: sábado, Anaheim
Juego 2: domingo, Anaheim
Juego 3: martes 22, Sn. Fco.
Juego 4: miérc. 23, Sn. Fco.
Juego 5: jueves 24, Sn. Fco.
Juego 6: sábado 26, Anaheim
Juego 7: dom. 27, Anaheim

El gran Benito

SAN FRANCISCO, E.U.A.
agencia afp

El receptor puertorriqueño Benito Santiago fue elegido como el Jugador Más Valioso del campeonato de la Nacional, luego de que sus Gigantes de San Francisco se consagraron campeones al vencer 2-1 a los Cardenales.

A pesar de irse en blanco el lunes, Santiago conectó la víspera un jonrón decisivo con Bonds en circulación para poner contra la pared a los Cardenales con un triunfo de 4-3.

Con el choque también empatado 2-2 en el final del 8º "inning", fue Santiago el héroe al botar la pelota en conteo máximo para enviarla al fondo del jardín central.

Santiago, de 37 años y quien sufrió un accidente que por poco lo cuesta su carrera profesional, promedió en las dos primeras rondas de "playoff" para .289 en 38 turnos al bate.

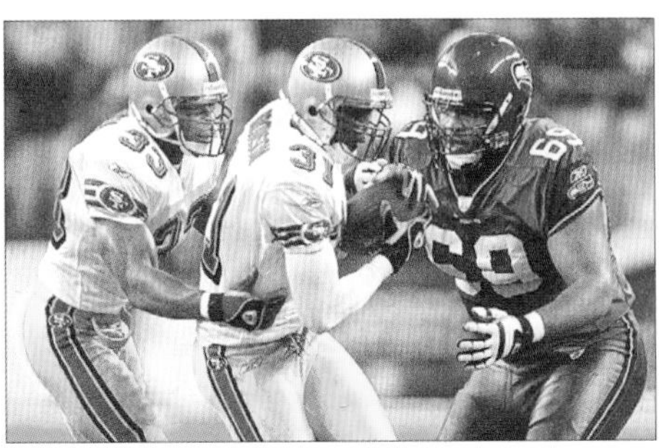

EL "SAFETY" DE LOS 49ERS, ZACK BRONSON (AL CENTRO)SUPERA A FLOYD WEDDERBURN, DE LOS SEAHAWKS DE SEATTLE.

Los 49ers desplumaron al halcón

» Terrell Owens y el salvadoreño José Cortez contribuyeron el lunes para darle a los 49ers la victoria sobre Seattle.

SEATTLE, E.U.A.
agencia efe

Terrell Owens capturó un pase de 37 yardas del mariscal de campo Jeff García en el 4º periodo para conducir el triunfo de los 49ers de San Francisco a la victoria 28-21 sobre los Halcones Marineros de Seattle, el lunes por la noche.

El mariscal de campo de los 49ers, Jeff García, brilló en el ataque con dos pases de anotación, mientras que el pateador salvadoreño José Cortez consiguió dos goles de campo, uno de 37 yardas en el primer cuarto y otro de 29 en el segundo, además de que anotó dos puntos extra.

Cortez tiene marca de 10 goles de campo en 12 intentos, para una efectividad del 83.3 por ciento y se mantuvo perfecto en los puntos extra con 11 en tantos intentos.

Asimismo, lleva marca perfecta en dos partidos de lunes por la noche, con seis anotaciones.

VIA SATELLITE FROM LORAL CYBERSTAR™

INTERNATIONAL

www.usatoday.com

Determined to win

For Shannon Dunn, snowboarding is a 'soul sport.' First in a series of 10 Olympians to watch, 9B

Burton Snowboards

AVAILABLE AROUND THE WORLD

By Melissa Moseley, Universal Studios

Talent to remember

Will a bravura performance in *Mulholland Drive* be enough to land Naomi Watts an Oscar nomination? Our annual look at longshots, 10B

Fri/Sat/Sun, January 25–27, 2002

Justice O'Connor downplays retirement from high court

USA TODAY

Supreme Court pioneer dismisses rumors that she'll soon retire or become chief justice. Interview, 4A.

Fed chairman more upbeat

Reuters

Federal Reserve chief Alan Greenspan tries to brighten up negative view of economy; 12th rate cut unlikely, 7A.

Dow, Nasdaq end day higher

Japan's Nikkei index jumps 33.14 points to 10,074.05. Hong Kong's Hang Seng falls 20.68 to 10,741.46. London's FTSE climbs 52.50 to 5233.10. Frankfurt's DAX rises 7.41 to 5170.44. 7A.

▸ Dow Jones industrial unofficially closes up 65.62 to 9796.48; Nasdaq rises 20.16 to 1942.54.

Campaign-finance bill going to House

Overhaul of laws regulating money in political campaigns gets backing of enough lawmakers to force House of Representatives to take up the issue; Senate has approved similar legislation. 4A.

Bush supports confinement of Arafat

As violence in Mideast continues to simmer, President Bush backs Israel's confinement of Palestinian leader Yasser Arafat; White House wants Arafat to show commitment to ending terrorism. 2A.

Wal-Mart to become biggest company

The giant Arkansas-based retailer will soon eclipse ExxonMobil as world's largest company, with about $220 billion in revenue. 7A.

Weather: Sunny in Rome, Los Angeles

European cities: London, showers; Rome, mostly sunny; Moscow, cloudy; Zurich, showers. Asian/Pacific cities: Tokyo, mostly cloudy; Hong Kong, mostly cloudy; Shanghai, showers. U.S. cities: New York, partly sunny; Los Angeles, sunny. 12A.

■ Money: Super Bowl, superstar

The people who create the ads shown during the big game, and those who star in them, could see their lives suddenly change. 7A.

■ Sports: Australian Open rematch

Defending champ Jennifer Capriati faces three-time Australian Open champ Martina Hingis in the finals of the Grand Slam event. Tennis. 1B.

▸ Several high school graduates have quickly made transition to college football. 1B.

■ Life: 'Mothman' a memorable movie

New Richard Gere vehicle about a creepy myth is a ★★★ sleeper of a film. 10B.

By John O. Buckley

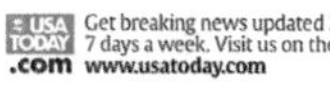

Get breaking news updated 24 hours a day, 7 days a week. Visit us on the web at www.usatoday.com

USA TODAY Snapshots®

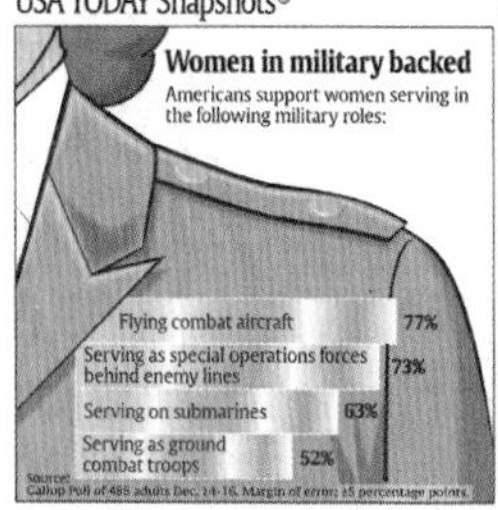

Source: Gallup Poll of 488 adults Dec. 14-16. Margin of error: ±5 percentage points.

By Lori Joseph and Marcy E. Mullins, USA TODAY

9 771051 740054 04

Crossword	8A
Editorial	11A
Nation	4A
State-by-state	6A
Stocks	10A
World	6A

€1.50 in all Euro Zone Countries

Austria, €1.50 20.64 S.	Iceland, 220Ikr	Poland, 6.50 PLZ
Belgium, €1.50 60.51 BF	Israel, 8.00 N.I.S.	Portugal, (Cont.) €1.50 300 Esc.
Cyprus, 1C£	Italy, €1.50 2904 Lire	Romania, 75,000 LEI
Czech Republic, 60 Cz. Kr.	Latvia, 1.75 Ls.	Russia, $3 U.S.
Denmark, 15.00 Kr.	Lebanon, LL 3000	Slovakia, 55 SK.
Estonia, 30 EEK	Lithuania, $2 U.S.	Spain, €1.50 250 Ptas.
Finland, €1.50 8.92 FIM	Luxembourg, €1.50 60.51 LF	Sweden, 16 S.Kr.
France, €1.50 9.84 F.	Malta, 60 Cents	Switzerland, 3.50 S.Fr.
Germany, €1.50 2.93 DM	Morocco, 16 Dh.	Turkey, C/V of $1.50
Greece, €1.50 511 Dr.	Netherlands, €1.50 3.31 Fl.	U.S. Military, $1.00
Hungary, 300 HUF	Norway, 20 N.Kr.	

Spedizione in A.P. -45% art.2 comma 20/B legge 662/96 - Milano

NFL Road to the Super Bowl

Win Sunday and they're in

Patriots at Steelers 12:20 p.m., CBS

Eagles at Rams 4:15 p.m., FOX

All times ET

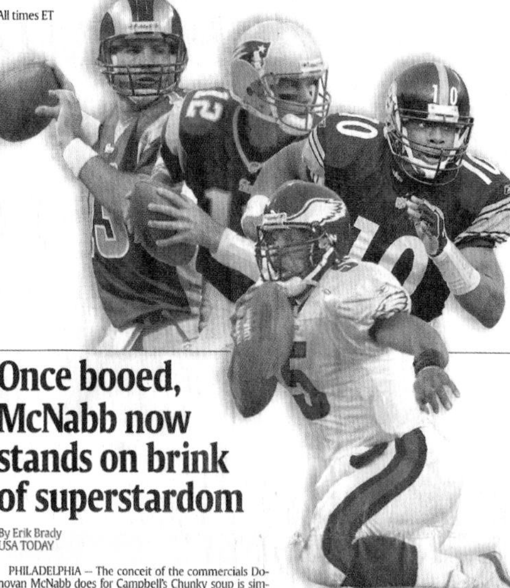

Patriots' **Tom Brady**, left; Steelers' **Kordell Stewart**; Rams' **Kurt Warner**; Eagles' **Donovan McNabb**

Brady by Getty Images; others by AP

Once booed, McNabb now stands on brink of superstardom

By Erik Brady
USA TODAY

PHILADELPHIA — The conceit of the commercials Donovan McNabb does for Campbell's Chunky soup is simple: This football hero is a mama's boy.

"That's not a bad thing to be," says Wilma McNabb, Donovan's mother. "It's what he is, though I'm not sure Donovan would agree."

Actually, he does. "Mom and I are tight," McNabb says. "She's my No. 1 fan and my No. 1 critic."

Lately there isn't much for other critics to say about McNabb — quarterback, seller of soup, superstar in waiting. Sunday he leads the Philadelphia Eagles into their first NFC Championship Game in a generation.

The Eagles are 12-point underdogs to the St. Louis Rams, whose quarterback, Kurt Warner, is Campbell's other NFL pitchman of the moment. Warner is Horatio Alger in cleats, gone from grocery store stock boy to Super Bowl hero — and from shelving soup to selling it. The two-time league MVP has one Super Bowl win to his credit and expects another in 10 days.

Standing in his way are McNabb's Eagles, who upset the Chicago Bears last week by ringing up 33 points on a de-

Please see COVER STORY next page ▸

Cover story

▸ Steelers' Stewart prepares for AFC title game, 1B

Fired auditor takes the Fifth

Andersen employees portray Duncan as a rogue

By Thomas A. Fogarty and Jayne O'Donnell
USA TODAY

WASHINGTON — A fired partner of auditing firm Arthur Andersen, accused by the company of shredding Enron-related documents, refused Thursday to testify before a House panel investigating the collapse of the once high-flying energy corporation.

"I respectfully decline," said David Duncan, citing his constitutional right against self-incrimination. Until he was fired Jan. 15, Duncan oversaw Enron audits as managing partner in the auditing company's Houston office.

Rep. Jim Greenwood, R-Pa., chairman of the House Energy and Commerce subcommittee on oversight and investigations, dismissed Duncan after expressing frustration over his refusal to testify.

Duncan has said previously, through his lawyer, that he was following instructions from Andersen in-house lawyer Nancy Temple to purge the documents and is cooperating with government investigators into the collapse of Enron.

His appearance before the panel came on the first day of a series of hearings on the Houston-based energy trader Enron, once the nation's seventh largest corporation. It also followed the announcement late Wednesday that Kenneth Lay, 59, had resigned as the firm's top executive.

With the reputation of the 88-year-old firm at stake, top Andersen employees who testified after Duncan portrayed him as a rogue executive who oversaw destruction of documents on his own authority.

"Enron robbed the bank, Arthur Andersen provided the getaway car and they say you were at the wheel," said Greenwood in introducing Duncan.

By Tim Dillon, USA TODAY

Duncan: Nothing to say.

▸ CEO resigns; workers file another suit, 9A

Dorsey Baskin Jr., an Andersen managing director, testified that Duncan oversaw destruction of "a very substantial volume of documents" over several days from Oct. 23, just after the Security and Exchange Commission announced an inquiry into Enron.

Baskin said Andersen "is not proud" of the destruction, but that Duncan, as head of the Houston office, bears primary responsibility. Duncan's actions "represent a failure of judgment that's simply unacceptable," he said.

Lawmakers, however, sought to chop away at the executives' contention that Duncan was solely to blame. Rep. Chris John, D-La., said their story left festering "an 18-day problem" — the period from the start of the shredding until Temple issued a directive Nov. 9 to preserve all Enron-related documents.

Temple insisted she "never counseled any destruction or shredding of documents." On Oct. 12, before the shredding began, Temple had issued a reminder to those involved with the Enron audit to review the firm's policy on document retention and destruction. That policy advises keeping documents that could be relevant to litigation or a government investigation. At that point, Temple said, no lawsuits had been filed by shareholders nor had an SEC probe been announced.

Contributing: Jim Drinkard

By J. Scott Applewhite, AP

In Alexandria: John Walker Lindh, with his head shaven, en route to his appearance in federal court.

Lindh has his 1st day in court

American Taliban held without bail

By Toni Locy
USA TODAY

ALEXANDRIA, Va. — In a firm, slightly accented voice, American Taliban fighter John Walker Lindh told a judge on Thursday that he understood the terrorism charges that could send him to prison for life.

Appearing in court for the first time to face charges that he conspired to kill Americans in Afghanistan and aided Osama bin Laden's al-Qaeda terrorism network, Lindh said, "Yes, I understand, judge," when the charges were summarized for him.

After a magistrate judge detailed the maximum penalties, Lindh said, "No sir, I don't have any questions."

Lindh, 20, whose head and face were shaven of the bushy hair and beard he had when he was captured in Afghanistan in November, wore a green jumpsuit with "PRISONER" stenciled on the back. He cut a slight figure as he stood before Magistrate Judge W. Curtis Sewell, who ordered him held without bail and set a bond hearing for Feb. 6.

▸ Jail already holds other infamous inmates, 4A

Lindh's court appearance began a new chapter in the story of the northern Californian who went abroad as a teenager two years ago to study Arabic and Islam, and wound up fighting for the Taliban in Afghanistan. It also set off what could be a sensational, high-stakes legal battle.

His attorney, James Brosnahan, wasted no time launching his offensive, complaining that Lindh had been denied access to a lawyer while being held for nearly eight weeks aboard Navy ships in the Arabian Sea. The criminal complaint against Lindh says that during that period, in interviews on Dec. 9-10, Lindh told FBI agents he had attended an al-Qaeda training camp and was among five trainees who met bin Laden, who thanked them "for taking part in jihad."

U.S. Attorney Paul McNulty said Thursday that Lindh signed a waiver of counsel when interviewed by the agents. McNulty said he has "great confidence" that Lindh is receiving "the full panoply of rights" given to all defendants, including the right to a lawyer.

But Brosnahan said after Thursday's hearing that Lindh had requested a lawyer as early as Dec. 2 or 3. "For 54 days he was held incommunicado," Brosnahan told reporters outside the courthouse.

Brosnahan accused the government of intercepting five letters he said Lindh tried to send to his parents via the Red Cross. Lindh's parents received one letter Wednesday; it was dated Jan. 8, Brosnahan said.

The lawyer also accused U.S. officials of improperly discussing the case against Lindh. Attorney General John Ashcroft has been the most vocal, saying Lindh aligned himself with terrorists.

"The officials who have commented on this case knew" that Lindh had asked for a lawyer and had not received one, Brosnahan said. He also said his client goes by the name Lindh, not his mother's last name of Walker. Lindh had used both names in the past; U.S. officials have called him Walker in news briefings and court documents.

Lindh's parents, Frank Lindh and Marilyn Walker, met with their son for about 20 minutes before the hearing. They spoke to him through a glass partition — with U.S. agents listening in.

"John loves America," Frank Lindh said. " John did not take up arms against America … and he did not harm any Americans." Marilyn Walker, who hadn't seen her son for two years, said, "My love for him is unconditional and absolute. I am grateful to God that he's been brought back to his family and his home."

The front page of *USA Today*, using Gulliver.

Gulliver's travels

John D. Berry

Two newspapers – one German, the other American – achieve entirely different looks using the same typeface

One typeface: two ways. Dutch type designer Gerard Unger created his Gulliver type family specifically for use in newspapers, and it has proven very popular. Like any news typeface, Gulliver gets used by different papers in very different ways – but the contrast between the *Stuttgarter Zeitung* and *USA Today*, both of which use Gulliver for their text and some of their headlines, could hardly be greater. Comparing them is an object lesson in how wildly varying the effect can be, depending on how you use the typeface.

Gulliver is an upright, sturdy typeface with roots in the Dutch tradition, dating from the 17th century, of practical typefaces with a sober structure but a subtle visual sparkle. Gulliver's italic is clearly cursive, but still upright and still with large spaces inside the letters. Unger considers Gulliver to be a "Latin" typeface, although it doesn't have the strictly pointed serifs that usually characterize that style. Like so many of Unger's type designs, Gulliver shows a lively tension where narrow strokes meet wide ones, where curves meet straight stems, and at the ends of curved strokes. It was designed to be economical – to fit more words on a page – by being "narrow without looking narrow," as Unger puts it, and appearing to be larger than it actually is. It has a large x-height and very open counters, so it stays legible when you shrink it down to a small size.

Unger anticipated what really happens to digital typefaces in everyday use, and designed Gulliver so that it would stand up to being squeezed or stretched horizontally (within reason). He gave it the spacing between letters – the fit – that he felt was optically correct, but that too is something that is often changed by the typesetter.

Which is exactly what happens with these two newspapers. *USA Today*'s text is set in an unusually large size of Gulliver, slightly condensed to fit more words on a line, and with very little space between lines. The effect is to make the text look big but crammed together. The *Stuttgarter Zeitung* took the opposite tack, keeping Gulliver at its normal width, but with very slightly more space between letters, and with more generous space between lines. The effects are so different that they don't look like the same typeface at all.

Gulliver is far from the only typeface designed specifically for newspaper work, and far from the only one that will look different in different settings. But it's not often that you have such a clear contrast of effect using the same typographic tools.

Schuldig schon vor der Tat – Spielbergs „Minority Report“ / *Seite 25*

STUTTGARTER ZEITUNG

Nr. 228 – 40. W. / 58. Jahrgang – E 4029

DIENSTAG, 1. OKTOBER 2002

€0,90 A/B/NL ▪ €1,00 F/I/P(cont.)/E/GR ▪ €1,40 sfr 2,20/Ft 270/TD 2,00/KN 12/TL 2000000

Rot-Grün schlägt Sparkurs ein

Koalition will zehn Milliarden Euro streichen – Eichel erwartet nur noch 1,5 Prozent Wachstum

BERLIN. Bei den Koalitionsverhandlungen hat sich Rot-Grün gestern auf einen rigiden Sparkurs verständigt. Im kommenden Jahr müssen im Bundeshaushalt zehn Milliarden Euro zusätzlich eingespart werden. Dies teilten Grünen-Parteichef Fritz Kuhn und SPD-Fraktionschef Franz Müntefering nach den rund zweistündigen Beratungen in Berlin mit.

Von Karl-Ludwig Günsche und Bärbel Krauß

Beide Vertreter der Koalition erklärten, dass die Wachstumserwartungen für die kommenden Jahre nach unten korrigiert werden. In den kommenden beiden Jahren rechnet Finanzminister Hans Eichel (SPD) nur noch mit 1,5 Prozent Wirtschaftswachstum; bisher waren 2,5 Prozent angesetzt. 2005 und 2006 seien zwei Prozent zu erwarten. An welcher Stelle genau die Koalition sparen will, ist nach Auskunft von Kuhn und Müntefering noch nicht beschlossen. Beide Partner stimmten aber darin überein, dass der Abbau von Privilegien und Subventionen, das Wachstum nicht negativ beeinflussen dürften.

Sowohl Müntefering als auch Kuhn bekräftigten, dass es keine Steuererhöhungen geben soll. „Diese Diskussion ist beendet“, sagte Müntefering. Die rot-grüne Regierung werde an ihrer Haushaltslinie festhalten und die Neuverschuldung bis zum Jahr 2006 auf Null reduzieren. Dies solle, so Müntefering, „im europäischen Geleitzug“ geschehen.

Bundesfinanzminister Hans Eichel (SPD) hatte in der Koalitionsrunde einen Überblick über die Haushaltslage und die finanziellen Spielräume gegeben. Nach seinen Berechnungen beläuft sich das Kürzungsvolumen auf etwa zehn Milliarden Euro. Im Jahr 2004 sind es laut Kuhn rund 15 Milliarden Euro. Der Grünen-Chef bezeichnete die wirtschaftliche Lage als ernst. Über Streichlisten und globale Minderausgaben sei gestern noch nicht gesprochen worden, betonten Müntefering und Kuhn übereinstimmend. Dies solle in den nächsten Tagen in einer Arbeitsgruppe geschehen, die von Kuhn und Finanzminister Hans Eichel geleitet werde. Dabei müsse das Gebot der Gerechtigkeit beachtet werden, sagte Kuhn. Wer mehr schultern könne, werde auch stärker belastet werden. Heute wollen die Koalitionäre einen Schnelldurchgang durch alle Politikfelder machen.

Die von einigen SPD-Ministerpräsidenten sowie Gesundheitsministerin Ulla Schmidt (SPD) angestoßene Steuererhöhungsdebatte nannte Bundeskanzler Schröder gestern nach einer Präsidiumssitzung eine „höchst ärgerliche Diskussion“. Er gehe davon aus, „dass sie beendet ist“. Die Ministerpräsidenten Sigmar Gabriel und Kurt Beck hatten vorgeschlagen, die Vermögensteuer wieder einzuführen und die Erbschaftsteuer zu erhöhen. Schröder lehnte diesen Vorschlag ebenso ab wie die Forderung der Gesundheitsministerin, die Tabaksteuer anzuheben. Es gehe um Einsparungen, die Streichung überflüssiger Privilegien und den Abbau von Subventionen. Dabei schloss Schröder die Kohlesubventionen allerdings ausdrücklich aus. Zentraler Punkt der Koalitionsgespräche sei die Schaffung von Arbeitsplätzen. Zunächst sollten die Hartz-Vorschläge zur Reform des Arbeitsmarktes umgesetzt werden.

Auch der CSU-Chef Edmund Stoiber forderte mehr Einsparungen statt Steuererhöhungen. Die Union würde eine Neuauflage der Vermögen- und eine Erhöhung der Erbschaftsteuer nicht mittragen. Unterdessen warnte das DGB-Vorstandsmitglied Heinz Putzhammer die Koalition davor, an der Entfernungspauschale oder der Steuerfreiheit von Sonntags-, Nacht- oder Feiertagszuschlägen zu rütteln. Er sprach sich für die Wiedereinführung der Vermögensteuer und eine höhere Erbschaftsteuer aus.

▪ Hintergrund: Höhere Steuern? Seite 2
▪ Kommentar: Das Machtwort Seite 3

Talfahrt an der Börse ungebremst

FRANKFURT (AP/rtr). Bis zu seinem letzten Tag hat sich der September in diesem Jahr als schwarzer Börsenmonat erwiesen: Auch am Montag bescherte er den Aktienmärkten massive Kursverluste. Die Diskussion um mögliche Steuererhöhungen in Deutschland, Unsicherheit über die Konjunkturentwicklung und die Irakkrise setzten die Börsen unter Druck. Der Dax fiel auf den schwächsten Stand seit fast sechs Jahren. Zum Handelsende hatte der Index 5,1 Prozent verloren und schloss bei 2769,03 Punkten. Am Neuen Markt gab der Auswahlindex Nemax 50 um 4,4 Prozent auf 339,26 Punkte nach.

„Egal, mit wem man spricht, überall heißt es, die Lage ist schlecht“, sagte ein Händler. Der Dow-Jones-Index notierte zum Handelsschluss 1,4 Prozent im Minus bei 7591,93 Punkten und lag auf dem niedrigsten Stand seit August 1998. Börsenfachleute erklärten, fast alle Konjunkturindikatoren deuteten darauf hin, dass die Erholung der Wirtschaft noch weiter auf sich warten lasse. Zugleich wurde darauf hingewiesen, dass sich der Dax in der letzten Zeit im Vergleich zur Wall Street, aber auch zu allen europäischen Börsen am schlechtesten entwickelt habe. Bei vielen Unternehmen sei der aktuelle Kurs nicht mehr gerechtfertigt. Es handele sich um eine Übertreibung nach unten.

▪ Börsenbericht: Dax im Keller Seite 13

Forschung und Fälschung

Brechen die Dämme?

Von Wolfgang Borgmann

Es hätte kaum schlimmer kommen können: Da bemühen sich die Max-Planck-Gesellschaft und ihr einstiger Präsident Hubert Markl höchstpersönlich um einen jungen, aufstrebenden Physiker, um ihn an das hoch angesehene Stuttgarter Max-Planck-Institut für Festkörperforschung zu holen. Und dann das: der umworbene Physiker, Anfang 30, ein Star der heiß umkämpften Nanowelt, hat in 16 von 24 Verdachtsfällen Daten manipuliert oder falsch dargestellt. Das hat nicht etwa ein Max-Planck-Gutachter herausgefunden, sondern eine Untersuchungskommission des berühmten Bell-Labors in New Jersey. Dort war der junge Mann bis vor kurzem beschäftigt. Jetzt ist er in Amerika gefeuert worden. Und der potenzielle Arbeitgeber in Deutschland ist froh, ihn endgültig nicht geheuert zu haben. Das ist weit mehr als ein Betriebsunfall in der Forschung.

Es ist erst einmal ein bitterer Vorgang für das Forschungsland Baden-Württemberg, auf dessen Bühne wieder einmal ein wichtiger Akt eines Fälschungsdramas gespielt wird. Fünf Jahre sind es her, da erschütterte der „Fall Herrmann“ nicht nur die Universitätsstadt Ulm, sondern die ganze deutsche Forschung. Der erfolgreiche Krebsforscher Friedhelm Herrmann und seine Mitarbeiterin Marion Brach wurden beschuldigt, Daten in mehr als neunzig Arbeiten gefälscht zu haben. Beide galten als Größen ihrer Branche. Das war ein schwerer Schlag für die gesamte Krebsforschung, die mit so vielen Hoffnungen beladen ist. In den Sog dieses Skandals wurde auch noch der bekannte Freiburger Gentherapeut Roland Mertelsmann gezogen und schwer belastet. So etwas, das schworen sich alle maßgebenden Forschungsorganisationen, sollte nie wieder passieren, und so bauten sie mit scharfen Regelungen Dämme gegen die befürchtete Flut. Und doch ist es passiert – und wieder in einem strategisch wichtigen Forschungsfeld.

In vielen Aspekten erinnert der Fall des Physikers Schön an den „Fall Herrmann“. Beide glänzten mit einer Menge von Veröffentlichungen, wurden zu Größen ihrer Branche, wurden bewundert und umworben. Doch als man sich schließlich anschickte, ihre angeblich glanzvollen Studien unter die Lupe zu nehmen, da stimmten schon die Grafiken nicht. Und es kamen noch viele andere Verdachtsmomente hinzu. Gutgläubig hatten sich Gutachter täuschen lassen, hatten Widersprüche übersehen. Der Krebsforscher Herrmann bestreitet bis heute eine Fälschungsabsicht. Und der Physiker Schön bedauert zwar seine Fehler, kann aber keine Fälschungsabsicht erkennen. Viele seiner Arbeiten, die seinen Weg nach Amerika ebneten, hat er in Konstanz angefertigt. Die Universität wird jetzt alle Mühe haben, den Spuren ihres einstigen Zöglings nachzugehen und zu klären, wer genau nachgeprüft hat, was der Forscher publiziert hat und wer dafür eigentlich die Verantwortung trägt.

Beim ersten Mal hatte es die Welt der Mediziner getroffen. Der „Fall Herrmann“ bebt bis heute nach. Beim zweiten Mal traf es die Gentechniker. Ausgerechnet in einem international erfolgreichen Institut der Max-Planck-Gesellschaft in Köln war es zu umfangreichen Manipulationen gekommen. Und nun dieser dritte Fall: Wieder geht es um einen Zweig der Forschung, in dem viel Ruhm erworben und viel Geld verdient werden kann. Winzige Schaltkreise aus Molekülen können in absehbarer Zeit die Zukunft der Computertechnik bestimmen. Viele Technologien sind an ihre physikalischen Grenzen gestoßen und verlangen nach neuen Antworten in Nanobereichen, in denen es um den millionsten Teil eines Millimeters geht. In diesem Brennpunkt arbeitete Schön und blendete offenbar auch angesehene Forscher. Manche waren bereits so beeindruckt, dass sie Jan Hendrik Schön schon auf dem besten Weg zum Nobelpreis sahen.

Und so hätte man sich das vorstellen können: ein zukünftiger Nobelpreisträger, der Seite an Seite mit Nobelpreisinhaber Klaus von Klitzing in Stuttgart-Büsnau zu Ruhm und Ehre der Region und der deutschen Forschung werkelt. Daraus wird nun nichts. Für Schadenfreude ist gewiss kein Anlass. Die Grundlagenforschung von heute, so heißt es, bestimmt die Zukunft der Gesellschaft. Damit wächst der Druck auf die Forscher, so schnell wie möglich gute Ergebnisse zu veröffentlichen. Im Kampf um Geld und Ansehen mag da manche Hemmung fallen. Und gerade in hoch spezialisierten Fächern wird der Kreis der Fachleute immer kleiner, die in der Lage sind, viel versprechende Arbeiten richtig einzuschätzen. Eine Voraussage sei gewagt: Wenn der Druck von Staat, Gesellschaft und Wirtschaft auf die Forschung weiter wächst, quasi auf Knopfdruck neue Ergebnisse zu erzielen, werden sich Fälschungen häufen. Forscher können, so gesehen, nicht nur zu Tätern, sondern wohl auch zu Opfern werden.

HEUTE

4 190402 900902 26040

Obrigheim soll länger am Netz bleiben

BERLIN (dpa). Das Atomkraftwerk Obrigheim soll nach dem Willen des Betreibers weit länger am Netz bleiben als bisher geplant. Die Energie Baden-Württemberg (EnBW) beantragte laut Bundesumweltministerium die Verlängerung der Betriebsdauer. Unterdessen kam es im ältesten deutschen Meiler zu einer Panne. Laut EnBW trat in Obrigheim ein Leck an einem Behälter im Abwassersystem auf. Radioaktivität sei nicht ausgetreten.

Die EnBW beantragte, ein Strommengen-Kontingent von 15 000 Gigawattstunden (GWh) vom AKW Neckarwestheim II auf Obrigheim zu übertragen. Das Ende der 60er Jahre ans Netz gegangene Kernkraftwerk könnte so auf Basis seiner derzeitigen Produktionsmengen rund fünf Jahre länger Strom produzieren. Andernfalls müsste Obrigheim Ende dieses oder Anfang nächsten Jahres den Betrieb einstellen. Nach dem Gesetz über den Atomausstieg hat jede Anlage eine Reststrommenge, nach deren Produktion die Genehmigung für den Betrieb erlischt. Sollte der Antrag genehmigt werden, würde sich die Betriebsdauer von Neckarwestheim II also verkürzen. Zu einer Entscheidung über den Antrag machte das Bundesumweltministerium gestern keine Angaben.

▪ Hintergrund: Verwirrspiel Seite 7

FDP: Kein Kompromiss mit Möllemann

BERLIN (gü). Im Machtkampf zwischen dem FDP-Vorsitzenden Guido Westerwelle und dem NRW-Landeschef Jürgen Möllemann geht es nach den Worten von Generalsekretärin Cornelia Pieper „um die Zukunft der FDP“. Das Verhalten Möllemanns im Wahlkampf sei ein „großer Vertrauensbruch“ gewesen. Dieser könne auch nicht durch eine Entschuldigung geheilt werden. Möllemann sei „ein Hauptgrund, aber nicht der alleinige“ dafür, dass die FDP bei der Bundestagswahl schlechter abgeschnitten habe als erwartet. In der FDP-Spitze wurde betont, es gebe keine Kompromissmöglichkeit mit Möllemann mehr.

Es sei jedoch eine „souveräne Entscheidung“ der Delegierten auf dem Sonderparteitag der NRW-FDP am kommenden Montag, ob sie Möllemann das Vertrauen aussprechen, betonte Pieper. Sie dementierte Berichte, dass Druck auf die Delegierten ausgeübt werde, gegen Möllemann zu stimmen. Wenn dieser die Vertrauensabstimmung gewinne, sei er weiterhin „der demokratisch legitimierte Vorsitzende“ in NRW. Zugleich bekräftigte Pieper, dass die FDP an der „Strategie 18“ festhalte. Gestern ist auch die Stellung Möllemanns als FDP-Fraktionsvorsitzender in NRW in Frage gestellt worden.

▪ Hintergrund: Der ideale Vize Seite 2

82 Millionen leben in Deutschland

WIESBADEN (AFP). Die Bevölkerung in Deutschland ist im vergangenen Jahr um 0,2 Prozent gewachsen. Wie das Statistische Bundesamt am Montag mitteilte, lebten zum 31. Dezember insgesamt 82 440 000 Menschen in der Bundesrepublik. Das waren 181 000 mehr als Ende 2000. Im Jahr 2000 war die Bevölkerungszahl um 0,1 Prozent gewachsen und im Jahr davor um 0,2 Prozent. Das leicht gestiegene Bevölkerungswachstum im vergangenen Jahr geht nach Angaben der Statistiker auf einen größeren Zuwanderungsüberschuss zurück. 2001 war die Zahl der zugewanderten Personen um 275 000 größer als die der Personen, die auswanderten.

Nach den Zahlen des Bundesamtes sind im vergangenen Jahr erneut mehr Menschen in Deutschland gestorben als geboren wurden. Die Zahl der Sterbefälle lag um 94 000 über der Geburtenzahl. Die Bevölkerungsentwicklung in den Bundesländern bietet ein uneinheitliches Bild. Während die Bevölkerung im vergangenen Jahr gegenüber 2000 in den neuen Länder um 0,9 Prozent sank, nahm sie im Westen um 0,5 Prozent zu. Im Osten war die Bevölkerung überall rückläufig, in den alten Ländern stieg die Zahl mit Ausnahme Bremens und des Saarlandes.

▪ *www.destatis.de*

Europa billigt Sonderrechte für US-Bürger

Im Streit mit den USA um internationalen Gerichtshof werden zweiseitige Abkommen möglich

Von Thomas Gack.

BRÜSSEL. Die EU hat sich im Streit mit den USA um die Befugnisse des Internationalen Strafgerichtshofes (ICC) auf eine einheitliche Linie geeinigt. Demnach können EU-Staaten unter strikten Bedingungen die von den USA geforderten zweiseitigen Abkommen abschließen, die einen Verzicht auf Auslieferung von US-Bürgern an den ICC festschreiben. Diesen Kompromiss haben die Außenminister gestern in Brüssel geschlossen.

Die 15 EU-Außenminister wollen offensichtlich verhindern, dass sich der Konflikt zwischen der EU und den USA weiter verschärft. Die Vereinigten Staaten hatten sich geweigert, dem Abkommen über den Internationalen Strafgerichtshof beizutreten. Stattdessen forderten sie weltweit Immunität für ihre Staatsangehörigen. Dagegen unterstützen die Europäer den Strafgerichtshof. Dieser wurde vor drei Monaten in Den Haag eingerichtet, um weltweit Kriegsverbrechen und Verbrechen gegen die Menschheit strafrechtlich zu ahnden.

Bisher lehnte die EU bilaterale Verträge mit den USA ab. In Brüssel wurde befürchtet, dass auf diese Weise die Internationale Strafgerichtsbarkeit unterlaufen werde. Unter dem Druck der Briten und der Italiener, die bilaterale Verträge mit den USA angekündigt hatten, sind die EU-Außenminister nun bereit, Washington weiter entgegenzukommen.

Bilaterale Verträge sollen nur unter strikten Bedingungen möglich sein. Sie sollen festhalten, dass US-Staatsangehörige, die Kriegsverbrechen oder Verbrechen gegen die Menschheit begangen haben, in den USA vor Gericht gestellt werden. Zum anderen müssen diejenigen Staaten, die ein Abkommen mit den USA abschließen, für ihre eigenen Bürger die internationale Gerichtsbarkeit akzeptieren. Drittens sollen die Sonderrechte nur den US-Bürgern gewährt werden, die als Soldaten oder Zivilpersonen von der US-Regierung in ein fremdes Land entsandt worden sind. US-Staatsangehörige, die als Privatpersonen reisen oder zum Beispiel als Söldner Verbrechen begangen haben, sind vom Verzicht auf Auslieferung ausgenommen.

„Es ist uns wichtig, dass wir einen gemeinsamen Standpunkt bezogen haben“, erklärte Bundesaußenminister Joschka Fischer. Die Gemeinschaft mache deutlich, dass sie ohne Einschränkung hinter dem Internationalen Gerichtshof stehe. Die Bundesregierung lehne allerdings weiterhin Separatverträge ab. Bisher haben rund ein halbes Dutzend Staaten solche Abkommen geschlossen.

▪ Kommentar: Politische Zwerge Seite 3

LUFF

Willkommen zur Inspektion

The *Stuttgarter Zeitung* (opposite) and *USA Today* (right).

2A · FRIDAY, JANUARY 25, 2002 · USA TODAY

Washington

White House backs Israel's confinement of Arafat

By Barry Schweid
The Associated Press

WASHINGTON — The White House gave its endorsement Thursday to Israel's confinement of Palestinian leader Yasser Arafat to a West Bank compound.

"The president understands the reason that Israel has taken the action that it takes, and it is up to Chairman Arafat to demonstrate the leadership to combat terrorism," spokesman Ari Fleischer said. "It is a threat not only to Israel, but to Chairman Arafat."

In the Middle East, three Palestinians were killed, two in a mysterious explosion and a third in a clash with Israeli soldiers.

Analysts on both sides predicted continuing violence. Because of the flareup, U.S. officials put a truce mediation effort by envoy Anthony Zinni on indefinite hold.

In Gaza, the mangled bodies of two Palestinians were found after daybreak. The militant Popular Front for the Liberation of Palestine said the two were killed in a "heroic martyrs' operation." Israel radio said it was apparently a failed suicide bomb attack.

In the West Bank town of Ramallah, a Palestinian intelligence officer was killed in a clash with Israeli forces. Israeli tanks are parked 70 yards from Arafat's headquarters there. Arafat has been under virtual house arrest for nearly two months. This deprives him of barnstorming the Middle East and Europe in search of support for the Palestinians. From his office window, Arafat can peer at Israeli soldiers posted just down the street.

"The president continues to believe that it is incumbent on Chairman Arafat to do more, take more steps, and show with action that he is committed to eliminating terrorism and combating it wherever it exists," Fleischer said.

With the Islamic militant group Hamas threatening to unleash "all-out war," Secretary of State Colin Powell telephoned Arafat on Wednesday to urge him to curb attacks.

The fighting has sidetracked mediation efforts by Zinni, a retired Marine general who has made two unsuccessful attempts to restore a cease-fire.

Meanwhile, a former Lebanese Christian warlord held responsible for a 1982 massacre of Palestinian refugees that for many symbolizes the outrages of Lebanon's civil war died in a car bombing at his house. Three bodyguards also died.

Elie Hobeika, 45, led the right-wing Lebanese Forces militia, which tore through the Sabra and Chatilla Palestinian refugee camps in Muslim west Beirut 20 years ago, slaughtering hundreds of men, women and children. An Israeli military post was nearby.

The militia was allied with Israel, and an Israeli commission of inquiry later found that then-defense minister Ariel Sharon — now the prime minister — was indirectly responsible for the killings.

There was no immediate claim of responsibility for the car blast.

Many in Lebanon blamed Israel, long accused of working to undermine stability here. Israeli Foreign Ministry spokeswoman Yaffa Ben-Ari denied those allegations.

By Nasser Nasser, AP

In Ramallah: Israeli soldiers have kept Palestinian leader Yasser Arafat confined to his West Bank compound for nearly two months.

Clinton defends U.S. policy on Middle East

Participants at forum criticize stance on Israel

By Bill Nichols
USA TODAY

NEW YORK — Former president Bill Clinton passionately defended the policies of his administration Thursday, as well as those of his successor, against criticism that U.S. foreign policy has helped create the kind of Islamic extremism that resulted in the terrorist attacks Sept. 11.

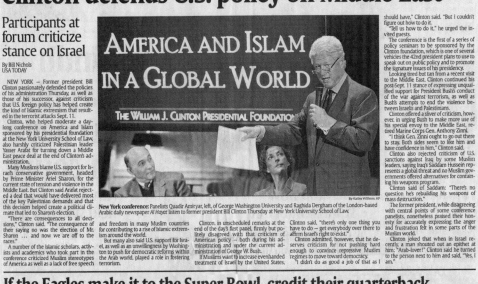

Clinton, who helped moderate a daylong conference on America and Islam sponsored by his presidential foundation at the New York University School of Law, also harshly criticized Palestinian leader Yasser Arafat for turning down a Middle East peace deal at the end of Clinton's administration.

Many Muslims blame U.S. support for Israel's conservative government, headed by Prime Minister Ariel Sharon, for the current state of tension and violence in the Middle East. But Clinton said Arafat rejected a deal that would have delivered most of the key Palestinian demands and that this decision helped create a political climate that led to Sharon's election.

"There are consequences to all decisions," Clinton said. "The consequence of their saying no was the election of Mr. Sharon … and now we are off to the races."

A number of the Islamic scholars, activists and academics who took part in the conference criticized Muslim stereotypes of America as well as a lack of free speech and freedom in many Muslim countries for contributing to a rise of Islamic extremism around the world.

But many also said U.S. support for Israel, as well as an unwillingness by Washington to push for democratic reforms within the Arab world, played a role in fostering terrorism.

AMERICA AND ISLAM
IN A GLOBAL WORLD
THE WILLIAM J. CLINTON PRESIDENTIAL FOUNDATION

By Kathy Willens, AP

New York conference: Panelists Quadir Amiryar, left, of George Washington University and Raghida Dergham of the London-based Arabic daily newspaper *Al Hayat* listen to former president Bill Clinton Thursday at New York University School of Law.

Clinton, in unscheduled remarks at the end of the day's first panel, firmly but politely disagreed with that criticism of American policy — both during his administration and under the current administration of George W. Bush.

If Muslims want to increase evenhanded treatment of Israel by the United States, Clinton said, "there's only one thing you have to do — get everybody over there to affirm Israel's right to exist."

Clinton admitted, however, that he deserves criticism for not pushing hard enough to convince repressive Muslim regimes to move toward democracy.

"I didn't do as good a job of that as I should have," Clinton said. "But I couldn't figure out how to do it.

"Tell us how to do it," he urged the invited guests.

The conference is the first of a series of policy seminars to be sponsored by the Clinton foundation, which is one of several vehicles the 42nd president plans to use to speak out on public policy and to promote the signature issues of his presidency.

Looking tired but tan from a recent visit to the Middle East, Clinton continued his post-Sept. 11 stance of expressing unqualified support for President Bush's conduct of the war against terrorism, as well as Bush's attempts to end the violence between Israelis and Palestinians.

Clinton offered a sliver of criticism, however, in urging Bush to make more use of his special envoy to the Middle East, retired Marine Corps Gen. Anthony Zinni.

"I think Gen. Zinni ought to go out there to stay. Both sides seem to like him and have confidence in him," Clinton said.

Clinton also rejected criticism of U.S. sanctions against Iraq by some Muslim leaders, saying Iraq's Saddam Hussein represents a global threat and no Muslim governments offered alternatives for containing his weapons program.

Clinton said of Saddam: "There's no question he's rebuilding his weapons of mass destruction."

The former president, while disagreeing with central points of some conference panelists, nonetheless praised their honesty for accurately expressing the anger and frustration felt in some parts of the Muslim world.

Clinton joked that when in Israel recently, a man shouted out an epithet at him: "Arab-lover!" Clinton said he turned to the person next to him and said, "Yes, I am."

If the Eagles make it to the Super Bowl, credit their quarterback

Continued from 1A

fense that yielded the fewest points in the NFL this season. McNabb ran or passed for 550 of Philly's 670 yards in playoff wins against the Tampa Bay Buccaneers and Chicago. That means he accounts for 82% of Philly's playoff offense. It also means the Eagles will go as far as their quarterback takes them.

McNabb is on the cusp of the kind of stardom that comes to those rare few who

Cover story

can make something out of nothing.

Watch him pull a rabbit out of his hat: Last week he danced away from a fierce pass rush, ducked one way, stutter-stepped another, drifted left and found running back Cecil Martin alone in a corner of the end zone for the go-ahead score. McNabb buys time as casually as you might buy milk.

McNabb, at 6-2 and 226 pounds, is "as close to a one-man gang" as anyone in the NFL since John Elway, Fox analyst John Madden says.

"I don't do this by myself by any means," McNabb objects. "We are coming together as a team at the right time."

They are coming together as a team that looks up to its young quarterback as unquestioned team leader — in just his third year in the NFL and second as a starter.

"People around the league feel he's one of the top quarterbacks" already, Eagles coach Andy Reid says. "But I still feel he's a year or year and a half from being a finished product. It takes four years for a quarterback to mature in this offense."

Reid refers to the quick-strike West Coast offense, pioneered by the San Francisco 49ers under Joe Montana, who was 25 when he won his first of four Super Bowls. McNabb is 25; he has a chance to be one of the NFL's best and brightest for the next dozen years.

"His upside is tremendous," says Ron Jaworski, an ESPN analyst who quarterbacked the Eagles in their last NFC Championship Game 21 years ago.

"I remember that game," McNabb says.

Really? You were a toddler then.

"Well, I don't mean I remember the actual game," he says. "I've seen the highlights. You see the highlights in Philadelphia all the time."

Which is exactly the point: The Eagles last won an NFL championship in 1960, before Super Bowls existed. They lost their only Super Bowl following the 1980 season. That last NFC title game — a 20-7 win against the hated Dallas Cowboys — is fondly recalled as emblematic of a golden age. Philadelphia hungers for another one.

Eagles fans will boo anybody, even (famously) Santa Claus. It was no big surprise they booed McNabb loud and long on the day he was taken as the second overall selection in the 1999 draft.

By Sue O'Grocki, Associated Press

Celebrating: Donovan McNabb led the Eagles' upset of the Chicago Bears.

"It wasn't really booing Donovan," Jaworski says. "It was booing not taking Ricky Williams," the Heisman Trophy winner from the University of Texas who wound up with the New Orleans Saints.

This week Philadelphia tried to atone for its original sin. Angelo Cataldi, a sports radio talk show host, held a pep rally that reenacted draft day, except with cheers this time. Cataldi was among those who wanted Williams; now he calls assembling the boo birds the dumbest thing he ever did.

"Dear Donovan," wrote *Philadelphia Daily News* features reporter Jim Nolan. "We know it's just a few days before The BIG Game, but is it too late to say we're sorry? Ol' buddy? Ol' pal?"

McNabb says it was no big deal. He didn't take it personally. But you get the sense he doesn't forget it. "It was embarrassing for my mom and dad," he allows.

Don't ever embarrass the mother of a mama's boy.

"Draft day is special in the life of any athlete, so, yeah, it's going to bother anyone," says Fletcher Smith, McNabb's agent. "But Donovan has the ability to take a negative and channel it into something positive."

And so on the ride from draft headquarters in New York to Philadelphia that day, he studied the Eagles' playbook. He has been a tireless worker since.

Reid says McNabb shows up at 6:30 most mornings and gets in a workout before team meetings at 9. He practices and studies videotape through the day — and often takes dinner with coaches. "We have to kick him out at night," Reid says.

McNabb lives with older brother Sean in Philadelphia's New Jersey suburbs.

Attacking defenses through the air and on the ground

In his third NFL season, Donovan McNabb is having a singular impact on his team's success in the postseason that seldom has been matched by other quarterbacks. He has become the third quarterback in the last 10 years to pass for 250 or more yards and rush for 35 or more yards in one playoff game:

Date	Round	Teams and score	Quarterback, team	Passing yards	Rushing yards
Jan. 23, 1994	Conference	Dallas 38, San Francisco 21	Steve Young, S.F.	287	38
Jan. 29, 1995	Super Bowl	San Francisco 49, San Diego 26	Steve Young, S.F.	325	49
Jan. 6, 1996	Division	Green Bay 27, San Francisco 17	Steve Young, S.F.	328	77
Jan. 6, 2001	Division	Minnesota 34, New Orleans 16	Daunte Culpepper, Minn.	302	51
Jan. 19, 2002	Division	Philadelphia 33, Chicago 19	Donovan McNabb, Phila.	262	37

McNabb also has become the fourth quarterback in the last 10 years to pass for 175 or more yards and rush for 50 or more yards in one playoff game:

Date	Round	Teams and score	Quarterback, team	Passing yards	Rushing yards
Jan. 9, 1993	Division	San Francisco 20, Washington 13	Steve Young, S.F.	227	73
Jan. 6, 1996	Division	Green Bay 27, San Francisco 17	Steve Young, S.F.	328	77
Jan. 30, 2000	Super Bowl	St. Louis 23, Tennessee 16	Steve McNair, Tenn.	214	64
Jan. 6, 2001	Division	Minnesota 34, New Orleans 16	Daunte Culpepper, Minn.	302	51
Jan. 12, 2002	Wild card	Philadelphia 31, Tampa Bay 9	Donovan McNabb, Phila.	194	57

Chasing a record

With totals of 456 yards passing and 94 yards rushing so far in this season's playoffs, McNabb is close to joining four of the NFL's all-time greats as the only quarterbacks to pass for 600 or more yards and rush for 100 or more yards in one postseason:

Season	Player, team	Passing yards	Rushing yards
1975	Roger Staubach, Dallas	670	100
1984	Joe Montana, S.F.	873	144
1986	John Elway, Denver	805	101
1994	Steve Young, S.F.	623	128

His offseason regimen is torturous. He spends much of it on his own in Phoenix, where he undergoes unorthodox workouts at MakePlays.com, a cutting-edge training firm. He is joined by some other NFL players, including Rams cornerback Aeneas Williams, against whom he'll throw passes Sunday.

McNabb throws passes from a balance beam and while restrained by a bungee cord. He lifts weights to strengthen his hips and back. He does eye exercises to sharpen his peripheral vision. And he gets dog toys thrown at him rapid fire.

Um, dog toys?

"Yeah, little rubber toys with nubs on them so you don't know how they're going to bounce," McNabb says. "They throw them at you, and you have to block them. It's good for your reflexes and reaction."

All of that helped, McNabb says, on that TD pass in Chicago when he pinballed around the pocket. "I could feel the pressure coming behind me," McNabb says. "It's all about vision and balance."

McNabb's point is clear: That kind of play is not just about talent and instinct. It is also about hard work — and dog toys.

McNabb wears many hats. He is quarterback, pitchman and triple-threat media star for TV, radio and the Web.

Take Monday of this week. First he taped *The Donovan McNabb Show* for local TV. Then he taped a segment for the Eagles' Web site. Next he talked to a gaggle of reporters. At night he did his local radio gig, also called *The Donovan McNabb Show*.

Philadelphians lap up this stuff. They love their Iggles — Philly talk for Eagles — and they love McNabb's easy demeanor.

His on-air persona is so affable that you hardly notice a lot of what he says is the same each time. His personality sparkles even when what he's saying doesn't.

He graduated from Syracuse with a degree in speech communications and says he wants to work in TV some day. "But not for a lot of years," he adds hastily.

In the meantime he'll work to get better as a quarterback. He has work to do.

"To have long-term success and win multiple championships, you have to be a pocket passer first," Jaworski says. "You have to be able read coverage and find your receivers and have the timing and anticipation. I have seen every game Donovan has played, and he's not there yet. But he's getting better.

"His escape ability and mobility when the pocket breaks down are exceptional. And the good thing is that he still looks to complete passes, which forces the defense to hold coverage and means more green grass if he does run."

He ran 5 yards for the last touchdown at Soldier Field last week — and then dunked the football over the goal post. Wilma and Samuel McNabb were there to cheer. They raised their sons in the Chicago suburbs and still live there.

McNabb says he gets his playful side from his mother, a nurse, and his fierce work ethic from his father, an electrical engineer. That split personality is in full view Sundays — McNabb often grins on the field even as he uses techniques honed by practice, drills and study.

"Donovan is like Brett Favre" that way, says Reid, a former assistant in Green Bay, where Favre quarterbacks. "Both can be the funniest guy on the bus but the most serious on the field when it's time to be."

McNabb cracks up teammates with dead-on impressions of his coaches. Reid caught one in progress last season. "I heard myself talking, and I asked someone, 'Who's that?' And they said, 'That's Donovan doing you.' "

McNabb doesn't understand why people are surprised at his smiling on-field demeanor. "I work hard all week," he says. "Sunday is fun time."

Mama couldn't have said it better herself. But that's not really Wilma McNabb in those soup commercials. Her role is played by actress Marcella Lowery.

Campbell's spokesman Jeff Bedard says actresses have played the mothers of all of the players in the series since its inception in 1997. He says that is done in the interest of time and efficiency, though Wilma wants to be play herself in future ads.

She'll be in St. Louis Sunday for McNabbvs. Warner — the Soup-er Bowl to decide which pitchman goes to the Super Bowl.

Although oddsmakers give Warner's Rams a big edge, one stat favors McNabb's Eagles: Philadelphians consume nearly three times as much Chunky soup as the citizens of St. Louis.

"Donovan likes Chunky soup just fine," Wilma says. "But he likes my red beans and rice better."

Of course he does, just like a good mama's boy.

Buchmesse Frankfurt: altbek

Die endlose Mission des Börsenvereins

Immer wieder gibt es Ärger mit der Buchpreisbindung

Seit gut einem Jahr ist die deutsche Buchpreisbindung gesetzlich verankert, vieles ist dadurch besser geworden. Trotzdem muss der gebundene Ladenpreis immer wieder gegen Angriffe verteidigt werden. Auch ein Streit mit den Bertelsmann-Clubs geht jetzt wohl vor Gericht.

Von Bettina Langer, Frankfurt

Die Spur führte dieses mal zum Azubi. Bei Ebay sind wieder einmal preisverminderte neue Bücher im Dutzend aufgetaucht, und der Börsenverein des deutschen Buchhandels hat sich gefragt: Wo kommen die jetzt wieder alle her? Das Online-Auktionshaus hat kooperiert und den Namen des Verkäufers herausgegeben. Und der wiederum hatte die Bücher von der Auszubildenden einer Buchhandlung, in der eben öfter ein paar Bücher weggekommen waren. Das Schlupfloch ist jetzt gestopft. Ein weiterer Fall sei dagegen noch in Arbeit, erzählt Oliver Schlimm, Rechtsanwalt des Börsenvereins bei einem Vortrag auf der Buchmesse. Der vom Börsenverein, beziehungsweise vom zuständigen Preisbindungstreuhänder beauftragte private Ermittler spüre dem Ebay-Händler noch immer hinterher.

Online-Verkauf, bei dem das Preisbindungsgesetz unterlaufen wird, ist nur eins der Probleme, mit dem sich der Verein als

aber auch einige Neuerungen, die beim Rest der Branche Unmut erzeugen. Erstens werden in den Filialen des Clubs jetzt auch Titel wie Madonnas Kinderbuch „Die Englischen Rosen" oder die neue Grönemeyer-Biografie zeitgleich mit der Auslieferung in normalen Buchhandlungen liegen – und nicht, wie bei solchen Titeln sonst üblich, erst nach sechs Monaten. Zweitens hat das Unternehmen angekündigt, dass seine rund vier Millionen Mitglieder in Deutschland ab November nicht nur die Club-Angebote, sondern auch alle hier zu Lande lieferbaren Bücher zum normalen Ladenpreis bei den Bertelsmann-Clubs bestellen können.

Dem Börsenverein geht das eindeutig zu weit. Justiziar Sprang meint, wenn Bertelsmann dieses Vorgehen durchsetze, sei für die normalen Buchkäufer nicht mehr nachvollziehbar, warum sie anderswo mehr bezahlen müssten, was das ganze System der Buchpreisbindung in Frage stellen würde.

Im Gesetz steht, dass Preisunterschiede bei Parallelausgaben „sachlich gerechtfertigt" sein müssen. Eine solche Rechtfertigung könnte, vereinfacht gesagt, sein, dass ein Buch erst ein halbes Jahr später auf den Markt kommt, anders aufgemacht ist oder nur einem begrenzten Nutzerkreis zugänglich gemacht wird. Diese Kriterien müssten immer gemeinsam betrachtet und gegeneinander aufgewogen werden, betont Sprang. Wenn der Buchclub Titel jetzt aktuell, aber

Marlins complete co
to prevail 9-6 for ber

By Chuck Johnson
USA TODAY

CHICAGO — Less than 24 hours after staging a dramatic rally to stay alive, the Florida Marlins dealt a deathblow to the Chicago Cubs' hopes of ending a 58-year drought without a World Series.

With Wednesday night's 9-6 victory in Game 7, the Marlins came all the way back from a 3-1 deficit to win the best-of-seven National League Championship Series.

The Marlins are headed to the World Series after beating Cubs co-ace Kerry Wood in the clincher, a night after they erupted for eight runs in the eighth to beat Mark Prior in Game 6.

hit 4-0 shutout Sunday
Game 5 and start the l
climb back in the series, v
standing again, coming b
two days' rest in relie
O'Leary's pinch-hit homer
seventh was Beckett's onl
ish in four innings of relief.

"There's no question (I
turned this series around,"
manager Jack McKeon sa
Cubs had a great deal of r
tum going for them when
them down Sunday. He wa
termined, he wanted t
again."

In losing their third in a
Cubs sent a Wrigley Field c
39,574 home to ponder th
World Series-less famine t

It's hard to believe they're both using the same typeface

Gulliver is used for the text of stories in both the *Stuttgarter Zeitung* (opposite) and *USA Today* (above). Giving the type a little space creates a quieter-looking page, while pumping up the type and squeezing it tightly gives it urgency.

Rocky Mountain News

THURSDAY, AUGUST 28, 2003 | ROCKYMOUNTAINNEWS.COM | ★ 50 cents in Denver

Steady rise
Average price for regular, self-serve unleaded in Colorado

LAST YEAR Aug. 28, 2002	LAST MONTH July 30, 2003	LAST WEEK Aug. 20, 2003	WEDNESDAY Aug. 27, 2003
1.46 2/10	1.54 9/10	1.63 3/10	1.68 1/10

Record gas prices

■ **Tight supplies** drive cost in Colorado to seasonal high; no relief in sight. **1B**

All eyes on historic Mars flyby

LINDA MCCONNELL/ROCKY MOUNTAIN NEWS

Cloudy night offers only quick glimpse

Jack Eastman, 64, of Sheridan, waits for the skies to clear before catching a glimpse of Mars from the University of Denver's Chamberlin Observatory on Wednesday night.

Eastman's telescope was made in 1877. Astronomy buffs around the world have watched the Red Planet make its closest approach to Earth in nearly 60,000 years. **23A**

COLORADO

AFA cadets reveal history of rapes. 5A

West Nile kills first male in state; Pueblo man 9th victim overall. 6A

SPECIAL SECTION

Grand Prix revs for racing

16-page guide. **1J**

NATION

Breathless from a case of recall fever

Mike Littwin in L.A. **7A**

Commandments display moved. 36A

Front page of the redesigned *Rocky Mountain News.*

The essence of *Rocky*-ness

Randall Roberts & Jonathon Berlin

In a two-newspaper town, readers call it "my paper"

Intensify. That was the key word as the *Rocky Mountain News* approached its redesign. Build on the strengths of the paper – dramatic photographs, bold headlines, clear, uncluttered design – and enhance its character with disciplined typography and more levels on the presentation volume dial.

The *Rocky* is not just another newspaper. It is Colorado's oldest, founded in 1859. It has a grand name and an unusual relationship with its readers, who are passionate about the paper, especially its tabloid format. In a two-newspaper town, they call it "my newspaper." But its basic typography hadn't changed since the introduction of an Atex publishing system in the late 1970s. Then, in 2000, the *Rocky* and its archrival, *The Denver Post*, declared a truce in a bitter newspaper war and asked permission from the federal government to enter into a joint operating agreement. The financial stability the deal provided made it possible for the *Rocky* newsroom to finally get a new publishing system. And that meant that for the first time in decades, it could reconsider completely the way it presented the news.

"The *Rocky* was at a turning point," said editor and publisher John Temple. "The JOA was a blow because we felt like we had the editorial edge in the newspaper war. We could have retreated. Instead, we focused on why we got into the business in the first place. It wasn't to win a newspaper war. It was to do great journalism. That meant using the new technology to produce a dramatically improved newspaper."

The *Rocky* turned to Roger Black, Nanette Bisher, and John Miller of Danilo Black for design help, and to Unisys Publishing Systems for a whole new approach to putting together the paper. The companies faced one unusual challenge: they would have to produce a tabloid and a broadsheet version of the same newspaper.

"The *Rocky Mountain News* has a great history, and a really strong identity," Black said. "Instead of 'redesigning' it, we set out to identify its basic character – *Rocky*-ness. And then we've tried to turn up the volume a bit, to make the newspaper even more *Rocky*."

The two companies – unbeknownst to one another – had one core idea in common: both believed that every element of the paper needed to be independent, a complete thought understandable in and of itself. This ultimately became a key concept in the redesign.

The *Rocky* first worked with Danilo Black and Urban and Associates to establish what it called "The Essence of *Rocky*-ness." Using years of reader surveys, market research, and the wisdom

Rocky Mountain News

TUESDAY

HAYMAN FIRE

Feds: Letter story a lie

Charges say forester deliberately set state's largest-ever blaze. 4A

Littwin: Rage swirls around fire, suspect. 11A

MISSIONARY RIDGE FIRE

Durango blaze escalates to top priority. 4A

Qwest stock up 20% on CEO's 1st day. 1B

Sordid side to Blagg

Affidavit: Murder suspect delved into paid sex, porn. 22A

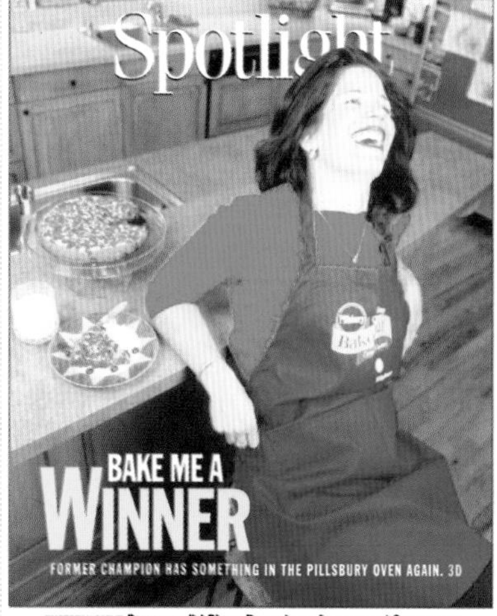

Spotlight

BAKE ME A WINNER

FORMER CHAMPION HAS SOMETHING IN THE PILLSBURY OVEN AGAIN. 3D

ENTERTAINMENT: Denver vocalist Dianne Reeves hopes for success at Grammys. 9D

Rocky Mountain News — Wednesday, February 27, 2002

SECTION B

Rocky Mountain News

Business

DOW 10,127.58 +12.32

NASDAQ 1,751.88 -14.96

SPORTS

THURSDAY • FEBRUARY 28 • 2002

Greenspan sees signs of hope

Vail earnings up 42 percent

Real estate sales help power resort past 9-11 slump that hit industry

Downtown projects hailed

Asian market, Invesco Field among six honored at group's 41st awards

of the staff, together they created a one-page sheet that was to be the guide for the redesign. The JOA requirement that the *Rocky* produce a broadsheet one day a week, on Saturdays, had forced the paper to examine what gave the paper its character beyond the tabloid format.

The guide defined seven characteristics that should apply no matter what format or platform the paper was using:

We're direct. This means conversational. We write to express, not to impress. We value clarity. In design, we're clear, legible, uncluttered, well organized. We use bold photos and short, direct headlines.

We belong here. In design, this means we emphasize local and our staff. We write stories with Colorado flavor. We're part of the community.

We own the "big stories." We are committed to dominating major breaking news. Big news gets dramatic treatment.

We have energy. We have a broad range of voices, visually and in writing. We have a high item count. We use dramatic photos. We get into the fray. We pursue enterprise with an edge. We're willing to mix it up, take on authority.

We're real. We're practical. People count on us to be a useful tool. We're concise, but conversational. We talk *to* people, not *at* them.

We like people. Our photos show human emotion and large faces. We're warm and compassionate in our approach. We're good, sensitive neighbors.

We have integrity. We don't try to make people look bad. We give sides equal treatment. We're committed to accuracy and fairness.

Danilo Black helped turn this vision of the newspaper into a functional redesign plan. Roger Black and his team worked with John Temple and design director Randall Roberts to build prototypes that could be shown to readers. Nothing would be done without reader feedback.

In interviews, readers were shown a prototyped newspaper – not individual proofs or pages. This gave them a more realistic experience. They were interviewed alone, one at a time, so that they could speak freely without any influence from others in the room.

What came out of the interviews was that *Rocky* readers had a strong connection with their newspaper and its tab format. And they hated the Saturday broadsheet version of the paper. The broadsheet would have to stay, but reader feedback could help reshape the design of both formats to serve readers better.

Readers reconfirmed many of the elements of *Rocky*-ness, and for the most part appeared to like the more intense approach of Danilo Black even better.

Readers often referred to "flipping" through the paper and to "flipping" from a story to where it jumped, so the editors decided to modify the jump-line style to reflect the readers' language. The jump lines now read: "Flip to BUSH on page 12A."

The interviews helped solidify goals for the redesign:

Enhance points of entry. They liked that we were making the paper easier and more fun to read. The paper did not put limits on story length, but rather tried to stretch its range by using more breakouts and more thoughtful display type, and by improving its approach to graphics.

Add more levels of volume. More contrast in image size, headline size, and item/story length.

Be more consistent. Keep typography and labeling the same throughout the paper. The flags, zippers, and topic labels are the same in every section. The paper

TUESDAY, MAY 20, 2003 — Rocky Mountain News 3D

HEALTH

MARIA COTE, LIFESTYLES EDITOR, 303.892.5169, E-MAIL: SPOTLIGHT@ROCKYMOUNTAINNEWS.COM

Short Cuts

SHOP SMART

- **What:** Sale of household items, clothing, shoes, books, starting at 10 cents; full bags $5 on Friday
- **Where:** St. Michael and All Angels Church, 1400 S. University Blvd.
- **When:** Presale (admission $5), 5 to 7 p.m. Wednesday; free 9 a.m. to 6 p.m. Thursday and 9 a.m. to noon Friday

Send shopping tips to Janet Simons, Simonsj@RockyMountainNews.com or (303) 892-2547.

LOSERS WANTED

If you've lost more than 60 pounds, the Discovery Health Channel wants to hear from you. The network is looking for Coloradans to profile on its new show *I Lost It!*, which offers inspirational stories to help others in their weight battles. If you'd like to share your story, call Gaylene Garcia at Colorado Production Group, (303) 455-5200, or e-mail her at gaylene@cpgtv.com.

HELP YOURSELF

"Nothing is more effective than a deep, slow inhale and release for surrendering what you can't control and focusing again on what is in front of you."

Oprah Winfrey

THE SUN'LL COME OUT

During May, Skin Cancer Awareness Month, the American Academy of Dermatology offers these reminders on protecting yourself from the sun:

- Wear sunscreen with a sun protection factor (SPF) of at least 15.
- Reapply sunscreen every two hours, even on cloudy days.
- Wear hats, long-sleeve shirts, sunglasses.
- Avoid sun between 10 a.m. and 4 p.m.
- Seek shade

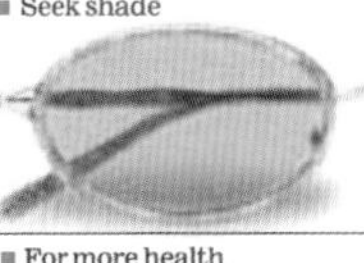

- For more health news, go to:

WWW. RockyMountainNews.com /drmn/health

Outdoor enthusiasts advised to gear up for battle against West Nile virus

Swat team

How to avoid West Nile virus

- Use a DEET-containing repellant when mosquitoes are present.
- Wear loose, light-colored, long-sleeved shirts and long pants.
- Have good screens and/or mosquito netting for tents and campers.
- Avoid low areas for campsites or rest areas, especially near stagnant water or swamps.
- Steer clear of hiking trails with high vegetation.
- Hunters should wear gloves when touching wild game, especially birds.
- Don't touch, or let kids touch, dead birds.

John Pape, Colorado Department of Public Health and Environment

By Debra Melani
ROCKY MOUNTAIN NEWS

Outdoor enthusiasts probably should tuck extra repellant and mosquito netting into their packs this year along with their climbing gear, camping equipment and fishing lures to fend off the newest threat: West Nile disease. The virus promises to continue its fast march across the United States.

Already named the country's second-greatest insect-borne malady behind Lyme disease, West Nile should be enough to change some behaviors among the state's thousands of outdoor recreationists, say experts bracing for a potentially larger Colorado outbreak this summer than last year's.

But it shouldn't be enough to keep people home, they say.

"Will we be telling people to stay inside, lock the doors and break out the duct tape? No," said John Pape, epidemiologist with the Colorado Department of Public Health and Environment. But the state will keep the public informed on high-risk areas and patterns, Pape said.

West Nile, which has yet to be detected in the state this year, is expected to peak in July and August. Experts will keep a watchful eye on the mountains, although the high country escaped the virus in 2002. The mosquito suspected of being the primary West Nile transmitter becomes scarcer at higher elevations.

The virus, spread mainly by mosquitoes that feed on infected birds, is eliminated from the systems of 80 percent of its victims with mild or no signs of illness. Of the remaining 20 percent, most will suffer flulike aches and pains, sometimes with a high fever and rash. Symptoms appear five to 15 days after infection, and patients usually recover in a few days.

About 1 percent of victims will have severe complications, generally from inflammation of the brain or its lining. Some will die or suffer permanent disabilities.

Four of last year's 14 Colorado victims were hospitalized. While none died, not all have fully recovered, Pape said. Lasting symptoms from the West Nile virus, first detected in the United States in New York in 1999, include cognitive or motor-skill problems and some polio-like paralysis.

Most infected mosquitoes and birds were found around the state's eastern riverbeds last summer, and those sections are likely to be the hardest hit again this year, said Michael McGinnis, president of Colorado Mosquito Control in Broomfield.

But this spring's wet weather could expand West Nile risk areas, McGinnis said. Because the virus is new and experts have little history to go on, predictions are hard to make, and experts often disagree.

Two Harvard researchers predicted last week that Colorado might have fewer human West Nile infections this summer than last year because of the high snowpack. Spring runoff could lower the number of stagnant pools where mosquitoes thrive, they said.

But all outdoor recreationists, regardless of their play area, should heed information about the virus, experts agree, especially since the nature of their sports boosts their risk of infection.

"It's not something to be afraid of; it's something to be aware of," said Pape, an outdoorsman himself, who intends to continue his excursions.

Although experts cannot pre-

Flip to WEST NILE on 5D

GETTY IMAGES

Moving around in the heat of the day will lessen your chances of being bitten.

All out for the outdoors

More than 149 million Americans ages 16 and over participate in outdoor recreation activities annually, according to a recent report by the Outdoor Industry Association. Here's the participation breakdown for Colorado by sport, along with how it ranks nationwide per capita.

Sport	Participants	No. 1 state	Colo. rank
Backpacking	541,560	Wyoming	2
Hiking	1.8 million	Wyoming	2
Kayaking, whitewater	136,221	Vermont	4
Rafting	511,658	Wyoming	4
Trail running	837,259	Montana	4
Rock climbing	136,221	Wyoming	5
Mtn. biking	730,940	Idaho	6
Camping	1.1 million	Idaho	6
Fly fishing	352,180	Wyoming	10
Bird watching	355,503	Rhode Island	14

Three examples of the old *Rocky* (opposite), before the redesign; and the front page of a section in the new design (above).

AMERICA AT WAR: SUMMARY

Day 12
Much of the day's fighting occurs south of Baghdad as American forces gather strength for a push toward the capital. American officials say about 3,000 bombs have been dropped in the past few days.
Approximate area under coalition control
Black Sea
Caspian Sea
TURKEY
SYRIA
IRAQ
IRAN
LEBANON
CYPRUS
JORDAN
ISRAEL
EGYPT
SAUDI ARABIA
KUWAIT
BAHRAIN
QATAR
U.A.E.
Mediterranean Sea
Sinai Peninsula
Red Sea
Persian Gulf
Beirut
Damascus
Amman
Jerusalem
Mosul
Kalak
Kirkuk
Tikrit
Tigris R.
Baghdad
Karbala
Hindiyah
Kut
Kifl
Najaf
Euphrates R.
Nasiriyah
Basra
Umm Qasr
Kuwait City
Manama
Doha
100 MILE RADIUS
KURDISH-CONTROLLED REGION
AREA CONTROLLED BY ANSAR AL-ISLAM
H1 airfield
H2 airfield
H3 airfield
Tallil airfield
101st AIRBORNE
5th AND 7th MARINES
1st MARINES
3rd INFANTRY
SPECIAL OPERATIONS FORCES
USS Truman battle group
USS T. Roosevelt battle group
USS Kitty Hawk battle group
USS Constellation battle group
USS Lincoln battle group
U.S. Central Command
Coalition aircraft hit Iraqi positions, aiding Kurdish fighters in their effort to force Iraqis from their positions. A Kurdish official says several thousand more U.S. soldiers are expected to help create a new, northern front.
U.S. warplanes continue to hit targets, including a ridge where Iraqi troops have been entrenched.
For the first time, long-range B-1, B-2 and B-52 aircraft carry out simultaneous raids on the same location as communication and command centers are attacked.
British forces continue to strike targets in and around the capital, hitting Iraqi troop positions and the Karada Intelligence Complex believed to be the headquarters of the Fedayeen Saddam, the paramilitary group known for its guerilla tactics.
U.S. forces stage a dawn raid, taking control of a key bridge over the Euphrates and battling elite Republican Guard units in street fighting as part of stepped-up air and ground strikes before a drive on Baghdad.
U.S. soldiers find a small cache of weapons in the city and tons of ammunition and hundreds of weapons at the local Baath Party headquarters, including boxes of American grenades marked "Property of the Ministry of Defence of Jordan" and maps showing Iraqi military positions and the expected route of the U.S. attack.
Clean water begins flowing through a pipeline from Kuwait to the port city after Iraqi forces cut off water supplies.
Around 4:30 p.m. a U.S. soldier is reported killed in battle. U.S. troops kill seven Iraqi women and children at a checkpoint near the city when their van would not stop as ordered. Two other civilians are injured.
American troops battle to isolate the Shiite holy city and destroy Iraqi divisions standing in the way of Baghdad. Troops from the 82nd Airborne Division kill about 100 "terror squad members" and capture 50 others.
Coalition forces continue to face stiff opposition here and in Basra.
SOUTHERN IRAQ
U.S. Marines stage raids looking for Iraqi Gen. Ali Hassan al Majeed, Saddam Hussein's cousin and a commander of Iraqi forces in the south. He is widely known as "Chemical Ali" for ordering the use of chemical weapons on Iraqi Kurds in 1988.
The International Red Cross visits a camp where 3,000 Iraqis are being held prisoner.

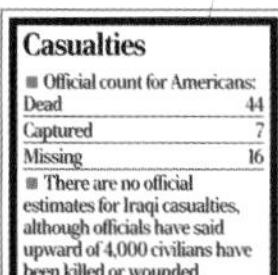

Two elite Iraqi divisions reduced by half

■ **U.S.-led troops** fought pitched battles with the Republican Guard in Hindiyah, within 50 miles of Baghdad. Two Republican Guard divisions south of Baghdad — the Medina and the Baghdad — had been reduced by half.
■ **U.S. troops shot and killed** at least seven Iraqi civilians — some of them children — in a van at a checkpoint in southern Iraq when the driver did not stop.
■ **Huge explosions rocked** central Baghdad late Monday. Earlier, an armada of B-1, B-2 and B-52 bombers struck communication and command centers in the capital.
■ **Iraq's foreign minister,** Naji Sabri, said Iraqi forces would defeat American and British forces, and only surrender would save coalition troops from the "holocaust." More than 5,000 Arabs have come to Iraq to help attack the invaders, he said.
■ **Iraqi television** aired footage of Saddam Hussein with sons Odai and Qusai at a meeting of top military commanders.
■ **The Pentagon said U.S. and British** airstrikes have caused "a very significant weakening" of Iraqi forces.
■ **The 82nd Airborne Division** killed about 100 "regime terror squad members" and captured about 50 prisoners at the Shiite holy city of Najaf and another town.
■ **Coalition commanders** said a U.S.-led assault on a compound controlled by an extremist Islamic group turned up a list of names of suspected militants living in the U.S. and evidence linking the group to al-Qaida. **6A**
■ **In northern Iraq,** U.S. aircraft pounded Iraqi positions near Kalak, aiding Kurdish fighters as they seized territory from Saddam Hussein's fleeing troops.
■ **British commandos** destroyed Iraqi tanks and seized equipment in a suburb of Basra.
■ **NBC fired journalist Peter Arnett** after he gave an interview to state-run Iraqi TV saying the U.S.-led coalition's first war plan had failed because of Iraq's resistance. **12A**
■ **President Hosni Mubarak** of Egypt warned that a drawn-out war in Iraq will lead to an increase in Islamic militancy. **14A**

Casualties

■ Official count for Americans:

Dead	44
Captured	7
Missing	16

■ There are no official estimates for Iraqi casualties, although officials have said upward of 4,000 civilians have been killed or wounded.

What they're saying around the world

■ **Pat Rabbitte, leader of the Labour Party, in *The Irish Times*, Dublin.**

We can see the suffering and fear on television nightly. The war in Iraq has already caused untold human damage and will do a lot more before it's over. But before the final toll of physical casualties can be counted, we can already see others.

The multilateral global system has been severely damaged. The United Nations has been seriously (in the eyes of some fatally) undermined. Europe is bitterly divided. Economic development throughout the world has been compromised.

And it has all happened in the name of two new concepts in international relations ("regime change" and "pre-emptive war") . . .

Where did these concepts come from? Have these new directions in global policy just sprung from the perceived threat of Saddam Hussein's weapons of mass destruction?

No. In fact, a small group of U.S. policymakers have been developing these dangerous ideas for several years. The brutal dictator Saddam Hussein is a good target and September 11th was the tragic catalyst they needed to put their policy into action.

These men are intent on world domination or, as they put it themselves, "American global leadership." They have an imperial agenda . . .

In the eyes of international law, this is an illegitimate war. But that does not concern these policymakers . . .

■ **Ibrahim Nafie in *Al-Ahram Weekly*, Cairo, Egypt.**

. . . It was clear from the outset that recourse to war would have disastrous consequences for all. It was clear that aerial and missile bombardments would claim a horrendous toll of Iraqi civilian lives as well as the lives of many of the young men and women engaged in battle. The tragedy is that all that horror could have been avoided.

The U.S. bears a large measure of responsibility for pushing matters to the brink. Bush and his cohort of hawks refused to hear the voice of reason, whether from the Arabs, Washington's NATO partners or other international powers. They had imagined that war would be a picnic — a few days of aerial bombardment after which the Iraqi command would lose control. . .

Washington's hawks donned rose-tinted glasses. They could only see a swift victory, a tumultuous welcome by the Iraqi people. How much greater their shock then to discover the heroic steadfastness of the Iraqi army. U.S. planners would have been wise, at the very least, to have taken into account that in this war Iraqis are not defending Saddam but their land, people and honour.

Rather than compounding its mistakes Washington should halt its aggression against the Iraqi people. The sooner it does so the easier it will be to repair the damage done, to rehabilitate international legitimacy and restore respect to the U.N. A rapid halt to the war would (end) the conjectures of the forces of extremism on both sides who have portrayed this war as a cultural clash in the hope of effecting a rupture between the U.S. and the Arab world. . . .

■ **To read more views** from around the world on the U.S.-led war on Iraq, go to: **http://pppp.net/links/news/**

Rocky Mountain News

Target: Baghdad

■ **Troops battle** sandstorms, ambushes; 50 miles from capital. **2A**

DISPATCHES

Nightmare of war

■ **Colorado:** State high court to hear Auman case. **24A** | ■ **Sports:** CU women win 86-67, sail into Sweet 16. **1C**

Rocky Mountain News

Baghdad falls

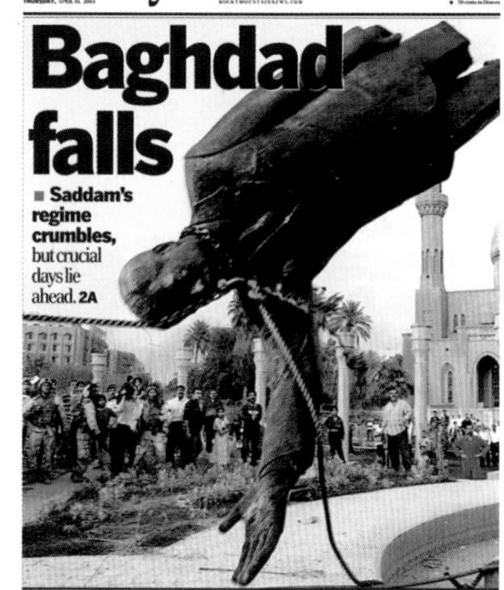

■ **Saddam's regime crumbles,** but crucial days lie ahead. **2A**

TRADE CENTER TRANSCRIPTS

9-11 tapes: Voices on verge of death

Callers pleaded for some way out as rescuers rushed in

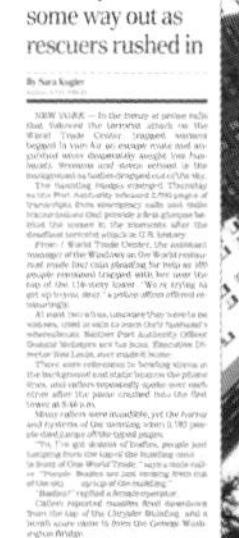

One. Two. Three. Four futile calls

'Fresh air going down fast,' reported restaurant manager

Excerpts from transcripts

Police officer tells mother 'This is bad'

'This makes your hair stand up'

Ninetieth floor told 'We're sending officers'

Debris and bodies falling from upper levels

'Is my husband in that building?'

Rocky Mountain News

MONDAY, JULY 22, 2002 ROCKYMOUNTAINNEWS.COM ★ 50 cents in Denver

Slurry bomber problems triple

BARRY GUTIERREZ/ROCKY MOUNTAIN NEWS

28 cases this year before Estes crash A bomber drops a load of slurry Sunday on the Big Elk Fire near Estes Park. Bombers carrying fire retardant in Colorado encountered mechanical breakdowns, broken parts or other problems 28 times between April 1 and last Wednesday – the day before a fatal air tanker crash. Officials are hoping that higher humidity and rain will continue to knock back the 4,000-acre blaze. **5A**

Telco giant tanks

■ **WorldCom** files for largest bankruptcy in U.S. history. **1B**

■ **Markets wary** over fallout in $4 billion accounting fiasco. **11B**

SPORTS

Ernie's tourney

Els wins British Open in four-way playoff. **6C**

■ Bernie Lincicome: It was a rare Sunday without Tiger. **1C**

Blazing hot finish in Mile-High Nationals at Bandimere. 1C

GREATER DENVER

Convicts in prostitution cases often granted early release. 4A

SPOTLIGHT

The long road

Teaching your teens to drive in Colorado takes more time than it used to. **3D**

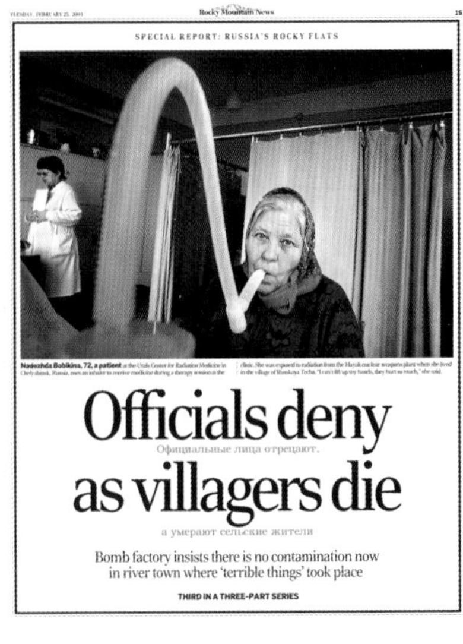

Rocky Mountain News

SPECIAL REPORT: RUSSIA'S ROCKY FLATS

Nadezhda Bobikina, 72, a patient

Officials deny as villagers die

Официальные лица отрицают, а умирают сельские жители

Bomb factory insists there is no contamination now in river town where 'terrible things' took place

THIRD IN A THREE-PART SERIES

Treatment of major stories

The *Rocky* deals with serious news – international, national, and local – on the front page, in infographics, in dramatic double-page spreads, and in special sections devoted to a single topic.

22A Rocky Mountain News ★ TUESDAY, NOVEMBER 12, 2002

WORLD & NATION

JOHN BOOGERT, NEWS EDITOR, 303.892.2728, E-MAIL: NEWSDESK@ROCKYMOUNTAINNEWS.COM

Globe

RATING TORNADOES

Tornadoes are rated from **F0 to F5 on the Fujita scale,** based on wind speed and damage. The scale was developed by Theodore Fujita of the University of Chicago.

- **F0:** Light damage, wind under 73 mph. Some damage to chimneys, branches broken off trees, sign boards damaged.
- **F1:** Moderate damage, wind 73-112 mph. Surfaces peeled off roofs, mobile homes pushed off foundations or overturned, moving autos blown off roads.
- **F2:** Considerable damage, wind 113-157 mph. Roofs torn off frame houses, mobile homes demolished, boxcars overturned, light objects become missiles.
- **F3:** Severe damage, wind 158-206 mph. Roofs and some walls torn off well-constructed houses, trains overturned, most trees in forest uprooted.
- **F4:** Devastating damage, wind 207-260 mph. Well-constructed houses leveled, cars thrown, large missiles generated.
- **F5:** Incredible damage, wind 261-318 mph. Strong frame houses swept away, automobile-sized missiles fly through the air more than 100 yards, trees debarked.

Associated Press

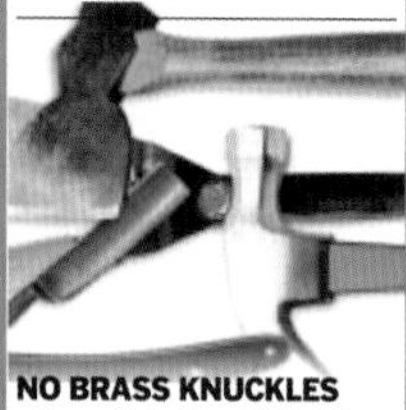

NO BRASS KNUCKLES

Items listed in a 1994 airline industry manual that passengers were forbidden to carry beyond airport checkpoints:

Ammunition, axes, box cutters, brass knuckles, carbon dioxide cartridges, dynamite, fireworks, gasoline, gun powder, hammers, hunting knives, Mace, meat cleavers, oxygen tanks, paint, pepper spray, pistols, plastic explosives, radioactive materials, revolvers, rifles, starter pistols, swords, tear gas, toy transformer robots (forms toy gun, toy weapons. See story, 25A

Associated Press

WWW.
RockyMountainNews.com

"I was trying to protect her. I was trying to give her a chance to survive."

Paul Roddy, telling how he shielded his wife in the hallway as a tornado ripped away parts of the walls and roof of a movie theater in Van Wert, Ohio. Both were unharmed.

JEFF MCCALL/BELLEFONTAINE EXAMINER

A tornado touches down Sunday near West Mansfield, Ohio, in the eastern part of Logan County. West Mansfield resident Jeff McCall, who was traveling at the time of the storm, said the tornado hit near the North Greenfield area and just missed West Mansfield.

Death from above

A swarm of twisters kills 35, devastates areas in eastern U.S.

By Duncan Mansfield
ASSOCIATED PRESS

MOSSY GROVE, Tenn. — Searchers and dazed survivors went from one shattered home to another Monday, picking through splintered lumber and torn sheet metal for any sign of the missing, after twisters and thunderstorms killed at least 35 people in five states.

More than 70 reported tornadoes cut a path of destruction from Louisiana to Pennsylvania over the weekend and into Monday. Sixteen deaths were reported in Tennessee, 12 in Alabama, five in Ohio and one each in Mississippi and Pennsylvania. More than 200 people were injured.

"Yesterday, we had a nice brick house and four vehicles. Today, we don't own a toothbrush," said Susan Henry of Mossy Grove, where seven people were killed and at least 40 were still unaccounted for as of mid-afternoon.

The tiny community 40 miles west of Knoxville was nearly wiped off the map, with about a dozen of the 20 or so homes reduced to concrete foundations and piles of rubble a few feet high.

Henry, her husband and two children survived after taking shelter in the basement of a neighbor's home that collapsed around them.

"It was just deafening it was so loud," said 17-year-old Tabatha Henry. "You could hear the wood pop in the house, and that was it. Then all you could hear was the screaming and praying."

Daylight brought a picture of destruction. In Mossy Grove, clothes fluttered from tree limbs. Power lines dangled from poles.

Cars lay crumpled after being tossed like toys. About the only sound was the bleating of a battery-operated smoke alarm buried deep in the rubble.

Searchers believed that most of the missing in and around Mossy Grove were OK and had simply been unable to get in touch with family members, said Steven Hamby, Morgan County director of emergen-

Continued on next page

ASSOCIATED PRESS

Front page of the World & Nation section, with additional, related information in the vertical channel on the left and the boxed map on the right.

limited itself to three core type families. Text and agate type do not vary from section to section or item to item just to make something fit.

Provide more complete information in display elements, such as captions, breakout boxes, and mug lines. Make every element on a page a complete thought. Such an approach pulls readers into stories. No more mugs with only name lines under them. Captions will be longer and tell a complete story.

Introduce "channels," a highly scannable collection of short, interesting, provocative items that people would talk about over lunch or coffee.

The type

The three type families are Sun Text for body; Benton Gothic, a sans serif, for headlines and agate; and Rocky, a serif, for secondary headlines, page flags, and some breakouts.

Even the body type is bolder. The *Rocky*'s new body type – Sun Text, 8.3 pt on 9.5 leading – blows away the old Century typeface. With a high x-height and stubby serifs, Sun packs a punch and jumps right off the page. The type reads smoothly and works well with the tabloid's smaller image area. Sun is also very efficient, allowing roughly 10 percent more characters per column inch.

One thing the *Rocky* does well is bold, direct headlines. With the Benton Gothic family, headlines carry much more pop and style. A stocky sans, Benton pulls its weight as a page-carrying banner or as 6-point agate. The stocks, entertainment listings and box scores are remarkably easier to read.

Also with Benton, the *Rocky*'s main daily headline has a stylistic flair and strength that its old face, ITC Franklin Gothic Condensed, had ceased to deliver. Black chose Benton because it was similar in

Hard work

For driller, pay dirt comes in form of freedom, pride

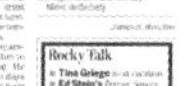

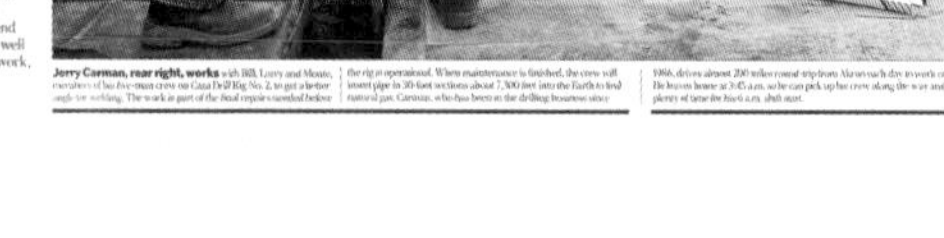

AMERICA AT WAR

AMERICA AT WAR

Day of blood and dust

A double-truck (printed across two pages on a single sheet; top) and a "false" double-truck (two facing pages, but on separate sheets; above).

WEDNESDAY, JULY 30, 2003 Rocky Mountain News 3D

FOOD

MARTY MEITUS, FOOD EDITOR, 303.892.5229, E-MAIL: SPOTLIGHT@ROCKYMOUNTAINNEWS.COM

Morsels

HILL AND BILL

$35 The cost of *The Clinton Presidential Center Cookbook: A Collection of Recipes for Family and Friends*, due in August. Recipe collection includes Hillary's recipe for chocolate chip cookies and 250 recipes from celebrities including Barbra Streisand, Muhammad Ali and Elizabeth Taylor. To order, go to **www.clintonpresidentialcenter.com**

OLÉ TO SPANISH SUMMER COOKING

What: A Taste of Spanish Summer Cooking Class, featuring tapas, gazpacho, and paella, crema Catalana and Sangria and Spanish wines, $35.
- **Who:** Chef Christopher Meier
- **When:** Monday, 7 to 9 p.m.
- **Where:** Wolfgang Puck's Grand Cafe, 500 16th St. (in the Pavilions)
- **Reservations:** 303-595-9653

HEALTHY HABITS

Nearly 1 million AOL members participated in a survey by *Food & Wine* magazine (results in the August issue) and America Online. Here's how they voted:
- **Burger and fries** is the quintessential American food
- **Merlot** is the favorite red wine
- **A pressure cooker** is the best time-saving gadget
- **Skinless chicken breast** is the food of choice for healthful cooking.

MOJITO-VILLE

Mojitos — a drink made of rum, lime juice, mint and club soda — comes home with a Mojitos kit, available at Bed, Bath and Beyond, $19.99. The kit comes with glasses; shaker top; lime reamer; sugar measure; muddler; stirring sticks; serving stand and a recipe.

www.RockyMountainNews.com/drmn/food

Burning desire

Author all fired up over love of barbecue

By Marty Meitus
ROCKY MOUNTAIN NEWS

When George Washington lost his first election for a seat in the House of Burgesses, there was a reason, says Steven Raichlen.

"He didn't provide refreshments (at the polls) and refreshments meant — barbecue."

Raichlen, it might be said, took his cues from Washington's oversight. Despite a string of successful cookbooks on other topics, barbecue has brought Raichlen the kind of celebrity that lands you gigs on public television — *Barbecue University with Steven Raichlen*, (KRMA-TV Channel 6, Saturday, 11:30 a.m.) — more cookbooks, and appearances each year at the *Food & Wine* Magazine Classic at Aspen, where he gives one of the more user-friendly demonstrations.

On a swing through Denver on his way to Aspen earlier in the summer, he burns red-hot on his favorite topic. His newly re-

Raichlen has written a number of user-friendly cookbooks.

Flip to BARBECUE on 7D

Grilled Shrimp Cocktail with Chipotle Orange Cocktail Sauce

Makes 6 servings
1½ pounds jumbo shrimp, peeled and deveined
3 tablespoons chopped fresh cilantro or parsley
2 garlic cloves, minced
1 teaspoon minced canned chipotle chile in adobo, plus 1 to 2 teaspoons adobo sauce from the jar or can
Coarse salt (kosher or sea) and cracked black pepper
2 tablespoons olive oil
2 tablespoons fresh lime juice
Cocktail Sauce:
1 cup ketchup
6 tablespoons fresh orange juice
2 tablespoons fresh lime juice
1 tablespoon Worcestershire sauce
1 to 2 chipotle chiles, minced, plus 1 to 2 teaspoons juices from the can
Salt and freshly ground black pepper
3 tablespoons diced white onion
6 sprigs fresh cilantro
6 limes, cut in half lengthwise
Mesquite chunks for building a fire or 2 cups mesquite chips for tossing on the coals, small bamboo skewers and a 12-by-18-inch sheet of aluminum foil folded in three to make a shield for the skewers

- Place the shrimp, cilantro or parsley, garlic, minced chipotle with juices, salt and pepper in a mixing bowl and toss to mix. Stir in the oil and lime juice and let marinate for 30 minutes.
- Meanwhile, place the ingredients for the cocktail sauce in a mixing bowl and whisk to mix. Correct the seasoning, adding salt or lime juice to taste. Divide the sauce among 6 tiny bowls or ramekins.
- Set up your grill for direct grilling and preheat to high. Thread the shrimp onto skewers. Clean and oil the grill grate. Grill the shrimp until cooked through, about 2 minutes per side.
- Place a half lime cut side down on each plate. Stick 2 or 3 shrimp skewers upright in each. Place a bowl of sauce on the plate and top each with a sprinkling of onion and cilantro sprig. The shrimp can be served hot or cold.

On the cover: Chef Steven Raichlen's Smoked Brisket with Coffee Beer Mop Sauce. See recipe on page **14D.** More recipes are on page **7D.** Photos by Barry Gutierrez/Rocky Mountain News

feel to Franklin Gothic but had more pop.

The serif Rocky was created by Matthew Carter through the Font Bureau specifically for the *Rocky Mountain News*. It's a distinctly Latin face that's elegant but strong, and thrives as the main headline on the Spotlight features section and as smaller heads for graphics and breakouts throughout the paper. Carter also redrew the page one masthead in Rocky, and he and Black restored a line drawing of the mountains – an image that had been removed in the mid-'70s. The new flag makes a bolder, stronger claim for the paper.

Each section uses the same basic styles for type, labels, flags, breakouts, and color palette. There is total consistency to the approach. The only variation is a large, all-lowercase flag for the Spotlight features section. But the flag's typeface is Rocky Bold, like all other section flags.

The channel

The *Rocky* is a tabloid with the news section wrapping the business section, wrapping the sports section, wrapping the features section, wrapping the classified ads. Pacing is important, and strong navigational devices are important.

A channel is used on the first page of every section break.

Channel content. A channel is a collection of short, non-narrative items that could include lists, graphics, charts, things to do, refers, quotes, background on the news, etc. – every item must be able to stand alone.

Items in the channel should provide information not found elsewhere in the section, or additional information from stories in the section. If the item is boring to an editor, it will be boring to readers – don't use it. Make them things people will talk about.

Goals of channels. Channels expand the range of the paper, and

TUESDAY, DECEMBER 10, 2002

Rocky Mountain News 1D

spotlight

Denver Art Museum incorporates collection of plant and floral paintings with two other botanical-themed exhibits of its own in a display of...

Natural color 8D

■ Botox has medical uses, too. 3D

■ Gram Parsons lives in music. 13D

Rocky Mountain News 1D

spotlight

Everything's coming up

STRIPES

Summer's hottest print goes vertical. 4D

Yoko Ono brings Lennon's legacy to town. 7D

Chautauqua's concert season ready to roll. 8D

Front page of the Food section (opposite), with a channel running down the left side, and front pages of the Spotlight features section (above and above right).

2A Rocky Mountain News ★ ● W A B C D E — MONDAY, MAY 12, 2003

NEWS

GREATER DENVER

Hepatitis drive aims message at Hispanics

Two health agencies say hepatitis C, which causes cirrhosis and cancer of the liver, is striking especially hard among Colorado's Hispanic population. This week will see the kickoff of an awareness campaign aimed at the state's Latinos. **5A**

Former IRA member fights deportation order

A former Irish Republican Army member who moved to Denver is in a jam after trying to get a green card. Immigration officials want to deport Ciaran Ferry, who says he is at risk if he returns to Belfast. **12A**

Suburb enlists kids, bats in war against West Nile

Pupils at Parker's Pine Lane Primary School are building bat boxes for their town, where officials hope to employ the mosquito-gobbling winged mammals in this summer's fight against West Nile virus. **18A**

WORLD & NATION

Midwest is punching bag for yet more tornadoes

Twisters again wreaked havoc over the weekend in Kentucky, Tennessee, Missouri and Illinois. **25A**

Kim Jong Il's vanishing act intrigues strategists

The Pentagon mulls new approaches to North Korean leader Kim Jong Il after learning he went into seclusion before the Iraq war for fear he, too, might be targeted. **26A**

COMMENTARY

Banish moratoriums on charter schools

Districts worried about losing students to charter schools should figure out what parents are looking for that they aren't providing. **34A**

ONLINE

ROCKYMOUNTAINNEWS.COM

NEWS

Watering restrictions

What are the restrictions for watering your lawn or washing your car? Go to **RockyMountainNews.com** to search our database for residential and community rules. Also:
- Drought special section
- Water rates
- Water district contacts

BUSINESS

Stock watch

Keep track of the ups and downs on Wall Street at **RockyMountainNews.com**. Create your own portfolio or see how local companies perform. Also, the day's gainers and losers.

BUSINESS

HD

MILE HIGH TECH

Denver being left behind in race for HDTV

A combination of hurdles — including zoning conflicts, community groups and the mountains — has turned the Denver area into a black hole for high-definition television among the nation's major cities. **1B**

MOVIE PIRACY

Film industry moves to protect its turf

Technology groups and digital rights advocates have discovered the motion picture industry isn't shy about pushing legislation in several states — including Colorado — to strengthen cable-TV piracy laws. **1B**

MOBILE PHONES

The ring's the thing

It's a new musical world out there, as companies embrace a trend to sign recording artists and bring old tunes out of mothballs to help cell-phone users make personal statements with their ring tones. **2B**

INTERNET

Japanese rapidly embrace broadband

With a push from the government and pressure from small providers, Japan has expanded its high-speed Internet connections tenfold. **11B**

SPORTS

BRONCOS

Smaller, faster Pryce could help out team

Denver Broncos defensive end Trevor Pryce has dropped 15 pounds in the off-season and has picked up some speed. Pryce expects to have a more productive season this year, and coaches are hoping he's right. **1C**

NFL

Cowboys running back dies at age 23

Dallas Cowboys running back Ennis Haywood, who had spent the past two days on life support, died of undisclosed causes Sunday. He was 23. **1C**

NBA

Lakers even series at 2-2 without Jackson

Shaquille O'Neal and Kobe Bryant combined for 64 points Sunday as the Los Angeles Lakers, with coach Phil Jackson at home following heart surgery, rallied to beat the San Antonio Spurs 99-95 and tie their second-round playoff series at two games apiece. Jackson had surgery to open a blocked cardiac artery. **14C**

■ **Around the NBA**
Philadelphia 95, Detroit 82
Sacramento 99, Dallas 83

SPOTLIGHT

FAMILY

Something old is new to a few local children

Youngsters who visit the Children's Museum of Denver are learning some old-fashioned games as the museum promotes four-square, jacks, hopscotch and jump-rope to promote motor skills, thinking and teamwork. **3D**

CRITTERS

Stray finds way to dream life of American dog

An Army national guardsman from the Denver area brought home a female from his overseas service. And he pulled a lot of strings for Lanya, a German shepherd he found in Hungary. **4D**

DUSTY SAUNDERS

May is planting season for big six networks

All six commercial networks will sow the seeds of their fall lineups this week and continue to plant rumors in the trade publications. Some of those are already growing. **2D**

STAGE

Moliere play gets new translation

A 333-year-old play by Moliere, *Scapin*, is on stage in Denver, thanks to Nagle Jackson, who has translated and directed the version presented by the Denver Center Theatre Company. **5D**

MUSIC

Scripture message rises with Third Day

Third Day balances its guitar-driven rock with straight-ahead, no-apologies Christian lines. The band joins forces with Michael W. Smith for a Pepsi Center concert on Tuesday. **6D**

CORRECTIONS

■ To notify the *Rocky Mountain News* of any inaccuracies, please call (303) 892-5201.

To Do

Youth to perform

The **Colorado Youth Symphony** will perform at 7 p.m. today at Gates Concert Hall, 2344 E. Iliff Ave., on the University of Denver Campus. Tickets: $6 to $10.

Time running out to see Bonnard

More than 100 of the colorful works of Pierre Bonnard are on display through May 25 at the Denver Art Museum. Tickets are $6 to $12 at the museum box office or online at www.denverartmuseum.org.

Partly cloudy
High 74, low 43
Complete weather: **39A**
24-hour line: (303)494-4221

INDEX

Break Time	11D	Movie times	6D
Classifieds	1G	Obituaries	10B
Comics	12D	People	38A
Dear Abby	2D	Rocky Talk	7A
Editorials	34A	TV listings	9D
Education	16A	World/Nation	24A

COLORADO LOTTERY

■ **Powerball: Saturday, May 10**
1-2-6-10-20
Powerball 38; Power Play 4
No ticket matched all five numbers plus the Powerball. Wednesday's jackpot is estimated at $12 million.

■ **Lotto: Saturday, May 10**
1-2-25-31-34-39
No ticket matched all six numbers. Wednesday's jackpot is estimated at $1.8 million.

Rocky Mountain News
John Temple
Editor, President & Publisher

How to reach us
All area codes (303)

Home delivery	892-6397
Outside (303)	(800) 892-6397
Classifieds	825-2525
Outside (303)	(800) 332-3327
Newsroom	892-5201
Arts, entertainment	892-2563
Lifestyles	892-5309
RockyPreps	892-5213
Outside (303)	(800) 315-6397
Sports	892-5100
Advertising	892-5227

Customer service, 892-6397
Monday - Friday, 6 a.m.-5 p.m.
Saturday, 7 a.m.-11 a.m.
Sunday, 7 a.m.-1 p.m.

USPS 469-280
145th year, Issue 17, May 12, 2003
© 2003 Denver Publishing Co.

Notice to readers

Denver Newspaper Agency LLP
Established 2001

Management Committee

Corporate Headquarters

■ Detailed agency directory **23A**

GREATER DENVER

Extra!

Tornado damage

Aurora hit by tornado

Late-summer storm floods streets, leaves many without power

58

Rainfall totals Thursday

WWW. RockyMountainNews.com

Channel-surfing

The redesign introduced "channels," vertical columns of small, provocative news items. A similar concept is used on the page-two visual index.

SPORTS

BARRY FORBIS, SPORTS EDITOR, 303.892.5100, E-MAIL: SPORTS@ROCKYMOUNTAINNEWS.COM

Sideline

RAGING BULLS

It was a Blue Sunday at the University of South Florida campus in Tampa, Fla. Despite a 9-2 record as a Division I-A independent and No. 23 ranking in the Bowl Championship Series standings, the Bulls were left without a bowl berth.

"It's just all about money," South Florida senior wide receiver **Ryan Hearn** told the *Tampa Tribune*. "I thought college football was about pride and respect."

HANDS OF VELVET

Indianapolis Colts receiver **Marvin Harrison** (118 catches) appears poised to gallop to the NFL single-season record for receptions, passing this elite group:

Player, Team	Year	No.
Herman Moore, Lions	1995	123
Cris Carter, Vikings	1994	122
Cris Carter, Vikings	1995	122
Jerry Rice, 49ers	1995	122

ROCKY/FSN POLL

■ **Monday's question**

Whom or what do you blame for the Broncos' loss to the Jets?

Coaches	58.1%
Offense	17.7%
Special teams	8.5%
Defense	5.8%
Something else	9.9%

■ **Today's question**

Who will win the Heisman Trophy?

See the results in Wednesday's News.

■ For the latest sports news or to vote in today's poll, go to

WWW. RockyMountainNews.com /sports

Thrown for a loop

Although confident, Broncos can't figure out meltdown roots

By Lee Rasizer
ROCKY MOUNTAIN NEWS

The scene in the Denver Broncos' locker room with each passing week becomes more and more like a clip from a dandruff commercial.

There's head scratching everywhere.

A 6-2 team, seemingly destined for a deep postseason run just a month ago, has been essentially reduced to an also-ran by losing four times in five weeks.

Imagine a house of cards in an earthquake and you get an idea of what kind of overall collapse is needed by other playoff contenders for Denver's season to continue beyond its scheduled season finale Dec. 29.

At least the Broncos can't be labeled the league's biggest disappointment: Super Bowl runner-up St. Louis has that title already wrapped up with its 5-8 start.

Yet, Denver would likely finish as the AFC's leading underachiever, without an opportunity to achieve the real thing because of daunting tiebreaker scenarios, even if the team takes consecutive wins against Kansas City, Oakland and Arizona down the stretch.

"We're the most talented team in the NFL, bar none," defensive end Trevor Pryce said Monday, less than 24 hours after the Broncos' 19-13 defeat to the New York Jets in East Rutherford, N.J. "There are places that might have a better right guard or better defensive end or long snapper. But overall, we're the most talented team in the NFL."

Flip to BRONCOS on 6C

More inside

■ ***win, lose & Drew:*** Broncos still caught in rut. **2C**

■ **Sam Adams:** Oakland loss left black-and-silver eye. **2C**

■ **UCLA might** come calling for assistant coach Dorrell. **6C**

Heisman race headed to photo finish

MARK J. TERRILL/ASSOCIATED PRESS

Final News poll gives USC's Palmer a narrow edge over McGahee, Banks

By Randy Holtz
ROCKY MOUNTAIN NEWS

It doesn't happen often, but when some old guy in a natty suit steps to a podium in Lower Manhattan on Saturday evening brandishing an envelope with the name of the 68th winner of the John W. Heisman Memorial Trophy Award, a football-crazed nation will watch with rapt attention.

Will it be Southern Cal's Carson Palmer hoisting the little stiff-arming bronze statue?

Miami's Willis McGahee? Maybe McGahee's backfield mate, Ken Dorsey?

Could it be Middle America's finest, Iowa quarterback Brad Banks?

We know this: ESPN won't be hurting for ratings for its annual dog-and-pony show, which airs live at 6 p.m. MST.

Because after doing this season-long Heisman Poll for 16 years now, there hasn't been anything as dumbfounding as this fall's manic free-for-all for what might be the most prestigious individual award in all of sports.

If the results are anything like our final survey of 10 voters, it could be the tightest Heisman finish in history.

Palmer, after being nowhere near the Heisman's radar screen the first three-quarters of the season, made a late charge to nip McGahee by a single point in the final *Rocky Mountain News* Heisman poll.

Flip to HEISMAN on 8C

The Heisman's leading men

■ The top five players in the *Rocky Mountain News* final poll. See the full results on 8C.

1 Carson Palmer
QB, Southern Cal

Cmp.	Att.	Yards	TD	Int.	Rat.
288	458	3,639	32	10	148.3

J. PAT CARTER/ASSOCIATED PRESS

2 Willis McGahee
RB, Miami, Fla.

Att.	Yards	TD	Rec.	Yards	TD
262	1,686	27	24	350	0

CHRIS DONAHUE/ASSOCIATED PRESS

3 Brad Banks
QB, Iowa

Cmp.	Att.	Yards	TD	Int.	Rat.
155	258	2,369	25	4	166.1

KEVIN RIVOLI/ASSOCIATED PRESS

4 Ken Dorsey
QB, Miami, Fla.

Cmp.	Att.	Yards	TD	Int.	Rat.
194	350	3,073	26	10	148.0

GENE J. PUSKAR/ASSOCIATED PRESS

5 Larry Johnson
RB, Penn State

Att.	Yards	TD	Rec.	Yards	TD
251	2,015	20	39	341	3

More inside

■ **Krieger:** Iowa's versatile Banks should win Heisman. **2C**

■ **UCLA** tells coach Toledo it is time to leave. **9C**

■ **Teams** below Buffs in Big 12 get to go to better bowls. **10C**

Left and opposite: examples of the new, longer broadsheet format for the Sunday edition, which is combined with the rival *Denver Post*.

Rocky Mountain News

& THE DENVER POST

SATURDAY, FEBRUARY 22, 2003 ★ 50 cents in Denver

SPECIAL SECTION: RUSSIA'S ROCKY FLATS

Radioactive hell

Death and sickness ravage the Chelyabinsk region of Russia. Bodies waste away. Children lie sick in bed, unable to attend school. Babies have birth defects.

After decades of secrecy, the area's villagers finally learned in the 1990s why they are suffering. They live next door to the Mayak nuclear weapons plant, a Cold War parallel to Denver's Rocky Flats.

Invisible radiation from Mayak has permeated their world, raining down nuclear waste after a horrific 1957 explosion, flowing through their rivers, seeping into their groundwater.

FIRST IN A 3-PART SERIES

Today, Mayak has reverted to denial. The people are no longer in danger, officials say.

That is not what *Rocky Mountain News* reporter Ann Imse and photographer Marc Piscotty heard and saw during their visit to the land ravaged by radioactive fallout. They found anger, sadness and little hope of escape from this nuclear hell.

A woman fighting for her health in a Russian hospital had a fervent wish for the people of Colorado. "I pray God this doesn't happen to you."

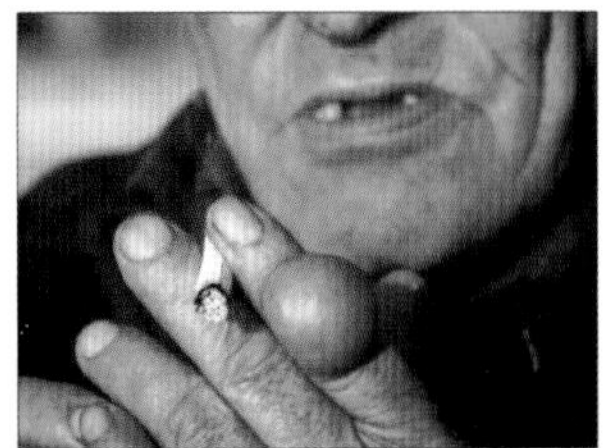

Islam Zainibasharov, who has a tumor on his finger, smokes on the main street of Tatar Karabolka. In the late 1950s, he helped bulldoze buildings in a nearby village evacuated after an explosion at the Mayak nuclear weapons plant.

PHOTOS BY MARC PISCOTTY/ROCKY MOUNTAIN NEWS

Sunset backlights the birch forest behind a fenced grave in the Russian village of Tatar Karabolka. The cemetery is a silent reminder of the thousands in the region who have died because of contamination from the nearby Mayak nuclear weapons plant. The town of 600, once home to several thousand people, has just built its eighth cemetery and many villagers are sick.

SECTION S WRAPS SPOTLIGHT

96 die in club inferno

- **'I never knew** a place could burn so fast,' survivor says. **25A**
- **Prevention** needs vigilance, inspections and sprinklers. **26A**
- **Missing guitarist** Longley was in Boulder-based band. **29A**

COURTESY WPRI-TV/ASSOCIATED PRESS

The band Great White performs Thursday night in a Rhode Island club. Their pyrotechnic display is blamed in a blaze that killed at least 96.

WORLD

Blix orders Iraqis to destroy missiles

March 1 deadline to dispose of weapons. **27A**

- **3rd Armored Cavalry** returns to Iraq. **4A**

WALL STREET WEST

Income tax guide: Be sure to read the laws' fine print. 1C

COLORADO

Barton gets 6 years in prison for starting Hayman Fire. 4A

BARRY GUTIERREZ/ROCKY MOUNTAIN NEWS

SPORTS

Ponderosa takes charge in Class 5A

State wrestling, 14B

Mikael Smith from Nucla pins Chad Gadillo of Mountain Valley.

- **Avs' hot streak derails with 4-1 loss to N.Y. Islanders. 1B**

ON THE WEB

For coverage of state high school wrestling finals and news, go to:

RockyMountainNews.com

DAILY 7 49377 10010 1

WEATHER

Becoming cloudy

High 46 ■ Low 19

Full forecast, **35A**

INDEX

Norah Jones

SPOTLIGHT

Grammys eclectic this year

No host, no front-runner equals safe but uncertain. **1D**

HOME FRONT

Ultra-cozy cabin is a rustic retreat. 1E

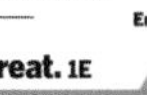

Eminem

they offer a different voice. The items are not opinions, but they are pointed. The channel is the newspaper directing readers to interesting, important, sometimes quirky items. It reflects the personality of the paper and allows us to show creativity, attitude, and a sense of humor.

The broadsheet

One challenge was to keep the look consistent from the tab to the broadsheet. This included how the broadsheet would be built for the 50-inch web. Rather than building the paper at the old 58-inch web standard and shrinking the width to fit the smaller SAU, as had been the practice, the *Rocky* decided to build the editorial templates at the 50-inch-web (12-inch-page) width. Ads would still be built at the larger size but then digitally shrunk and married to the editorial portion. This way at least editorial type and visuals would be spared the 92% anamorphic squish that many papers, including the *Rocky*'s JOA rival, *The Denver Post*, inflict on their pages.

The rollout

The project was more than a redesign. The *Rocky* used the change as a chance to revamp its workflow, its newsroom organization, and the tools it used to create the newspaper. Editors studied how the paper was being put out and determined that the new technology could have a bigger impact if the newsroom was structured differently. The newspaper would be better if journalists had more direct responsibility for content in section teams, rather than through a universal presentation desk.

The new Unisys Publishing system allowed the *Rocky* to make journalists' jobs more varied and satisfying by diminishing the assembly-line approach to production. For example, editors could link stories to pages and even

spotlight

Spot check

$177

681

Body builders

Automotive works of art are rolling off a different kind of assembly line

MEGA GIVEAWAY! MEGA SAVINGS! SEE PAGE 7 FOR DETAILS!

WALL STREET WEST

Ticker

United chasing $1.8B

Airline flexes its political muscles to win loan guarantee

When large companies like DataPlay fall, little ones can go tumbling after

Domino effect

Entrepreneur grasps value of timing, risk

Holy grail of hot cars

Rare Ferrari GTOs fuel pride, privacy prices in millions

Glitch makes Dish dark for thousands

Uplink equipment sends out signal that cuts service

Rocky Mountain News

HARDBALL

191

Although records are made to be broken, no one recently has come close to the RBI mark. Will anyone get a crack at Hack Wilson's magic number? **4H**

Top RBI seasons by active players

147 Ken Griffey Jr. & Todd Helton

148 Rafael Palmeiro

150 Andres Galarraga

157 Juan Gonzalez

160 158 Sammy Sosa

165 Manny Ramirez

100 YEARS OF THE WORLD SERIES

Red Sox: Eighty-four years of failure in Boston prove there's nothing worse than the Curse. **8H**

TUESDAY, JANUARY 14, 2003 — Rocky Mountain News 1C

SPORTS

BARRY FORBIS, SPORTS EDITOR, 303.892.5100, E-MAIL: SPORTS@ROCKYMOUNTAINNEWS.COM

Sideline

COACH CLASS

Three of the head coaches in Sunday's NFL conference championship games never have coached a team to a conference title.

Only Tennessee's **Jeff Fisher**, who guided the Titans to the AFC title in the 1999 season, has won a conference crown.

Since the NFL adopted its current alignment in 1970, the record for coaching victories in conference title games is five, shared by **Tom Landry** and **Don Shula**. Landry also shares the record of five losses with **John Madden**.

■ Most coaching victories in conference title games:

Coach, team(s)	Record
Don Shula, Miami	5-2
Tom Landry, Dallas	5-5
Joe Gibbs, Washington	4-1
Marv Levy, Buffalo	4-1
Dan Reeves, Denver-Atlanta	**4-1**
Chuck Noll, Pittsburgh	4-3

THEY SAID IT

"It is good to represent the fans and if I get a chance to do that, I will do that. But if I don't, there will be no remorse, no ill feelings, no animosity . . . I'll enjoy my week."

Michael Jordan, above, on his chances of playing in All-Star Game

ROCKY/FSN POLL

■ **Monday's question**

Should U.S. Olympic Committee CEO Lloyd Ward be fired?

Yes	72.7%
No	9.1%
I'm not sure	18.2%

■ **Today's question**

What team looks to be in the driver's seat to win the Super Bowl?

See the results in Wednesday's News.

■ For the latest sports news or to vote in today's poll, go to

WWW. RockyMountainNews.com /sports

At halfway point, Avs are playing just average

Struggles put team in unusual position

ANALYSIS

By Rick Sadowski
ROCKY MOUNTAIN NEWS

While the Colorado Avalanche will spend the second half of the season "Pursuing History," the Northwest Division-leading Vancouver Canucks might use the title of a current film as their rallying cry:

"Catch Me If You Can."

The Avalanche trails Vancouver by seven points — and eight victories — with 38 games remaining, so it will take some doing to overtake the Canucks and win a record ninth consecutive division championship.

Otherwise, the Avalanche will have to pull ahead of several other teams just to finish fourth in the Western Conference and earn home-ice advantage for one playoff round. The Avalanche stands fourth in the division and eighth in the conference, four points ahead of ninth-place Anaheim.

This is foreign territory for a team that isn't used to playing average hockey, and it rates no better than a "C" grade for its first-half performance, one that prompted general

Flip to AVALANCHE on 9C

Avs' midseason report card

■ **Team gets** a grade of 'C' for first half. **9C**

NHL inside

■ **Hartley, above,** to take over as coach at Atlanta. **9C**

■ **Sabres join** Senators in filing for bankruptcy. **9C**

DAVID CALLOW/ASSOCIATED PRESS

Title run comes to a bitter end

Jennifer Capriati lets out a cry of frustration during her first-round match against Marlene Weingartner at the Australian Open tennis tournament in Melbourne, Australia, on Monday night. Capriati, who had won the women's singles title the past two years, lost 2-6, 7-6 (8-6), 6-4. Weingartner reached the fourth round at Australia last year, but more often has struggled on the women's tour and entered this year's tournament ranked 90th. **10C**

Agent starts shopping Grbac

By Lee Rasizer
ROCKY MOUNTAIN NEWS

Elvis Grbac has made it clear he wants back in the NFL after a year off, and the Denver Broncos are a possible destination.

Now the quarterback's agent, Jim Steiner, is busy spreading the word.

"I've begun to make phone calls, not only to the Broncos but other teams, regarding Elvis' interest in playing," Steiner said Monday. "But I don't know what's going to be available."

Without specifically confirming a conversation with Denver coach Mike Shanahan regarding Grbac, who retired after one rocky season (2001) with the Baltimore Ravens, Steiner delivered a message.

"Mike knows Elvis is available," Steiner said, adding the Broncos haven't yet expressed an interest or lack thereof.

Grbac, a nine-year NFL veteran who was selected to the Pro Bowl in 2000 in his last of five seasons with the Kansas City Chiefs, could make sense for Denver if the team releases incumbent starter Brian Griese, a move that's likely in June.

Broncos offensive coordinator Gary Kubiak was Grbac's position coach with San Francisco in 1994, when Shanahan served as the 49ers offensive coordinator. Grbac played 12 games that season in relief of

Flip to BRONCOS on 5C

Front page of the Sports section (above) and a special baseball section (above left).

write headlines. Copyeditors could generate content and do simple design. Designers could copy-edit and generate content. The previous Quark/Atex/PC-network system made it extremely difficult for staffers to work outside their niche; one person had to wait for the other before he could do his part. Under the new system, a team shares responsibility for getting a section done and does whatever task is needed at the moment.

Finally, the paper created its own web-based news budgeting system, which allows more timely and more easily shared budgets, and an Intranet site to act as the basic reference resource for all employees.

The *Rocky* rolled out all of these changes from May 22 through July 13, 2003, when it produced its first complete broadsheet paper. The transition was remarkably smooth. On the first day it started with Spotlight, the paper received less than 50 calls and e-mails – nothing when compared to the more than 200 it got when it test-dropped the comic strip "Annie" or the thousands it received when "For Better or For Worse" introduced a gay character. Then came Sports, Business, National and International, and Commentary.

The editor responded to every e-mail. In one case, a reader wrote: "What have you done to my paper? I could put up with the rest of the paper looking like a souvenir edition of a 19th-century paper. But you've really gone too far with the Commentary section. It's awful."

"I'm sorry you feel this way," Temple wrote back. "I'd ask that you give it a few days to get over the shock. We're actually trying to use modern technology to produce a better-edited newspaper that meets the needs of busy people."

Three days later Temple got this response:

"I got over the shock, and I actually like what I see very much. Maybe it's just hard to change old habits when you're near your seventh decade."

Each step of the way the response became even quieter. Only about a dozen calls or e-mails about Business, for example. On the day of the final changes – to page one and the local section – the response was muted: about three dozen calls came.

The idea of the redesign had not been a radical transformation. Readers already liked their *Rocky*. But the paper needed to be able to compete better in the modern media blast of the Internet/cable era.

Now comes the tweaking, to explore the dimensions of the new design and to refine the paper's approach to presenting the news.

"It's been a great experience," Temple said. "We've re-examined every detail of our paper. Every act is intentional now." ‹

Segunda-feira, 29 de maio de 2000 | Ano 1 | Número 20 | R$ 1,50*

Valor ECONÔMICO

Área de saúde sai na frente na corrida do ensino virtual D4

Júlio Gagliardi (foto) dá a receita do Aché, o maior laboratório brasileiro B7

www.valoronline.com.br

Destaques

Força estrangeira
Caso o Banespa seja vendido para um dos cinco bancos estrangeiros interessados em sua privatização, a participação externa no sistema financeiro nacional atingirá 26% do total de ativos e 22% dos depósitos. **Página C1**

Pressa no setor elétrico
O Ministério de Minas e Energia anuncia nos próximos dias um programa de antecipação de obras para evitar riscos de racionamento em 2001. Deverão ser incluídos empreendimentos nas áreas de transmissão e geração. **Página A3**

Importação de talentos
Mais imigrantes legalizados entraram nos Estados Unidos a partir de 1980 do que nos 60 anos anteriores. O programa que acolhe mão-de-obra especializada, a pedido das empresas, já preencheu a cota deste semestre. **Página A9**

Peru realiza eleição
O Peru realizou ontem o segundo turno da eleição presidencial, apesar de pedidos dos EUA e da OEA para que a votação fosse adiada. O presidente Alberto Fujimori, virtual candidato único, deve ser reeleito para um terceiro mandato consecutivo. **Página A-8**

Franceses querem a Light
A francesa EDF está negociando a compra das participações da CSN e da Relliant na Light, além da troca de ações da Eletropaulo pelas da distribuidora fluminense em poder da AES. **Página B1**

White Martins sai da bolsa
A CVM autorizou o fechamento de capital da White Martins, que a partir de hoje sai da Bovespa. Por seis meses a Praxair terá de comprar as ações dos minoritários que desejarem vendê-las, ao preço do leilão de 3 de maio. **Página C2**

Concentração reduz preços
O processo de concentração no comércio varejista — de supermercados a farmácias, açougues e lavanderias — tem ajudado a conter os índices de inflação. Os ganhos de escala estão sendo repassados ao consumidor. **Página A4**

Dólar		
Comercial (Mercado)		1,8360/1,8370
Comercial (BC)		1,8447/1,8455
Paralelo	São Paulo	1,9100/1,9250
	Rio	1,8700/1,9000
Turismo	São Paulo	1,8350/1,8900
	Rio	1,8500/1,8700
Juros		
Taxa Selic meta		18,50 % ao ano
Taxa Selic efetiva		18,51 % ao ano
DI over (taxa efetiva)		18,44 % ao ano
DI futuro (set/00)		19,74 % ao ano
TR (25/05 a 25/06)		0,2190 %

Índice

***PREÇO DE VENDA AVULSA**
$1,50 DF/ES/MG/PR/RJ/SP
$2,00 BA/GO/MT/MS/RS/SC/TO
$2,25 AC/AL/AP/AM/CE/MA/PA/PE/PI/RN/RO/RR/SE

ISSN 1517-9710

RAFAEL JACINTO/VALOR

Szajman vendeu sua participação no Real por R$ 200 milhões: preço acima do mercado

A jogada milionária de um grande minoritário

Mara Luquet
De São Paulo

Abram Szajman, o controlador do grupo VR e presidente da Federação do Comércio do Estado de São Paulo, vendeu sua participação de 17% no Banco Real por cerca de R$ 200 milhões.

O Real foi comprado em 1998 pelo holandês ABN-Amro Bank, que fez uma oferta para comprar as ações dos minoritários ao preço unitário de R$1,38. A ação na época estava sendo negociada ao preço de R$ 1,10.

Szajman não aceitou a oferta e fez sua negociação individualmente. Conseguiu que o ABN-Amro pagasse por seus papéis cerca de R$ 1,80, o que significa um ganho de 63,64% em relação ao preço que a ação estava sendo negociada no mercado e 30% acima do que os outros minoritários embolsaram.

"Ele tinha quase 20% do banco, era natural que recebesse um tratamento diferente", observa um dos executivos do ABN-Amro.

Szajman diz que não precisou brigar. "Eles são muito corretos e estão acostumados a negociar com minoritários no seu país de origem". **Página D1**

Crise agravada na Argentina afeta o Brasil

De São Paulo e Buenos Aires

O agravamento da crise econômica da Argentina, o segundo maior importador de produtos brasileiros, tende a prejudicar os setores mais dinâmicos da economia nacional — a indústria de manufaturados, que está aumentando suas exportações em ritmo acelerado neste ano, puxando a retomada do setor industrial. Correm riscos a médio prazo as vendas de veículos, de autopeças e de eletroeletrônicos.

Mais do que isso, um aprofundamento da crise na Argentina pode afetar também a imagem do Brasil no exterior porque para o mercado financeiro é cada vez mais comum a análise dos países do Mercosul como bloco econômico.

O governo argentino adiou para hoje o anúncio do pacote de corte de gastos públicos previsto para sábado.

A expectativa é de que as medidas adotadas serão recessivas — com impacto, portanto, sobre a capacidade da Argentina de importar. O economista da consultoria Tendências Roberto Padovani vê relação direta entre a renda dos argentinos e as exportações brasileiras de manufaturados. Assim, se ocorrer forte desaquecimento, tudo indica que a balança comercial piore.

Já o economista sênior do Unibanco Eduardo Figueiredo de Freitas não acredita que vá haver ataque especulativo contra a Argentina, mas alerta para o risco do desemprego. "Ninguém pode prever quando o governo vai mudar o rumo da política econômica, pelas crescentes pressões da sociedade."

Bernardo Macedo, da LCA Consultores, diz que a Argentina está, novamente, sob forte desconfiança dos mercados. "Como o câmbio não pode absorver choques externos, o impacto cai sobre o nível de atividade. O efeito é perverso: desemprego."

Nos mercados internacionais, a percepção de que a situação fiscal na Argentina deteriorou-se e de que as metas com o Fundo Monetário Internacional (FMI) podem não ser atingidas provocou um aumento nas taxas de juros que medem o risco argentino.

Páginas A3, C5 e C6

Por que o pacote foi adiado

Cláudia Trevisan
De Buenos Aires

O governo argentino adiou a divulgação do corte de gastos de pelo menos US$ 600 milhões por divergências em relação ao valor do piso a partir do qual haverá redução salarial e por dúvidas sobre a conveniência de divulgar outras medidas que, embora sem impacto fiscal, promovem reformas estruturais.

O anúncio deve ser feito hoje, antevéspera da chegada da missão do FMI encarregada de monitorar as contas públicas.

Os ministros se dividem entre reduzir salários superiores a US$ 700 ou a US$ 1.000. A tendência ontem era a opção pelo menor valor, posição defendida pela equipe econômica.

A medida vai fortalecer a manifestação que a CGT dissidente fará contra o FMI na quarta-feira, em um protesto que já tem a adesão da Igreja Católica.

O adiamento foi provocado também pela resistência de uma ala do governo em incluir no pacote a regra que permitirá a empresas de medicina privada competir com as obras sociais dos sindicatos, que hoje prestam assistência médica aos trabalhadores. Esse grupo teme que se amplie o confronto com os sindicalistas. **Página A8**

Petrobras vende minipoços

Cláudia Schüffner
De Aracaju

O presidente da Petrobras, Philippe Reichstul, apresentará amanhã o primeiro programa de venda de campos em bacias maduras ao conselho de administração da estatal, presidido pelo ministro de Minas e Energia, Rodolpho Tourinho, um dos maiores defensores da criação de um mercado de empresas independentes no Brasil. Tourinho sonha ver no Nordeste uma situação parecida com a do Texas, nos Estados Unidos, onde algumas famílias conseguem sobreviver da produção de pequenos poços de petróleo.

Uma fonte ouvida pelo **Valor** revelou que a Petrobras espera arrecadar até US$ 500 milhões com a venda desses ativos. A estatal não confirma. No portfólio estão 73 campos com 763 poços perfurados cuja produção está em declínio. Por isso, a exploração se tornou antieconômica para uma empresa do porte da Petrobras. Esses campos são conhecidos no mercado como marginais e vêm sendo erroneamente chamados de campos maduros, uma incorreção geológica, segundo especialistas.

São considerados campos marginais os de pequeno porte em que os poços já perfurados estão com baixa produtividade, precisando de investimentos para aumentar a produção. Eles podem ser operados de forma mais eficiente e econômica pelos pequenos produtores, porque estes não têm os custos das grandes empresas. **Página B8**

A guerra de tarifas nos portos do NE

Luiz Herrisson e Heliana Frazão
De Recife e Salvador

A necessidade de atrair mais clientes está acirrando a competição dos portos nordestinos e provocando a redução de tarifas. Os terminais de Salvador, Recife, Fortaleza e Natal estão investindo milhões de reais na ampliação da capacidade de carga e em infra-estrutura para receber embarcações maiores e concentrar as cargas destinadas à região. Em 2001, a briga se acirra, com o início da operação de Pecém. **Página A5**

Privatização de quatro bancos será adiada

Mônica Izaguirre
De Brasília

O governo brasileiro e o Fundo Monetário Internacional vão revisar esta semana o memorando técnico assinado em dezembro de 1999, na parte que trata da privatização de bancos estaduais. O governo havia se comprometido a vender à iniciativa privada sete instituições financeiras ainda este ano. No entanto, o Banco Central já admite que o máximo que vai conseguir — se tudo der certo — é a privatização de três bancos: Banespa, Banco do Estado do Maranhão e o Banestado, do Paraná. A lista apresentada anteriormente ao FMI previa também a venda dos bancos dos estados de Goiás, Ceará, Amazonas e Piauí. Mas estes vão ficar para o ano que vem. **Página C4**

Rei da soja vira socialista

EVILÁSIO S. ALVES/FOLHA IMAGEM

Filiado ao PPS há pouco mais de seis meses, Blairo Maggi, um dos maiores proprietários rurais do país, quer ser governador do Mato Grosso e eleger Ciro Gomes Página A12

Sara Lee já tem 21% do café em pó brasileiro

Juliano Basile
De Brasília

Em uma ofensiva rápida e silenciosa, a americana Sara Lee passou a dominar 21% do mercado nacional de café em pó, ao adquirir os negócios da União. Os órgãos antitruste do governo devem aprovar a compra, porque o mercado ainda é pulverizado. No ano passado, a Sara Lee arrematou as marcas Café do Ponto e Seleto e agora, ao levar os negócios de café da União, terá também as tradicionalíssimas Pilão e Caboclo. **Página B11**

Profile: *Valor*

Simon Esterson

Crisp type and dynamic graphics give punch to a new Brazilian financial paper

Valor (it means "value"), launched in 2000, is now the leading Brazilian business daily, the equivalent of the *Financial Times* or the *Wall Street Journal* for the younger but no less dynamic Brazilian economy. Based in São Paulo, the paper is a joint venture between the *Folha de S. Paulo* and *O Globo* publishing groups.

Valor is a four-section paper. Its main section carries news and comment, while two others carry company news and stock-market tables. The fourth section, "EU&," covers personal finance and carries general features about life outside business for its readers.

The headline and main text font is Gerard Unger's serif font Coranto, where the slightly condensed bold headline weight gives a good character count on this US-style narrow-width page. The sans-serif Griffith Gothic is used for captions, labeling, and the many charts and tables a financial newspaper needs.

Under art director Silas Botelho, the paper has pioneered using information graphics and magazine-style portrait and reportage photography for daily business subjects, working hard to avoid the visual trap of having every businessman photographed sitting behind a desk.

A monthly color magazine, *Estampa,* was launched a year after the newspaper's own launch. ‹

Editor:
Celso Pinto
Consulting Art Directors:
John Belknap, Simon Esterson, Ally Palmer
Art Director:
Silas Botelho

Opposite: Front page of the business paper *Valor*.

Valor's page two (right), with Brazilian economic news, an opinion column, and an index to businesses mentioned in this issue; and the front page of the general-news section EU& (opposite).

A2 | **Valor** | Quarta-feira, 4 de setembro de 2002

Brasil

Estoques da Embraer caem cerca de US$ 200 milhões e vão para US$ 1 bilhão **Página B5**

Safra 2001/2002 de grãos no Brasil deve fechar em 98,7 milhões de toneladas **Página B10**

MICHAEL REID

A batalha de Fox pelas reformas

Nos últimos meses, à medida que o "contágio" do colapso argentino se alastrou pela América do Sul, o México permaneceu, aparentemente, imune. De abril para cá, o peso sofreu uma desvalorização de 10%. O spread dos bônus mexicanos registrou ligeiro aumento, mas depois cedeu para algo em torno de 350 pontos base acima dos bônus do Tesouro dos EUA. Em comparação com a maioria das economias da América do Sul, esse desempenho equivale a um modelo de estabilidade. Será que ele poderá se manter assim?

Não são difíceis de identificar as razões da relativa estabilidade financeira mexicana. Desde a crise do peso, em 1994-5, o México adotou políticas macroeconômicas responsáveis. Dois fatores convenceram os investidores de que essas políticas vieram para ficar. Em primeiro lugar, o Nafta, que vincula a economia mexicana à dos EUA, assegurou um fluxo contínuo de investimentos estrangeiros diretos, e torna um retorno ao populismo macroeconômico ao um só tempo oneroso e improvável. E em segundo lugar, uma transição para a democracia culminou pacificamente na eleição de Vicente Fox em 2000, pondo fim às sete décadas em que o Partido Revolucionário Institucional (PRI) se manteve no poder. Esses fatores estão por trás da decisão das agências de classificação de crédito, de recomendar investimentos em papéis da dívida mexicana.

Ainda assim, seria um pouco apressado demais concluir que o México transformou-se numa economia norte-americana desenvolvida e que deixou de ser uma economia latino-americana ainda emergente. Graças principalmente ao Nafta, o México registrou um crescimento econômico acelerado na segunda metade da década de 1990. Mas com a desaceleração da economia americana no ano passado, o México entrou em uma recessão da qual está, agora, tendo dificuldades para sair. Embora a economia tenha crescido 1,16% no segundo trimestre, em comparação com o mesmo período do ano anterior, vários analistas estão céticos em relação ao vigor da recuperação.

Algumas maquiladoras mudaram para a China

Uma preocupação está no fato de que os próprios EUA poderão entrar num "duplo mergulho recessivo", arrastando o México junto consigo. Mas há também problemas no plano doméstico. Fox chegou à presidência prometendo promover um crescimento anual de 7% através de uma modernização das finanças públicas, e de uma melhoria na competitividade das empresas mexicanas através de uma reforma estrutural. Há, porém, um aspecto relevante: com o aumento nos salários reais no México, algumas das "maquiladoras", como são denominadas as indústrias montadoras estabelecidas ao longo da fronteira com os EUA, migraram para a China.

Mas diante de uma oposição que predomina no Congresso onde o PRI continua sendo o maior partido, Fox tem encontrado dificuldades para implementar sua agenda de reformas. No ano passado, o Congresso desfigurou os aumentos de impostos propostos, deixando o governo federal ainda perigosamente dependente das voláteis receitas do petróleo. O governo não encontrará mais facilidade para viabilizar os itens seguintes de sua agenda. O novo período de atividades do Congresso iniciado em 2 de setembro será dominado por uma batalha envolvendo uma reforma na Constituição para afrouxar os controles sobre os investimentos privados no setor de geração de eletricidade. Em seguida virão medidas para reformar a legislação vigente relativa aos setores do petróleo e gás, telecomunicações e reformas trabalhistas.

"Assim como o gerenciamento macroeconômico diminuiu o 'risco país', essas reformas baixarão o 'custo país'", diz Luis Ernesto Derbez, ministro da Economia. Segundo ele, os custos serão reduzidos pelas reformas ou, no longo prazo, uma desvalorização do câmbio se encarregará disso — mas ao preço de empobrecer os mexicanos e sob o risco de elevar a inflação.

Esse dilema é bastante familiar ao Brasil. E também no México tais reformas provocam resistência dos tradicionalistas. Muito ficará na dependência de Fox demonstrar maior habilidade em suas negociações com o PRI do que anteriormente. O presidente deu mostras de uma nova humildade. Em seu discurso sobre o estado-da-nação, no domingo passado, ele admitiu que o México exige "melhores resultados" de seu governo.

Há sinais de que o novo líder do PRI, Roberto Madrazo, está disposto a negociar um acordo no que diz respeito ao setor de eletricidade. Quanto às reformas tributárias, Fox provavelmente terá de aceitar mudanças incrementais. Tendo em vista o Nafta e a solidez da economia mexicana, isso deverá ser o suficiente para assegurar um crescimento moderado e para manter a estabilidade financeira. Mas talvez não o seja.

Michael Reid, editor de Américas da revista "The Economist", em Londres, escreve às quartas-feiras

Curtas

Bancários

Representantes de bancários de todo o país consideraram "insuficiente" a primeira proposta de reajuste salarial apresentada pela Federação Nacional dos Bancos (Fenaban) nesta campanha salarial. Os sindicalistas querem aumento de 13,39%, equivalente à reposição da inflação, produtividade e resíduo inflacionário, mas a Fenaban propôs 6% de reajuste, mais abono único de R$ 1.150.

Inadimplência

O índice de inadimplência deverá ser menor no período do Natal deste ano. É o que prevê o assessor econômico da Serasa, Carlos Henrique de Almeida, levando em consideração três fatos: o consumidor está acertando seus débitos; está retraído nas compras; e evitando dívidas grandes que se estendam até o próximo ano. A última pesquisa mostrou que em julho foram devolvidos 13,8 cheques para cada mil compensados.

Aneel define critério para revisão ordinária das tarifas das elétricas

Roberto Rockmann e Vinícius Dória
De São Paulo e de Brasília

A Agência Nacional de Energia Elétrica (Aneel) deve publicar hoje no Diário Oficial resolução que define o custo de reposição a valor de mercado como método para calcular a remuneração dos ativos a ser usada na revisão ordinária de tarifas das elétricas.

A decisão é contrária à proposta da Associação Brasileira das Distribuidoras de Energia Elétrica (Abradee), que desejava usar o preço mínimo dos leilões de privatização como metodologia a ser usada na revisão. É vista também pelos agentes como mudança nas regras do jogo. As distribuidoras alegam que a diferença entre a idéia sugerida pela agência e a delas é de R$ 13,1 bilhões. Ou seja, elas reclamam que seus ativos serão subavaliados, com isso, as tarifas também subiriam menos, o que teria impacto sobre suas contas, já bastante fragilizadas.

Há mais de um mês, o diretor da Abradee, Luiz Carlos Guimarães, disse que as empresas poderiam quebrar com uma decisão diferente da proposta pela entidade. A medida era considerada como a mais importante pelas distribuidoras, que destacavam que um parecer contrário ao delas significaria ruptura nas regras do jogo e implicaria redução na vinda de investimentos. Agora, mesmo com a publicação da resolução, a queda-de-braço entre Aneel e empresas deve se intensificar. Representantes das distribuidoras devem mostrar seu descontentamento a altos funcionários do governo.

A escolha da Aneel, pelo valor de mercado das empresas, fará as tarifas subirem menos em 2003. A desvalorização do real (muitas elétricas compram energia de Itaipu, em dólar) e os leilões de energia (que permitem reajustes extras fora dos aniversários das concessões) já são ingredientes explosivos e que poderão fazer os preços subirem mais de 20%. Caso concordasse com a proposta das distribuidoras, as pressões sobre os preços seriam ainda maiores e as tarifas poderiam ultrapassar 25% em 2003, nos cálculos de um especialista.

A revisão ordinária ocorre de quatro em quatro anos. No próximo ano, quase 20 concessionárias passarão por isso. Dessas, 11 já começaram a ter suas tarifas analisadas pela Aneel. Em 2004, será a vez de mais de 40 distribuidoras.

O próximo passo da agência na revisão ordinária é a realização de audiência pública sobre o polêmico "Fator X", que visa ao compartilhamento de ganhos de produtividade com o consumidor na tarifa, o que reduziria seu percentual de alta. As elétricas alegam que sua produtividade foi abalada pelo racionamento e pela demora no repasse dos custos não-gerenciáveis às tarifas depois da máxidesvalorização de 1999. Esses dois fatores terem dado baixa remuneração a seus ativos. Outro ponto em que as discordâncias devem surgir.

www.aneel.gov.br

Costa Leite volta ao STJ como advogado

Juliano Basile
De Brasília

Os bancos contrataram o ex-presidente do Superior Tribunal de Justiça (STJ), Paulo Costa Leite, para defendê-los no julgamento que definirá qual índice deve corrigir os contratos de financiamento imobiliário durante o chamado Plano Collor, em março de 1990. O caso volta a ser julgado hoje pela Corte Especial, órgão máximo do do STJ

Costa Leite fará sustentação oral perante os antigos colegas no STJ. Ele foi contratado pelo Banco Itaú e falará a favor da Associação Brasileira das Entidades de Crédito Imobiliário e Poupança (Abecip).

O ex-presidente defenderá uma causa avaliada em R$ 20 bilhões. A Corte Especial terá de definir entre a correção pelo Índice de Preços ao Consumidor (IPC), que era de 84,32%, em março de 90, ou pelo Bônus do Tesouro Nacional Fiscal (BTNF), de 41,23%.

Os bancos defendem a aplicação do IPC para corrigir os contratos imobiliários. Assim, não ficariam obrigados a desembolsar a diferença entre esse índice e o BTNF aos mutuários. Seus advogados alegam que o IPC foi usado nesses contratos por ser o índice de reajuste da caderneta de poupança, até o advento do Plano Collor. Os mutuários alegam que o plano determinou que as poupanças passassem a ser corrigidas pelo BTNF e cobram a diferença entre os índices.

Costa Leite deixou o STJ em 3 de abril deste ano para ser o vice na chapa de Anthony Garotinho (PSB) à Presidência da República. Ele desistiu da disputa política depois que reportagens revelaram sua participação no Serviço Nacional de Informações (SNI) do regime militar.

A gestão de Costa Leite foi marcada por uma série de iniciativas voltadas ao cidadão comum, como a busca por um acordo entre governo e trabalhadores para o pagamento do FGTS expurgado dos correntistas nos planos Verão (janeiro de 89) e Collor. Hoje, ele advogará contra a pretensão dos mutuários.

ROBERTO JAYME/VALOR

Paulo Costa Leite: "Sinto-me feliz de advogar perante o tribunal"

O ex-presidente do STJ disse ao **Valor** que se impôs uma quarentena e agora, está satisfeito em voltar a advogar. "É uma situação interessante e me sinto feliz de advogar perante o tribunal", declarou.

Em 1º de julho deste ano, a Corte Especial do STJ retomou o julgamento do índice de correção dos contratos de financiamento imobiliário ao julgar dois processos. No primeiro, deu IPC, ou seja, decisão a favor dos bancos. Houve um intervalo e o chamado horário de lanche dos ministros. Os ministros retornaram do lanche, em composição diversa, para julgar um segundo caso. Como não eram os mesmos ministros que julgaram o primeiro processo, a decisão acabou sendo pelo BTNF, beneficiando, assim, os mutuários.

Como a Corte Especial julgou dois processos de forma distinta, o presidente do STJ, ministro Nilson Naves, informou que só julgaria uma terceira ação sobre o caso quando a Corte estivesse completa, com 21 ministros presentes. Assim, ele pretende definir um entendimento consolidado sobre o índice a ser aplicado.

Costa Leite informou que esse entendimento não deverá sair hoje porque os ministros julgarão um processo sobre a primeira quinzena de março do Plano Collor, na qual há várias decisões judiciais a favor do IPC. A definição sairá, segundo o ex-presidente, quando o STJ julgar um caso envolvendo a segunda quinzena.

CNI prevê estagnação no emprego

Daniel Rittner
De Brasília

O nível de emprego industrial deve terminar o ano estagnado ou com pequena queda na comparação com 2001, segundo projeções da Confederação Nacional da Indústria (CNI). Sem novos postos de trabalho e com redução dos salários médios reais, a soma de todos os rendimentos dos trabalhadores — a chamada massa salarial — está diminuindo e dificulta a recuperação da economia, afirma relatório divulgado ontem pela entidade.

De acordo com os economistas da CNI, o mercado de trabalho "inverteu a tendência de melhoria" apresentada desde o fim do ano passado. A virada negativa ocorreu em abril. O início das turbulências no mercado financeiro contaminou rapidamente a economia real e a instabilidade trazida pelas eleições presidenciais não deve mudar o cenário, diz o relatório. "A reversão desse quadro nos próximos meses é improvável."

No primeiro semestre, o emprego industrial caiu 0,74% em relação à igual período do ano passado. Segundo os analistas, trata-se do resultado do ajuste empreendido pelo setor após o racionamento de energia elétrica. A perspectiva é de que o desempenho da segunda metade do ano se mostre um pouco melhor, até por causa da base de comparação mais fraca.

A CNI avalia, porém, que essa possível melhoria seria "apenas suficiente para compensar a queda do primeiro semestre". De janeiro a junho, 14 dos 18 setores industriais pesquisados tiveram diminuição do emprego. Os mais afetados foram os ramos de máquinas e aparelhos elétricos e eletrônicos. "Ao contrário do que se observou nos dois últimos anos, dificilmente será registrado crescimento do emprego na indústria de transformação em 2002."

Índice de empresas citadas em textos nesta edição

ABN Amro **C2**
Accenture **B3**
AES Sul **B8**
AGF **C5**
Alba **B5**
Allianz **C5**
Alpes **C2**
Amerada Hess **A6**
Aracruz Celulose **C2**
Arno **B6**
AT&T **B4**
ATL **C14**
AtoFina **B6**
Audi **B7**
Audi/Volkswagen **A3**
Avon **B3**
Axa **C5**
BAe Systems **B5**
Bahia Sul **C2**
Banco Pactual **C14**
BBA **D2**
BBC **C5**
BBV **A3**
BCP **B4**
Bertelsmann **B4**
BHP Billiton **A6**
Biobrás **C1**
Biomm **C1**
BNDES **B6**
Bombril **B5**
Borden Chemical **B5**
BR Distribuidora **A6**
Bradesco **C2**
Brasil Telecom **B4, C2**
BREED Technologies **B1**
Britânia **B6**
British Gas **D2**
BSH International **C14**
Case New Holland **A3**
CEF **C2**
Cimefor **B7**
Cirio **B5**
CIT Group **C5**
Citibank **A3**
Citigroup **C1**
Citroën **B7**
Clorox **B5**
Comgás **D2**
Concrefor Participações **B7**
Copel **B8**
Credit Suisse Asset Management **D1**
D. Araújo Loducca **B2**
Dassault **B5**
Datasul Tecnologia **B2**
Dell Computer **B4**
Delphi **B1**
Deutsche Bank **C5**
Döhler Indústria Têxtil **B2**
DSM **B6**
DuPont Chemical Solutions Enterprise **B6**
Eliane Revestimentos Cerâmicos **B2**
Embraer **A4, B5, B7**
Embratel **B4**
Engemix **B7**
Enron **B3, C1**
EPGE Participações **B7**
F2b **C2**
Fence **A8**
Fiat **B2, B7**
FNP **B10**
Ford **B7, C1**
Friedland Capital **C2**
Gartner **B4**
General Electric **C5**
General Motors **B2, B7**
Geral de Concreto **B7**
Gerdau **C2**
Globo S.A. **B2**
Grupo Pestana **D2**
H2R **D4**
Habib's **B3**
Halliburton Energy Services **A6**
Hedging Griffo **D1**
Henkel **B5**
Honda **B7**
HP **B4**
HSBC **A3, D2**
IBM **B4**
Intel **C1**
Ipiranga **A6, B3**
Itaú **A2, C2**
Jaguar **B1**
JP Morgan Chase **C1, C2**
KBR **A6**
Lehman Brothers **C1**
Leo Burnett **B2**
Lloyd's **C5**
Loducca **B2**
Lokheed-Martin **B5**
Mallory **B6**
Manguinhos **A6**
Marcopolo **B7, D2**
Marks & Spencer **C5**
McDonald's **B3**
Mckinsey **B1**
Medabil Tessenderlo **B3**
Mellon Financial **C5**
Metron **B4**
Microsoft **C14**
Mizuho **C1**
Mundial **B6**
Moody's **C5**
Morgan Stanley **C2**
Moulinex **B6**
Munich Re **C5**
MVC **B7**
Napster **B4**
Odebrecht **B3**
Oi **B4, B6**
Opportunity **B4**
Pacific Investment **C5**
Petrobras **A6, C2**
Philips **B6**
Portugal Telecom **B1, B4**
Powell, Goldstein, Frazer & Murphy LLP **B10**
PriceWaterhouseCoopers **B4**
Procter & Gamble Co. **B3**
Prodam **B4**
Prudential Securities **C1**
Quick House **B3**
Rabo Securities **B6**
Rede Record **B2**
Renault **A3**
Renault/Nissan **A3**
Repsol YPF **A6**
Roche **B6**
Rosoboronexport **B5**
Rothschild **C5**
Saab **B5**
Santista Têxtil **C14**
São Carlos **C2**
Saudi Aramco **A6**
Siemens **A4**
SNL Financial **C5**
Socopa **D2**
Sony Ericsson **B4**
Standard & Poor's **C5**
Suzano **C2**
Symnetics **D4**
TCO **B4**
Teather & Greenwood **C5**
Tecelagem Blumenau **C2**
Tele Norte Leste **C2**
Telecom Italia **B1, B4**
Telefônica **B4**
Telefônica Celular **B4**
Telemar **B4, B6**
Telesp Celular Participações **B1**
Tendências **A3**
Terra **B6**
The Lowe Group **B2**
TIM **B4**
TotalFinaElf **B6**
Traffic **B2**
TV7 Vídeo Comunicação **B2**
UBS Warburg **C2**
Unibanco **A3, B2, B8, C2**
Usiminas **B1**
Usiminas Mecânica **B1**
Varit **B4**
Varig **B1**
Virtual Cred **C2**
Volkswagen **B1, B2, B7**
Volvo **A3**
Votorantim **B7**
Walita **B6**
Westpac **C5**

EU&

Uma aventura na África para aprender inglês e curso de marcenaria são opções de presentes para os pais D5

NO GRAMADO

Na filosofia do capotão, a "pátria de chuteiras" parece estar sem cadarço. É o que discutem um sociólogo, um antropólogo, um cineasta e o saudoso Tostão. Pág. D6

MARISA CAUDURO/VALOR

O antropólogo Luiz Henrique de Toledo, autor de "No País do Futebol", acredita que as mudanças de tabelas, troca de técnicos, transformação do jogo num negócios de cifras milionárias e interesses de patrocinadores prejudicam o "futebol mito"

MEUS INVESTIMENTOS

As mulheres invadem o mercado

Elas são até 30% dos investidores no Brasil. Nos EUA, crecimento é de 85% em 15 anos. Por **Rachel Rubin**, de São Paulo

As mulheres estão crescendo no mundo das finanças. Um estudo encomendado pela Merrill Lynch (ML) mostra que o número de mulheres investidoras, nos Estados Unidos, cresceu 85%, de 1985 até o ano passado. O resultado, acreditam os executivos da instituição, é o prenúncio de uma tendência mundial. Para Winthrop H. Smith, "chairman" da ML Internacional, o número de mulheres no mercados financeiro deve duplicar, em breve.

No Brasil, o crescimento da participação feminina não é tão expressivo quanto nos Estados Unidos, mas já há uma mudança cultural. "Há dez anos, apenas 5% dos investidores daqui eram mulheres. Agora, o percentual está entre 25% e 30%", observa João Luiz de Medeiros, vice-presidente da ML.

Uma das razões para esse crescimento, em todo o mundo, é o fato das mulheres representarem boa fatia do mercado de trabalho. E, assim como os homens, elas também estão se conscientizando da necessidade de organizar as finanças e garantir o futuro. O que só acontece através da participação ativa na escolha dos investimentos, não dependendo somente de um sistema de pensão, público ou oferecido pela empresa na qual trabalha.

A pesquisa se baseou em dados da Investment Company Institute - a entidade de classe das indústrias de fundos americanas - e da Securities Industry Association.

O vice-presidente da ML observa que há algumas diferenças no estilo feminino de investir: "De uma forma geral, elas são mais cautelosas, preferem os investimentos conservadores. E, depois que ingressam no mercado, tendem a acompanhá-lo mais de perto do que os homens". No Brasil, boa parte das investidoras são profissionais do mercado, como analistas e gestoras, diz ele.

O portal financeiro Patagon, por exemplo, já registrou aumento no número de mulheres que investem via internet. Do total de usuários cadastrados, 15% são mulheres, percentual 6,7% maior do que em 1999, no lançamento.

Medeiros explica que, culturalmente,

> "As mulheres são mais cautelosas, preferem o investimento conservador. Depois, tendem a acompanhá-lo mais de perto do que os homens".

o brasileiro é mais conservador do que o americano. Por isso, as mulheres brasileiras são ainda mais cautelosas do que as americanas. Assim, estre os preferidos estão aqueles produtos ao estilo dos fundos DI, por exemplo, que acompanham as variações das taxas de juros.

O investimento em imóveis, apesar de não ser o foco da ML, costuma ter uma maior demanda por quem não quer correr muitos riscos - mas também tem os seus perigos. Por aqui, as mulheres estão liderando a procura por eles. No portal imobiliário Planetaimovel.com, por exemplo, 60% dos compradores de imóveis são mulheres, diz Flávio Suplicy, diretor do site.

Outro fator determinante para o intenso ingresso das mulheres rumo aos mercados é a maior divulgação que se tem feito sobre o assunto, o que acaba esclarecendo dúvidas e aumentando o conhecimento delas sobre os macetes financeiros.

Já estão sendo criados, no Brasil, clubes de investimento exclusivos para mulheres, em que há reuniões periódicas para discutir os ativos a serem selecionados para os investimentos.

A Merrill Lynch realiza, desde a década de 50, programas voltados para o ensino de investimentos para as mulheres, além de elaborar livros dedicados só para elas.

A cultura dos clubes de investimento é nova no Brasil, enquanto que, nos Estados Unidos, durante a década de 90, os clubes femininos se tornaram tão populares que representaram metade dos clubes cadastrados na "National Association of Investors Corporation " (Naic).

Segundo a Naic, a rentabilidade média dos clubes de mulheres ultrapassou a dos homens em quase dois pontos percentuais. Parece uma tendência: a pesquisa encomendada pela ML cita um estudo, feito pela Universidade da Califórnia, em 1998, cuja conclusão é a deque, como as mulheres trocam menos de ativos, acabam pagando menos taxas e conseguem retornos anuais 1,4% maiores do que aqueles obtidos pelos homens.

PÁGINA 3

MINHA CARREIRA

Vereadores como o presidente da Câmara, José Cardozo (foto), vão aprender política pelo ensino virtual

PÁGINA 4

MINHA ESTRATÉGIA

Imaginarium investe em vitrines conceituais para vender objetos de decoração

PÁGINA 7

LITERATURA

O ex-senador ACM e a agência de publicidade W/Brasil terão biografia de Fernando Morais (foto)

EU&

Archbisho
the druids

TH

No. 67507

air fights to
al rift with

Times Classic: a new type for the old *Times*

John D. Berry

Following in its own tradition, the venerable *Times* commissions a new typeface family as part of its gradual redesign

Opposite: an enlarged detail of the front page of *The Times*.

The most famous redesign of a newspaper, without any doubt, is the introduction of Times Roman (originally called Times New Roman) as the new typeface of *The Times* in London on October 3, 1932. It wasn't even a full redesign in the modern sense; very little changed except the typeface. (The nameplate went from blackletter to roman caps – a radical change of the paper's image – but it would still be years before *The Times* would put actual news on the front page, in place of the classified ads.)

The typeface that most of us know simply as "Times" was developed specifically for the use of the grand old lady of British newspapers, at the instigation of the influential typographic consultant Stanley Morison; but it didn't remain a proprietary typeface for long, and since the '30s it has been, in one form or another, the typeface for text and sometimes display in numerous newspapers and magazines all over the world. Times Roman was already the most ubiquitous typeface in the printing business when it was chosen as one of the core set of PostScript typefaces in the original Laserwriter; since then, it has become as common in everyday use, by amateurs as well as professionals, as file folders or PostIt™ notes.

But *The Times* itself has switched typefaces several times since 1932, responding to new technology and new tastes. Times Roman was designed for the printing conditions of *The Times* in 1932, but by the 1960s the changes in paper stock and press techniques had made the once-sharp text type look wan and gray on the page, and in 1972 *The Times* replaced it with a new design by Walter Tracy called Times Europa. Although Times Roman was re-introduced for a while in a phototype version in 1981, the next turn in the technological road brought another new typeface: in 1991, Aurobind Patel and Gunnlaugur Briem created and digitized a lively new family of related typefaces, Times Millennium.

But Times Millennium, despite its name, only lasted a decade. (It did see in the new millennium in the paper's pages.) By the late 1990s, Times Millennium was already beginning to run into problems, as technology relentlessly changed. In particular, the introduction of color made a huge difference in the look of the page. On color pages, the press operators could cut back on the amount of ink used in the black areas by as much as 20 percent – but this meant that the regular text weight of Times Millennium, which was already delicate in its design, started to look thin and anemic. It was the same thing that changing print technologies had done to the original Times Roman, only on a faster track: the pages no longer looked crisp and clear. On top of this and other problems, News International, which publishes *The Times*, was planning changes in its entire production system, so this seemed the right time for a typographic overhaul.

Associate design head David Wadmore commissioned a wholly new type family, to be designed by Dave Farey and Richard Dawson of HouseStyle Graphics. The new face was introduced gradually at first, in a few places such as section heads; then, on February 11, 2002, *The Times* appeared fully dressed in its new livery: Times Classic.

A nearly impossible task

At a newspaper, the decision to introduce a new typeface is never made lightly. The typeface affects every aspect of the paper in subtle ways, and it's an integral part of the readers' experience, even if few readers are consciously aware of this. But every time the printing technology changes, the type has to change with it, and often the best solution is to design a new typeface from scratch.

Creating any typeface, especially one that will be used in text, is a balancing act between tradition and innovation, distinctiveness and invisibility, and a newspaper face takes this inherent tension to impossible lengths. What Dave Farey and Richard Dawson were faced with was the same problem that faces every designer of a news typeface: how to create a text typeface for a newspaper that combines the robustness and sturdiness of a workhorse face, the comfortable familiarity of text presented in a way that the readers are used to, and a very, very subtle stylishness and panache that will distinguish this particular newspaper from all the others on the stands.

That is part of the brief. The rest can get quite detailed. For *The Times*, there was the baggage of history: not only two centuries of publication, but the fairly widespread knowledge (even among supposedly casual readers) that at one point in the past, *The Times* had commissioned its own typeface, and that this typeface took on a life of its own and became the most commonly used typeface in the world. Any new typeface that the paper might adopt, whether designed specially for it or not, must somehow carry on a historical dialogue with the original Times Roman.

Newspaper faces need to be "economical," that is, fairly narrow, so that they don't take up too much room, and a large number of words can fit on each line of the paper's (usually) narrow columns. But the design can't sacrifice everything else on the Procrustean bed of space-saving. For one thing, the readers of newspapers are not necessarily young people with young eyes; we may admonish those who are creeping into middle age to use their reading glasses, but the sad fact is that for many people, if they can't read the paper easily however they choose – with or without their glasses – they'll just throw it down and start complaining. (In fact, they're liable to complain vehemently no matter what the designer does.)

As Farey and Dawson point out, another factor is the tendency of high-speed offset presses to lay down a fairly light layer of ink, which makes the type look lighter, grayer, than it ought to. The design of the typeface has to compensate for this, by being clearer, darker, and more robust. Subtle details need to give sparkle and life to the letters, yet at the same time the overall effect has to be solid and functional; anything else strikes readers as affected.

Originally, Farey and Dawson were commissioned to produce three weights of the new typeface,

THE TIMES

THE TIMES

The newly revised nameplate of *The Times* (top), using Times Classic Titling, and the old design (bottom), which used Times Millennium Bold. Details of the crest have also been tidied up.

Order, order

IF YOU THOUGHT OUR Prime Minister's Questions was a tempestuous affair, you should visit the Northern Territory state legislature in Darwin. Andrew Kilvert, a media adviser to the Labor Government, celebrated his resignation last week by having sex in the debating chamber of Parliament House. Finding the Speaker's chair too awkward, Kilvert and his unidentified partner moved on to one of the benches.

"Video cameras record some of the ingress and egress from the main entrance and the rear entrance," said Ian McNeil, the assembly clerk, who has been going through the footage in preparation for a full briefing for the outraged Speaker. Kilvert is unrepentant. "I wanted to go with a bang," he said.

Order, order

IF YOU THOUGHT OUR Prime Minister's Questions was a tempestuous affair, you should visit the Northern Territory state legislature in Darwin. Andrew Kilvert, a media adviser to the Labor Government, celebrated his resignation last week by having sex in the debating chamber of Parliament House. Finding the Speaker's chair too awkward, Kilvert and his unidentified partner moved on to one of the benches.

"Video cameras record some of the ingress and egress from the main entrance and the rear entrance," said Ian McNeil, the assembly clerk, who has been going through the footage in preparation for a full briefing for the outraged Speaker. Kilvert is unrepentant. "I wanted to go with a bang," he said.

Order, order

IF YOU THOUGHT OUR Prime Minister's Questions was a tempestuous affair, you should visit the Northern Territory state legislature in Darwin. Andrew Kilvert, a media adviser to the Labor Government, celebrated his resignation last week by having sex in the debating chamber of Parliament House. Finding the Speaker's chair too awkward, Kilvert and his unidentified partner moved on to one of the benches.

"Video cameras record some of the ingress and egress from the main entrance and the rear entrance," said Ian McNeil, the assembly clerk, who has been going through the footage in preparation for a full briefing for the outraged Speaker. Kilvert is unrepentant. "I wanted to go with a bang," he said.

Times Classic Text [8.6/9pt] regular, medium, and bold weights, respectively, showing their accompanying small caps and italics. (This item appeared in *The Times* on March 15, 2002.)

THE TIMES
weekend

THE TIMES
business

Headings for special sections (above), where Times Classic was first introduced; and a full front page (opposite) using the new typefaces.

with italics and small caps for each, and corresponding display versions in roman only. The new faces had to be at least as economical in space as their predecessor (this must be the ever-present requirement in all newspaper faces: "Fit in as much text per page as we had before, or more!") while having more of that amorphous quality, "color," and that even more indefinable quality, "Britishness."

How it should look

Getting the right look in the type on a newspaper page is a hard task. It not only has to convey the actual information, it has to promise the kind of reading experience that the reader expects and that the paper does, in fact, deliver. Nothing is more disruptive of reader loyalty than a redesign that changes the terms of the transaction between paper and reader: that promises something different from what it delivers. The Times Classic typefaces, and the redesign that they were a part of, had to deliver, in essence, "more of the same, only better."

As Farey and Dawson wrote in an internal memo ("The Times Vernacular 2002") circulated just prior to the introduction of the new typeface: "The design guidelines and art direction for developing the series of Times Classic as text and display typefaces for *The Times* were, in a sense, both specific and general. The specific requirements were in relation to the ambiance of *The Times*, that a new typeface needed to be slightly heavier than Times Millennium in its basic roman text weight, that it was to be as economical of word usage as Times Millennium and [that] it would conform to a 9-point grid – its physical size being placed within a clear space of 9 points, allowing a sufficient balance of white and black for ocular satisfaction."

COUNTRY STRIFE
Charles and Camilla's hunting row
Andrew Pierce reports PAGE 3

THE NEW GRUMPIES
Libby Purves on the
Victor Meldrew generation PAGE 16

THE  TIMES

40P
NEWSPAPER OF THE YEAR

No. 67540 | TUESDAY AUGUST 27 2002 | 2W | www.timesonline.co.uk

Attack on Saddam cannot wait, says Cheney

By Tim Reid in Washington **and Richard Beeston** Diplomatic Editor

AMERICA'S Vice-President launched a spirited counter-attack yesterday on those urging caution over an Iraqi invasion, saying that pre-emptive military action against Saddam Hussein was imperative to stop him acquiring nuclear weapons.

"The risk of inaction [is] far greater than the risk of action," Dick Cheney said in a speech to army veterans. "What we must not do in the face of a mortal threat is to give in to wishful thinking or wilful blindness."

Mr Cheney's remarks came as Iraqi opposition leaders told *The Times* that Washington had given them a clear signal in recent private talks that the US is pressing ahead with preparations for military action against the Iraqi dictator.

Sharif Ali bin Hussein, a leader of the Iraqi National Congress (INC), said US funding, co-ordination and other preparations were well advanced for action, which he believed would take place sooner rather than later. "[Washington] made it clear there will be no turning back," he said.

President Bush will make a fresh attempt today to win the support of Saudi Arabia for his plans when he holds talks with Prince Bandar, the Saudi Ambassador to the US, at his Texas ranch. In his speech in Nashville, Tennessee, Mr Cheney said he was familiar with the arguments urging caution or opposition towards any action against Saddam but he said their logic was "deeply flawed".

Making a relatively rare public appearance and even rarer public comments on the Iraqi situation, Mr Cheney said he agreed fully with the recent assertion by Dr Henry Kissinger, the former Secretary of State, who said pre-emptive action was imperative.

His strong words, the clearest signal yet from within the Bush Administration that an invasion of Iraq is unavoidable, came after mounting opposition, both within the Republican Party and internationally, to a unilateral US invasion.

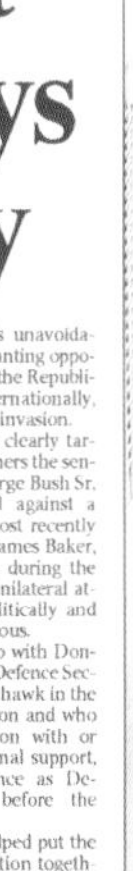

Mr Cheney was clearly targeting above all others the senior advisers of George Bush Sr, who have argued against a lone US attack, most recently on Sunday when James Baker, Secretary of State during the Gulf War, said a unilateral attack would be politically and economically perilous.

Mr Cheney, who with Donald Rumsfeld, the Defence Secretary, is a leading hawk in the Bush Administration and who favours an invasion with or without international support, cited his experience as Defence Secretary before the Gulf War in 1991.

"As one who helped put the international coalition together it would have been infinitely more difficult if he [Saddam] had had nuclear weapons," Mr Cheney said. "If we did wait [now] Saddam would become emboldened and it would become harder to get allies."

He said inaction could have devastating consequences and that regime change in Iraq, far from destabilising the region and damaging the Middle East peace process, "as many argue", would have a number of benefits.

Sharif Ali and other Iraqi opposition leaders met Colin Powell, the US Secretary of State, and Mr Rumsfeld a few weeks ago as well as holding a videoconference with Mr Cheney. "We were very encouraged by our meetings in Washington earlier this month," he told *The Times*. "The Administration spoke with one voice on the issue."

Washington has told the Iraqi opposition that it is determined to use force to change the regime in Baghdad. The only decisions left are when to strike and how to effect the overthrow of the Iraqi leader.

The Iraqi opposition has experienced a love-hate relationship with Washington. It felt betrayed by Mr Bush Sr, who failed to support the 1991 uprising against Saddam, which was ruthlessly put down. A second operation mounted by the CIA during the Clinton Administration was also defeated.

"This time we all felt very strongly that the Bush Administration regards Iraq as a priority. They are committed to it. They made it clear there will be no turning back. We did not sense any hesitation on their part. Rather the contrary, the process seems to be accelerating," said Sharif Ali.

The role of the opposition in the overthrow is still not clear. While some have likened the INC to the Northern Alliance in Afghanistan, which spearheaded the attack on the Taleban, in Iraq government forces are much stronger and the opposition much weaker.

Sharif Ali admitted that the invasion force would be a US operation but said the opposition could be vital in urban centres where Saddam's loyalists are likely to make a stand.

Iraq said US and British warplanes attacked civilian targets in the south of the country yesterday for the second consecutive day, wounding a civilian and damaging his house.

The aircraft had flown 59 sorties, a military spokesman said.

Bush loophole, page 12

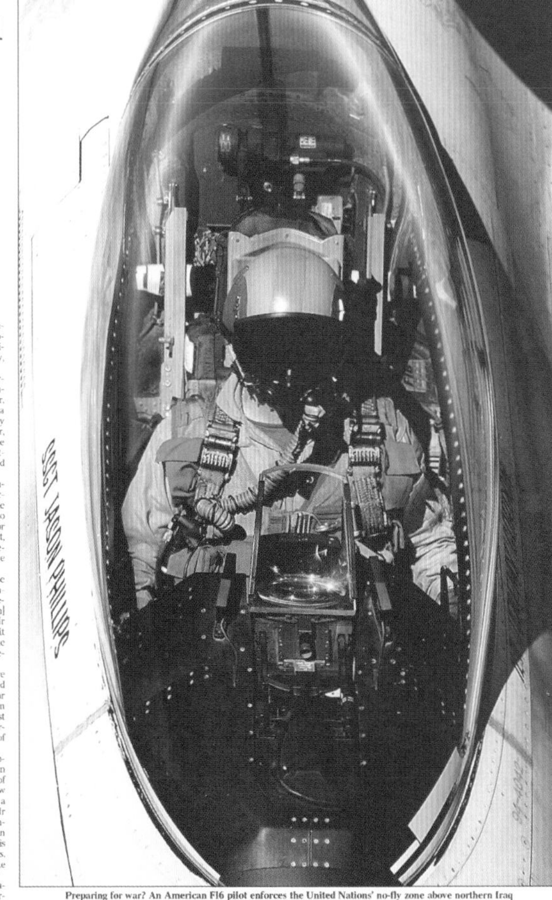

AP

Preparing for war? An American F16 pilot enforces the United Nations' no-fly zone above northern Iraq

Cancer policy on knife edge, say specialists

By Nigel Hawkes and Greg Hurst

THE Government's flagship cancer policy faces a crisis of confidence as specialists complain that money to treat the disease is not reaching front-line services for a second successive year.

Alan Milburn, the Health Secretary, made cancer his priority along with tackling heart disease yet some clinicians said they had received little or none of £255 million earmarked for cancer last year and feared that this year's £76 million could also disappear.

Professor Mike Richards, the National Cancer Director (previously known as the cancer czar), admitted that the Health Department did not know if the £255 million earmarked for cancer care last year had reached the front line. "We think in the end it has not," he said, "which is why we are now trying to find out what actually reached the front line."

Of a nationwide team of 34 cancer networks set up to lead the fight against the disease and co-ordinate services in regional areas, at least half have been left short of money, according to Professor Anthony Goldstone, lead clinician in the North London Cancer Network. "The very existence of the Cancer Networks is on a knife edge," he said. "We have spent two years building up confidence but it is all going to drift away."

His own network put in a bid for £16 million for 142 projects this year and was granted £2.2 million. More than half of that amount went to pay debts at a local hospitals. "This is not what Mr Milburn was talking about when he launched the Cancer Plan," Professor Goldstone said.

When he launched the plan at the Labour Party conference in Brighton two years ago Mr Milburn declared that his aim was the fastest improvement in cancer services in Europe and cancer survival rates among the best in Europe by 2010.

An investigation by *Health Service Journal* found cancer specialists despairing. Professor Hilary Thomas, lead clinician of the Surrey, West Sussex and Hampshire Cancer Network, said: "We've seen none of the £76 million. We were led to expect that sort of spend and we have seen nothing of it."

Earmarking was meaningless because large financial deficits meant that health authority managers used the money to pay off debts, she said.

Death rates will be the real test for cancer plan 4

Peter Reeves, acting finance director for Eastbourne Downs Primary Care Trust, said: "In common with lots of places, we did not find it possible to put this year's earmarked funding for the purpose for which it was intended.

"The reason is very simple. It's just that when push comes to shove, the perceived most important targets are the Government's waiting list and waiting time targets."

The department has at least three ways of targeting funds: they can be hypothecated, earmarked, or ring-fenced (in order of increasing compulsion). Last year's £255 million was hypothecated, which meant ministers pronounced it cancer money but authorities and trusts could spend it in different ways.

Of this year's new money, totalling £407 million, £76 million has been earmarked, which should make sure that it is spent on cancer.

Liam Fox, the Shadow Health Secretary, said: "The monolithic structure of the NHS has turned into a black hole which swallows up cancer money. Ministers keep announcing initiatives as though that will be enough. There is no attempt to make sure the money reaches the patient."

INSIDE

Omagh inquiry

Rosemary Ingram, 53, a victim of the Omagh bombing, was forced to strip to her underwear by lawyers who were assessing her compensation claim. Ministers have ordered an inquiry 4

India walk it

India strolled to a deserved innings victory over England after a superb all-round performance that levelled the series with one game to play, which will be at the Oval. It was only India's fourth Test victory in England 36

INSIDE TODAY
FANTASY LEAGUE SCORES
See how your team has done so far
Page 13

Gone with the wind in Essex

By Robin Young

THERE is a Toby Belch lurking within us all, it seems. A survey of Britons' personal habits has confirmed that nose-picking, burping and passing wind in public are the rule rather than the exception.

Six thousand people, asked about their everyday behaviour, took no shame in revealing a vulgarity of Falstaffian proportions. More than 60 per cent admitted picking their noses more than five times a day; 34 per cent said they ate what they excavated.

A similar proportion claimed to see no shame in burping loudly in public; 29 per cent said they would not hesitate to pass wind indiscreetly.

The survey was conducted in conjunction with a popular exhibition at the Science Museum in London entitled *Grossology: The (Impolite) Science of the Human Body*. The exhibition shocked some squeamish adults by revelling in schoolboy delights such as intimate body functions, mucus, excretions and smelly parts.

After the survey was published yesterday a spokeswoman for the museum said: "Overall, we are all pretty gross. But it was a fun survey and I don't think anybody should take it too seriously."

According to the survey, Northern Ireland can claim the grossest addiction to nosepicking in the UK, with 44 per cent confessing to digging around more than five times a day. The Rabelaisian residents of the Six Counties also top the league for public belching (44 per cent) and breaking wind (34 per cent).

The Welsh came top (61 per cent) in the willingness to transfer the blame for their smells on to others.

Among the English, it is Essex man who tops the lewd league. Almost half that county's male population admitted burping noisily and passing wind blatantly in public.

The exhibition continues until September 6.

Mbeki attacks West's 'survival of the fittest'

From Anthony Browne Environment Editor in Johannesburg

PRESIDENT MBEKI of South Africa launched a thinly veiled attack on the West yesterday, calling for the end of a world political system based on "survival of the fittest" and demanding one that was caring and humane.

He made the demands as he opened the Earth Summit in Johannesburg, where there is growing despair among developing nations about the West's political will to help to combat world poverty.

Mr Mbeki told the opening session of the ten-day World Summit on Sustainable Development that the current imbalances of wealth in the world could not be allowed to continue. "A global human society characterised by islands of wealth surrounded by a sea of poverty is unsustainable," he said.

His comments echoed those he made at the grand opening ceremony on Sunday night comparing the division of the world into haves and have-nots to "global apartheid".

NOT EVERYONE WANTS TO SAVE THE WORLD, MR BOND
EARTH SUMMIT

Developing nations are becoming increasingly critical of what they say is Western governments' lack of commitment to the summit. The West has ruled out any new aid money, or making it easier for developing nations to sell agricultural produce to them.

The United States has delivered the biggest snub. President George Bush has refused to attend, sending Colin Powell, his Secretary of State, in his place and the US delegation has repeatedly said that it does not want to agree to any binding targets.

Tony Blair has also been criticised for planning to attend for just 24 hours to make a five-minute speech towards the end of the conference.

However, Mr Mbeki said that failure was not an option. "The peoples of the world expect that this world summit will live up to its promise of being a fitting culmination to a decade of hope," he said.

"We do not accept that human society should be constructed on the basis of a savage principle of the survival of the fittest." He said that society had for the first time in human history the capacity, knowledge and resources to eradicate poverty.

Another planet, page 11
Eat and be merry, page 16

The Times Today: page 2. Crossword: page 18. Law Report: page 29. TV & radio: T2, pages 27-32

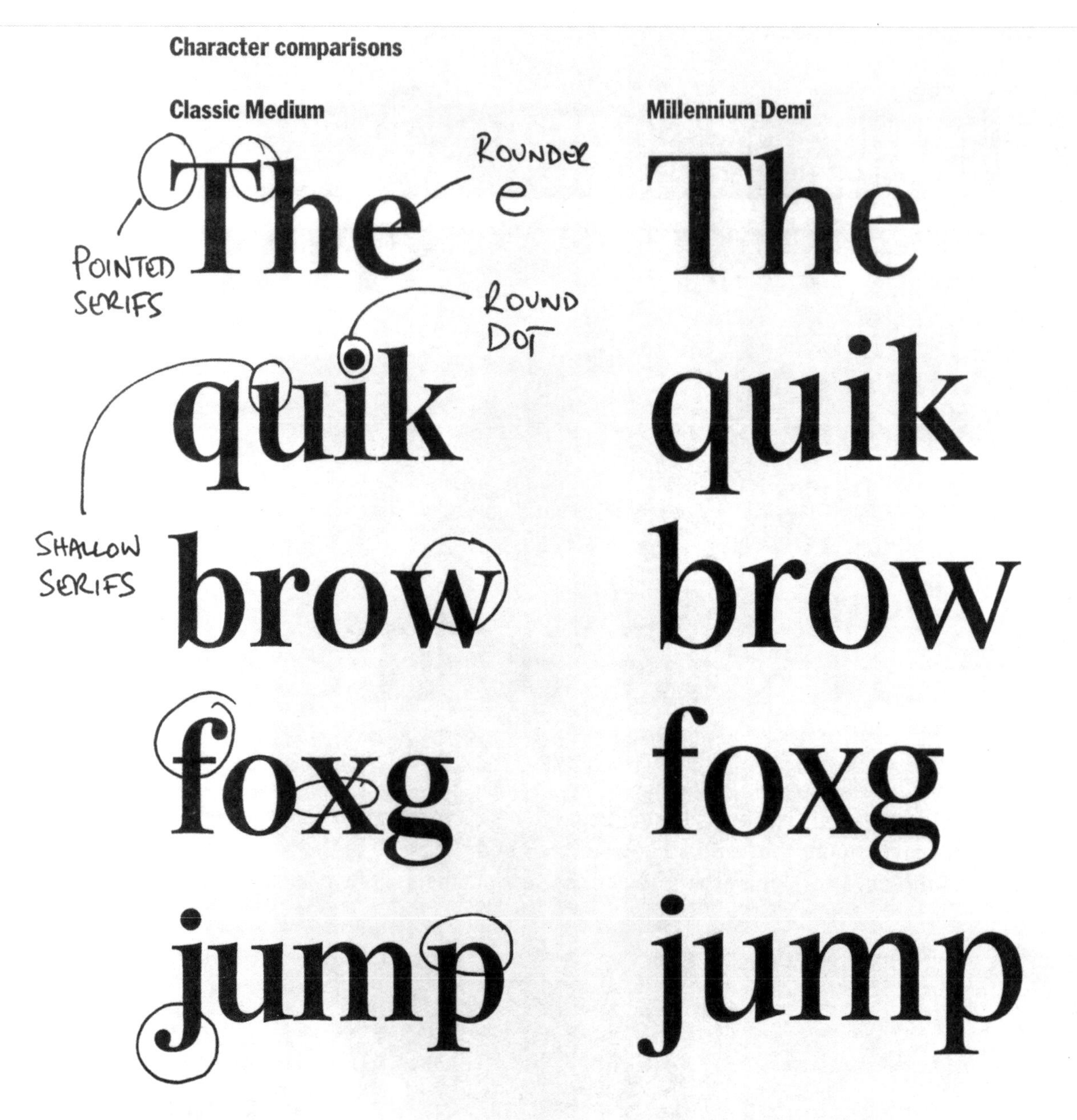

Times Millennium vs. Times Classic
Some of the design features of the old Times Millennium become exaggerated as the weights progress – for instance, the crossed **w**, the high crossbar on the **e**, the pointed top to the **t**, and the changing shape of the dot of the **i**. The details of Times Classic's design look more consistent across the weights.

weathering
weathering
weathering

weathering
weathering
weathering

The three weights of Times Millennium (top) and Times Classic (bottom).

RED ALERT

Blair must beware of a new trade union threat

his the summer of our discontent? The of the vote to make the left-winger ɾek Simpson general secretary of the en- ɛering union Amicus in place of the Blair- Sir Ken Jackson would be a victory for itancy in any season. It looks particularly ouraging for the Left coming after its ture of the communication workers', fire brigades' and civil service unions. ɛre is a temptation to see the increasing itancy of Britain's trade unions as 1970s ory revisited. There are real dangers for Prime Minister in the current climate, they are of a different kind.

he economic reforms of the Thatcher rs have transformed Britain's economy, dering unthinkable a return to the failed omes policies, industrial paralysis and cri- of ungovernability which blighted the enties. The challenges now mounted by strength in public sector monopolies has helped to ensure that nearly two-thirds of increased public sector spending has already gone in higher prices and wages. Public-sector inflation is running at 6.5 per cent, three times the level of the rest of the economy. The capacity of managers to reform institutions charged with innovation, such as PFI hospitals or specialist schools, is impeded by the union-rigged wage and bargaining positions of certain workers.

The new militants in the trade union movement wish to capitalise on these positions by, among other things, demanding ever-higher minimum wages, less managerial flexibility in fixing employment patterns, a curtailment of the use of the private sector in public-service delivery and further income rises ahead of inflation in the public sector. If Mr Blair seeks to stand in the way

LETTERS TO THE EDITOR

1 Pennington Street, London E98 1TA. Telephone: 020-7782 5000
Fax: 020-7782 5046 e-mail: letters@thetimes.co.uk

Nato and Europe's defence capability

From Sir Brian Crowe

Sir, It is not, as Sir John Weston maintains (letter, July 15), "that we shall end up with two collective defence policies and defence organisations for Europe", with neither working properly when really needed. It is rather that we shall have a European military capability which we Europeans can choose to use, with recourse to Nato assets as appropriate, when the other defence organisation, ie, Nato with US involvement, does not want to be engaged.

Sir John argues that this result should have been achieved "within Nato", and prays in aid Nato's 1999 Washington Summit communiqué. This indeed referred to further en-

NHS treatment of immigrants and visitors with HIV

From Dr David Parsons

Sir, Visitors to the UK are entitled to free treatment under the NHS only, I believe, for illnesses which afflict them after arriving here, eg, appendicitis and pneumonia. Conditions they bring with them should not be treated free.

The venereal diseases legislation of earlier years offered free treatment to anyone with such an infection, regardless of nationality or status, as a means of protecting the resident population. About 15 years ago I and other medical colleagues pointed out that HIV/Aids was a venereal disease, which meant that the whole world could come to the UK and claim free treatment (reports and leading article, July 15).

leagues complain at having to treat those whom they suspect are not entitled to NHS services.

Yours faithfully,
DAVID PARSONS,
Two Ridges,
Summerhill, Chislehurst BR7 5NY.
July 16.

From Mr David Thompson

Sir, The figures for new cases of HIV give serious cause for concern. There are already more than 5,000 immigrants with the disease here, and under the Human Rights Act they cannot be returned to their own country. Since newcomers to Britain are not subject to health checks, there is a huge potential influx of HIV sufferers,

the past have initiated community-based seminars to address some of these issues, including the disproportionately high incidence of other sexually transmitted diseases in black communities.

More needs to be done. We urgently need imaginative, culturally and gender-sensitive public information advertisements to defuse the slowly ticking time-bomb of an undiagnosed heterosexual epidemic among Britain's black communities.

Yours faithfully,
TUBONYE C. HARRY
(Secretary),
African Caribbean Medical Society,
Ash Lodge, Hall Road,
Oulton Broad, Lowestoft NR32 3NR.
July 16.

The very traditional look of *The Times*'s editorial and letters-to-the-editor page, using the new typefaces in familiar ways (above; and a close-up detail, opposite).

luxury *with Lucia*

Here I am after all these years, tootling around the luxury goods industry (whose iconic products as we know are always handbags), and I'm still searching for that elusive thing, the perfect tote or working woman's holdall.

I've never really cracked the conundrum of turning up at a meeting with all papers in place, looking effortlessly pot of moisturiser, several fragrances, Muji felt-tip pens (because they're brilliant), Post-it Notes, eyelash curlers, toy trucks to amuse her child, and anybody else's, a bar of chocolate or a walnut whip, Marks & Spencer sandalwood and geranium tissues ... so you see, it's not easy.

Notting Hill yummie mummies are spoilt for choice — they can carry enchanting baskets or whimsical carry- the Hermès imprimatur, there's the Herbag, in canvas and leather, which comes in two parts — you put the two together when you need to carry your laptop, otherwise you just use a single part. It looks good — not too formal — has shoulder straps and its price (£700) is very different from the Birkin's.

Take a look at Tanner Krolle — it has a delicious summery tote in red and orange called The Knightsbridge

Times Classic in use (along with Franklin Gothic) in the style and feature sections, where a much more dynamic layout is appropriate.

Contemporary Roman

They traced the history of newspaper typefaces in Britain, and they found that most of them fell into one of two design categories, which they call "Ionic" and "Contemporary Roman." In Ionic typefaces, the body of most lowercase letters tends to be wide, with the character's width about the same as the x-height, and the difference between thick and thin strokes in the letters is minimal. Where many newspapers, in the UK as elsewhere, use Ionic faces, like Nimrod or the more recent Miller, *The Times* has followed an alternate line of development, the Contemporary Roman. In fact, Farey and Dawson make the point that Times Roman itself set the style:

"Contemporary Roman styles are without question best exemplified by the 20th-century design of Times (New) Roman, where the design structure and characteristics are based upon the classic stress and relationship of angle and weight for legibility, where the thicker parts of a curve can be made heavier without encroaching upon the interior counters, as it is as much upon the inside of a letter as [upon] the overall outline of a character that separation and identity depends. Within this regard the model of a contemporary roman combines legibility, a strong color, and space economy. It is also aesthetically satisfying for headline purposes, with finer terminal serifs than the Ionic model, where larger sizes do not have optical or balance problems, and where subtle design features within letters produce a separate appreciation of the typeface apart from its text solutions and value."

Once they had decided to proceed along the lines of a Contemporary Roman, they looked at where the problems were in the typeface they were replacing, Times Millennium. (They also, of course, looked back to Times

LETTERS TO

1 Pennington Street, London E9
Fax: 020-7782 5046 e-ma

Europe's
:apability

we

ohn Weston main-
15), "that we shall
lective defence pol-
ganisations for Eu-
working properly
d It is rather that

NHS treatment of

From Dr David Parsons

Sir, Visitors to the UK are entitled to free treatment under the NHS only, I believe, for illnesses which afflict them after arriving here, eg, appendicitis and pneumonia. Conditions they bring with them should not be treated free.

Text faces and headline faces

Times Classic has a compatible set of display weights of Roman, Medium, and Bold, where the weight structures are in each case heavier in the main strokes and lighter in the lighter strokes than the equivalent Times Classic Roman, Medium, and Bold text family. This provides for more contrast and delicacy within the display family, while still retaining a perfect conjunction with the accompanying Times Classic text.

Comparison of text and display versions of Times Classic (right; Text on top), showing differences in details like the ball on the a and the thickness of serifs; the three weights of Times Classic Display, plus Titling (right, above), with the "classic British R shape"; a comparison of Times Classic Display and Text (top right; Display above Text), with superimposed outlines of Display Bold (in red) and Text Bold; and a showing of the typographic system of *The Times*, for internal use (opposite).

TIMES CLASSIC *Fount numbers*

Headline Founts (14pt+)

Times Classic Bold Fount 78 / 704

Times Classic Medium Fount 76 / 702

Times Classic Roman Fount 77 / 700

Italic Founts

Times Classic Roman Fount 71 / 701

Times Classic Medium Fount 73 / 703

Times Classic Bold Fount 75 / 705

Text Founts

Times Classic Roman Fount 70 / 700
Times Classic Medium Fount 72 / 702
Times Classic Bold Fount 74 / 704

CLASSIC FRANKLIN *Fount numbers*

This is Franklin 50 /100
This is Franklin 54 /102
This is Franklin 56 /104

This is Franklin 58 /106
This is Franklin 59 /107

Plus there are italics

Franklin 51
Franklin 55
Franklin 57

ABCDEFGHIJKLMNOPQRSTUVWXYZ&

1234567890abcdefghijklmnopqrstuvwxyz:;?!

Times Classic's contemporary italic

The 20th-century contemporary italic can be seen to some extent within Times Roman italic, where the serifs slope at a natural writing angle, creating a pattern from one letter to the next. Because the actual shapes of lowercase letters between roman and italic have different forms, where the italic are calligraphic – such as the *a e m* and *u* – there is no need to angle the slope to an extreme; the letterforms alone are enough to show a difference of typeface between roman and italic. The angle of Times Classic italic is only 9°, whereas Times Millennium's is 13° and Times Roman's is 16°. The letterforms of Times Classic italic are more simplified than its predecessors', but no less functional.

water *water*
water *water*
water *water*

Italic examples that tend toward the 19th-century roundhand style (first column, top to bottom: Miller, Times Europa, and Nimrod), and the simpler, less cursive style that can be described as contemporary roman italic (second column: Times New Roman, Times Millennium, and Times Classic).

William Rees-Mogg

The Plague that has cursed Europe for **centuries**

"To square the circle with a complete typographic identity for *The Times*": a display version of a Garamond italic with swash characters, and an adjustment of the complementary sans serif, Franklin Gothic, to optically match the size of Times Classic.

Roman.) "The first observations, common to Times Roman and Times Millennium, were that the capitals were, in both instances, too heavy for the accompanying lower case. This is perhaps a 21st-century observation, but once determined, it could not be ignored – the balances were not quite right. Although the prevailing tendency is to set headlines in lower case, and [although] obviously, in natural text, lower case dominates by around 95%, the capitals for the new Times Classic needed to be well proportioned to the lower case, more so than the existing models. The second consideration was the dimension of the lower case in relation to the capitals. Times Roman, by today's standards, has a slightly small x-height, whereas Times Millennium's x-height is considerably larger. [...] There is an important balance to be struck between the ascenders and x-height for ease of reading, and it was necessary to reduce the x-height of Times Classic by around 4% in measurable terms compared to Times Millennium but a hairswidth in visual terms at text sizes, which gave the Times Classic lower case text setting a discernibly more satisfying appearance when sited correctly on a 9pt grid compared to Times Roman or Times Millennium."

No detail too small

Farey and Dawson paid close attention to small details of individual letters, looking for exactly the right characteristics to make the typeface easy and comfortable to read en masse on the page. One of the most important is the intersection of curved strokes with straight stems in many letters. As they put it, "there is a predominance of curves which have to move away from a vertical line within the lower case of typefaces, and how that is resolved is a major factor in relation to the accumulative

Three decks of thirty point (makes depth of 90pt)

New fount will tend to leave more space before the start of the text

Balancing sizery to 21pt testg solig setty

Monica Reiter
Political correspondent

NIALL Quinn is poised to win his 83rd international cap when the Republic of Ireland take on Cyprus in their vital Group Two World Cup qualifier on March 24.

The veteran Sunderland striker has been suffering a recurrence of a back injury in recent weeks and is awaiting the

Skyros suffers third earthquake in eight days

Nikos Loukamades
in Athens

NIALL Quinn is poised to win his 83rd international cap when the Republic of Ireland take on Cyprus in their vital Group Two World Cup qualifier on March 24.

The veteran Sunderland striker has been suffering a recurrence of a back injury in recent weeks and is awaiting the

ager Peter Reid will do all in his power to get Niall over to link up with the rest of the panel before we fly out to Nicosia next Tuesday."

Much will depend on whether Quinn plays for Sunderland against Chelsea in the Premiership game at Stamford Bridge on Saturday. If the 34-year-old is again sidelined by injury, Tottenham's Gary Doherty is the likely replacement to part-

It's visualy test for a balancery 21 sgt solid

Roux Merassit
Political Editor

NIALL Quinn is poised to win his 83rd international cap when the Republic of Ireland take on Cyprus in their vital Group Two World Cup qualifier on March 24.

The veteran Sunderland striker has been suffering a recurrence of a back injury in recent weeks and is awaiting the

A graphic illustration of headline styles, from a *Visual Style Guide* (March 2002) to the Times Classic fonts and how to use them in *The Times*.

Times Classic Display Regular

Times Classic Display Medium

Times Classic Display Bold

The three weights of Times Classic Display (left), and a showing of Times Classic Text roman (opposite) with its small caps and italic.

pattern when used in text." The letters where this meeting of curves and uprights makes the most difference are h, n, m, r, and u, with b, d, p, and q close behind.

"Among other minor decisions that have helped to provide a smoothness to the typeface," write Dawson and Farey, "in regard of eccentricity or interruption while reading, is the shape of the lowercase t. The Times Classic t has an oblong rising above the x-height junction, so above the crossbar there is a rising flat-topped stroke. This is a break from convention or the traditional pointed terminal used in both Times Roman and Times Millennium. The treatment of letters partially containing diagonal strokes or constructed wholly with diagonal strokes has been considered carefully for their relationship with non-diagonal letters. For example, and in particular, the w is not constructed from two overlapping v's, but is designed within its own integral shape, which in turn allows for the exterior diagonals to be able to fit harmoniously alongside the variously curved shapes of letters, and alternatively the straight-sided letters, that will randomly accompany the w."

Fine points, perhaps, but it's these little details, repeated thousands of times per page, that make all the difference in readability.

How Times Classic stacks up

Compared to Times Millennium, the Times Classic roman is a little smoother and calmer in text, harking back in some ways to Times Roman, as well as giving a darker, more readable impression on the page. "The Times Classic faces," according to a little booklet entitled *The Times Typography in the 21st Century*, "were designed to fit the same measures as their Millennium counterparts and to be a fraction heavier and allow slightly more inter-line spacing." Times Classic's italic is noticeably

Times Classic Text Roman

ABCDEFGHIJKLM
NOPQRSTUVWXYZ
abcdefghijklm
nopqrstuvwxyz
ABCDEFGHIJKLM
NOPQRSTUVWXYZ
1234567890£$&?!:;-/""()
1234567890£$&?!:;-/""()

Times Classic Text Roman Italic

ABCDEFGHIJKLM
NOPQRSTUVWXYZ
abcdefghijklm
nopqrstuvwxyz
1234567890£$&?!:;-/""()

Examples of the different text weights of Times Classic in use (right), and a mix of text and display versions, with dramatic use of photography, on the front page (opposite).

narrower and less steeply inclined than Times Millennium italic, and much less rounded than Times Roman italic, which was influenced by 19th-century handwriting. Since Times Classic italic uses distinctly italic letter shapes, visually different from the roman, it doesn't need to have such a pronounced slant to distinguish it from surrounding roman text.

Compared to some of the typefaces being used by *The Times*'s competitors in the UK newspaper market, Times Classic stands out by combining three different weights in closely coordinated designs (most UK papers use only two weights, and sometimes the different weights aren't even related typefaces) with variant designs for text and display.

As Dawson and Farey put it (naturally with a somewhat biased perspective): "The Times Classic romans and italics, viewed as a complete typeface family, as they are intended to be used in the *Times* newspaper, will have a distinct identity developed from historic models which have, as a natural inclusion through a reappraisal of 20th-century typeface innovations and developments, the characteristics and style capable of providing for a continuing British vernacular as the livery for *The Times*." ‹

.media
Diary

■ THERE are signs of efforts being made to save Artsworld, the TV arts channel founded by Sir Jeremy Isaacs, which announced its closure this week. If it collapses, the assassin will have been the Guardian Media Group, which owns 24 per cent of the venture and decided against putting in more money. The Guardian board pulled the plug only 18 months after launch. The misfortune is a chance for the Digital Classics channel, which is free-to-air and might be tempted to try to start charging again, as Artsworld did.

■ SO MUCH for open government. Treasury Chief Secretary Paul Boateng gave ITN producers the runaround on Monday after the Government's spending announcement. Boateng agreed to go on Channel 4 and Channel 5 News, but insisted that he would not engage directly in debate with other guests in the studio. This meant that on Channel 4 News he had to be sat on one side of the table with Jon Snow, while Tory and Lib Dem spokesmen were kept at a sterile distance on the other. On Channel 5 the first half of the show was given over almost entirely to Boateng, while other guests waited in the wings.

Archbishop joins the druids NEWS PAGE 3

Lux
My en
LUCIA

THE

HONI·SOIT·QUI·MAL·Y·PENSE
DIEU·ET MON·DROIT

No. 67507

FRIDAY JULY 19 2002

Blair fights to heal rift with angry unions

By Tom Baldwin
and Christine Buckley

TONY Blair held crisis talks with union leaders last night in an attempt to halt militancy which is endangering his public service reforms and Labour's financial future.

The meeting came at the end of a day in which strikes paralysed the London Underground, and the Prime Minister's most loyal union ally refused to accept that he had lost his job to an unknown left-winger.

The AEEU was mired in chaos and confusion after a fourth recount showed that Sir Ken Jackson had been defeated by Derek Simpson in the union's election for the post of general secretary.

Attempts by Sir Ken's supporters on the union's executive committee to challenge the result and hold a new election were halted temporarily when left-wingers walked out, causing the meeting to be abandoned.

Downing Street has been stunned by Sir Ken's defeat which many Labour MPs believe was caused by his closeness to the Government.

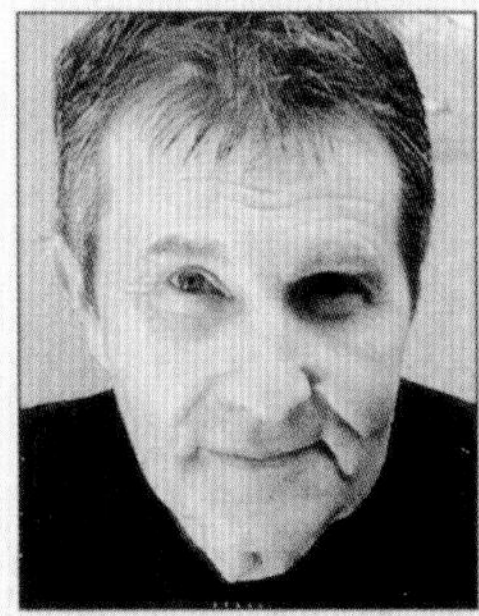

Simpson: won AEEU poll but faces challenge

include dismissing up to 20 per cent of its staff.

It is understood that Labour is seeking a "transitional" multi-million pound funding from the unions to bail it out in the short term. The Communication Workers' Union, one of the three which have cut donations in recent months, has already indicated that it may release some extra money. But others insist that they will want concessions before dipping into their pockets.

As disclosed by *The Times* yesterday, the Trades Union Congress has drawn up a document

beginning with hints that public services could be privatised during the last election.

In the last Parliament negotiations were conducted behind the scenes by a "quadrant" consisting of John Monks, the TUC General Secretary, Ian McCartney, the then Industry Minister, Jon Cruddas, a Number 10 aide, and Gerry Sutcliffe, representing union-sponsored Labour MPs.

Since then Mr McCartney has been moved to the Department for Work and Pensions, Mr Cruddas has become an MP, Mr Sutcliffe has beeen given a junior ministerial job, while Mr Monks has announced his resignation.

A senior government adviser said last night: "The problem is that we have no system and the lines of communication have broken down. Things are very bad. It is like two warring armies."

Senior government figures believe that Sir Ken was too autocratic and had been "egotistical" in seeking another term as general secretary.

Sir Ken lost the leadership of the AEEU — half of the new Amicus union — by just 406 votes to Mr Simpson.

Tiger snaps:

NZZ am Sonntag • 15. Dezember 2002

NZZ am Sonntag

Stil

Merlot-Duell
Die Tessiner gegen die Franzosen. Eine Partie der Besten mit erstaunlichem Ausgang
95

Queen's Car
Drei Monate feinste Handarbeit, bis der neue Bentley gleitet
91

Skisaison
Die wichtigste Sportart findet an der Bar statt
92

Herrin der Ringe: Jade Jagger, Tochter des Stones-Chefs, soll die Juwelenbranche aufpolieren

FOTOS: MARY MCCARTNEY, DONALD, JONATHAN HEYER, GETTY IMAGES

Profile: *NZZ am Sonntag*

Simon Esterson

Creating a colorful new Sunday companion to an established Swiss daily

Opposite: the front page of the Style section.

The design of the new *NZZ am Sonntag* ("NZZ on Sunday"), launched in March 2002, was an attempt to respect the journalistic traditions of its Zurich-based daily stable-mate, the *Neue Zurcher Zeitung*, known to all its readers as the *NZZ*. The 222-year-old *NZZ* is deliberately very austere in its presentation of the news, with page make-up devoid of the tricks and devices that other papers use to make their pages look less daunting.

The brief to design the new Sunday paper for the publishing house called for an approach that respected this history without simply creating a pastiche of the daily paper's look. In the *NZZ am Sonntag*, headline sizes are larger and there are more pictures than in the daily, but the spirit of the design is a contemporary clarity that, in the words of one of its editors, is about "information, not entertainment."

The design of the eight-section paper is based around a five-column grid. Display sizes are deliberately restricted, and a mid-weight of Poynter Display was created by Font Bureau so that headlines would not be too bold on the page. Griffith Gothic (and later Benton) were used as the supplementary sans-serif fonts. Typography is justified, with ranged-left setting for display, captions, and selected text.

Section fronts are deliberately controlled, with a contents listing down the first left-hand column: the different pictures tell the story rather than extravagant typography. The *Sonntag* is never afraid of words, but balances dense blocks of copy with controlled use of space and sub-stories.

The style section (Stil) uses the same typographic vocabulary as the other sections, but in a bolder way, with Benton becoming the main display font, a grid that allows for more white space, and a greater use of color in the typography. ‹

Editor:
Felix Muller
Consulting Art Directors:
Simon Esterson
Mark Porter
Art Director:
Hans Peter Hosli

Brighter on Sunday

NZZ am Sonntag takes its news just as seriously as its much older daily sibling, but the new Sunday edition presents it with contemporary clarity.

Der Zürcher Zeitung
222. Jahrgang

Freitag, 2. November 2001
Nr. 255

Neue Zürcher Zeitung

SCHWEIZER AUSGABE

Fr. 2.20 inkl. MWSt · DM 4.–, S 30.–, L 4300.–, fFr. 15.–, Pta. 380.– NZZ Online: www.nzz.ch

Redaktion und Verlag: Neue Zürcher Zeitung, Falkenstrasse 11, Postfach, 8021 Zürich, Tel. 01 258 11 11 · Redaktion: Telefax 01 252 13 29, E-Mail: redaktion@nzz.ch · Verlag: Telefax 01 258 13 23, E-Mail: verlag@nzz.ch
Abonnements: Tel. 01 258 15 30, Telefax 01 258 18 39, E-Mail: leserservice-schweiz@nzz.ch · Anzeigen: Tel. 01 258 16 98, Rubriken: Tel. 01 258 16 70 · Weitere Angaben im Impressum (Inlandteil)

HEUTE

Umfang 90 Seiten

Keine Ermittlungen gegen Schäuble
Die Ermittlungen gegen den CDU-Politiker Schäuble in der Finanzaffäre sind eingestellt worden. Prompt wird Schäubles Name mit einer möglichen Kanzlerkandidatur für die nächsten Wahlen in Verbindung gebracht.
AUSLAND 2

Märtyrer, Bösewicht, Dämon?
Es ist den USA offenbar noch nicht gelungen, bei den Muslimen des Mittleren Ostens den Kampf gegen bin Ladin als Krieg gegen den Terror darzustellen.
AUSLAND 7

Mühen mit Milosevics Erbmasse
Serbisch-montenegrinische Gespräche über eine gemeinsame Zukunft sind gescheitert. Montenegro will weiterhin die vollständige Unabhängigkeit.
AUSLAND 9

Verlad statt zweite Gotthard-Röhre
Ein Lastwagenbrand, diesmal auf der San-Bernardino-Route, lässt die Nutzung des Gotthardbasistunnels für die Bahn auch für Autotransporte noch sinnvoller erscheinen. Die Kapazität des Tunnels reicht dafür aus.
INLAND 13

Steigende Löhne im nächsten Jahr
Wie schon 2000 und 2001 dürften die Löhne in der Schweiz gemäss Lohnumfrage der UBS auch im kommenden Jahr stärker wachsen als die Teuerung.
WIRTSCHAFT 19

Gegen Zürcher Munitions-Alleingang
Für den Zürcher Regierungsrat überwiegen zwar die Vorteile der Mannstopp-Munition, er will das Polizeikorps aber nicht im Alleingang damit ausrüsten.
ZÜRICH UND REGION 43

Servette und GC eine Runde weiter

Servette und der Grasshopper-Club stehen im Uefa-Cup in der 3. Runde, der FC St. Gallen (im Bild rechts der Stürmer Gane) ist nach einer 2:4-Niederlage gegen den SC Freiburg ausgeschieden. *(Bild Reuters)*
SPORT 49

Heftige Unwetter in Mittelamerika
Schwere Niederschläge haben die Atlantikküste von Honduras und Nicaragua heimgesucht. In den beiden Ländern kamen mehrere Personen ums Leben.
VERMISCHTE MELDUNGEN 60

Retrospektive Jean Dubuffet in Paris
Die Schau zum 100. Geburtstag Dubuffets im Centre Pompidou breitet das Werk mustergültig aus. Die brüskierende Archaik Dubuffets, in der sich Witz und Kulturkritik vereinigen, hat nichts an Aktualität verloren.
FEUILLETON 61

BEILAGEN

Klagen über «.info»-Adressvergabe
Vor wenigen Wochen hat das Verzeichnis der «.info»-Internetadressen den regulären Betrieb aufgenommen. Doch schon häufen sich Klagen über Missbräuche.
MEDIEN UND INFORMATIK 79

Symbole für Schottland und Wales
Die politische Autonomie weckte in Edinburg und Cardiff den Wunsch nach neuen Parlamentsgebäuden. Deren Genese erweist sich nun als äusserst kompliziert.
PLANEN · BAUEN · WOHNEN 81

Börsen 31 · Stadtzürcher Gottesdienste 48 · Sportresultate 53 · Wetter 59 · Briefe an die NZZ 65 Fernseh- und Radioprogramme 66 · Schach 69 Philatelie 71 Impressum 14

Anzeigen: Dienstleistungen 46 · Multimedia 46 · Fahrzeuge 50 · Finanzmarkt 58 · Kunsthandel 68 · Kino 70 Veranstaltungen 72 · Immobilien 74 Todesanzeigen 57

9 771420 531009 01255

Schewardnadse an einer Pressekonferenz in Tbilissi am Montag. (Bild ap)

Offene politische Krise in Georgien

Schewardnadse in Bedrängnis – Regierung entlassen

Die staatliche Gängelung eines regierungskritischen Fernsehsenders hat in der georgischen Hauptstadt Tbilissi eine Grossdemonstration ausgelöst. Als Folge ist Präsident Schewardnadse unter starken politischen Druck geraten. Am Donnerstag entliess er seine gesamte Regierung. Schewardnadse selber will jedoch nicht zurücktreten.

A. R. Moskau, 1. November

In Georgien sind seit langem schwelende politische Konflikte in den letzten Tagen aufgeflammt und haben das Land in eine akute Krise gestürzt. Bedrängt von Parlament und Tausenden von Demonstranten, sah sich Präsident Schewardnadse am Donnerstag zur Entlassung seiner Regierung und damit auch zur Absetzung seines umstrittenen Innenministers Targamadse gezwungen. Unmittelbarer Anlass der Krise war am Dienstag der Versuch von Sicherheitskräften, eine Hausdurchsuchung beim regierungsunabhängigen Fernsehsender Rustawi-2 zu veranstalten. Die private Station hat die Behörden mit ihren kritischen Berichten immer wieder in Rage gebracht und war vor allem vom Innenminister unter Druck gesetzt worden. Im Sommer war einer ihrer Journalisten Opfer eines wohl politisch motivierten Mordanschlags geworden. Vor zwei Wochen hatten die Fernsehleute eine Inspektion der Steuerbehörden über sich ergehen lassen müssen, die aber keine Unregelmässigkeiten an den Tag brachte.

Von früheren Freunden verlassen

Die jüngste Einschüchterungsaktion rief nun zahlreiche Demonstranten auf den Plan. Sie konnten das Eindringen der Ordnungskräfte in das Fernsehgebäude verhindern und lancierten einen Protest gegen die Bedrohung der Medienfreiheit, der auch am Donnerstagabend anhielt.

Sicherheitsminister Kutateladse, der die Durchsuchung veranlasst hatte, reichte noch am selben Tag seinen Rücktritt ein. Die Demonstranten und ihre Sympathisanten forderten jedoch auch die Absetzung des Innenministers und des Generalstaatsanwalts. Präsident Schewardnadse kam damit in akute Bedrängnis. Er witterte einen Umsturzversuch und wertete das Geschehen in einem Fernsehinterview als Teil eines Plans, ihn von der Macht zu entfernen. Er stellte sich vor die beiden angeschuldigten Behördenleiter und drohte für den Fall, dass das Parlament ihnen das Misstrauen ausspreche, mit seinem eigenen Rücktritt.

Schewardnadses Putschtheorie scheint nicht völlig aus der Luft gegriffen zu sein. Jedenfalls fiel auf, wie sich ein Teil seiner früheren Getreuen öffentlich gegen ihn stellten und aus der TV-Affäre politisches Kapital zu schlagen versuchten. Parlamentspräsident Schwania berief eine Sondersitzung ein und warf dem mittlerweile 73-jährigen früheren sowjetischen Aussenminister mangelnden Realitätssinn und die Entfremdung von der Bevölkerung vor. Schwania, ein langjähriger Vertrauter Schewardnadses, scheint damit mit seinem politischen Ziehvater gebrochen zu haben. Prompt verhöhnte ihn dieser als Karrieristen. Ob Schwanias Rechnung aufgeht und er die Macht in Tbilissi pflücken kann, scheint aber mehr als fraglich. Der als prowestlicher Reformer geltende Magistrat, der seine politischen Sporen Anfang der neunziger Jahre in der grünen Bewegung des Landes abverdient hatte, ist innerhalb der georgischen Elite umstritten. Er verfügt auch nicht über das taktische Geschick Schewardnadses, der in seiner Zeit als kommunistischer Parteifunktionär alle Schliche des Machtspiels erlernt hatte. Schwania bot seinen Rücktritt an, falls auch der Kopf des Innenministers rolle. Als dies geschah, legte er seinen Posten nieder.

Anders Schewardnadse: Am Donnerstagnachmittag erklärte er, als verantwortungsbewusster Mensch könne er nach dem Rücktritt der Regierung nicht auch noch sein Amt niederlegen. Obwohl es nun scheint, dass er aus der ärgsten Bedrängnis herausgefunden hat, ist die Erosion seiner Machtstellung dennoch offenkundig. Noch vor einigen Monaten hatte er mit Hilfe seiner Partei, der Bürgerunion, das Parlament beherrscht und die verschiedenen politischen Clans des Landes souverän ausbalanciert. Mittlerweile zeigt die Bürgerunion deutliche Zerfallserscheinungen. Schewardnadse hat in Reaktion auf innerparteiliche Kritik den Parteivorsitz aufgegeben, und die laufende Krise offenbarte einen beträchtlichen Unmut im Parlament und in der Bevölkerung.

Die Krise ereignet sich vor dem Hintergrund gravierender Wirtschaftsprobleme und einer verbreiteten Wut über die Selbstbereicherung der herrschenden Elite. Frustriert über den mangelnden Willen der Staatschefs zur Korruptionsbekämpfung, hatte der junge Justizminister Saakaschwili, ein Anhänger Schwanias, im Sommer das Handtuch geworfen. Ein anderer enttäuschter Politiker sprach am Sender Rustawi-2 von einem verrotteten politischen System, für das er sich nicht mehr länger einsetzen wolle.

Geschwächte Staatsführung

Ob Georgien nach den jüngsten Ereignissen regierbar bleibt, muss sich weisen. In der jetzigen Lage ist die Staatsführung jedoch schlecht gerüstet, um mit den anstehenden Problemen fertig zu werden. Neben drängenden sozialen Fragen betrifft dies vor allem die beunruhigende Lage im Nordwesten des Landes, wo der Konflikt mit den abchasischen Separatisten neu aufgeflammt ist. In die Kodori-Schlucht sollen angeblich mehrere hundert Freischärler, vor allem Tschetschenen, eingedrungen sein. Der Abschuss eines Helikopters mit Uno-Beobachtern an Bord soll damit in Zusammenhang stehen. Verlässliche Informationen aus der Region fehlen. Bekannt ist, dass sowohl die georgische als auch die abchasische Führung Truppen in das Tal beorderten. Georgien beschuldigt zudem die russische Luftwaffe, sie sei in den georgischen Luftraum eingedrungen und habe vermutete Lagerplätze von Freischärlern mit Helikoptern und Kampfflugzeugen angegriffen.

Amerikanisch-russischer Konsens über A-Waffen?

Treffen Powells mit Iwanow

Washington, 1. Nov. (ap) Die USA und Russland streben offenbar eine Reduktion ihrer Atomsprengköpfe um etwa zwei Drittel an. Wie am Donnerstag aus amerikanischen Regierungskreisen verlautete, soll bei dem für Mitte November geplanten Gipfeltreffen über ein entsprechendes Abkommen verhandelt werden. Abrüstungsfragen standen auch im Mittelpunkt eines Treffens von Staatssekretär Powell mit dem russischen Aussenminister Iwanow in Washington. Ein ranghoher Vertreter des Weissen Hauses sagte, es kristallisiere sich ein Konsens heraus, die Anzahl der Sprengköpfe von derzeit 6000 auf 1750 bis 2250 zu verringern. Allerdings könne sich diese Zahl bis zum Beginn des Gipfeltreffens zwischen den Präsidenten Bush und Putin noch ändern. Putin und Bush wollen vom 13. bis zum 15. November in Washington sowie auf Bushs Ranch in der texanischen Stadt Crawford zusammenkommen.

Intensivierte US-Luftangriffe in Afghanistan

Verstärktes Vorgehen gegen Stellungen der Taliban

Die amerikanischen Streitkräfte haben ihre Luftangriffe auf Afghanistan in den letzten Tagen intensiviert, nachdem die Verfolgung politischer und militärischer Ziele entkoppelt worden ist. Verteidigungsminister Rumsfeld hat inzwischen Lehren für die Verteidigungsstrategie der Vereinigten Staaten in künftigen Kriegen gezogen.

brü. Washington, 1. November

Die Vereinigten Staaten haben die Intensität ihrer Luftangriffe auf Ziele in Afghanistan in den letzten Tagen merklich erhöht. Dabei wurden auch Langstreckenbomber des Typs B-52 eingesetzt, die grosse Flächen bombardieren können. Die Aktionen konzentrieren sich auf Truppenansammlungen der Taliban nördlich von Kabul sowie auf die Umgebung der Stadt Mazar-e Sharif. Die Verstärkung der Bombardements sowie der Einsatz der B-52 sind die Folge einer veränderten Strategie der Amerikaner. Sie besteht nach Angaben aus Regierungskreisen in einer Entkoppelung von politischen und militärischen Überlegungen.

Strategiewechsel

In den ersten Wochen hatten die Streitkräfte auf Wunsch des Weissen Hauses und des Aussenministeriums die Auswahl der Ziele limitiert, weil die Politiker die Sorge hatten, dass durch einen plötzlichen Zusammenbruch des Taliban-Regimes ein gefährliches Machtvakuum entstehen könnte. Vor allem sollte der Eindruck vermieden werden, dass die amerikanischen Angriffe die Nord-Allianz begünstigten, weil sie darin das Risiko sahen, dass andere ethnische Gruppierungen im Süden Afghanistans sich deswegen hinter die Taliban scharen könnten.

Mittlerweile hat sich jedoch herausgestellt, dass der Versuch, eine breit angelegte Koalition aus oppositionellen Gruppen zu bilden, so schnell keine Ergebnisse bringen wird. Es herrsche ein grosses Durcheinander, erklärte ein hoher Regierungsvertreter, in dem zahlreiche Gruppierungen und intrigierende Warlords eigene Interessen verfolgten. Die Vereinigten Staaten müssten militärisch «jetzt tun, was sie tun müssen», um die Angelegenheit hinter sich zu bringen.

Mehr Spielraum für das Pentagon

Diese Erkenntnis hat in Washington offensichtlich zu der Entscheidung geführt, militärische und politische Ziele nicht länger parallel, sondern auf unterschiedlichen Wegen anzustreben. Dies habe zur Folge, so sagte der Regierungsvertreter, dass das Pentagon für seine Aktionen einen grösseren Spielraum erhalten habe. Es sei einfach nicht rea-

17. März 2002
1. Jahrgang • Nr. 1
Fr 3.50 • € 2.50

NZZ am Sonntag

Sport

WALTER BIERI/KEYSTONE

Zürcher Hockeyklubs gleichen Serie aus

Sowohl die ZSC Lions (gegen Lugano) als auch Kloten (gegen Davos) gewinnen ihre ersten Heimspiele in den Play-off-Halbfinals. Damit stehen beide Serien jetzt 1:1. ▶ Seite 33

Wirtschaft

Vom Euro umgeben

Jean-Pierre Roth, der Präsident der Nationalbank, ist überzeugt, dass eine eigenständige Geldpolitik inmitten des riesigen Euro-Raums der Schweizer Wirtschaft einen Mehrwert bringt. ▶ Seite 57

Geld

Bill Gates im Gespräch

Der Software-Gigant Microsoft will weiter wachsen. Ziel sei es, alle Haushalte via Breitband-Kabel permanent ans Internet anzuschliessen, sagt Bill Gates im Interview. ▶ Seite 65

Gesellschaft

Egoismus und Liebe

Auch in der Liebe herrsche das Prinzip Eigennutz, schreibt der Zürcher Paartherapeut Jürg Willi in seinem neuesten Buch, das nächste Woche in die Buchläden kommt. ▶ Seite 114

Sport

Kehrt Karl Frehsner in die Schweiz zurück?

Als Nachfolger des zurückgetretenen Herren-Alpinchefs Dieter Bartsch scheint Karl Frehsner die besten Aussichten zu haben. Frehsner war zuletzt Frauenchef in Österreich. ▶ Seite 35

Sportresultate

Fussball-Finalrunde		
Zürich - St. Gallen	1:0	
Basel - FC Sion	4:0	

Eishockey-Play-offs		
Kloten - HC Davos	3:2	Serie 1:1
ZSC Lions - Lugano	6:1	Serie 1:1

Wetter

Alpennordseite	Alpensüdseite
Max 17°	Max 15°
Min 5°	Min 7°

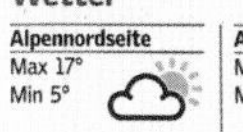

Wetter ▶ Seite 52

NZZ am Sonntag
Falkenstr. 11, Postfach 8021 Zürich, www.nzz.ch/sonntag
Redaktion: Tel. 01 258 11 11, redaktion.sonntag@nzz.ch
Abonnements: Tel. 01 258 15 30, www.nzz.ch/abo

9771660085003 11

Investoren bieten für Swissair 1,2 Milliarden

Berkeley Group will auch die Crossair bestehen lassen

Die amerikanisch-niederländische Beratungsfirma Berkeley Group will die Swissair kaufen. Das Angebot wurde Mario Corti formell unterbreitet.

Peter Keller

Der Sachwalter der zusammengebrochenen Swissair Group sucht einen Käufer für die Marke Swissair. Bis jetzt war lediglich bekannt geworden, dass mindestens ein seriöser Interessent mit der Swissair im Gespräch sei. Jetzt ist bekannt, um wen es sich dabei handelt: um die amerikanisch-niederländische Luftfahrt-Beratungsfirma Berkeley Group, die ihren Sitz in Bethesda (USA) hat. Sie hat am 24. Januar ihr Angebot dem Swissair-Chef Mario Corti in Anwesenheit von Verwaltungsrat Bénédict Hentsch und Sachwalter Karl Wüthrich unterbreitet.

Laut dem Businessplan will Berkeley nicht nur die Marke, sondern die ganze Swissair mit 26 Kurzstrecken- und Mittelstreckenflugzeugen sowie 26 Langstreckenmaschinen übernehmen. Die Airline soll mit 1,2 Milliarden Franken rekapitalisiert werden. Berkeley will dabei mit der geplanten Swiss nicht konkurrieren, sondern in Zusammenarbeit mit Crossair die bisherigen Marken Swissair und Crossair bestehen lassen.

Die Basler Airline ist allerdings bis jetzt offiziell nicht kontaktiert worden. Er könne zu einem Projekt, das ihm offiziell noch nie präsentiert worden sei, nicht Stellung beziehen, erklärt Crossair-Chef André Dosé auf Anfrage. Dazu komme, dass die Swissair-Nachfolgefirma Swiss bereits bestehe und am 31. März ihren Betrieb aufnehmen werde.

Als weiteres Handicap für Berkeley kommt dazu, dass die Betriebsbewilligung und die Streckenkonzessionen der Swissair an diesem Datum sistiert werden. Die Voraussetzungen für den Betrieb einer Airline sind dann nicht mehr gegeben, weil sie über kein Personal und über keinen finanziellen Hintergrund mehr verfügt. «Die entsprechenden Streckenkonzessionen sind nach dem in der Luftfahrtverordnung vorgesehenen normalen Erteilungsprozess an die Crossair respektive Swiss vergeben worden», sagt Daniel Göring, Informationsbeauftragter beim Bundesamt für Zivilluftfahrt (Bazl). Ein Zurückbuchstabieren sei in dieser kurzen Zeit kaum mehr zu realisieren. Hingegen habe jeder Interessent das Recht, eine neue Betriebsbewilligung zu beantragen. Er müsse aber über die nötigen technischen und operationellen Voraussetzungen verfügen.

Diese Variante kommt für Berkeley jedoch nicht in Frage, weil sie keine neue Airline aus der Taufe heben will. Eine weitere Schwierigkeit ist, dass Crossair weiterhin ein Vorkaufsrecht auf die Marke Swissair hält. Die Fluggesellschaft kann allerdings einen Verkauf nicht blockieren, falls sie den von einem Interessenten vorgeschlagenen Preis nicht bezahlen will. Eine Hypothek für die Marke Swissair könnte zudem das Durchgriffsrecht der Gläubiger darstellen.

▶ Kommentar Seite 23
▶ Bericht Seite 53

Forscher wollen Fruchtbarkeit der Schweizer testen

Die Zeugungsfähigkeit des starken Geschlechts sei bedroht, warnen Mediziner und Wissenschafter. Internationale Untersuchungen deuten nämlich darauf hin, dass die Männer aus den Industrieländern im Durchschnitt immer weniger Spermien haben. Schuld daran sollen allgegenwärtige Umweltgifte sein, die schon in kleinsten Konzentrationen das empfindliche menschliche Hormonsystem beeinflussen können.

Doch die Datenbasis für gesicherte Aussagen ist dünn, vor allem in der Schweiz. Im Auftrag des Bundesrates hat der Schweizerische Nationalfonds deshalb das Forschungsprogramm NFP50 zu diesen sogenannten hormonaktiven Stoffen in Angriff genommen. Darin enthalten ist auch ein brisantes Projekt: Marc Germond vom Universitätsspital Lausanne will mit Spermienanalysen von Freiwilligen aus Rekruten-, Unteroffiziers- und Offiziersschulen herausfinden, ob auch die Fruchtbarkeit der Schweizer gelitten hat. Ähnliche Studien sind bereits in Dänemark durchgeführt worden. Germonds Versuch ist vorläufig auf drei Jahre angelegt und kostet 600 000 Franken. Was noch fehlt, ist die definitive Zusage des Eidgenössischen Departementes für Verteidigung, Bevölkerungsschutz und Sport. *(mam.)*

▶ Seite 97

Hoffnung auf Waffenruhe im Nahen Osten

Im Nahen Osten hat sich die Lage etwas beruhigt. Im Westjordanland wurde ein Sicherheitsoffizier von Arafats Leibgarde zu Grabe getragen. Der Nahost-Vermittler Zinni sprach mit beiden Konfliktparteien. US-Vizepräsident Cheney traf in Saudiarabien ein. (Muhammed Muheisen/Getty)

▶ Berichte und Analysen Seite 2 und 3

Durchbruch für freien Strommarkt

Zustimmung zu neuem Verordnungstext

Der Streit um die Strommarkt-Verordnung ist beigelegt. Der Bund kommt Umwelt und Konsumenten entgegen, die Wirtschaft ist einverstanden. Das verbessert die Chancen für die Öffnung des Strommarkts.

Pascal Hollenstein und Erich Aschwanden

Nach monatelangem Gezänk und unzähligen Verhandlungsrunden hat das Bundesamt für Energie am Freitag dem Bundesrat die Strommarkt-Verordnung vorgelegt. Mit der neuen Fassung der umstrittenen Verordnung kommt der Bund der Wirtschaft und den Konsumenten entgegen.

Zahlreiche Vorkehren sollen sicherstellen, dass der Strom für Industrie, Gewerbe und private Haushalte tendenziell günstiger wird. Die Grundlagen für die Berechnung der Durchleitungstarife wurden so angepasst, dass die Stromwirtschaft wenigstens auf einen Teil ihrer früheren Monopol-Gewinne verzichten muss. Für sechs Jahre verbietet die Verordnung Tariferhöhungen für die Stromdurchleitung gänzlich; später müssen sich die Stromunternehmen nationalen und internationalen Preisvergleichen aussetzen.

Die Elektrizitätswirtschaft hat diese bitteren Pillen offenbar geschluckt. Der Bund hat ihr im Gegenzug mehr Freiheiten in der Umsetzung dieser Bestimmungen eingeräumt.

Zu den Gewinnern gehören aber auch die Umweltorganisationen. Sie haben sich mit allen Postulaten durchgesetzt. Die Elektrizitätswerke werden verpflichtet, Strom aus Wind, Sonne, Biomasse und Kleinwasserkraftwerken gratis durch ihr Netz zu leiten. Zudem erfahren die Konsumenten auf ihrer Stromrechnung, aus welchen Quellen ihre Energie stammt. Die Umweltorganisationen erhoffen sich von diesen Massnahmen bessere Chancen für ökologisch produzierten Strom.

Die Verordnung zum Strommarktgesetz gilt als Knackpunkt bei der Liberalisierung des Strommarkts. Zwar stimmen die Stimmbürgerinnen und Stimmbürger am 22. September formell über das übergeordnete Gesetz ab. Da dieses aber in zentralen Bereichen recht vage bleibt, beschloss Bundesrat Moritz Leuenberger in einer in der Geschichte der modernen Schweiz einzigartigen Aktion, die Verordnung vorgängig auszuarbeiten und in die Vernehmlassung zu schicken. «Die Bürger sollen wissen, worüber sie genau abstimmen», begründet der Sprecher von Moritz Leuenberger, Hugo Schittenhelm, dieses Vorgehen.

Moritz Leuenbergers Taktik zielte darauf ab, die liberalisierungskritische Linke einzubinden. Der Schachzug missglückte allerdings gründlich: Kaum jemand mochte sich vorbehaltlos hinter den ersten Verordnungsentwurf stellen. Stattdessen schalteten auch die Vertreter der Wirtschaft auf Opposition: «Zu interventionistisch», wertete der damalige Präsident von Economiesuisse, Andres F. Leuenberger, den Entwurf.

Die nun ausgearbeitete Verordnung scheint jetzt die Wende gebracht zu haben. Walter Steiner, Chef des Bundesamts für Energie, spricht von einem «Durchbruch». Vertreter der Elektrizitätswirtschaft und von Umwelt- und Konsumentenorganisationen bezeichnen das Ergebnis einmütig als «tragfähigen Kompromiss». Das letzte Wort hat der Bundesrat. Er behandelt die Vorlage voraussichtlich an der Sitzung vom 27. März.

▶ Seite 14

Mode

Style Watch
Big Woman

Was sind das für Leute, die bei H&M kaufen? Der Fachzeitschrift «Textilwirtschaft» zufolge sind sie «erlebnisorientiert» und finden Begriffe wie «nackt», «verführen» und «wild» anziehend – im Gegensatz zu «Vaterland» und «Moral». Der typische H&M-Fan ist 34-jährig, weiblich (70%), und nicht alle sind dünn wie Models. Jetzt haben sich die Schweden dazu durchgerungen, auch ihre Big-is-Beautiful-Kollektion für grosse Grössen trendig zu designen: mit Cargopants und Chiffontuniken, Kimonoblusen und Armeejacken. *(aur.)*

Gefühl und Utilitarismus: Bestickte Baumwollbluse, Cargohose und Kruzifix-Kette.

Tunika, Hose aus gebürstetem Mikro-Nylon und Schal, jeweils nur ab Grösse 42 und unter 50 Fr.

Trend meets Klassik: Tunika aus Georgette zur Five-Pocket-Jeans (oben), Tunika mit Kimono-Ärmeln zur Leinenhose mit Tunnelzug, deren Schlag anno 2003 in die Stiefeletten gehört (unten).

Eleganz und Extravaganz in Kombination: Kragenkaskaden von Viktor & Rolf an den Pariser Schauen. (Pierre Verdy/Keystone)

Klassiker in Opulenz

Das Designerduo Viktor & Rolf hat die Formel des neuen Looks gefunden: Moderne Klassik

An allzu vieles, das in den zurückliegenden Tagen der Prêt-à-porter-Schauen in Paris gezeigt wurde, braucht man sich nicht en détail zu erinnern. Die grossen Linien sind so klar wie schon lange nicht mehr. Neben den bereits für diesen Sommer angekündigten Miniröcken feiern kommenden Herbst vor allem die Sechziger ein grosses Comeback. Die Modewelt spricht von einer «neuen Couture», obgleich vieles im Grunde nicht viel mehr als eine ästhetische Anleihe bei den alten Vorbildern ist. Auch das niederländische Designerduo Viktor & Rolf beschreitet den Weg in Richtung neuer Klassik – doch sie gehen dabei ein gutes Stück weiter.

Denn Viktor Horsting und Rolf Snoeren aus Amsterdam haben mit einer reifen Kollektion und einer spektakulär schönen Schau die Regentschaft in Sachen Stil übernommen. Sie stehen damit auf der vorläufig höchsten Stufe einer persönlichen Entwicklung, die sie von den Rändern der Avantgarde über ihre Rolle als Konzeptkunst veranstaltende Eigenbrötler und gehypte «Nouveaux Couturiers» bis an die Spitze der Prêt-à-porter geführt hat. Praktisch zum ersten Mal veranstaltete das Duo dieses Mal in Paris eine «konventionelle» Modenschau statt einer Art-Performance. Ort des Geschehens war eine geräumige Eventhalle am Pariser Stadtrand, der Laufsteg in einem neutralen Grau gehalten und der Hintergrund von einem überdimensionierten Viktor-&-Rolf-Logo geschmückt, einem roten Lacksiegel. Smoking-

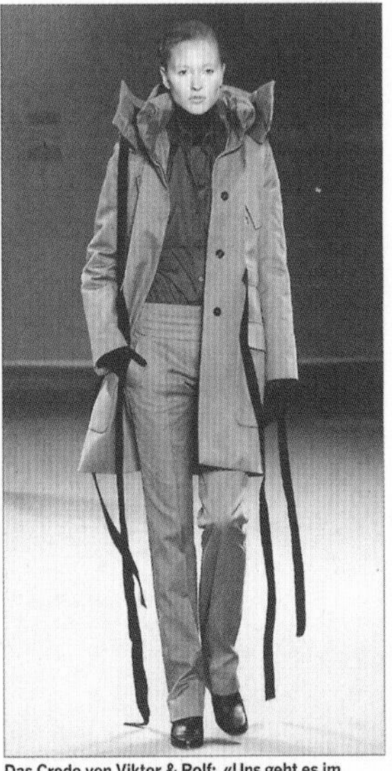

Das Credo von Viktor & Rolf: «Uns geht es im Grunde nur um die Kleider und die handwerkliche Technik der Couture, denn sie ist die höchste Form der Mode.» (Jack Dabaghian/Reuters)

Kombinationen in schlichtem Schwarzweiss zum Auftakt der Show. Dann setzt eine Frauenstimme mit dem Rezital von Textpassagen ein. Ein erster sehr weiter Kragen taucht auf, befestigt an einem Hemd, dessen Manschette genauso aus der Proportion gerutscht und ungefähr 20 Zentimeter breit geschnitten ist. Es folgen weisse Blusen, deren Kragenvolumen sich entsprechend der akustischen Untermalung langsam steigern. Zur Stimme kommt ein Beat, ein Instrument, der Sound wächst zu einer Klangwolke, während eine schwarze Jeansweste mit multiplen Kragen und ein Parka mit Riesenkapuze die Botschaft der Show kontinuierlich zuspitzen.

Der Look: eine moderne Klassik, sorgfältig geschnitten, feminin tailliert, erwachsen, fast durchgehend in Schwarz – und eben mit diesem wunderbaren Effekt der geschichteten und fast bis zum Scheitel reichenden Kragenkaskaden, die die Gesichter der Models wie eine Blüte umrahmen. Die Botschaft von Viktor & Rolf trifft den Nagel der Zeit auf den Kopf. Sogar die mächtige «International Herald Tribune» anerkennt: Viktor & Rolf verkörpern mit einer dramatischen Präsentation die Rückkehr eines smarten, schlichteren Looks. Die Konsumenten sind nach Jahren teilweise absurder Extravaganz reif für eine Neuinterpretation der Basisgarderobe. Man sucht nach einfachen Kreationen von einer gestandenen Eleganz, nach Lieblingsstücken. Die bieten Viktor & Rolf in Hülle und Fülle. Denn wenn man die Überzeichnung des Looks wegnimmt, die acht übereinander gelegten Smokingjacken einzeln aufhängt und alles für sich betrachtet, schaffen die Holländer nichts als die reine Vernunft. Die Extravaganzen sind nur noch Reminiszenz an ihre eigenen Wurzeln, ein feiner Fingerzeig zurück in die Richtung, aus der das Duo gekommen ist.

Jeroen van Roojien

Kreative Erneuerer

Das Duo Viktor & Rolf, bestehend aus Viktor Horsting und Rolf Snoeren (beide 34), begann seine Laufbahn 1999 in Amsterdam. Anders als bei vielen ihrer Zeitgenossen führte ihr Weg dabei aber nicht durch diverse Ateliers der grossen Meister, sondern war seit ihrem Diplom an der Kunstakademie in Arnhem eine konsequente Arbeit am eigenen Label. Statt auf die Unterstützung durch private Gelder bauten sie dabei auf die verschiedenen Förderprogramme für junges Design. Als eigentlicher Karriereturbo wirkte die Auszeichnung am internationalen Newcomer-Festival von Hyères. Seither haben sich die beiden als Erneuerer der zeitgenössischen Mode profiliert, nicht zuletzt dank der Teilnahme an internationalen Kunstausstellungen. Für kommenden Winter kommt erstmals auch eine komplette Männerkollektion der Niederländer in den Handel. *(jvr.)*

Auftritt casual oder glamourös: Viktor (l.) und Rolf als Teil der Show. (Giovannozzi, Bucco/Keystone)

NZZ am Sonntag • 23. März 2003

85

Glück aus dem Crèmetopf

Besser als Schokolade essen. Die Kosmetik-Industrie nimmt sich der Psyche an

«Meine Haut hat genau wie ich ein Faible für Glücksgefühle.» Dieser Satz stammt nicht etwa aus einem Kiosk-Roman, sondern aus der Kosmetikwerbung. Denn die neue Zauberformel im Kampf gegen Falten, Furchen und fahle Haut heisst Glück. Dabei geht es ganz konkret um eine Verbesserung der Hautstruktur und nicht allein um die viel zitierte «Schönheit von innen». Nach Fruchtsäuren, Enzymen, Vitaminen und Mineralstoffen sind jetzt die Endorphine an der Reihe, für einen makellosen Teint zu sorgen. Dass die Neurohormone durch Schokolade-Essen aktiviert werden, ist längst bekannt. Nun also «Glück aus dem Topf». Die frohe Kunde kommt von der französischen Kosmetikfirma Guerlain, die vor kurzem das Glücksprodukt «Happylogy»› lancierte (Serum 30 ml 124 Fr., Crème 30 ml 84 Fr.). Es basiert auf der relativ neuen wissenschaftlichen Erkenntnis, dass neben dem Gehirn auch die Haut in der Lage ist, Endorphine freizusetzen. Diese natürlichen Neurotransmitter, die als chemische Überbringer für alle angenehmen Empfindungen verantwortlich sind, werden von den Keratinozyten (verantwortlich für die Zellerneuerung), den Langerhans-Zellen (sensorische Zellen der Haut), den Melanozyten (Pigmentzellen), den Merkel-Zellen (neuroendokrine Zellen) und von den Fibroblasten (Kollagen und Elastin produzierende Zellen der Lederhaut) hergestellt.

Wie Dr. Laurent Misery, Leiter des Labors für Hautneurobiologie und der Abteilung Dermatologie der Universitätsklinik Brest, in einer von Guerlain verbreiteten Veröffentlichung festhält, kurbeln diese Endorphine die Aktivität der Keratinozyten an – Zellen, die das Erscheinungsbild der Hautoberfläche und die Feinheit des Hautbilds entscheidend mitbestimmen und deren Vermehrung sich bei der Hautalterung verlangsamt. Zudem stimulieren sie die Fibroblasten, jene Zellen der Lederhaut, welche die Hautbeschaffenheit im Bindegewebe mitprägen. Endorphine besitzen auch hemmende Eigenschaften gegenüber den Nervenfasern und wirken so entzündungshemmend beziehungsweise beruhigend bei Hautentzündungen. Laut Dr. Paul Bigliardi, klinischer Leiter des Forschungslabors der Dermatologischen Klinik der Universität Basel, der sich seit Jahren mit entsprechenden Untersuchungen beschäftigt, können Endorphine die Wundheilung und den Aufbau der Haut sowie verschiedene juckende Hauterkrankungen beeinflussen. Auch hätten gewisse klinische Beobachtungen gezeigt, dass die Wundheilung bei glücklichen Menschen besser ablaufe als bei unglücklichen.

Wie aber kann die Haut zur Bildung von Endorphinen stimuliert werden? Die diesbezügliche Forschung steckt noch in den Anfängen. Guerlain scheint jedoch einen möglichen Schlüssel dazu entdeckt zu haben. Zentraler Bestandteil von «Happylogy», so wird mitgeteilt, sei ein Wirkstoffkomplex mit Pro-Endorphinen, der die Produktion von Beta-Endorphinen in der Haut ankurble und einen wahren «Glückstaumel» auslöse, der das Hautbild schnell glätte, verfeinere und in gesunder Frische erstrahlen lasse. Guerlains Produkt ist somit eine Premiere in der Kosmetik. Der Gedanke dahinter ist indessen nicht neu. Seit langem werden Möglichkeiten gesucht, mittels Glücksgefühlen die Haut zu verschönern. Bis anhin wurde dies jedoch via Tastsinn, Nase und Augen zu erreichen versucht. Der «emotionale Eindruck» einer Crème ist erwiesenermassen von grosser Bedeutung für das psychische Wohlbefinden (und natürlich somit auch für die Kaufentscheidung). Die Textur einer Crème spielt genauso eine Rolle wie ihr Geruch und ihr Aussehen. Den Beweis dafür liefern Messungen mit dem sogenannten PET-Scan, einem Instrument, das die durch gewisse Produkte stimulierten Gehirnbereiche identifiziert. Die meisten neuen Gesichtspflegeprodukte zielen auch auf Polysensorialität. Neben den eigentlichen Wirkstoffen werden noch andere Steuerungsmechanismen angewendet. So soll beispielsweise Shisedos «Future Solution» durch das Zusammenspiel von Wirkstoffen, Textur und Duft die Sinne gleichermassen ansprechen.

Bleibt die Frage, ob eine «glückliche» Haut tatsächlich straffer und reiner ist als eine «unglückliche» und ob die Hautalterung bei glücklichen Menschen langsamer vor sich geht als bei unglücklichen. Klinische Beweise gibt es nicht. Bigliardi weist darauf hin, dass Endorphine in der Haut schwierig nachzuweisen und ihre Mechanismen noch wenig bekannt sind. «Aber vielleicht», so der Dermatologe, «schauen glückliche Menschen einfach weniger kritisch in den Spiegel.» *Christa Arnet*

Glücksmomente für die Haut: Wirkstoffe der Crèmes oder innere Einstellung? (Lars Matzen/Jump)

Stimulierend: «Happylogy» von Guerlain setzt auf die Wirkung von Endorphin (30 ml 84 Fr).

Pflegen durch Entspannung: «Crème de Nuit Relaxante» von Carita (50 ml ca. 130 Fr).

«Resilience Lift» von Estée Lauder setzt auf entspannende Düfte (50 ml 115 Fr).

Einstreicheln: «Wohlfühltextur» nennt Dior den Inhalt von «Capture» R60/80TM (30 ml 72 Fr).

«Shiseido Future Solution» (50 ml 298 Fr.) will mit Form, Duft und Textur alle Sinne ansprechen.

Lancaster verspricht mit «Suractif Excellence Rich Lifting Revitalizer» sofortiges Wohlergehen (50 ml 280 Fr).

Schönheit

Tyler Brûlés Kanon der Populärkultur

Stilvoll, schweizerisch und schützenswert

Von Zeit zu Zeit wächst in mir das Bedürfnis, mein Leben dem Naturschutz zu widmen. Gewiss, ich liebe Pandas, seltene Pflanzen und vom Aussterben bedrohte Völker ebenso wie meinen Nächsten, aber mir scheint doch, dass die Schutzwürdigkeit dieser Gruppen im globalen Bewusstsein hinreichend verankert ist. Mein Interesse richtet sich deshalb auf Dinge, die mehr mit meinem Alltag zu tun haben.

Noch bin ich nicht so weit, dass ich mit anderen Aktivisten auf der Bahnhofstrasse demonstriere oder für eine Petition werbe. Aber die Zeit ist nicht mehr fern. Die Schweiz steht bekanntlich in dem Ruf, Menschen zu helfen, ihnen Asyl zu bieten. Die Schweizer gelten weltweit als eine der grosszügigsten Nationen, und Genf ist Sitz unzähliger Nichtregierungsorganisationen. Das alles ist gut und schön, aber ich finde, dass sich die Schweizer nicht genug um sich selbst kümmern, vor allem um ihr Erbe in den Bereichen Architektur und Design.

In Krisenzeiten kann sich die Schweiz als Hort von Sicherheit und Stabilität empfehlen, in besseren Zeiten wird sie mit ihrer Infrastruktur werben, ihren Verkehrsverbindungen, der Hotellerie und ihrem weltweit anerkannten Industriedesign. Es ist jedoch bedauerlich und frustrierend, mit ansehen zu müssen, in welch rasantem Tempo das Fundament schweizerischen Designs ausgehöhlt wird. Wohlstand und der Trend zum Innovativen verlangen unablässig Neues, Abschied vom Alten. Das ist gut und schön, aber vielleicht sollte man nicht immer ersetzen, was überhaupt nicht kaputt ist.

Wenn ich sofort aus meinen beruflichen Verpflichtungen aussteigen könnte, würde ich mit meiner Freundin Laura Houseley und einem guten Photographen, vielleicht David Willen, jeden Quadratmeter der Eidgenossenschaft dokumentieren – beispielsweise das imitierte Walnussfurnier in den Badezimmern des Suvretta House, die merkwürdige Beleuchtung der Cafés in Ilanz, die wunderbaren Reklameschriften in Biel und die bizarren, aber fabelhaften Ticket-Kioske in Genf.

Da der französische Stil der Vierziger und Fünfziger ebenso ausführlich dokumentiert ist wie der skandinavische Modernismus und das italienische Industriedesign der Siebziger, wird es Zeit, dass jemand den ganz besonderen Schweizer Stil festhält, der sich in den Nachkriegsjahren entwickelt hat.

Am Mittwochabend hatte ich ein paar Gäste in meiner Londoner Wohnung. Wir tranken einen anständigen chilenischen Rotwein, schauten, was in der BBC über den Krieg berichtet wurde, und ergingen uns in Erinnerungen, indem wir Fotos betrachteten von interessantem Design, die ich im Laufe der Jahre gemacht habe. Neal, ein relativ neues Gesicht in unserer Runde, überraschte uns, als er auf ein Foto zeigte und fragte: «Sind das nicht Dachziegel von einer Kirche in St. Moritz? Typisch schweizerisch. Ganz toll.» Erstaunlicherweise war Neal noch nie in der Schweiz, und doch sprachen allem Anschein nach ein paar weiss-gelbe Tessiner Ziegel Bände über eine bisher weitgehend nicht dokumentierte Schweizer Spezialität.

Viele Menschen, die ich auf meinen Reisen durch die Schweiz kennen lerne, finden, dass die auffälligen Ziegel, die Kaffeebrauntöne und die nüchterne Typographie hässlich sind und möglichst schnell ersetzt werden sollten. Für mich gehören sie zum schweizerischen Design-Erbe, und sie sind ebenso erhaltenswert wie ein Schloss im Waadtland oder ein nepalesischer Albino-Tiger.

Die Schweizer kümmern sich nicht genug um ihr Design-Erbe und ihre Architektur.

Tyler Brûlé ist CEO / Creative Director der Winkorp AG und Gründer der Zeitschrift «Wallpaper». Er lebt zwischen Zürich, London und Stockholm.

NZZ am Sonntag

Stil

Mode Das Design-Duo Viktor & Rolf interpretiert die Klassik neu. Die Modewelt war lange nicht mehr so begeistert 84

Reisen Birkenwälder und Gurkensalat ohne Ende. Stille Tage in der Transsibirischen Eisenbahn 86

Auto Der imposante Kühlergrill feiert in diesem Sommer ein Revival 89

Schönheit: Glücklichmacher auf der Haut

Seite 85

Pages on fashion (opposite) and beauty (left), and a cover of the Style section (above).

Colorful, structured, lively

Pages on fashion, beauty, and style all reflect a tightly controlled grid where the visual elements seem to break out.

21

NZZ am Sonntag

Hintergrund

Ventil Leserbrief

Leserbriefe sind ein individuelles Genre und mitunter auch einfach ein politisches Ventil. Ab nächsten Sonntag auch bei uns.
Seite 25

Landung im Markt

DINO PANATO/ANSA

Wird Simon Ammann, der Lausbub aus dem Toggenburg, jetzt so richtig reich? Kaum, schreibt der Ökonom und Olympiasieger Hippolyt Kempf.
Seite 28

Der New Yorker

Er personifiziert den Willen einer ganzen Stadt, sich nicht kleinkriegen zu lassen: Der ehemalige Bürgermeister New Yorks, Rudolph Giuliani.
Seite 29

Schlachtgefühle

Das Schächtverbot bleibt – die Stimmung war zu vergiftet. Was macht Schlachtungen so emotionsgeladen? Ein Streifzug durch die Kulturgeschichte.
Seite 31

Nur wer die Fakten kennt, kann eine fundierte Meinung haben

Felix E. Müller über die Aufgabe der Medien in einer demokratischen Gesellschaft

Das zwischen 1835 und 1840 erschienene Werk «De la démocratie en Amérique» von Alexis de Tocqueville gehört noch heute zu den Standardwerken der Amerikanistik, weil es der französische Schriftsteller scharfsinnig verstand, die konstitutiven Elemente der amerikanischen Gesellschaft herauszuschälen und zu analysieren. Deshalb äussert sich Tocqueville auch über die Presse, mit spürbarer Verwunderung darüber, dass sich die Alte und die Neue Welt in diesem Punkt durchaus ähnlich seien: «In Amerika wie in Frankreich stellt die Presse eine besondere Macht dar, die so eigenartig gemischt ist aus Gutem und Bösem und von der man weiss, dass ohne sie die Freiheit nicht existieren könnte und mit ihr die öffentliche Ordnung sich kaum behaupten kann.»

Die Freiheit der Presse ist eine Grundbedingung für eine demokratische Gesellschaft. Aus diesem Grund bemerkte schon vor de Tocqueville Thomas Jefferson, er würde nicht zögern, eine durch die Presse ausgelöste öffentliche Unordnung einer Unterdrückung der Meinungsfreiheit vorzuziehen. Aber beide Denker haben gleichzeitig auch das destruktive Potenzial klar erkannt, das der verantwortungslose Umgang mit der Pressefreiheit in sich birgt.

Diese Gefahr ist uns heute, im Zeitalter des Kampagnenjournalismus und der «Reality»-Shows, wohl noch bewusster geworden. Wir können beobachten, dass die Überpräsenz des Negativen in den Medien das Vertrauen in die gesellschaftlichen Institutionen zu unterhöhlen droht; wir erleben, wie der gelegentlich fahrlässige Umgang mit den Tatsachen und Fakten die Tür zu einer manipulativen Beeinflussung der öffentlichen Meinung aufsperrt; wir verfolgen, mit welcher Anmassung und Überheblichkeit heute die Presse teilweise auftritt.

Es hat dies damit zu tun, dass die Medien seit Watergate ihre zentrale Aufgabe in der Kontrolle der Mächtigen sehen. Vergessen geht dabei, dass sie daneben eine mindestens so wichtige, aber weniger spektakuläre Aufgabe erfüllen sollten: die Vermittlung von Informationen. Dass die Auflagen gerade der gedruckten Presse in den USA nach dem 11. September gestiegen sind, ist Ausdruck dieses Bedürfnisses, sich in unübersichtlichen Zeiten besser zu informieren, damit man sich besser orientieren kann.

Eine Zeitung, die diese beiden zentralen Funktionen einer freien Presse erfüllen will, muss über ein Grundkapital verfügen: Glaubwürdigkeit. Nur wer glaubwürdig ist, der wird als kritische Instanz anerkannt und dem vertraut man, verlässliche Informationen zu vermitteln. Zeitungen, die sich diesen Ruf erwerben wollen, müssen als ihre primäre Aufgabe die Beschaffung und wahrheitsgemässe Wiedergabe der Fakten sehen.

Meinungen zu haben, ist nicht schwer, weil jeder Mensch über solche verfügt. Wer sich darauf beschränkt, als Journalist einfach seine Gesinnung auf einem Silbertablett vor sich herzutragen, der hat eine einfache Disziplin gewählt. Schwieriger ist es, Meinungen zu haben, die vor den Fakten bestehen können.

Die Versuchung, etwas zu meinen, bevor man etwas weiss, ist eine grosse Versuchung in diesem Metier. Es resultieren daraus eine Aufgeregtheit in der Sache und eine Überspanntheit der Tonalität, die den Journalismus in der Öffentlichkeit teilweise in Verruf gebracht haben. Umfragen zeigen immer wieder, dass das Publikum das Medienangebot gerne nutzt, den Inhalten aber generell eher misstraut und die Medien und mit ihnen die Journalisten als arrogant empfindet.

Das ist allerdings keine neue Entwicklung. In den von Goethe und Schiller gemeinsam im Jahre 1796 herausgegebenen Xenien findet sich die bissige Bemerkung über den Journalismus: «Wieviel Staub! Und wie wenig Gepäck!» Bereits sechzehn Jahre früher notierte ein Leitartikler etwas prosaischer: «Es wird uns zwar, so wie andern Zeitungsschreibern, nicht möglich sein, die Weltbegebenheiten früher anzuzeigen, als sie geschehen sind.» Mit diesem Satz setzte sich die neu gegründete «Zürcher Zeitung» vor 222 Jahren von dem ab, was man neuerdings «mid-risk journalism» nennt – von der Versuchung, die Fakten imaginativ dermassen zu ergänzen, damit sich daraus eine schnittige Schlagzeile gewinnen lässt.

> Wer sich als Journalist darauf beschränkt, einfach seine Gesinnung vor sich herzutragen, der hat eine einfache Disziplin gewählt.

Ohne Treue zu den Tatsachen, ohne redliche Absicht, diese so zu präsentieren, wie sie sich auf Grund der Recherche darstellen, wird sich Glaubwürdigkeit nicht einstellen – und ohne gesicherten Standpunkt zur Beurteilung dieser Fakten ebenso wenig. Zur Glaubwürdigkeit trägt schliesslich eine Eigenschaft bei, die im heutigen Journalismus nicht sehr weit verbreitet ist: Selbstkritik. Mass halten kann nur, wer sich selbst in Frage stellen kann; Verständnis für den andern vermag nur aufzubringen, wer die Bedingtheit des eigenen Standpunktes erkennt.

Nur wo diese drei zentralen Elemente einer Selbstkontrolle vorhanden sind, kann sich die Pressefreiheit zum Vorteil der Gesellschaft auswirken. Qualitätsjournalismus ist jedoch kein Zustand, sondern das Ergebnis eines ständigen Bemühens – genau so, wie dies schon die «Zürcher Zeitung» 1780 in ihrem Leitartikel festhielt: **«Und wenn wir anfänglich eben nicht das leisten, was wir gerne leisten wollten, so bitten wir zu bedenken, dass aller Anfänge schwer seyen, und dass wir von einer Woche bis zur andern unsre Einrichtung verbessern und der Zeitung selbst dadurch mehr Interesse geben werden.»**

Präservative gegen die Korruption

Ingrid Betancourt, entführte Präsidentschaftskandidatin. *Von Richard Bauer*

Manche Autofahrer im Zentrum der kolumbianischen Hauptstadt Bogotá staunten, als vor ein paar Jahren eine attraktive jüngere Frau ihnen bei Rotlicht Präservative durchs Wagenfenster reichte. Wer glaubte, es handle sich um eine Kampagne für Familienplanung oder gegen Aids, hatte sich geirrt. Die Gummiware war Überbringer einer politischen Botschaft. Ingrid Betancourt – damals 33 Jahre alt, Tochter eines ehemaligen Erziehungsministers und einer sozial engagierten Schönheitskönigin – hatte genug von der Verlogenheit der Politikerklasse und kandidierte mutterseelenallein für einen Sitz im Parlament.

Korruption im Staat sei mit Aids gleichzusetzen, erklärte die Aktivistin zwischen Abgasen und Hupkonzerten ihrer potenziellen Wählerschaft: «Ich schenke Ihnen ein Präservativ, auf diese Weise werden Sie am Wahltag an mich denken.» Und wie: Innert kürzester Zeit hatte sich die unkonventionelle Politnovize in den Medien als glaubwürdige Kämpferin gegen Machtmissbrauch und Klüngelwirtschaft profiliert. Sie erzielte das beste Wahlergebnis auf der liberalen Parteiliste, in die sie sich der Form halber hatte eintragen lassen. Dann schaffte sie vom Abgeordnetenhaus den Sprung in den Senat. Jetzt kandidiert sie für das Amt des Staatspräsidenten.

Statt des Parisers ist diesmal Viagra als Propagandamittel angesagt. An Wahlveranstaltungen wurden die Pillen verteilt. Dem von Kleinkrieg, Attentaten und Wirtschaftskrise demoralisierten Kolumbien sollte die alte Spannkraft zurückgegeben werden. Um der unbequemen Kandidatin und ihrem Wahlbündnis «Neues Kolumbien» die Flügel zu stutzen, erreichten politische Gegner ein Verbot für die rezeptfreie Abgabe der Potenzdroge.

Ingrid Betancourts Kampagne ging abrupt zu Ende, als sie vor wenigen Wochen von einem Kommando der grössten Guerillagruppe des Landes, der Fuerzas Armadas Revolucionarias de Colombia (Farc), als Geisel entführt wurde. Auf der Strasse zwischen Florencia und San Vicente del Caguán war sie in eine Sperre der Farc geraten. Dabei hatte man ihr dringend davon abgeraten, den Landweg in dieser unruhigen Gegend zu benützen.

Nur kurz zuvor hatte Präsident Pastrana die Rückeroberung der entmilitarisierten Zone im Süden und das Ende der dreijährigen Friedensverhandlungen mit den Rebellen bekannt gegeben. Was man als «Friedenslabor» entworfen hatte, war zu einem rechtsfreien Raum verkommen, in dem die Farc frei schalten und walten konnten. Pastrana kritisierte, das Gebiet, das so gross wie die Schweiz ist, sei von den Farc als Zufluchtsstätte für Geiselnehmer, Drogenlabor und Waffenlager sowie als Schmugglernest missbraucht worden.

Über Nacht eskalierte Mitte Februar der jahrzehntealte Konflikt. Die Armee lancierte die «Operation Thanatos». Tausende Soldaten drangen in die Hochburg der Guerilla ein, Flugzeuge bombardierten Dschungellager und besprühten Kokainfelder mit Unkrautvertilgungsmitteln. Die Kolumbianer befürchteten den «totalen Krieg» zwischen marxistischen Guerilleros, rechtsextremen Paramilitärs und den von den USA im Rahmen des «Plan Colombia» unterstützten Streitkräften. In dieser aufgewühlten Situation wollte Betancourt zugunsten der unbeteiligten Zivilbevölkerung vor Ort Partei ergreifen. Dabei hatte sie die Situation falsch eingeschätzt. Sie galt als dialogfreudige Vermittlerin zu den Farc, mit deren Führungsspitze sie mehrmals zusammengetroffen war. Jetzt ist sie das Faustpfand der Aufständischen. Diese wollen die Regierung zwingen, ein Gesetz über den Austausch von gefangenen Guerilleros gegen entführte Politiker, Soldaten und Polizisten zu verabschieden.

In den letzten Jahren hat Ingrid Betancourt am eigenen Leib erfahren, was es heisst, sich in Kolumbien politisch zu exponieren. Sich gegen Korruption stark zu machen, für Veränderungen im Staatsapparat und soziale Reformen einzustehen, hat ihr immer wieder Drohungen, nicht zuletzt vom politisch tonangebenden Establishment, eingebracht. Einem Attentat ist die rebellische, manchmal allzu naive Frau, die an der Pariser Science-Po, der Elitehochschule für politische Wissenschaften, studiert hat, einmal knapp entkommen. Ihre beiden Kinder leben aus Sicherheitsgründen getrennt von der Mutter im Ausland. Gegen die traditionellen Wahlmaschinerien der Liberalen und der Konservativen hatte Frau Betancourts Sprengkandidatur um die Präsidentschaft nie eine Chance. In Umfragen lag sie bei knapp zwei Prozent. Trotz Geiselhaft können die Wähler für sie stimmen. Dies bestimmt ein Ende letzten Jahres verabschiedetes, wohl nur in Kolumbien denkbares Gesetz.

2 International

In Kürze

Brisanter irischer Korruptionsbericht

Köpferollen in Polens Regierung

Die Uno will in Asylstreit vermitteln

Briefbomben in Mailänder Post

Farc-Guerilla zeigt Geiseln auf Video

Afrikas Hoffnung auf Frieden

In Durban wird die Afrikanische Union aus der Taufe gehoben

Nach 39 Jahren soll am kommenden Dienstag in Südafrika die Organisation für die Einheit Afrikas durch die Afrikanische Union ersetzt werden. Ob dies den erhofften Neuanfang auf dem Kontinent signalisiert, bleibt abzuwarten.

Treffen der Vilnius-Staaten zum Nato-Beitritt

Afghanischer Vizepräsident bei Anschlag in Kabul getötet

Abschied von Kohl und seiner Garde

Im Deutschen Bundestag haben sich vergangene Woche einige Spitzenpolitiker verabschiedet. Sie werden bei den Wahlen im September nicht mehr antreten. Einige haben die Jahre der Ära Kohl entscheidend mitgeprägt.

International 3

Friedenssicherung Blauhelme werden zunehmend verdrängt durch multinationale Kampfverbände

Neues Krisenmanagement im Balkan

Die Balkanstaaten sehen sich heute vermehrt einer privatisierten Gewalt gegenüber. Nato und EU versuchen ihre Friedenssicherung dieser neuen Bedrohungslage anzupassen.

Schwache Staaten

Verschiedene Trends

Will London den Frieden privatisieren?

Die britische Regierung zieht in Betracht, lizenzierte Söldner-Firmen an Konfliktherden für Stabilität sorgen zu lassen und so die angespannten eigenen Ressourcen zu ergänzen.

US-Generäle als Berater von Söldnern

International news pages (above) and a section called Background (opposite).

Front pages of the Science (left) and Culture (opposite) sections.

97

NZZ am Sonntag • 17. März 2002

NZZ am Sonntag

Wissen

Atomstrom

Kernenergie hat eine neue Zukunft – dank sicheren Kugelhaufenreaktoren.
Seite 99

Kultstätte des Stiers

Das Rätsel um die Höhle von Zillis ist gelöst: Hier verehrten die Römer Mithras.
Seite 101

Daniel Bernoulli

Der berühmte Basler Mathematiker und seine bizarren Familienverhältnisse.
Seite 103

Pilzmekka Schweiz

Im Kanton Neuenburg ist das weltweit erste Mycorama geplant: ein Museum der Pilze.
Seite 106

Fürsorgliche Tiere

Je tiefere Löcher Erdhörnchen graben, desto fetter werden ihre Kinder.
Seite 111

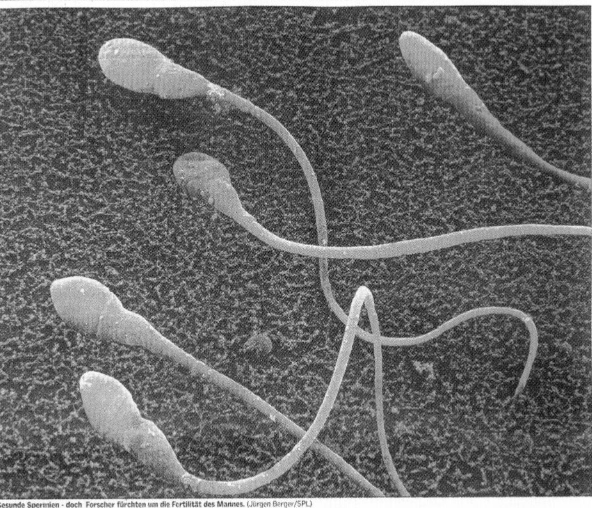

Gesunde Spermien – doch Forscher fürchten um die Fertilität des Mannes. (Jürgen Berger/SPL)

Was ist mit den Spermien los?

Die Fruchtbarkeit von Schweizer Rekruten soll getestet werden. *Von Matthias Meili*

Rekruten sind für vieles gut: Man kann sie auf ihre Intelligenz testen. Man kann sie auch laufen, klettern und schwimmen lassen. Oder aber man nimmt sie als das, was sie sind, nämlich geschlechstreife Männer mit der Aufgabe, einmal Kinder zu zeugen, und testet ihre Fruchtbarkeit. Genau das möchten jetzt Schweizer Forscher tun.

Im Rahmen des Nationalen Forschungsprogramms «Hormonaktive Substanzen: Wirkungen auf Tiere, Menschen und Ökosysteme» (NFP50, siehe Kasten) plant der Lausanner Reproduktionsmediziner Marc Germond in Zusammenarbeit mit der Armee eine Reihenuntersuchung zur Fitness der Spermien von Schweizer Männern. Das Projekt ist bis ins Detail ausgefeilt und hat alle wissenschaftlichen Hürden geschafft, wie Philippe Trinchan vom Schweizerischen Nationalfonds auf Anfrage bestätigt. Die zuständige Ethikkommission hat ihre prinzipielle Zustimmung erklärt. Der Entscheid des Militärdepartementes steht noch aus.

Die Frage, ob die Fruchtbarkeit bei Männern generell abnimmt, ist seit geraumer Zeit heiss umstritten. Das ist nicht selbstverständlich. Denn bis weit in die zweite Hälfte des vergangenen Jahrhunderts wurde für alles, was mit Fortpflanzung und deren Misslingen zu tun hat, die Frau verantwortlich gemacht. Nichts könnte falscher sein. Viele Studien, die vor allem im Zuge der modernen Reproduktionstechnologien gemacht wurden, haben gezeigt, dass die «Schuld» in der Hälfte der Fälle beim Mann zu suchen ist. Ein – aus heutiger Sicht – einleuchtendes Ergebnis. Doch laut Marc Germond wird das Problem der männlichen Unfruchtbarkeit immer noch massiv unterschätzt.

Pro Sekunde produziert ein gesunder Mann in seinen Hoden Tausende von Samenzellen. Bei der Ejakulation werden – nach einigen Tagen sexueller Abstinenz – zwei bis sechs Milliliter der milchig-weissen, Vitamin-C-reichen und leicht basischen Suspension ausgestossen, kaum mehr als ein halber Esslöffel. In jedem Milliliter Samenflüssigkeit sollten mindestens vierzig Millionen Samenzellen sein. Fällt die Gesamtzahl unter zwanzig Millionen leidet der Mann an Oligozoospermie oder reduzierter Fruchtbarkeit. Sinkt der Bestand unter fünf Millionen Spermien pro Milliliter, wird Unfruchtbarkeit diagnostiziert.

Vor genau zehn Jahren hatte der dänische Kinderarzt Niels Skakkebaek die Debatte um die sinkende Fruchtbarkeit der Männer in den Industrienationen neu entfacht. In seiner berühmten Meta-Studie, die er im renommierten Fachblatt «British Medical Journal» veröffentlichte, stellte er bei der Auswertung von 61 seit den dreissiger Jahren erschienenen Arbeiten (mit über 150 000 Probanden) über die Spermienqualität und -quantität fest, dass die Anzahl Spermien pro Milliliter bei Männern der westlichen Welt seit den dreissiger Jahren durchschnittlich um drei Prozent pro Jahr gesunken ist.

Skakkebaeks Arbeit inspirierte andere Forscher zu weiteren Studien. In der Folge traf aus vielen Ländern ähnlich deprimierende Kunde ein. Doch gleichzeitig schien in anderen Teilen der Welt – Finnland, gewisse Regionen der USA, aber auch Frankreich – die Fruchtbarkeit, zumindest was die Menge und Vitalität der Spermien betraf, nicht zu stagnieren, sondern zum Teil sogar zuzunehmen. Die Kritik an allen Studien liess nicht lange auf sich warten. Eine holländische Forschergruppe um Aldert H. Piersma kam vor allem zu einem Schluss: Alle bisherigen Studien sind nur bedingt aussagekräftig gewesen, weil die getesteten Männer schlicht nicht repräsentativ waren. Viele Daten stammten aus Fruchtbarkeitskliniken, deren Kunden selbstverständlich an irgendwelchen Fruchtbarkeitsstörungen litten. Oft sei das Alter und der allgemeine Gesundheitszustand nicht berücksichtigt oder die Zeit der sexuellen Abstinenz vor der Probennahme nur ungenügend kontrolliert worden.

Skakkebaek hat darauf Testpersonen gesucht, die am ehesten den Durchschnitt der männlichen Gesellschaft widerspiegeln: Soldaten. Vor wenigen Monaten veröffentlichte er die Ergebnisse einer Nachfolgestudie mit über 700 Dänen im Alter zwischen 18 und 20 Jahren, die er bei der Aushebung zum Militärdienst zur Samenabgabe bat. Ergebnis: Selbst bei einer strengen Kontrolle der sexuellen Abstinenzfrist lag die Spermienkonzentration bei fast der

► Fortsetzung Seite 99

Den Hormonteufelchen auf der Spur

Hormonaktive Gifte, auch endokrine Disruptoren genannt, beeinflussen das Hormonsystem des Körpers und somit sein Signalsystem. Sie können deshalb schon in äusserst geringen Konzentrationen schädlich sein. An Fischen und Reptilien wurden direkte Auswirkungen schon mehrfach festgestellt. Wie die Zusammenhänge und Mechanismen genau beschaffen sind, ist aber weitgehend unbekannt. Um das Problem fachübergreifend anzugehen, hat der Nationalfonds das Nationale Forschungsprogramm 50 (NFP50) «Hormonaktive Stoffe: Bedeutung für Menschen, Tiere und Ökosysteme» zusammengestellt. Für fünf Jahre werden Forschungsvorhaben mit insgesamt 15 Millionen Franken unterstützt. Bisher hat der Nationalfonds 17 Projekte bewilligt, unter anderem für die Erforschung der molekularen Mechanismen und der Folgen auf Ökosysteme und auf Menschen und für die Entwicklung besserer Analysemethoden. In einer späteren Phase soll die «Risikobeurteilung» in den Vordergrund rücken.

Am 22. April findet an der Uni Zürich eine öffentliche Tagung statt, um den aktuellen Stand der Forschung zu präsentieren. (www.snf.ch/NFP/NFP50/Home_d.html)

Fische in Not: Bachforelle (Ullstein)

Space for ideas

The Science and Culture sections are more spacious and focused than the news pages, balancing white space against dense type, with a single boldly cropped photograph dominating the page, and smaller cropped or silhouetted visual elements clearly subordinate.

NZZ am Sonntag

Kultur

Marcel Duchamp: Roue de Bicyclette (Pro Litteris/AKG)

Bester Film? Beste Regie? Robert Altmans «Gosford Park» hat sieben Oscar-Nominationen. (Fabrice Trombert/Retna)

Der Herr von Gosford Park

Robert Altman lässt Agatha Christie und Jean Renoir sich begegnen, hält Englands beste Darstellerriege bei Laune – und uns auch. *Von Martin Walder*

Sir William McCordle ist das, was man einen Kotzbrocken nennt: *Owner of Gosford Park. New money. Title from wife.* So schmeichelt ihm das Personenverzeichnis des Films. Ein autistischer Patriarch mit Schosshund – der schrötige Michael Gambon ist Spezialist für diese Rollen. Die Gouvernante Elsie (Emily Watson) wüsste mehr, Gattin Lady Sylvia (Kristin Scott Thomas) auch, aber die eine darf und die andere will nichts sagen. Als Sir William tot in seiner Bibliothek aufgefunden wird, mag kaum jemand weinen. Aber dass es einstmals Tränen gegeben hat und wo und in welcher Weise, enträtselt der Film wie beiläufig und offenbart dabei sein eigentliches Geheimnis.

Das Haus von Gosford Park mit seinen Salons und Treppenhäusern, Zimmern und Kellern; seine Bewohner und Jagd-Weekend-Gäste samt Personal: Sie sind die Protagonisten. Lauter Hauptrollen, Nebenrollen gibt es keine. *Above stairs* die Welt der feinen Gesellschaft und *below stairs* die Welt des Dienstpersonals. Zwei soziale Systeme unter einem Dach, sexuell natürlich durchlässig (was der Film blendend kalt zeigt), beide hierarchisch strukturiert, das untere noch viel strenger und komplizierter als das obere, wie Robert Altman im Gespräch betont.

Mord – doppelt gemoppelt

Er hat sich kundig gemacht. Als Amerikaner in England die britische Klassengesellschaft in einer bestimmten historischen Zeitspanne nicht richtig zu zeigen, könne man sich schlicht nicht leisten. Ein Butler, eine Haushälterin und ein Koch, alle weit in ihren Achtzigern, waren ständig auf dem Drehplatz und haben die Schauspieler beraten.

Eigentlich könnte der 77-jährige Regiemeister aus Kansas City (wie sein anglophiler Kollege James Ivory) selber gut als englischer Landadliger durchgehen: Er gibt sich distinguiert und auch beim hundertsten Interview geduldig. Sir Robert persönlich. Sagt er dann aber *Gasford* statt Gosford Park, hat uns Amerika gleich wieder.

Zum Projekt gekommen ist es auf Anstoss des Produzenten Bob Balaban, der im Film mitspielt: «Damals nannten wir es ‹*Ten Little Indians* trifft *La règle du jeu*›.» Die Koordinaten Agatha Christie und Jean Renoir sind gesetzt. So einschlägig Ambiente und Personal sind, so wenig ist das *Whodunit?* im Agatha-Christie-Stil jedoch wirklich ernst zu nehmen. Ein Mord, wiewohl doppelt gemoppelt, genügt. Der Pfeifen rauchende Kommissar (Stephen Fry) tritt marginal in Erscheinung und erweist sich als blasierter Trottel; ein kluges Paar Zimmermädchenaugen hat längst viel mehr gesehen und erkannt.

«Angelpunkt des Dramas», sagt Altman, «ist die soziale Struktur der Menschen im Haus, und erst im Verlauf der Arbeit hat sich ergeben, dass auch ein Mord passiert.» So hätte denn «Gosford Park» vielleicht vom *Whodunit-Genre* die ironische Natur und von Renoirs gewalttätig unterspülten Konventionen der *règles du jeu* die sozialkritische Statur?

Die Reverenzen an diesen epochalen Film sind klar: die Jagdgesellschaft, der mit tödlichen Folgen über die gesellschaftlichen Standesgrenzen und moralischen Ambivalenzen hinwegspielende Zufall. Doch bleibt es auch hier bei der lässig knappen Verbeugung. Renoirs Film spielt 1939, unmittelbar vor dem Zweiten Weltkrieg, «Gosford Park» im November 1932, wenige Wochen vor dem Reichstagsbrand jenseits des Kanals. Warum?

Nicht Hitler (und die Haltung der englischen Aristokratie zu ihm) sollte ins Zentrum rücken, sagt der Regisseur; ihn interessierte der Umbruch im sozialen und im Bildungsgefüge der Bedienstetenklasse. Junge Mädchen vom Lande, ehedem ihrer Herrschaft auf Gedeih und Verderb ausgeliefert, oft als ledige Mütter, hätten in der Zwischenkriegszeit mehr und mehr alternative Möglichkeiten in der Stadt erhalten – beispielsweise in Manufakturen, doziert er vielsagend mit Seitenblick auf seinen Film. Denn Sir William hat da seine eigenen Usanzen.

Wieder gelingt es Altman, in einer Verschränkung von *short cuts* auf Geschichten und Figuren einen sozialen Kosmos zu entwerfen und zum Vibrieren zu bringen, bis sich Risse ausbreiten. Gesteuert ist diese komplexe Dramaturgie durch den Blick von mehreren Kameras und überlappend geführte, nach Bedarf anwählbare Tonspuren. Sein Markenzeichen seit «Nashville».

In seinem satirischen Porträt der Country-Metropole war er 1975 berühmt damit geworden, hatte Erfolg und liess vor zehn Jahren in «The Player» unter Aufbietung einer ganzen Stargarde in Statistenfunktion ein Bündel herrlicher Blitze auf die selbstverliebte Hollywood Community herunterfahren – auf jenes Hollywood, mit dem sich die grosse Spielernatur Altman immer schwer getan hat. Und umgekehrt, die ganzen achtziger Jahre hindurch. Doch darüber mag er sich eigentlich gar nicht mehr auslassen: «Die sind schon okay in den Studios; sie tun, was sie tun.»

Dem Adel zur Hand gehen: Maggie Smith (oben), Kristin Scott Thomas. (pwe)

Feiner Voyeurismus

«Gosford Park» ist ganz in England produziert worden: «Die beste Erfahrung, die ich je gemacht habe – mit der Technik, mit den Schauspielern.» Ein exquisiteres Ensemble ist denn auch kaum vorstellbar: Sir Derek Jacobi und Sir Michael Gambon, Dame Eileen Atkins und Dame Maggie Smith (in einer triumphal unterspielten Snob-Satire). Und Helen Mirren, die wunderbar mausgraue und doch dominante Haushälterin: Ihr gebührt die Krone – und ihr gilt auch das wenige wahre Gefühl, das Altman sich leistet; zu viel Empathie ist ja seine Sache nie gewesen. Mirrens kurze Tränen am Schluss wirken nur um so stärker nach.

Wie ist der amerikanische Filmemacher mit den englischen Schauspielern zurechtgekommen? Nur Lob. Gerade weil sie im Gegensatz zu vielen US-Kollegen Bühnenerfahrung mitbringen und Altman sie eher der multiplen Wahrnehmung einer Bühnenaufführung ausgesetzt sehen will als dem fokussierten Blick des Films: «Sie sollen auch nicht zum Publikum hin spielen, sondern dieses soll ihnen beim Spielen zuschauen.» Hübsches Lehrstück: wie das bühnengemäss Gedachte zum Filmischen werden kann.

Was auch für uns, das Publikum, die echte, feine Art des Voyeurismus ist – mit Auge und Ohr für alle Sottisen und Snobistereien. Man ist angesichts des geballt aufkreuzenden Personals von «Gosford Park» massiv gefordert, um nicht zu sagen überfordert, bei aller Lust. Den alten Herrn kümmert's nicht. Er hat seinen Spass gehabt, diesen Film zu drehen: eine Laune, «just a caprice».

LE DEVOIR

À VOIR

LE DEVOIR, LE VENDREDI 17 SEPTEMBRE 1993

Théâtre

Début de saison. Rien de marquant en ce début de saison théâtrale. Mais ici et là quelques morceaux réussis: Jean-Louis Millette dans le rôle de Clov, avec son métier, sauve du désastre un *Fin de partie* bien académique au Café de la Place; Normand Canac-Marquis se donne à fond dans une interprétation nerveuse du meurtrier Gary Gilmore dans une pièce trop anecdotique sur cette histoire qui intéressa l'Amérique des années 76 et 77, *Gilmore, Que vaut la vie d'un homme?* à La Licorne. Mais le seul spectacle à recommander demeure *La Trahison orale* de Mauricio Kagel mis en scène par Denis Marleau du Théâtre Ubu, au Monument National.
Robert Lévesque

Danse

FIND. Un avant-goût du Festival International de Nouvelle Danse 93, au cinéma Parallèle, qui diffuse, à partir d'aujourd'hui, 19 heures, un cycle de vidéos de danse, présentant plusieurs des chorégraphes invités cet automne. À voir aussi, les premières représentations de la série *Émergences* de l'Espace Tangente, dédiée aux jeunes créateurs, jusqu'à dimanche.
Valérie Lehmann

Opéra

Le Vaisseau fantôme. Les choeurs, l'OSM dirigé par Spiros Argiris, la mise en scène de Bernard Uzan font du *Vaisseau fantôme*, cet opéra romantique de Richard Wagner, une production exceptionnelle. La prestation de la basse Victor von Halem en Daland est remarquable et les autres interprètes défendent fort bien leur personnage. À voir absolument à l'Opéra de Montréal, Place des Arts, samedi 20 h et aussi les 22 et 25 septembre.
Marie Laurier

Musique classique

Sons et Brioches. Pour leur premier Sons et Brioches, les Jeunesses musicales du Canada offrent un concert gratuit dimanche à 11h sur l'esplanade de la PdA, avec une initiation à l'art du *taiko*, ou tambour japonais avec le groupe montréalais Arashi Daiko.
75 ans en chant choral. La Société chorale de Saint-Lambert souligne dimanche à midi son 75e anniversaire sous forme d'un brunch-récital-bénéfice au 250 rue Saint-Laurent, à Saint-Lambert. Le directeur artistique David Christiani dévoilera les activités de la prochaine saison.
Sarah Chang. On connaît l'engouement de Charles Dutoit pour la violoniste Sarah Chang, engouemenet qu'il a communiqué au public de l'OSM. Le mæstro nous la présente à la télévision radio-canadienne dimanche à 15h. Aussi un reportage sur l'IRCAM et la présentation des *Oiseaux exotiques* d'Olivier Messiaen.
Marie Laurier

Rock

Marc Cohn. On l'a bombardé James Taylor des années quatre-vingt-dix, et on n'a pas tort. Comme Taylor, Cohn est un calme, un réfléchi, un introspectif, un brillant auteur-compositeur-interprète qui chante sur un ton feutré. Mais alors que Taylor est un Nordiste de Boston, nourri de *doo-wop*, Cohn est un véritable Sudiste, avec le Mississippi qui lui coule dans les veines. Son étonnant amalgame de pop, de folk, de country, de blues et de gospel en fait foi. Dans le genre, *Walking In Memphis*, la chanson qui l'a lancé en 1990, vaut à elle seule le déplacement au Club Soda, ce soir à 20h30.
Sylvain Cormier

Arts visuels

Anne Deguelle. Miroir, miroir dis-moi qui est Montréal... Ce que je dis deux fois est vrai, écrit Anne Deguelle, une artiste française qui expose pour la première fois ici des œuvres *in situ*, des vues tirées sur verre qui parlent avec des monochromes, un lieu fictif qui confronte le réel, une mouvance architecturale qui ne manque ni de piquant ni de poésie. À la Galerie Yves le Roux Art Contemporain, 5505 boulevard Saint-Laurent, espace 4136. Jusqu'au 2 octobre.
Marie-Michèle Cron

Cinéma

Trahir, de Radu Mihaileanu, dont c'est le premier long métrage. Un écrivain dissident roumain jeté en prison retrouve la liberté et la respectabilité en vendant son âme au diable, c'est-à-dire à la Securitate. L'imparable emprise d'un régime totalitaire sur ses citoyens pris en otages. Ce film, éprouvant pour les spectateurs, a d'ailleurs remporté le Grand Prix des Amériques lors de la récente édition du Festival du film de Montréal. Terrifiant.
Francine Laurendeau

PHOTO LA FONDATION DE DANSE MARGIE GILLIS

Margie Gillis, la danse de la vie

«Un théatre, c'est le lieu idéal pour le rituel et la célébration qui constituent l'essentiel de ma danse. Spirituel, intellectuel et émotionnel doivent s'y mélanger. La scène offre une opportunité unique de parler de notre condition et d'être en connection avec les choses qui nous donnent la grâce, le courage, la beauté, l'amour.» Ainsi parle Margie Gillis. Parce que sa vision de la danse ne prend pas le chemin habituel, de ses chorégraphies et de ses interprétations découlent des sensations inattendues. Lorsqu'un quelconque mortel regarde cette femme déployer ses ailes sur un plateau, une sorte de magie s'opère instantanément. Margie possède un charme qui confère à l'envoûtement. Dans chacun de ses gestes, empreints tantôt d'une lenteur extrême, tantôt d'une légèreté coquine, réside l'énergie vitale. Comme les thèmes favoris de l'artiste sont la mort, la tendresse, la vieillesse, la naissance, l'amour, la solitude... chaque danse n'est pas loin de signifier l'accord parfait, et davantage encore lorsque la chorégraphie a été composée par un œil extérieur, c'est-à-dire quand la danseuse se permet de se perdre dans les méandres de l'interprétation.

Dans le spectacle que la Margie Gillis Fondation propose ce soir et demain à la Place des Arts figurent quatre solos isssus du répertoire classique de la danseuse, particulièrement représentatif du style Gillis: *Mara*, imaginé par Stéphanie Ballard, qui conte peut-être la solitude d'une sirène, *Variations* et *Slipstreams*, chorégraphiés par Margie Gillis, qui chacun à leur manière expriment liberté et fébrilité, *Valsig Mathilda*, signé de Margie également, qui met en scène l'étrange passion d'une femme amoureuse.

Un cinquième solo inscrit au programme a été créé, début janvier 1993, par le danseur Christopher Gillis — le frère et l'ami aujourd'hui disparu. Il s'intitule *Landscape*, raconte la douleur d'une femme face à la maladie, la souffrance dans l'impuissance.

Mais pour célébrer dignement son retour à Montréal après deux ans d'absence, l'artiste a également choisi de présenter à la Place des Arts un nouveau duo et un quintet inédit. *Vers la Glace*, une œuvre composée à trois, duo symbole parce qu'il a toujours été dansé par les Gillis frère et sœur, est joué par Margie et le meilleur ami de son frère, Juan, membre de la Paul Taylor Company. .

A gathering, la dernière création de Stéphanie Ballard, est interprété par cinq femmes. Giocanda Barbuto, Andréa Boardman, Danielle Sturk et Suzanne Trépanier y donnent la réplique à Margie Gillis. Plus qu'une exploration du monde féminin, il s'agit, aux yeux de la créatrice canadienne, «d'un rituel d'initation surtout, qui explique l'idée du passage et le phénomène de la transformation».

Il faut dire que depuis la mort de son complice de frère, emporté par le sida cet été, Margie Gillis n'a pas cessé de chercher comment continuer la route entamée avec ce dernier. Danser pour la cause du sida était pendant les deux dernières années une préoccupation immédiate de cette missionnaire de l'Art. À ce titre, elle a participé à de nombreux galas-bénéfices, partout dans le monde. «J'ai essayé d'aider, je ne sais pas si j'en suis capable, c'est un défi pour moi de continuer à lutter pour les choses fondamentales de la vie. Ma vision de la danse ne change pas, elle se perpétue au contraire à travers la notion de célébration. Mais... en ce moment précis de septembre, je ne pense qu'à la Marche pour le sida du 3 octobre organisée à Montréal, pour laquelle je suis "ambassadrice". Là est l'important pour moi.»

Valérie Lehmann

À FAIRE

LES POMMES

La tête dans les feuilles, avec un bon chandail de laine, à ramasser tout ce qu'on a besoin pour la meilleure gelée de l'année, quel plaisir! La saison des pommes bat son plein, et c'est l'activité idéale pour la famillé, puisque plusieurs producteurs encouragent le public à l'auto-cueillette. De toute façon, aller acheter des pommes sur le bord de la route peut-être le prétexte à une ballade en auto si la fin de semaine est belle. La majorité des producteurs se retrouvent dans la Montérégie, dans les secteurs de Saint-Hilaire et Rougemont, quoiqu'on peut également en trouver plusieurs dans la région de Hemmingford près de la frontière américaine, et dans la région d'Oka. Renseignements: Fédération des producteurs de pommes du Québec, 679-0530.
Paul Cauchon

À LIRE

Tout Denys Arcand. À la sortie de son film *Love and Human Remains*, Denys Arcand a refusé d'accorder des entrevues à la presse. La raison en est fort simple: il a tout dit à Michel Coulombe. Les Éditions du Boréal viennent de publier ces entretiens dans un court ouvrage intitulé *Denys Arcand, La vraie nature du cinéaste*. Le cinéaste y explique largement sa vision du monde, avec une franchise qui en dérange déjà plusieurs. «Si l'anglais doit être la langue dominante au XXIe siècle, ce sera comme la lave d'un volcan. On pourra soit être enseveli, soit être enseveli en protestant», dit-il. Toute la ville en parle. À lire de toute urgence!
Pierre Cayouette

LE MARATHON

Surveillez bien vos déplacements dimanche dans les rues des villes hautes d'Outremont, Mont-Royal et Saint-Laurent. Ils pourraient être perturbés par la tenue du marathon de Montréal. Quelque 6000 coureurs sont attendus et le public est invité à applaudir ces braves en les regardant bien en toute sécurité sur les abords du parcours. Le départ se fait à 9h, face à la station de métro Édouard-Montpetit et les participants étrangers d'Europe, d'Asie et des États-Unis se mêleront aux Québécois pour lui donner ce caractère international que l'on recherche et aussi en faire une fête de la bonne forme physique. C'est aussi télévisé. Noter que les chicanes et les barrières qui bloquent ou détournent la circulation seront levées en fin d'après-midi. Avertis d'avance, les automobilistes peuvent davantage être conciliants et s'éviter une crise d'apoplexie.
Marie Laurier

LES Z'AMOURS

Hot-dogs, bière et odeur de championnat, samedi soir, au Stade Olympique, où le Québécois Denis Boucher, le petit nouveau des Expos, sera le lanceur partant face aux redoutables Phillies de Philadelphie. Pour la chaleur de la foule, l'ambiance et un aperçu — sait-on jamais? — de la folie qui s'emparerait des amateurs si jamais l'équipe montréalaise se rendait jusqu'au bout.
Benoît Munger

À PIED

La rue Saint-Paul, entre Saint-Laurent et McGill, dans le Vieux-Montréal, est laissée au piétons durant tout le week-end. L'idée est de permettre aux familles de visiter tranquillement ce tronçon de rue historique et de flâner devant le travail des artisans installés sur les trottoirs. On peut aussi arrêter voir le Théâtre Biscuit pour enfants et l'animation d'époque du Musée Pointe-à-Callière. On propose également une exposition de voitures anciennes, des cerf-volants, de la musique et des clowns.
Stéphane Baillargeon

CHAMPIGNONS

Cueillir ou ne pas cueillir tel ou tel champignon? Pour s'y retrouver et garder la santé, il suffit d'aller s'initier à la clinique Provigo du Jardin botanique samedi (10h à 14h) et dimanche (midi à 17h), à la grande serre et à la salle Jacques-Rousseau. Par ailleurs, dès midi, durant les deux jours du week-end, le Pavillon Japonais offre des séance de dégustation de légumes nippons, à frais minimes.
Stéphane Baillargeon

Profile: *Le Devoir*

John D. Berry

Redefining what's "classic" in the thoughtful voice of Québec

Opposite: The "what's happening" section has a double pun in its title: *à voir* (to see) sounds much like *avoir* (to have) and also echoes the paper's name: *Le Devoir.*

"I think after *USA Today*," says Lucie Lacava, "newspapers went a little too far. Everybody wanted that colorful look with graphs and charts all over the place. I tend to be very classic in my approach to typography and design."

With the highly respected French-language Montreal daily *Le Devoir*, one of the most literate newspapers in North America, a classic approach was clearly in order. But "classic" does not mean dull or staid. With Lacava's 1993 redesign, *Le Devoir* presented a lively and startling new face to the world – one with more reference to the look of European newspapers than is usually seen in North America. It has been much imitated since.

Le Devoir has nearly a century of history as the intellectual voice of francophone Québec, so any redesign had to reflect the paper's traditions as well as the directions its editors wanted it to go in. "Like the city it serves," says Lacava, "a newspaper also has a history that a designer has to respect." But the paper was in deep trouble, and management was hoping that a dramatic new design could help pull *Le Devoir* back from the brink.

"In the early '90s," says Lacava, "the paper was in a very difficult financial situation; its circulation was at an all-time low. Even though it was still read by the political and intellectual elite, it no longer appealed to the younger generation, who perceived it as institutional and stodgy. It was practically on its death bed. As one columnist once wrote, the redesign was going to make it or break it for *Le Devoir*." The publisher at the time, Lise Bissonnette, led a two-year restructuring plan that included the sale of the historic building where the paper had been housed for several decades, to help finance the move to newly renovated rental premises and a new page-makeup system, as well as the redesign itself.

"The redesign was first commissioned to an agency, but the early prototypes were rejected by the union of journalists," explains Lacava. "Four months before the launch, I was hired as in-house design consultant to help implement the redesign. After having seen the final version of the prototype, I tried to convince management that it was preferable to stay with the old design rather than adopting the new proposal – it was wrong, and it didn't reflect the personality of the paper; they had totally missed the mark.

"But the relaunch date had already been announced, and there was no going back. With only four months left to go, management asked me to take over the redesign task."

Lacava had neither the time nor the budget to get custom typefaces designed, so she chose

The nameplate of *Le Devoir* as it has evolved through the years: 1910 (top), 1940 (middle), and 1950 (bottom). Opposite: a full front page from 1993.

LE DEVOIR

Directeur: HENRI BOURASSA — FAIS CE QUE DOIS!

La Canonisation des M… fixée au 2…

LE DEVOIR

Le DEVOIR est membre de la "Canadian Press", de l'"A.B.C." et de la "C.D.N.A."

Les villes françaises de plus de 20,000 âmes déclarées "villes ouvertes"

L'armée française poursuit sa résistance — Les Allemands à Cherbourg et à Rennes

Les puissants forts de la ligne Maginot, au nord de Bâle, abandonnés par leurs garnisons

LE DEVOIR

Directeur: Gérard FILION — FAIS CE QUE DOIS — Rédacteur en chef: Omer HEROUX

MONTREAL, VENDREDI, 23 JUIN 1950

Washington met ses armes les plus nouvelles à la disposition de l'Europe

Ce n'est qu'en agissant ainsi qu'on évitera de mobiliser autant d'hommes que la Russie — Connally présente le bill de réarmement européen au Sénat

Trois jeunes gens seront soumis à la peine du fouet

"Pas d'espoir de paix tant que Moscou ne laissera pas les autres régimes subsister à côté du sien"

LE DEVOIR

Vol. LXXXIV — No 18 · Montréal, samedi 23 janvier 1993 · 4 CAHIERS — 1,30$ + TPS + TVQ

CULTURE

Une grande rentrée... ordinaire

Oui, il y a, ou plutôt il y avait la récession dont les échos se font encore entendre derrière les rideaux de scène. Mais, malgré les restrictions et les compressions budgétaires, c'est à un étonnant foisonnement de spectacles que nous assisterons dans les mois qui viennent. Notre Cahier du samedi y est consacré.

Arthur Buies, le gentleman chroniqueur

Grand orphelin, bohème et célibataire, Arthur Buies passa sa vie dans l'instabilité complète, entre le bonheur de connaître et le mal de vivre. L'édition de ses chroniques par les Presses de l'Université de Montréal nous offre la prose d'un des esprits les plus originaux du 19e siècle québécois, écrit Robert Lévesque.

Page C-21

ÉCONOMIE

Nationair complice d'Air Canada?

Et si Nationair se faisait complice d'Air Canada? Le président de Nationair résume la situation: «Je tire sur le marché, j'affaiblis davantage Canadien, Air Canada réplique en prétextant réagir à la concurrence, et il tue Canadien».

À lire en page B1

ÉDUCATION

J'aime l'école

Notre cahier spécial ÉDUCATION de 12 pages

Après deux mois de flottement
Mulroney se ressaisit

- Il resterait en selle pour la prochaine élection
- Les aspirants doivent rentrer dans le rang

Chantal Hébert
de notre bureau d'Ottawa

MALGRÉ les sondages et une conjoncture difficile, Brian Mulroney aurait résolu de rester en selle pour une troisième campagne électorale, ont indiqué au DEVOIR plusieurs sources bien placées dans la capitale fédérale.

Après deux mois d'incertitude, le premier ministre, indique-t-on, mettra son parti et ses députés sur un pied d'alerte la semaine prochaine en vue du déclenchement d'une élection n'importe quand à compter du 1er avril prochain.

Un remaniement ministériel d'envergure, un Discours du trône et un budget précéderaient le déclenchement d'une élection générale.

Le premier ministre mettra son parti sur un pied d'alerte la semaine prochaine

Dans les rangs de l'opposition, on s'attend généralement à ce que le vote ait lieu dès au mois de juin plutôt qu'à l'extrême limite de l'automne prochain.

En attendant, depuis le milieu de la semaine, des signaux destinés à mettre fin aux rumeurs de départ qui entourent Brian Mulroney depuis son échec référendaire ont commencé à être envoyés.

Le chef de cabinet du premier ministre Hugh Segal aurait ainsi enjoint en termes «sans équivoque» les principaux aspirants à sa succession de mettre un terme à leurs campagnes officieuses, indique-t-on de source ministérielle.

Quatre ministres, Perrin Beatty, Kim Campbell, Michael Wilson et Jean Charest, avaient commencé à tâter le terrain d'une course au leadership.

Après plusieurs semaines de flottements, l'entourage du premier ministre serait également rassuré sur ses intentions.

Voir page A-4 : Mulroney

Première salve de Clinton contre le Canada

Washington revient à la charge dans le conflit du porc

Marie Tison
de la Presse canadienne

WASHINGTON — À peine entrée en fonction, l'administration Clinton a tiré sa première salve commerciale contre le Canada.

Tard jeudi soir, les États-Unis ont demandé une révision d'un jugement rendu en vertu de l'Accord bilatéral canado-américain qui donnait raison au Canada dans un conflit commercial sur le porc vivant.

Les États-Unis ont fait valoir que le groupe spécial d'experts responsable de ce jugement n'avait pas suivi une règle de procédure fondamentale, ou qu'il avait excédé sa juridiction.

L'administration américaine a ainsi suivi une procédure de contestation extraordinaire qui n'avait été utilisée qu'une seule autre fois, en 1991, dans un conflit sur le porc gelé et surgelé.

Le Canada avait remporté cette partie.

Selon deux spécialistes, le Québec et le Canada ne sont pas des priorités pour Clinton

Voir page A-5

Le nouveau conflit porte sur le porc vivant exporté du 1er avril 1988 au 31 mars 1989. Le département américain du Commerce a statué en juin 1991 que le programme tripartite canadien d'assistance aux producteurs de porcs vivants constituait une subvention déloyale qui permettait à ces producteurs d'écouler leur marchandise à un coût avantageux sur le marché américain.

Le 30 octobre dernier, un groupe spécial composé de cinq experts des deux pays a déterminé que ce programme, financé par le gouvernement fédéral, les provinces et les producteurs eux-mêmes, ne constituait pas une subvention déloyale. Il a ordonné au département américain du Commerce de recalculer les droits compensatoires imposés sur les exportations canadiennes de porcs vivants pour l'année 88-89 et de rembourser environ 8 millions$

Voir page A-4 : Clinton

Les jeunes du PQ veulent «brasser la cage»

Ce n'est plus le parti de la jeunesse, affirme leur président

Pierre O'Neill

INTITULÉ *Brassons la cage*, mis de l'avant par l'exécutif du comité national des jeunes du PQ, un document de réflexion porteur d'une virulente critique sera porté à l'attention des membres du conseil national du parti, dont les assises se tiennent en fin de semaine à Québec. «Le PQ n'est plus le parti de la jeunesse», proclame leur président, Christian Picard.

Le comité national des jeunes péquistes invite les dirigeants du parti à une profonde remise en question, à créer un environnement favorable aux jeunes, à élaborer une structure accueillante où ils seront associés aux grandes orientations et décisions politiques. «Nous désirons devenir le porte-parole des jeunes auprès du parti et non du parti auprès des jeunes», peut-on lire dans le document dont LE DEVOIR a obtenu copie.

Remontant jusqu'à la naissance du parti, rappelant quelques-uns des épisodes qui ont marqué son évolution, les auteurs du texte insistent sur le rôle prépondérant qui leur a toujours été dévolu dans le passé. «Non seulement les jeunes étaient-ils les bienvenus au PQ, mais ce parti était le leur.

Christian Picard, président du Comité national des jeunes du Parti québécois

Pour René Lévesque, comme pour plusieurs leaders péquistes de sa génération, le PQ était l'unique porte-parole de la jeunesse du Québec sur le plan politique.

Un préjugé favorable qui, selon eux, a prévalu aussi longtemps que le parti est demeuré dans l'opposition. «Tant que le parti ne prit pas le pouvoir, tout était permis dans l'imaginaire des jeunes. Le fossé entre le discours du parti et ce que les jeunes voulaient était quasiment inexistant. Les jeunes sentaient que leur influence était significative. Le PQ, pour un jeune de l'époque, en plus d'être un instrument de regroupement, était un lieu de haute socialisation où l'on se sentait chez soi, où le conflit intergénérationnel n'existait pas, puisque l'on possédait la force du nombre et que c'était en notre nom que l'on construirait un Québec neuf».

À travers cette analyse de l'évolution de leur parti, les jeunes péquistes constatent que leur influence a diminué, d'abord avec l'accession au

Voir page A-4 : Jeunes

Les Haïtiens commencent à se sentir moins seuls

Jesse Jackson leur apporte le soutien de la communauté noire américaine

Sylviane Tramier
Envoyée du DEVOIR

PORT AU PRINCE — S'il fallait une nouvelle preuve que décidément la communauté internationale se soucie du sort d'Haïti, elle est arrivée hier à Port-au-Prince, en la personne du révérend Jesse Jackson qui a mis pour la première fois le pied sur le sol haïtien.

Invité par la «Plate-forme haïtienne des organismes de défense des droits humains» composée de proches du président Aristide, Jesse Jackson vient renforcer la conviction qu'ont les partisans du père Aristide que leur message a trouvé un écho dans la population noire américaine. «Le traitement spécial réservé aux réfugiés haïtiens aux États-Unis est perçu comme une discrimination envers toute la communauté noire», dit Paul Dejean, animateur d'un centre d'alphabétisation et membre de la Plate-forme.

S'il était arrivé un peu plus tôt dans la journée, Jesse Jackson aurait pu assister à l'aéroport à une scène qui à elle seule résume la situation de ces réfugiés. À deux reprises hier se sont posés des avions de Miami Air, amenant chacun 171 rapatriés. Aujourd'hui, ils arrivaient des Bahamas.

En rang, deux par deux, leurs baluchons à la main, ils sont conduits

Ces Haïtiens rapatriés attendent au bureau d'Immigration de l'aéroport de Port-au-Prince. Ils font partie des quelque 2000 réfugiés qui ont été refoulés de Cuba, des Bahamas et des États-Unis depuis un mois. Le sort qu'on leur réserve aux États-Unis commence à être vu comme une forme de discrimination par la communauté noire de ce pays.

par un responsable du Haut commissariat des Nations unies aux réfugiés (HCR) dans des installations de l'aéroport à quelques centaines de mètres de l'avion. Là, un par un, ils passent devant les autorités de l'immigration haïtienne qui vérifie leur identité, puis ils reçoivent de la Croix-Rouge un sac de trente livres de vivres (de l'huile, du riz, du sucre et de l'avoine) et une allocation de sept dollars US pour prendre le *tap-tap* qui les ramènera chez eux.

Le gouvernement haïtien est là aussi, discrètement. Une élégante responsable refuse de parler à la presse, mais distribue à chaque rapatrié un petit sac de papier contenant deux paquets de biscuits soda et sur lequel est inscrit: «Bienvenue Nan Peyi ou — Ayiti Kontan Wè ou — Ayiti Bezwen ou».

Les rapatriés ont tous à peu près la même histoire à raconter: ils sont partis sur un bateau, certains ont payé 500 dollars pour leur passage. Ils ont été interceptés au bout de six à huit jours en haute mer, certains ont été déposés sur une île voisine des Bahamas. Ils ont été mis en prison, plusieurs mois, puis placés dans des camps de détention.

Sur le vol de l'après-midi, il y a beaucoup de femmes. Jeunes, la vingtaine à peine, parties seules pour Miami. Il y a Ivanise, de Saint-Louis-du-Nord, près de l'Île de la

Voir page A-4 : Haïti

FONDÉ EN 1910

LE DEVOIR

Vol. LXXXIV · No 282 — MONTRÉAL, LE LUNDI 6 DÉCEMBRE 1993 — 65¢ + TPS + TVQ / Toronto 85¢

PERSPECTIVES

Poly, entre le sens et l'insensé

Martine Turenne
Roland-Yves Carignan

L'ENTREVUE
Une dame très digne: Gretta Chambers
PAGE B 1

L'ÉCONOMIE
Semaine cruciale pour les agriculteurs
PAGE B 3

CULTURE
Les FrancoFolies, en été et dans la rue
PAGE B 7

Chirurgie dans l'espace

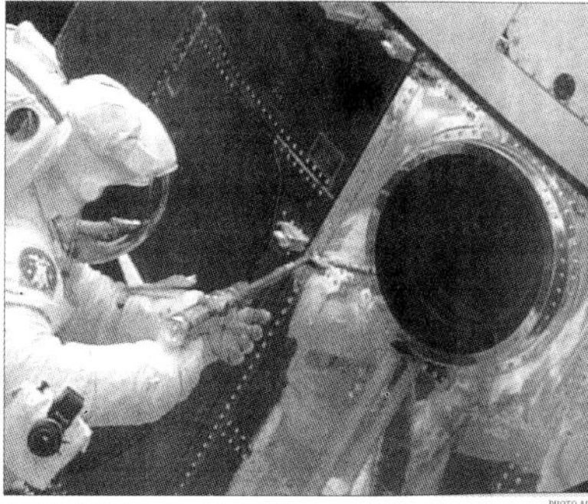

L'astronaute Jeff Hoffman travaille avec un outil électrique sur un des panneaux du télescope Hubble afin d'aller remplacer, à l'intérieur, des gyroscopes défectueux. Aujourd'hui, les astronautes doivent entrer dans l'essentiel de leur mission et aller changer les panneaux solaires du télescope.

Mission Hubble: ça roule

VOIR PAGE A 10: HUBBLE

Les hostilités reprennent entre la CSN et la FTQ

La mésentente est totale sur le projet de loi 116

SYLVAIN BLANCHARD
LE DEVOIR

Clément Godbout

Gérald Larose

VOIR PAGE A 10: HOSTILITÉS

La gauche l'emporte dans les villes italiennes

VOIR PAGE A 10: ITALIE

Les nouveaux propriétaires du Manoir Richelieu ne sont pas des hôteliers
PAGE A 4

Le maire L'Allier présente la candidature de Québec aux autorités du CIO
PAGE A 4

Le futur président mexicain sera l'homme des Canadiens

BRIGITTE MORISSETTE
COLLABORATION SPÉCIALE

VOIR PAGE A 10: MEXIQUE

Luis Donaldo Colosio: le plus sympathique aux «Latins du Grand Nord».

INDEX

Météo
Ciel variable
Max. 4
Détails en B5

Front pages from just after the introduction of the new design in 1993 (above) and from 1994 (opposite).

off-the-shelf fonts that were already available on the system: Century Old Style for headlines and text, Torino and Industrial for navigation and feature headlines. "Fortunately," she says, "my prototypes were a go-ahead from the start, since there was no time left to dwell on this latest remake."

The launch was overwhelmingly successful for the small but influential paper. A year later, according to the Audit Bureau of Circulation, *Le Devoir* had experienced, in both percentages and numbers, the largest circulation increase in Canada.

Lacava remained on the staff of *Le Devoir* for another year and a half, in a hands-on position as Assistant Managing Editor ("Rédacteur en chef adjoint, direction artistique"). During that time, she trained the entire newsroom.

Le Devoir's design is modular, built on a 24-column grid. Since French text and headlines generally take up 30% more space than English, Lacava created a design where the headlines appear in multiple layers (label/overline/headline/deck). This serves the dual purpose of keeping the main heads short and providing multiple points of entry for the reader.

The dramatic use of display type and photography throughout the paper, especially in the features sections, contrasts with and complements the sober approach to the text. The treatment of display type is consistent, from the newspaper's nameplate to the major heads in the arts section; the Torino typeface is striking, yet reminiscent of classical French typography. And the text throughout the paper is meant to be read and thought about.

"A newspaper should look like a newspaper," as Lacava put it in a profile in *Le 30*. "A newspaper should look believable, it should give an impression of immediacy,

PHOTOS JACQUES NADEAU

◆ FONDÉ EN 1910 ◆

LE DEVOIR

Vol. LXXXV - No 109★ MONTRÉAL, LE MERCREDI 11 MAI 1994 65¢ + TPS + TVQ / Toronto 85¢

PERSPECTIVES

Le *sitcom* dévastateur de Tremblay

Robert Lévesque

Sensationnel retour de Key West pour Michel Tremblay! De son hiver floridien il a ramené dans son sac à malice un pur pamphlet contre la magouille et la médiocrité dans le monde de la télévision publique, qui, dès sa lecture publique lundi dernier sur la scène du Théâtre du Nouveau Monde, a créé rien de moins que l'événement politique et théâtral de l'année culturelle.

Une salle bondée, curieuse, inquiète, jouissante, ravie, frustrée, délirante, secouée par l'audace et l'ironie pessimiste, n'a rien ménagé de ses rires, de ses cris, de ses applaudissements complices, de ses bravos d'honneur, aux huit acteurs alignés derrière des lutrins, textes en mains, qui disaient, avec des fous rires et des trébuchements, un dialogue vif, osé, franc, décapant et cynique au carré, où tout ce qui bouge dans les coulisses de la télévision publique est présenté comme pourri à l'os, pitoyable univers de protection, de fricotage et de conflit d'intérêts gigognes. On se serait cru le jour où Molière fit jouer *L'Imposteur...*, les curés et dévôts d'alors étant ici des journalistes nerveux de s'y retrouver et des producteurs inquiets de s'y reconnaître...

Événement politique dans le beau sens du terme — ce qui est relatif à la cité — parce que Tremblay, retrouvant avec *En circuit fermé* le souffle agressif de ses — et de nos — années 60, livre le premier état d'une pièce-choc comme il le fit en 1968 avec *Les Belles-soeurs*, une pièce qui cogne et dérange parce qu'elle expose des vérités gardées dans le giron des happy few, et parce qu'elle dessine à la manière de l'auteur du *Vrai monde?* ce portrait cru et saisissant d'un panier de crabes où l'homme est un loup pour l'homme, comme disait Brecht, où le pouvoir est la fin en soi pour ceux qui le courtisent, l'attrapent et s'y maintiennent comme dans la grande mécanique de l'escalier chez Shakespeare.

On se serait cru le jour où Molière fit jouer *L'Imposteur*

Événement théâtral, malgré ou à cause de ce caractère improvisé, spectacle vite préparé, livré dans une nervosité réelle, qui transformait le TNM en une agora où l'on se rassemble pour entendre le discours vif, l'histoire nouvelle d'un auteur aimé, pour voir en toute complicité un théâtre qui pouvait faire penser aux représentations vites réglées du temps du grand Will. Un théâtre où ce qui se dit et va se dire est, dans l'instant, plus important que la façon dont on le dit. Un théâtre vivant.

Pourquoi cette salle si allumée? Parce que Tremblay touche — encore une fois — un point sensible de la condition humaine, parce qu'il ose stigmatiser un monde circonscrit dans sa suffisance médiocre, et que le public veut et attend ce genre d'attentat pour compenser la rectitude politique de l'époque. On veut voir casser les habitudes d'un théâtre trop beau et trop muet. Le théâtre des années 80 et 90, pour remarquable qu'il soit esthétiquement, a tourné le dos à ses fonctions politiques. Avec *En circuit fermé* Tremblay nous y ramène, signant un pamphlet avec toute la mauvaise foi que peut contenir un pamphlet, il le disait lui-même lundi soir — on n'échappe pas au genre —, un pamphlet qui dépeint à gros traits le moteur et le fonctionnement d'un milieu — ce pourrait être tout autre milieu, l'université, les hôpitaux, etc. — où l'on abuse de son pouvoir, où l'on ne pense qu'à se remplir les poches et les narines dans une furie où la réussite finit par ressembler à l'hécatombe de ses illusions.

Dans ce vaudeville-choc — qui a l'intelligence de ressembler quant à la forme à celle des *sitcom* dont il dénonce le vide — Tremblay montre un monde qui se fait le fossoyeur de ses rêves avant de sombrer dans le trou du compromis et du profit, et c'est pour cela que, dans cette pièce où la presse va d'abord chercher à savoir qui est qui (comme dans les salons au temps de Molière), on trouvera vite que l'anecdotique est largement dépassé et que Tremblay — encore une fois — prouve qu'il est un dramaturge essentiel, qui avec un art consommé de la communication populiste (mais jamais malhonnête) jette son regard derrière les fausses apparences, débusquant le drame là où l'homme et la femme — en perpétuels combats où celle-ci manipule celui-là — sont les vaincus d'une guerre très ancienne et dont ils s'illusionnent encore sur les enjeux prochains.

On dira que Tremblay s'inscrit dans un retour du pamphlet. Depuis peu au Québec, l'utilisation du mot pamphlet est la dernière illusion à la mode. Ces pamphlets sur la droite culturelle ou l'anti-américanisme sont le fait de nouveaux moralistes qui utilisent le genre pour proposer une attitude à corriger ici et là. Avec Tremblay — c'est le choc formidable de lundi au TNM — on est pour la première fois depuis très longtemps en face d'un vrai pamphlet, un pamphlet qui cogne dur et ne fait pas dans le subtil, un pamphlet qui ne recèle aucune moralisation autre que celle du miroir.

INDEX

Météo
Ciel variable
Max: 15
Détails en **B4**

LES ACTUALITÉS

Rae reconnaît les conjoints homosexuels

PAGE A 4

LE MONDE

Cinq ministères pour les néo-fascistes italiens

PAGE A 7

L'ÉCONOMIE

Hausse de 34 points du taux d'escompte

PAGE B 2

Des dossiers d'assurés dans les poubelles du complexe Desjardins

Des centaines de dossiers confidentiels à la portée du premier venu

LAURENT SOUMIS
LE DEVOIR

Le Groupe Desjardins d'assurances générales laisse sans surveillance et à portée de la main du premier venu des centaines de dossiers d'assurés qui contiennent des informations confidentielles protégées par la loi sur les renseignements personnels et qui peuvent s'avérer d'un commerce fort lucratif pour les fraudeurs.

Plutôt que d'être mis sous clé et détruits dans des conditions sécuritaires conformément à la loi, ces documents garnissent les poubelles du premier sous-sol du Complexe Desjardins sous la Tour sud où loge le plus important assureur de dommage au Québec.

Plusieurs témoins dignes de foi ont rapporté au DEVOIR qu'au cours des derniers mois, de nombreux conteneurs emplis à ras bords ont ainsi séjourné durant plusieurs jours dans un corridor d'accès au stationnement souterrain du complexe, à proximité d'une cantine devant laquelle passent quotidiennement employés, usagers et visiteurs des tours à bureaux.

À preuve de leurs dires, ces personnes ont remis au DEVOIR un dossier de réclamation d'un automobiliste d'Iberville qui contient une multitude d'informations confidentielles. On y trouve notamment, les noms de l'as

VOIR PAGE A 10: **DESJARDINS**

Le peuple du soleil

PHOTO JACQUES NADEAU

PLUSIEURS *centaines de personnes étaient réunies au Planétarium de Montréal hier, pour observer la fameuse éclipse solaire qui est apparue dans le ciel de Montréal, de 11h55 à 15h17. Jacques Beaulieu avait coiffé un casque de soudeur pour observer le phénomène, tandis que d'autres portaient des lunettes spécialement conçues à cet effet. Le tout se déroulait sous l'oeil impassible de Nicolas Copernic.*

On pouvait même observer Vénus

CAROLINE MONTPETIT
LE DEVOIR

Pendant l'éclipse solaire d'hier, Celso H. Delago-Ramirez, consul général du Mexique à Montréal, se tenait debout sur la pelouse du Planétarium, le plus sérieusement du monde, en complet cravate, les paumes levées vers les deux astres, en position de salut, d'adoration.

«Nous, Mexicains, nous sommes le peuple du soleil, disait-il, posté à côté d'un télescope, avec plusieurs centaines d'amateurs d'astronomie, pour observer l'éclipse solaire. Les Aztèques, les Teotihuacan, et les Mayas, tous les Indiens du Mexique, levaient les mains au ciel pour recevoir et saluer le soleil. Pendant l'éclipse, le soleil récupère, les plantes, les fleurs et les arbres s'ouvrent».

Le consul du Mexique à Montréal n'était pas le seul hier à observer les bienfaits de la réunion des astres en éclipse solaire.

La fameuse éclipse, qui a duré plus de trois heures, et que les spécialistes attendaient avec impatience depuis plusieurs années, n'a finalement déçu personne.

Vers midi, alors que les nuages couvraient le ciel et que quelques gouttes arrosaient les télescopes, on croyait la partie perdue.

Puis, ce fut l'éclaircie.

Au plus fort de l'éclipse (la lune cachait 88% de la surface du soleil), une lumière bleutée, moins dense qu'à l'accoutumée, baignait les rues de Montréal.

Dans le ciel, à travers les lunettes conçues à cet effet, on ne voyait plus qu'un croissant de soleil, découpé dans la surface opaque de la

VOIR PAGE A 10: **SOLEIL**

Exaspéré par le CRTC, Malofilm se tourne vers les États-Unis

Le producteur lance le Parents Channel *à la télé américaine*

PAULE DES RIVIÈRES
LE DEVOIR

Exaspéré par les lenteurs du CRTC, Malofilm s'est tourné vers les États-Unis pour réaliser sa brillante idée. Il y lancera prochainement un nouveau canal de télévision, destiné aux parents. Des dernières recherches en pédo-psychiatrie aux grands-parents trop ou pas assez présents, le *Parents Channel* ne négligera aucun aspect du rôle de parent, promet le président du producteur de films, M. René Malo.

Ce dernier a conclu une entente avec un des plus importants câblodistributeurs américains, qui s'est engagé à lui faire une place d'ici quelques mois sur son réseau.

«L'idée m'est venue lorsque je discutais avec un groupe d'amis. J'ai réalisé que nous passions 90% de notre temps à parler des enfants. J'achète entre cinq et dix revues de parents par mois, la bibliothèque est remplie de livres sur les enfants mais à la télé, il n'y a que quelques

VOIR PAGE A 10: **MALO**

Le nom magique qui fait trembler le pouvoir

Candidat à la présidence, Cuauhtemoc Cardenas récolte le fruit du mécontentement mexicain

ADAPTÉ DU NEW YORK TIMES

Villa de Garcia — Selon les normes habituelles, Cuauhtemoc Cardenas ne semble pas avoir le profil d'un candidat charismatique. Le candidat du PRD (Parti révolutionnaire démocratique) aux élections présidentielles du 21 août élève rarement la voix. On sent qu'il n'est pas du genre à dire des banalités pour soulever un auditoire. Bien des observateurs n'en pensent pas moins que Cardenas est la personne qui peut le plus sérieusement menacer la férule que maintient le PRI (Parti révolutionnaire institutionnel) depuis 65 ans sur le Mexique.

Le PRI, dont le candidat désigné en décembre, Luis Donaldo Colosio, a été assassiné à Tijuana, compte sur Ernesto Zedillo, un économiste tout aussi peu flamboyant que son rival du PRD, pour conserver le pouvoir.

Cardenas est un nom magique au Mexique, il évoque le nom du général Lazaro Cardenas auquel le Mexique doit la nationalisation de l'industrie du pétrole dans les années 30. Son fils, maintenant âgé de 60 ans, a comme

VOIR PAGE A 10: **MEXIQUE**

LES ACTUALITÉS

M3i: la tête de Mario Bertrand roule

PAGE A 2

LE DEVOIR

CAHIER C

◆ ◆ ◆

CINEMA

LES ARTS

Élise Guilbault et Monique Miller en Oreste.

Un monument d'angoisse effritée

Sami Frey joue Antonin Artaud

ODILE TREMBLAY
LE DEVOIR

Il a les yeux d'Artaud. La même intensité fiévreuse. La même démarche, les mêmes cheveux. Où est-ce sa convaincante interprétation du poète maudit dans le film de Mordillat qui me le fait confondre avec son modèle? Qui mieux que Sami Frey pouvait incarner à l'écran le damné sur terre que fut l'auteur du *Théâtre de la cruauté*?

À Montréal, on rencontre le comédien dans une auberge urbaine, assis dans une chambre au fond d'un couloir extérieur où le froid s'engouffre. Il fume une longue cigarette étroite et des [illegible] de *jobber* et il dit que ce sont vos yeux à vous qui transpercent l'autre dans à la vérité. Frey dégage quelque chose d'incandescent et d'agité qui l'apparente à son personnage.

En entrevue, il digresse un peu, s'égare, ses mots se chevauchent. L'air un peu bizarre. À l'écran, ça se traduira par les flammes dans un regard d'enfer, les joues creuses, une agitation physique perpétuelle. Dérangeante. Comme le fut, on l'imagine, celle d'Artaud.

Depuis ses débuts au cinéma à l'aube des années 60, Sami Frey a joué aux côtés de Godard (*Bande à part*), de Clouzot (*La Vérité*), de Doillon (*La Vie de famille*), de Von Trotta (*L'Africaine*), de bien d'autres, Deville, Sautet. Au théâtre, il a interprété Claudel, Racine, Brecht et Pirandello. Il fut mis en scène par Marguerite Duras, Jean-Louis Barrault, Roger Planchon voire par lui-même dans ce *Je me souviens* de Georges Perec où tout seul sur un vélo, se souvenant à perpète, il a conquis les scènes du monde.

Sami Frey dégage quelque chose d'incandescent et d'agité qui l'apparente à son personnage.

Mais à travers ce rôle d'Artaud, c'est la première fois, me confie-t-il, qu'il va aussi loin en lui-même. «En les rives de moi où j'hésite à courir», comme disait Vigneault. «Voyez-vous, un acteur a toujours peur de basculer de l'autre côté du ridicule. Cette fois, j'ai pris le risque d'y tomber.» Et il a gagné sa mise.

Le poète noir ressuscité

Si vous voulez voir revivre Artaud, faites un détour par le cinéma Parisien cette semaine. Vous le rencontrerez en noir et blanc sous les traits de Sami Frey dans un film qui parle de douleur, de poésie et de silence, sur une performance illuminée de l'interprète. *En compagnie d'Antonin Artaud* de Gérard Mordillat évoque les dernières années de la vie du poète, frais extirpé de l'hospice, cancéreux, perclus de douleur, assoiffé de laudanum, errant en 1946 dans Paris en compagnie de ses disciples, dont un certain Jacques Prevel, poète de son état, qui racontera ces errances et ces fulgurances dans son journal intime.

Artaud, Frey le connaissait, comme tout le monde, pour son travail au théâtre, pour sa correspondance avec Jacques Rivière à travers laquelle l'écorché vif s'affolait de son grand vide intérieur qui lui fut une cause de tourment infini.

Mais après avoir lu le scénario de Jérôme Prieur et de Gérard Mordillat inspiré du journal de Prevel, le comédien a protesté: «Non, vraiment, je ne suis pas le bon choix.» Devenir un monument, surtout un monument d'angoisse effritée, trop peu pour lui. Puis acteur et cinéaste ont parlé, durant des mois et des mois, du dernier livre lu, du dernier film vu, d'Artaud, de Prevel surtout. Jamais Frey n'a admis: «Je suis d'accord». Mais petit à petit le poète noir ressuscitait à travers lui.

VOIR PAGE C6: FREY

ANDROMAQUE quand le TNM joue avec la tragédie

ROBERT LÉVESQUE
LE DEVOIR

Lorraine Pintal parle épouvantablement d'abondance, cette énergique défenderesse de la cause théâtre est intarrissable, et on ne la prendra jamais en défaut de vivacité verbale, mais je n'apprend pas grand chose, en deux heures avec elle mercredi dernier (à 48 heures de la première de son *Andromaque* unisexe), sur la situation de plus en plus occulte (ou tabou?) du Théâtre du Nouveau Monde.

La directrice artistique du TNM, qui vient tout juste (prudente?) de signer un second et court contrat d'un an et demi à la barre de la plus importante compagnie de théâtre québécoise, «garde l'espoir», dit-elle, mais elle garde la langue dans sa poche lorsqu'on veut vraiment savoir ce qui arrive, ou ce qui arrivera du TNM qui traîne un déficit de près d'un million et demi de dollars, qui vit une situation aberrante avec des bureaux administratifs et des salles de répétition au fin fond de Saint-Henri alors que sa salle de théâtre est au centre-ville, une salle qui se détériore de saison en saison.

Le TNM, à ce que l'on sache, n'apparaît pas dans les préoccupations majeures du gouvernement québécois qui ira bientôt aux urnes (alors qu'à Ottawa on coupe) et s'il y a un bouillon de culture au cabinet Johnson il ne mijote pas fort fort. Pintal me dit: «croyez-vous que Daniel Johnson s'intéresse à la culture, vous? moi je ne le sais pas».

Mais il ne faut pas demander à Lorraine Pintal de dénoncer une situation de plus en plus tragique pour le TNM, et de se lancer dans des déclarations à l'emporte-pièce sur l'urgence de sauver et de réhabiliter le TNM au rang de première scène la mieux équipée du Québec, avec les moyens adéquats à une pratique professionnelle et progressiste du théâtre — comme, toutes proportions gardées, la Schaubühne à Berlin ou les Amandiers à Nanterre — non, Lorraine Pintal préfère défendre, en général «la pratique du théâtre à Montréal», qu'elle trouve en voie de sous-développement puisqu'on gèle partout et que l'on coupe chez les plus petits («qui sont la relève de demain, que l'on est en train d'étouffer»), plutôt que de défendre uniquement ou prioritairement la situation particulière du TNM.

Missionnaire du théâtre

C'est une missionnaire du théâtre, une animatrice et cheftaine dans l'âme, une marraine de toutes les troupes, Pintal, et il faut la croire lorsqu'elle dit clairement que le Théâtre du Nouveau Monde — qu'elle quittera dans un an et demi «si rien n'a bougé», imaginant très bien sa vie après le TNM — n'a pas à être «privilégié» par rapport aux autres compagnies de théâtre. Elle dit: «il ne faut pas en enlever aux autres pour sauver le TNM».

On a beau lui dire qu'il ne s'agit pas nécessairement d'en enlever aux autres pour faire du TNM une scène à la fine pointe du théâtre au Québec, que cela est affaire de choix éclairés, culturels et politiques, elle n'entre pas dans ces raisonnements pour la simple raison qu'elle croit qu'au Québec «il n'y a pas de fonctionnaires

VOIR PAGE C7: ANDROMAQUE

Élise Guilbault dans le rôle d'Hermione.

it should be close to the news – but it should also offer depth, analysis, opinion. Not instant information, like television."

The 1993 redesign is still being used, a decade later (though perhaps not quite as elegantly or in as polished a fashion as in the beginning – a common fate of bold newspaper designs). *Le Devoir* has won four gold medals from the Society of Newspaper Designers, three silver medals, and a Best of Show award, and it was nominated by SND as the "world's best designed newspaper."‹

CAHIER
C

Télévision Page C2
Cinéma Page C3
Théâtre Page C6
Danse Page C7
Opéra Page C8
Disques Page C9
Agenda culturel Page C10
Arts visuels Page C12
Architecture Page C14

VARIÉTÉS

Rirolarma!

Sur toutes les scènes, tous les écrans, le rire est roi. Pourquoi?

LES Ag

randeur misèr d'un cinéas québéc de pren plan

Un film est ur

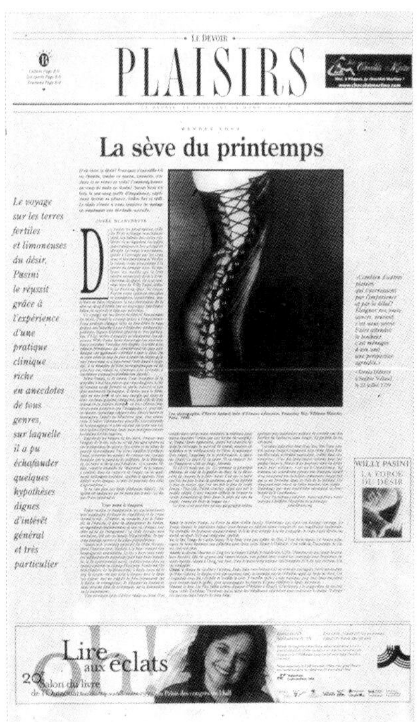
LE DEVOIR

PLAISIRS

La sève du printemps

Le voyage sur les terres fertiles et limoneuses du désir, Pasini le réussit grâce à l'expérience d'une pratique clinique riche en anecdotes de tous genres, sur laquelle il a pu échafauder quelques hypothèses dignes d'intérêt général et très particulier

WILLY PASINI
LA FORCE DU DÉSIR

Lire aux éclats
20e Salon du livre de l'Outaouais

Dramatic use of type and photography in the Arts and Entertainment sections.

El Gráfico

PRENSA LIBRE

EL MERCURIO

ILTA-SANOMAT

THE NATIONAL
ENQUIRER

More than you ever wanted to know about nameplates

Jim Parkinson

With technological changes causing many newspapers to reconsider their typography, there may be a nameplate redesign in your future.

Opposite (from the top): a new cursive design for Mario Garcia's redesign of an Argentine sports weekly; a restoration for a redesign prototype; a careful restoration for a Chilean daily; a restoration and repair for a Helsinki daily; a nameplate redesign that restored the eagle to the *San Francisco Examiner*; a redesign done with David Matt.

A newspaper's nameplate, as Allen Hutt pointed out, is one of the most important elements in its typography, but also one of the most neglected. Papers that redesign themselves with more elegant and readable typography often retain an out-of-date and badly deteriorated logo at the top of the front page. It's a position that few other businesses would tolerate.

A nameplate is the face of the institution and should demand as much care as the design of any other product name or company logo. The nameplate is often called the logo or flag, and for good reason: it requires just those qualities, to act as a symbol for the organization and to draw attention and excite curiosity.

Nameplates deteriorate through years of heavy use and technological changes at a paper. Many of today's nameplates originally existed as a steel engraving or as a single custom-made type-high brass printing plate. The harder metals were used to help the nameplate withstand constant heavy letterpress usage.

A proof taken from this printing plate to produce camera-ready art for offset printing would reflect any damage to the plate: softened edges, broken hairlines, and all. Over the years, the proof is veloxed, the original is lost, the velox is veloxed, and so on – each generation degrading the nameplate a little more. A well-meaning artist with limited lettering skills may be engaged to *fix it*, with modest results. The results of trying to modernize something that was intentionally designed to look old can be quite strange. Many generations later, the nameplate, beaten down and disfigured, abused and mistreated at every turn, a mere shadow of its former self, may suffer a further indignity. It is *auto-traced*. This is usually the kiss of death.

Some newspapers, with nameplates that have deteriorated to the point where they are ineffective, hesitate to change for fear that change would impair the trademark value that long usage of the old nameplate has given them. Changes for the better are not likely to have adverse consequences. Many long-established and successful newspapers have changed their nameplates repeatedly during the course of their existence, with few, if any, ill effects.

Eventually, a newspaper designer may be asked to try and restore the nameplate or to replace it with a new design. Sometimes this can be accomplished using type, but more often, the nameplate is designed and drawn by hand. This may require the help of a typographic designer who specializes in drawing letterforms.

Frederic Goudy and Matthew Carter, two of America's great-

The Detroit Free Press
The Detroit Free Press
The Detroit Free Press
Detroit Free Press

The nameplate history of the *Detroit Free Press*. From the top: 1929, 1945, 1960, and 1970.

Dallas
Dallas

Original above, restoration below. The original looked as if had been dipped in chocolate.

est typographic designers, have, at one time or another, designed nameplates. Matthew Carter's very elegant design currently graces the front of the *Boston Globe*. (FYI: *Fred's dead.*)

A very brief nameplate history

The earliest newspaper nameplates were simple and restrained. They were made from plain roman types that harmonized with the other typographic elements of the paper. Set in classic roman capitals or caps and lowercase, they were often merely larger sizes of the same typeface used for the body matter. As competition between papers increased, the nameplates of many papers became bolder and more ornate, to attract attention. Blackletter was the blackest type then available in most printing shops.

The first plain blackletter nameplate appeared in England in about 1680. When several influential newspapers shifted to blackletter for their nameplates, English printer John Bell introduced the first ornamented blackletter, with a white inline. It was immediately popular, and it remains so today. The *Detroit Free Press* and the *Montreal Gazette* are similar to Mr. Bell's nameplate in their ornamentation. In North America and Britain, the blackletter and plain roman nameplate styles still dominate today. All other nameplate styles combined, including cursive, slab serif, sans serif, art nouveau styles, and decorative forms, seem to make up only a small proportion of nameplate designs.

What is blackletter?

Blackletter is also known as gothic, Old English, and textura. *Textura* is an Italian term derived from the "woven" appearance of a page of blackletter. The letterforms evolved in manuscripts from the ninth to the fifteenth century. The first moveable type was in the style of

Detroit Free Press

The *Detroit Free Press* nameplate was developed with Deborah Withey. It began as a restoration and evolved into a new design.

The Gazette

Designed with Lucie Lacava, this nameplate reflects the character of the *Montreal Gazette*'s original nameplate from 1778.

textura (think "Gutenberg Bible"). Blackletter continued to evolve and become somewhat standardized. In the late nineteenth century, there was an astonishing variety of blackletter styles available from printers and type founders.

Blackletter still has connections with formality and authority. It survived in liturgical and legal printing (in the English tradition) long after the roman letter had won out. It is still used today in diplomas and certificates, because it connotes authority, dignity, formality, and tradition.

There are three good blackletter designs available today: Engraver's Old English and Cloister Black, by Morris Benton or Joseph Phinney (depending on who you ask), and Goudy Text by Frederic Goudy. But none of them work well as nameplates. They are too light, too wide, and too old-fashioned in their detailing. Blackletter as it is traditionally used in newspapers today is not readily available as type.

It's a letter style that is supposed to look old, so trying to modernize it can be a risky proposition. Most of the little thingamabobs and doodads on the letters were not put there just for kicks. These letterforms have evolved over a thousand years, and all those strange little things are there for reasons: usually to improve spacing, color, balance, and of course *readability*. If you don't know why they are there, maybe you should leave them alone. To remove letter details indiscriminately can invite disaster. One of the few ways to soften a blackletter type is to replace certain angular features with curves. A worn-out blackletter nameplate, once restored, can look dramatically different. The *St. Petersburg Times* is a good example. A newspaper's nameplate history may often give clues that may help in a redesign.

ABCDEFGHIJK
LMNOPQRSTUVWXYZ
abcdefghijklmnopqrstuvwxyz

ABCDEFGHIJK
LMNOPQRSTUVWXYZ
abcdefghijklmnopqrstuvwxyz

Engraver's Old English (top) and Cloister Black (bottom).

St. Petersburg Times

St. Petersburg Times

Before, after. A nameplate in very bad condition (top) is restored and updated.

ton ton

Some blackletter styles can be softened by making them less angular.

The Hamilton Spectator

The Hamilton Spectator

THE HAMILTON SPECTATOR

Development of a new nameplate for *The Hamilton Spectator*. The original nameplate (top), then an attempt to salvage the old. At bottom, the new nameplate, hand-lettered.

From blackletter to roman

Some newspapers hesitate to change from blackletter because they want to retain a long-established look, or they're reluctant to let go of the trademark value of the nameplate.

Other papers make the leap from blackletter to roman letterforms. *The Hamilton Spectator* experimented with "cleaning up" a rather frightening old blackletter nameplate before deciding to go with a more contemporary look. The new nameplate is not type, but hand-drawn. In comparing the three versions, it's interesting to note how much more readable the roman is, and how much larger it appears in basically the same amount of space.

The Journal of Commerce is another example of a paper with a blackletter nameplate changing over to roman letterforms. The roman in this case is again hand-lettering, based on Perpetua.

Nameplates from roman letters

Nameplates can be made from typefaces, of course. But it can get tricky. Many typefaces have character shapes that have been compromised in order to achieve universal character fit (sacrificing the few for the many). This makes for better type, but, depending on the name of the paper (the character relationships) and the typeface, there may be awkward letter combinations, weight problems, kerning issues, or any number of other problems that may appear when the type is viewed as a logo. But, carefully done, typefaces can make great nameplates.

Roger Black's elegant nameplate for the *Baltimore Sun* is a perfect example of a successful nameplate designed with a typeface. In this case, the typeface is Miller, designed by Matthew Carter. A pictorial element drawn by British illustrator Bill Sanderson

The Journal of Commerce

THE JOURNAL OF
COMMERCE

The Journal of Commerce: a restoration of the existing logo (top), and a new design art-directed by David Matt and Roger Black.

POST

POST

POST

The *National Post* nameplate was first set in the typeface Miller (top). Then it was horizontally scaled until it achieved the desired width. Finally, the nameplate was redrawn using the scaled type as a template.

is positioned between the words THE and SUN.

The nameplate for the *National Post* was developed with Lucie Lacava. It's based on a severe horizontal scaling of the typeface Miller. Horizontal scaling is a great design tool, but it alters the type so insensitively that the letters will probably need to be redrawn to restore weight, proportion, and style.

To be effective, a typographic nameplate should be presented in a typeface or hand-lettering in the same family used for the main news heads on the front page, or in a *decidedly different* typeface or lettering style. If it is somewhere in between, it's likely to be incompatible with the rest of the typography on the page.

Using pictorial elements

Some early newspapers used a pictorial device in their nameplates, usually in the form of a woodcut or a steel engraving. While many of today's nameplate illustrations continue to have an engraver's or a wood-cut quality, others are illustrated with more contemporary drawings or photographs.

Whenever an illustrative element is added to the nameplate, the design and color of the illustration should be compatible with the design and color or value of the typeface or lettering. The illustration should read instantly, and it shouldn't attract too much attention to itself and away from the name of the paper.

Individuality and timelessness

Not all nameplates are either plain roman or blackletter. There are many successful designs made with all manner of ornamented and shadowed roman letters, italics, cursives, sans and slab serifs, plain and ornamented and shaded. These logos usually stand out because they vary from the norm. They offer a publication

NATIONAL POST

The *National Post* nameplate was designed with Lucie Lacava, from the typeface Miller.

The Brownsville Herald

BROWNSVILLE
The Herald

The new nameplate for *The Brownsville Herald* was designed with Pam Marshak and illustrated by Don Breeden. A simplified blackletter with BROWNSVILLE arched over the illustration of historic Brownsville buildings make the nameplate.

The Metropolitan

DE FINANCIËLE MORGEN

Η ΚΑΘΗΜΕΡΙΝΗ

The Dallas Morning News

From the top: a short-lived nameplate for a San Francisco tabloid; a new design for a Brussels financial paper; a nameplate redesign for an Athens daily; a restoration.

some individuality in its identity. A unique nameplate can give a paper the image of uniqueness. These logos are also a not-so-subtle example of the expressiveness of letters beyond what they spell.

No matter what style of lettering is chosen for a nameplate, the design should be made to appear timeless (as much as that's possible): not wanting to appear too old, but also not wanting to appear new and not established. Beware of typographic fads.

Anything can happen... and usually does

Some nameplate redesigns go very smoothly, but anything can happen. The nameplate is something everybody wants to sign-off on. Prototypes are printed. Individuals who at one time thought the nameplate was fine the way it was may suddenly morph into influential designers, no matter how unqualified. Focus groups may be convened. The project may start, stall out, and then start up again. Or not. One newspaper actually took eighteen months to decide between two sketches. During the course of a nameplate project, publishers or key editors may be replaced. The paper may even be sold. Major changes topside often mean a new vision for the paper, and that includes the nameplate.

It's worth the effort

The nameplate is the first piece of typography the reader sees. As the product logo, it should represent a paper in the best possible way. A properly restored nameplate can revitalize a paper's visual image. A brand-new design can represent either a fresh start or a step from the past into the future (or into the present). It should be clean, crisp, and instantly readable. It should, in its execution, reflect tradition, authority, and dignity.

Even the most subtle differences in a nameplate design make a large difference in terms of the subliminal/subconscious impression they leave on their audience... *the readers.* ‹

contributors

Over the last 15 years, Roger Black's design studios have rebuilt some of the most prestigious magazines and newspapers in the world, including *Reader's Digest*, *Esquire*, *Premiere*, the *Straits Times* (Singapore), *Tages Anzeiger* (Zurich) and the *Baltimore Sun*. He is chairman of Danilo Black, Inc. (daniloblackusa.com), with offices in New York and Monterrey, Mexico.

Simon Esterson is an editorial designer based on London. He has worked on newspaper and magazine projects for *The Guardian*, *The Times*, and the *Evening Standard* in London, *Valor* in São Paulo, and the *NZZ am Sonntag* in Zurich. He has also been creative director of the Italian architecture magazine *Domus*. He is a Royal Designer for Industry and a member of the AGI.

Miguel Angel Gómez is Art Director for newspapers at Danilo Black. He has worked on more than 40 design and redesign projects in Latin America, the USA, Asia, and Europe, including the award-winning *Reforma* and *Mural* in Mexico, and *Nuestro Diario* in Guatemala. His expertise is not only design, but also empowerment and training of the people involved.

Lucie Lacava is a Newspaper Architect and President of Lacava Design Inc. She has redesigned more than forty publications across Canada, the US, and Europe. Her architectural and streamlined approach to the redesign process has translated into over 100 national and international awards. Her redesigns have been praised and awarded for typography usage. She is past president of the Society for News Design.

Ole Munk is a graphic designer and newspaper consultant, and a partner in Ribergård & Munk Graphic Design (www.ribmunk.dk), where he has done design & redesign projects at more than twenty papers all over Scandinavia. He is the author of *Reporter or Artist* (1992), *Sæt Billeder På* (1999), and *Avis-layout & Redigering* (2003), as well as numerous articles and reviews on newspaper design.

Jim Parkinson specializes in the design of typefaces and typographic logos. He has designed newspaper nameplates for the *Wall Street Journal*, the *National Post*, and the *Los Angeles Times*; magazine logos for *Newsweek*, *Rolling Stone*, and *New York*; and display typefaces for *Rolling Stone*, *Newsweek*, and the *National Post*. He is principal of Parkinson Type Design in Oakland, California (www.typedesign.com).

Randall K. Roberts is Presentation Director for the *Rocky Mountain News*, where he oversees the newspaper's design, copy-editing, and graphics. He was a key player in implementing Danilo Black's redesign of the *Rocky*. In 2002, Roberts oversaw the presentation and assisted in picture editing for the *Rocky*'s coverage of a summer of wildfires in Colorado, which won a Pulitzer Prize for Breaking News Photography.

Jonathon Berlin rides his bike to work rain or shine. Whereas self-propulsion is important as an assistant design director at the *Rocky Mountain News* in Denver, making the newspaper is more like a tandem bike with many riders. Most of the time, uphill or downhill, it's a good ride. Jonathon is also editor of the Society of News Design's *Update* newsletter.

John D. Berry is an editor/typographer who works both sides of the design/content divide. He is the former editor and publisher of *U&lc* (*Upper and lower case*) and *U&lc Online*, and editor of the book *Language Culture Type*, on international typeface design. He writes and consults extensively on typography, and he has won numerous awards for his book designs.

| index

M

N

O

P

Q

R

S

Colophon

Book design and composition by John D. Berry and Carl Juarez.
The typefaces are Miller Text and Miller Display, designed by Matthew Carter, and Knockout, designed by Jonathan Hoefler. The typefaces used on the end-papers are all from the Balboa family designed by Jim Parkinson.

There is a special edition of 50 copies of this book, which has been hand bound in half cloth. It is accompanied by a folder containing ephemera relating to the projects and typefaces mentioned in this book. Both the book and the folder are housed in a hand-made slipcase.

Dead Man Found in Cemetery

RAINS DELAY UMBRELLA SHOW

Dinosaur Faces Grand Jury Probe

Cops Halt Doughnut Shop Robbery

STEALS CLOCK, FACES TIME

Missouri Woman Big Winner

TWO SOVIET SHIPS COLLID

Something Went Wrong in Jet Cra

THREE AMBULANCES TAKE BLAST VICT

Stolen Painting Found

PANTS MAN TO EXPAND AT THE REAR

Man Disputes Government Claim He's Dead

Typhoon Rips Through Cemetery

HUNDREDS DEAD